DAUGHTER OF THE ENEMY

For Leonora —
with best wishes.
Marie
9.9.18

Siehe, ich lebe. Woraus? Weder Kindheit noch Zukunft
Werden weniger . . . überzähliges Dasein
Entspringt mir im Herzen.

Die Neunte Elegie
Rainer Maria Rilke

Look, I am living. Out of what? Neither childhood nor future
Grows any smaller . . . Abundant being
Wells up in my heart.

The Ninth Elegy
Rainer Maria Rilke

Daughter of the Enemy

A Memoir

Marie Pal-Brown

LAGOON
HOUSE
PRESS

Daughter Of The Enemy
Marie Pal-Brown

ISBN 978-0-9972609-5-3

Note to the reader:
This is a work of memory. Actual names of persons and places were
used in most cases. My recollections of events may differ from those
of others who witnessed or were part of these same events.

All translations by the author.

Printed in the United States
Lagoon House Press
Long Beach, CA
lagoonhousepress.com

For our children and their partners
Alison & Andrea
Jeremy & Laura
Daniela & Peter
Ryan & Greg
For our grandchildren
Greta, Caterina, Remi

For the children in worn-torn countries everywhere
and all the other children throughout the world
in hopes that they may never have to suffer the
consequences of war

Acknowledgments

In the 1990s, I was seeking to understand how my father's death had impacted my young life and shaped the adult I became. I was in therapy with the Jungian analyst Dianne Cordic, when my then-husband brought home a flyer for a one-day workshop with the poet Doraine Poretz. The flyer stated that the writing theme of the day would be the warrior archetype. Participants were instructed to bring a photo of a person of their choosing. I took this as a synchronistic parallel I was meant to heed: my father had died as a soldier, a warrior. I chose a photo of him in his uniform to take with me to the workshop.

Seated around a table in a sunlight-flooded studio, we each introduced ourselves at the beginning of the workshop. The other five participants – one woman and four men – all had Jewish-sounding surnames. My slight German accent seemed to arouse no one's curiosity.

I thought immediately of the photo of my father, tucked away in my notebook. How could I possibly find the courage to expose him as a soldier in the German *Wehrmacht* and myself as a daughter of the enemy? Was I not, in some way, representative of the evil committed in my country's name – to anybody, but especially to anyone Jewish? Off and on during the day, I obsessed over what to do when the time came for the writing exercise related to the photo. I wavered between pretending that I had forgotten to bring a photograph and refusing to read aloud whatever writing was going to ensue. In the end, after much wrestling with myself, I came to a resolution: I must stand accountable as someone of German birth and accountable as well for Germany's ugly past.

Near the end of the day, and after many different exercises – none of them related to the photographs we'd been instructed to bring – it seemed unlikely there would be enough time for another exercise. I thought I had been saved from exposure. Then, Doraine's instruction came: "Write a letter to the person in the photo you brought."

I waited to be the last to share my letter. Finally, Doraine called on me. The room was quiet as I opened my notebook. "Dear Daddy," I read out loud. I couldn't control the quivering in my voice, and yet I felt brave at the same time, exposed as I was in that sunlit circle. In the letter to my father, I recounted the story of the day in 1945, in Rockensußra, when my mother, with me eavesdropping, learned that he had been killed at the Soviet front.

No one spoke for an uncomfortably long time. Then, a man in his seventies, sitting across from me, said, "I never thought about the children."

Others followed with similarly kind remarks.

I wish to acknowledge and thank those workshop participants – in particular the woman, a generation older than I, who sat next to me. Originally from Greece, she'd addressed her letter to the uniformed young man in a black-and-white snapshot: her brother, who had been shot down and killed over Germany by the German *Luftwaffe* near the end of the war. I don't remember her words, only her gesture of reconciliation: how she put her arms around me and wept. If not for the compassion shown to me by that woman and the other people in the workshop, I would not have found the courage to tell this story.

And, if it hadn't been for a call from Doraine the following day, my "Dear Daddy" letter would have ended up in a folder of miscellaneous writings, never to be looked at again. As it was, Doraine encouraged me to expand the story of one who'd lost her father in WWII – a different kind of "victim," one whose story promised to shed light on that terrible history from the perspective of a German child.

I'm grateful to Doraine Poretz for igniting the flame that set me on the course to writing this memoir.

My deepest appreciation and admiration go to Holly Prado, my writing mentor who, with her wisdom and guidance, kept the flame burning. Always supportive, she helped moderate my often ruthless inner critical voice; but she also never stopped reminding me to minimize the use of run-on sentences, that multi-clausal structure prevalent among many German-speaking writers.

I also want to thank the women and men in Holly Prado's writing workshops for their input and encouragement over the years: Gina Battaglia, Linda Berg, Kathleen Bevacqua, Garrett M. Brown (fellow workshop participant before he was my husband), Barbara Crane, Toni Fuhrman, Susan Hayden, Richard Heller, Toke Hoppenbrowers, Joan Isaacson, Kathy Lazarus, the late Leonard Levy, Edith Light, Mary Ann McFadden, Vicki Mizel, Marlene Saile, Pamela Shandel, Jill Singer, Rae Wilken, Cecilia Woloch.

My sister, Brigitte Khalil, and my cousin Marco Feinendegen provided valuable assistance with my rendering of Rhenish *Plattdeutsch* dialog.

Pamela Borchert, Grazia McEwan and the late Hector Kingston read installments of the earlier version of this work. Their enthusiasm – without a critical word ever – gave me much needed encouragement.

My appreciation also to E.E. Bustamante who, throughout the years, in his no-nonsense way, urged me to stay the course, "You got to keep with it."

My first husband, David Pal, put up with me when I spent day and night behind the closed door of my study. He deserves my apology and my gratitude.

After I had put the earlier version aside for more than ten years, Eric Nystrom asked to read it. Unbeknownst to him, his approval of it motivated me to revise the manuscript a final time.

I thank Hannah Friederich, Kathy Lazarus, and Arlen Stahlberg for their close reading of the manuscript.

I'm thankful to Cecilia Woloch for editing the manuscript. Her compassion for the child who then became the adult described in my recollections enabled her to offer invaluable suggestions and to ask germane questions with insight and sensitivity.

I thank Glenna Morrison, Toni Fuhrman and Marjie MacFarlin for their meticulous proofreading.

My gratitude always to Lagoon House Press for believing in my work.

My husband, Garrett M. Brown, a fine writer himself, stepped up on the many occasions when I lost faith in my ability as a writer, especially as I was writing in a language other than my native German. He offered his sometimes gentle, sometimes tough-love, encouragement. As my first reader, Garrett's editorial notes were never short of imaginative ideas. His studio door was always open, making me feel welcome to interrupt him with questions about an English word or a turn of phrase, when dictionaries didn't suffice. I owe him more than words can say.

PROLOGUE

This story began when I was still a child. The event that prompted it had already passed. When I was no longer a child, I had a dream that foretold the ending:

It is autumn. I travel through rural areas in a remote country, and happen upon the battlefield where my father was killed. The old peasants I encounter don't speak my language. But when they understand that I am searching for my father's grave, they lead me to an unmarked burial site on a rise, not far from a stand of trees. I scoop up a handful of earth. It is dark and moist. In the nearby meadow, my mother, young and lovely as I remember her from my early childhood, rakes pebbles into piles. I pick up the smoothest and shapeliest, gather them in my apron pocket. I arrange them on my father's bare plot to spell his initials:

J S

PART ONE

Rockensußra
1944 – 1945

1

Rockensußra, January 7, 1945, the Monday after Epiphany, the Christian feast day commemorating the Adoration of the Magi, marking the end of the Christmas season. It was the day on which it was customary to dismantle the Christmas tree. Once decorated with shiny ornaments, beeswax candles, and an angel crowning its top, the tree was bare now, except for the odd piece of tinsel. Gone was the celebratory glow that had shone in the modest front room of the Köppel farmhouse. The tree stood shunted aside in a corner, ready to be cut into kindling.

A fire was burning in the wood stove. Herr Köppel put on a heavy coat and headed for the door. The sudden sound of his work boots on the wood-planked floor startled the women, who turned their heads. Frau Köppel, her face furrowed beyond her years by a life of hard work and sorrow, and her two daughters, both of marrying age, were shelling dried kidney beans into wicker bowls on their laps. Mother walked in from the hallway, having completed her chores around the house. She closed the door quickly to keep the warmth in the room, and joined the women with a cheerful, *"Guten Morgen."*

Kurtie was the Köppel's nine-year old son. He sat at the table, furiously whittling away at another toy building block with a pocket knife, a Christmas gift that now was his most prized possession.

"What are they for?" I asked, looking up from my drawing.

"A cabin," he mumbled in that dismissive way in which he showed that he wanted nothing to do with a five-year-old girl like me. His perpetually runny nose disgusted me, but how I ached for his attention nonetheless.

My one-year-old sister, Brigitte, whom we called Gitta, was crawling in fast circles on the floor. To Mother's obvious delight, she made periodic attempts at raising herself to a wobbly standing position. She would fall back on her bottom each time, then raise her arms and shriek at the top of her lungs.

Snowflakes tumbled past the only window in the room, settling on the exterior sill and blanketing the winter-brown meadow and the footpath to the highway below. Stillness enveloped everything but for the occasional bleating of a sheep from the barn. It was a stillness so deep, it hushed the ordinary sounds in the front room.

My drawing finished, I dragged a chair to the window. I climbed on the seat and, with my finger, traced snowmen on the steamed-up glass. Small ones and larger ones, as many as would fit in between the wooden mullions, on as many panes as I could reach.

A figure in the distance caught my eye. Pressing my face close to the glass, I was able to make out a man trudging along the path toward the house. He wore a long military coat and cap. He walked deliberately, slowly pulling his boots out of the deep snow with each step.

"A soldier!" I cried out, delighted at the prospect of having a visitor.

The Köppel's older daughter rushed over, abandoning her basket of beans. She wiped a pane with the side of her hand, blotting out my snowmen, and peered into the white landscape. In a voice, high-pitched with cheer, she turned to my mother. *"Das muss Ihr Mann sein! Aus dem Krieg zurück!* – That must be your husband! Back from the war!"

I scrambled off the chair. I wanted to be the one to open the front door and greet my father. But Mother grabbed my arm. She held me back. It startled me.

"No! It's not him," she said, as if she were afraid to jinx the small odds that it was her husband, were she to give credence to any hope she had.

She walked out into the hallway, having decided, it seemed, to answer the door anyway.

I followed, puzzled by Mother's apparent change of mind, and by the women's abrupt silence.

Flat winter light from the transom above the front door spread across the black and white tiles, spotless except for a few footprints closest to the outdoors. Every Saturday, the sisters scrubbed the floor on their knees.

Mother opened the door. The stranger stood there waiting, silhouetted against an empty sky. It had stopped snowing. He took off his cap. He stamped and shuffled his feet. Snow fell off his boots. He stepped inside and closed the door behind him. His face, now visible in the interior light, was that of a serious looking man in his middle years.

"Frau Schupp?" he said.

Mother nodded.

"Ich habe die traurige Pflicht, Ihnen mitteilen zu müssen, dass Ihr Gatte gefallen ist. – It is my sad duty to inform you that your husband has been killed in action." His words sounded rehearsed, his speech clipped.

Mother cried out, just a little. I reached for her hand with mine, but she shook it off impatiently, as if to say, *Not now, not now.*

The stranger pulled a letter from his coat's breast pocket. He unfolded it and read its contents in a solemn manner. I heard the words, but they were only words, words beyond my comprehension. Even when he said, *"Kopfschuss. Ihr Gatte war auf der Stelle tot.* – Shot in the head. Your husband died instantly," it meant nothing.

He finished reading, handed Mother the letter and dropped his head in silence. After a polite pause, he shook her hand and stroked my head lightly.

"My deepest sympathies," he said and, raising his arm, saluted, *"Heil Hitler!"*

He turned sharply on his heels. He opened the door and, stepping outside, pulled it shut behind him. It closed with a dull thud.

Mother turned away from me. She buried her face in her hands. I could hear her sobs. Her body shook.

I watched her, a wild fear coming over me, a fear I had never known before.

Then, as if suddenly remembering me, she pressed my head into the softness of her belly. *"Dein Papa ist tot.* – Your Papa is dead." And recognizing, maybe, that the meaning of her words went beyond my understanding, she rephrased what she had said, *"Er kommt nie wieder nach Hause.* – He'll never come home again." The hollow tone in her voice frightened me even more. I wrapped my arms around her thighs and held on as tightly as I could.

In reality, I knew my father had always been an absence, a memory, kept alive as a promise less tangible than Christmases to come, and waiting for him to return home on leave had been little more than a wish included in my bedtime prayer.

At periodic intervals, the promise of his visits had been fulfilled; but as these visits inevitably came to a quick end, they bore the mark of fantasy in my little-girl life.

Dressed in our prettiest outfits, Mother and I would go to meet him at the train station back home in Delrath. A fine looking man in his *Wehrmacht* uniform, he'd lift me up high above his head. I'd look down into his face, shy, at first, then overjoyed. *"Wie groß du geworden bist. –* How tall you've grown," he'd say with a father's proud smile.

Though brief, his furloughs were magical. He'd bring gifts from faraway places, like Paris, where he had been stationed: a porcelain doll with eyes that opened and closed; a red French winter coat.

He held my hand on our walks through the streets of Delrath. People stopped us to say hello and to ask him about the war. How tall I stood, proud to be his daughter! We called at Grandmother and Grandfather's house for cocoa and pastry. On good weather days, we walked along the meadows of the River Rhine and in the woods outside of town. We all attended Mass together, like a real family. Mother, a reluctant Catholic, came along just to comply with her husband's wishes. Afterwards, my father would join the old men – those still left in town, who were beyond drafting age – in the pub across the street from our flat.

At the end of each of his leaves, Mother and I walked my father back to the train station. We waved goodbye from the platform as he leaned out the compartment window, fluttering a white handkerchief in the breeze. Both of us holding back our tears, Mother and I watched the train pull away and disappear around the bend further up in the fields. We were without my father again. When the war escalated and he was deployed to his regiment's headquarters in East Prussia, his visits became even less frequent, and then they stopped altogether.

'Dead' was only a word.

With my face still buried in the folds of Mother's skirt, I began to weep – out of pity for my weeping mother. Weeping with her, I wanted to comfort her, or to make things right again. At the same time, I felt the first stirrings of fate's cruel and random ways. Something imponderable had struck, whose repercussions went beyond my ability to measure but whose enormity I sensed.

If only Mother had not gone to answer the door, none of this would have come to pass. That became my magical thinking and my escape, which allowed me to believe that what had happened could un-happen, could be undone. My father would come home after the war; Mother would be mine again.

We stood there together, Mother and I, on the black and white checkered floor in the cold hallway. We cried together for a long time. When there were no more tears, small whimpers came from my throat. Then those, too, ebbed. Mother took a handkerchief from her skirt pocket. She wiped my eyes, then hers. Lifting her head high and straightening her shoulders, she said, *"Komm."*

She led the way into the front room. The women had resumed shelling beans. Gitta was asleep on the floor near the stove. Kurtie's carving project and pocket knife lay abandoned on the table. The women raised their heads. Their anxious faces betrayed that they knew already what had transpired in the hallway.

"My husband . . ." Mother said, voice breaking. She began to sob again.

Frau Köppel was the first to leave her chair and approach us. The coarse texture of her homespun woolen skirt brushed against my cheek. She clasped Mother's hand with both of hers.

"Be brave," Frau Köppel said. Face furrowing, lips tightening, she picked up the hem of her apron and wiped her eyes. When she spoke again, an edge of anger hardened her tone.

"So many of our men have died already," and, lowering her voice, as if she were broaching something unutterable or forbidden, "Many more will pay with their lives before this wretched war is over . . ."

"Red' nicht so, Mutter. – Don't speak that way, Mother," the older of the sisters interrupted, glancing at the door.

We'd come to Rockensußra five months earlier, in August of 1944, leaving behind Delrath at the height of the Allied bombing raids in the

Rhineland region. Changing trains along the way, we made the long journey to Erfurt, the capital of Thuringia. From there, we continued by bus to Rockensußra. Late one evening, we knocked on the door of the Köppel farmhouse.

Rockensußra was a hamlet of no more than a couple of farmsteads, a Lutheran church and a dozen or so shabby, low-slung houses along an unpaved street. There we would spend the remainder of the war and two months after Germany's defeat, until June 1945.

Reflecting on those times in later years, my mother always emphasized that we had not made the move under the auspices of the official evacuation order issued in 1943, that we had not been "poor, bombed out" evacuees. But that my father, in his letters from the front, had urged her to leave the war-threatened west, assuring her we'd be safer in the eastern part of Germany, where the war had not yet spread. Reluctantly, she'd looked for a suitable opportunity.

In her younger years, Mother had been active in the *BDM,* the *Bund Deutscher Mädel* – the girls' division of the Hitler Youth. Through its network, she was referred to a farming family in Rockensußra. Arrangements for our stay were made. In exchange for our upkeep, Mother would pay a monthly stipend and work in the Köppel household.

Thus, we escaped the Allied bombing.

Krieg, meaning war, like *Tod,* meaning death, was a word beyond my understanding. Still, in my early childhood, the word "war," like "death," was prevalent in everyday parlance. Its undercurrent of horror leaked into the games we invented. Back in Delrath, playing hide and seek, my little friends and I had pretended running from low-flying bombers; we took cover behind the living room sofa. A drawing I made that survived the years depicts cone-shaped objects falling from the sky and a child with short blonde braids in front of a burning house.

Yet, the Allied bombings in the Rhineland, the terror of air raid sirens howling, of my mother's hand gripping my hand as we ran for shelter in the school basement at night, of artillery shells ripping through my grandparents' house – while these, in all reality, were part of the war, in my imagination, none of them were the war itself.

The war was far away. My father was in the war, in East Prussia, where he had been stationed, and later in Latvia, where he had been deployed during his regiment's retreat from the siege of Leningrad. *Kurland* – the Latvian province of *Kurzeme* – was the name by which Mother would always refer to the place where my father had become a casualty of the war. So, *Kurland* was the name by which the war became real for me, a child of five. It evoked a landscape eternally covered in snow, as it must have been late in the afternoon of December 26, 1944, when the shot rang out that killed my father. *Kurland,* where he lay buried, *"unter einer Handbreit Erde verscharrt* – under a hand's breadth of dirt,"* Mother would say, without trying to hide the contempt with which she always talked about the war – the war that had widowed her and irreversibly altered her life and the lives of millions of women like her.

For years to come, my idea of the war remained shrunk to the Latvian province of Kurzeme – from where my father had not returned. Compared to the actual proportions of World War II, *my* war was a small war – until much later, when I learned about the horror that had been perpetrated and the unimaginable numbers of casualties it had claimed.

2

After the stranger's call, Mother seldom spoke about my father. On the rare occasions she did, she would tilt her head away from whomever she was speaking to. Or an angry frown would come over her face. Her tone accusing, she would say, "My husband had two children and a wife, seniority in his company back home – he would've been deferred from military service. Instead he joined, voluntarily." She lifted her hands in resignation, "I pleaded with him not to go."

Years later, when it was safe again to speak one's mind, she blamed not only my father, but the system in which he'd gotten caught up and its ideology. *"Wahnvorstellungen* – Monstrous delusions!"

In the night, Mother's stifled sobbing sometimes woke me in the narrow bed we shared. Then I'd snuggle tightly into the curves of her body. I'd wait quietly for her sobbing to stop and for her breath to become shallow and smooth again. But before long, I'd fall back into sleep.

During the day, I didn't let her out of my sight. I followed her every step. She indulged my neediness and allowed me to be the indispensable helpmate I so wanted to be. She taught me how to hold the dustpan's edge closely angled to the floor so she could sweep dirt onto it with her broom. I set the table for meals. We'd make our bed together; she'd shake the featherbed, I'd fluff the pillows. I played with Gitta in the kitchen, while Mother peeled potatoes or chopped cabbage for our meals. I amused Gitta by clapping my hands to the rhythm of *Backe, backe Kuchen* – Patty cake, patty cake. But I was happiest when Gitta was napping in her crib upstairs, and I had Mother all to myself.

Often I just watched her, as I did one early afternoon, sitting at the kitchen table, my chin propped on my forearms. A soot-crusted cauldron of water stood heating on the cooking stove. Mother added a dark powder, stirring the mix with a large wooden spoon. Steam rose. Its sour odor permeated the room.

A piece at a time, she dropped an armful of her clothes into the boiling water. Her face looked self-absorbed, at once absent and intent on the task. Her movements were slow and measured as she swirled the garments in the black brew. Every so often, she paused to retrieve random pieces, draping them over a wooden spoon, from which they hung like shapeless rags. Magically, their colors changed, darker each time, until eventually, after more boiling and stirring, when she pulled them out of the cauldron, each piece was pitch black.

She transferred the steaming, dripping clothes into a tub of cold water, swooshed them around with both hands, and, removing them, squeezed out the excess water. She rinsed them several times over. Her hands turned red from the icy water as she wrung out each piece separately and held up for final inspection. She looked pleased as she tossed one after another into a wicker basket.

Grasping both handles, she lugged it up the stairs to the landing and then up the attic staircase, steep and barely wide enough to maneuver. The attic was kept closed off by a folding door, except on bad weather days when the women took up the laundry to dry. I followed Mother, clutching the banister with each tall step.

Meager daylight crept through the louvered boards on both gables. Spider webs clung to the rafters. The floor creaked under our weight. I shivered as an eerie dread paired with the allure of mystery. It was near pleasurable, the way I remembered feeling in Grandmother's attic, strewn with discarded treasures, piles of books and old furniture.

Mother set down the basket. She hung the freshly dyed garments on lines strung across the rafters. She tied a bag of clothes pegs around my waist. I took out two at a time and handed them to her. Mother pinned up first her dresses, then her skirts and blouses, followed by slips and panties. When we were done, she lifted me inside the basket and carried me downstairs. How I loved Mother at that moment, playful again the way she used to be.

We returned to the attic two mornings later. Mother held my hand. I felt safe as we climbed the stairs. Dark shapes hung stiffly from the clotheslines. Mother made a few random checks to assure that all her garments were dry. One by one, she took them down, folded them and stacked them in the basket. I collected the clothes pegs.

Back in the kitchen, she layered blankets on the dining table, then covered them with a bed sheet. Two flat irons were heating on the back plate of the stove. She wetted her middle finger with her tongue, and quickly touched the underside of one of the irons. When it made a small hissing sound, she began pressing her newly dyed clothes with practiced motion. After the first iron had cooled, she set it back on the stove to reheat, while continuing to press with the second. In this way, she rotated the irons until the basket was empty, and her dresses and skirts hung from a rack on the kitchen wall, lifeless effigies of my mother. Everything else – her undergarments and blouses she stacked in neatly folded piles on a bench under the window.

Mother looked fragile in her mourning attire. Her face was paler than before, her dark blonde hair without the playful curl to one side. She went about her chores quietly, without the cheerful humming I was used to hearing.

Perhaps she had told me that widows, while they mourned for their dead husbands, wore black, like the old women who dressed in long dark clothes and pulled their gray hair back into tightly twisted buns. Perhaps I had begun to sense then that widowhood accorded something special, something the loss of one's father did not: a kind of entitlement to grieving and to displaying one's grief to the outside world. Mother's status was different now. The farm women, Kurtie, even Herr Köppel, gruff as his manners were, treated her with distance and consideration. The villagers we encountered in the street respected her separateness with a bare nod. Walking down to the village, she sometimes stopped to talk to other women dressed in black, whose stories were much like her own, although most of them had lost their husbands earlier, in the Battle of Stalingrad.

Worse than being fatherless, I felt I was no longer one with my mother. If only I could join her in her separate world. I wanted to be special the way she was. I wanted my clothes dyed black like hers, but she wouldn't hear of it. I begged for at least a black ribbon in my hair. "*Sei nicht albern.* – Don't be silly," she said, reproachfully, as if my suggestion made light of my father's death, or of her misfortune.

She had become the widow she would remain for the rest of her life, robbed of the promise of a happy and prosperous future with her husband, left alone to raise her two girls in times of hardship. She deplored her own fate then, but particularly in the ensuing years, when she condemned the war and cursed its consequences.

Later, much later, I speculated that my mother, seeking to protect her children, had blinded herself to certain things, hoping that Gitta and I would also not see the truth of our tarnished, fatherless experience. Not speaking of our father in terms of her children's loss, she glossed over the tragedy that was ours as well. She was a *Kriegerwitwe* – a war widow; we were *Halbwaisen* – half orphans, by official definition: the former a term she would endorse as her identity, the latter, a word she did not allow in her vocabulary.

Out of deep love for her children, my mother wanted their world to be intact, ignorant of the high cost of pretending this was so. She rarely spoke of my father. She avoided activities that typically involved a whole family, like going to Mass or on walks on Sunday afternoons. Unable to articulate the lack, it created a sense in me of being not only less fortunate, but also less worthy than other children who had fathers, who I secretly envied.

3

It was well into January. The sky shone a crisp blue, crisper even than on summer days. The new snow had transformed the shabby farmyard into an idyllic playground.

"Komm, wir machen Schnee-Engel," Kurtie said. He showed me how to lie on my back and flap my arms to create impressions of angel wings in the snow.

Mother stepped outside. She was carrying a bucket of kitchen scraps to empty into the pigs' trough in the barn. Seeing us, she called out, "You'll catch cold," but she didn't make us stop.

It was the postman who got me to my feet. I heard him call out, in the manner of a town-crier, "From the front." He leaned his bicycle against the half-timbered wall of the farmhouse. I abandoned Kurtie and the angels and ran, half falling in the snow, wanting to collect the letter he was waving in his hand.

Mother stopped me, *"Nein."* She spoke tersely, and took the letter from the postman, without so much as a nod to thank him.

The envelope bore my father's familiar handwriting, finely penned in royal blue ink.

My father was alive, after all. He had written to us. The letter proved it.

"Von meinem Papa. – From my Papa."

Mother covered her mouth with her hand, to stifle a cry, it looked like. Turning away, she folded the envelope, stuffed it into her coat pocket and went inside the house. As if nothing had happened. As if the postman hadn't come. As if she hadn't heard me.

The letter, I would learn much later, was my father's last letter. It was dated December 19, 1944, seven days before he was killed on December 26, the *Zweite Weihnachtstag,* the Second Christmas Day, as it is known and observed in Germany. A *memento mori,* Mother kept it tucked away in the inner pocket of her handbag.

A week or two passed. The snow had begun to melt. Brown blotches marred the formerly pristine winter landscape. Rivulets of dirty water washed along the path, leaving large puddles near the dunghill in the courtyard. From the barn, a cow's mooing broke the silence now and then.

Mother was sweeping the brick entryway. I was waiting to help her with the dustpan. She looked up when the postman approached on his bicycle, a parcel strapped to the back rack. Swinging his leg over the seat, he came to a running stop. He handed the parcel to Mother with a wordless nod, knowing perhaps that he was not the bearer of welcome gifts. Mother accepted it, wordlessly also. With the parcel clasped against her chest, she headed into the house. I tagged along behind her.

Upstairs in our room, Mother placed the parcel at the foot of the bed. She seemed unaware of my presence. Her movements were painstakingly slow, as if she wanted to delay what she knew was ahead. She undid the packing twine, looped it around her index and middle fingers a few times, and secured it with a knot and bow. She removed the brown wrapping paper, folded it neatly, then put it to one side.

At last she opened the flaps of the box. She hesitated before she lifted out a folded mass of an army green military coat. She spread it on the bed, smoothing out the wrinkles with her palms.

Mother didn't explain, she didn't have to: my father's belongings sent home from the front, I realized. The coat had been his. I climbed on the chair behind the bed and leaned over the now half-empty box. Mother didn't stop me.

Atop a small jumble of things, I spotted my father's silver cigarette case. Its lid was dented. Mother sighed audibly as she rubbed it and caressed the engraved initials, *JS*. 'It must have been in his back pocket when he fell,' she said, not for my ears, and barely loud enough for me to hear. It brought to life, for the first time in my fantasy, a partial re-creation of how my father had died: Not the shot in the forehead – that part I did not envision, not yet – but his falling backwards in the trench, in fading late-afternoon light. Mother opened the cigarette case. An elasticized ribbon held three cigarettes in place, slightly crushed but intact.

She sat down on the bed, her thoughts elsewhere, until, after a while, she resumed her task and took from the box a tin canteen with a moss-green felt cover. She shook it. It sounded empty, but when she unscrewed the top, a musty smell escaped, a smell reminiscent of Grandmother's root cellar.

A portfolio, its brown leather worn at the edges, came next. It contained neatly folded letters with Mother's handwriting, larger than my father's, rounder and more generous; a black fountain pen under a loop in the center crease; unused *Feldpost,* the *Wehrmacht*-issued writing paper; a couple of photos.

"Das bin ich. – That's me," I said, thrilled to see myself, a little girl holding a bunch of wild flowers. Mother seemed to take notice of me for the first time. She looked up. She smiled at me, with her eyes.

"He loved you very much," she said.

Reaching deeper into the box, she retrieved a black wallet, a few bills and coins inside. Something shiny sparkled from a small inside compartment: my father's gold wedding band. Mother took off her own and, placing it on top of his, slid both on her right-hand ring finger, the finger traditionally reserved for one's wedding band. From that day on, until the day she died, she wore the two rings as a visible sign of her widowhood.

The parcel was empty now but for a long, black and silver-colored object at the very bottom.

"Was ist das, Mama?" I asked, half-knowing it was a weapon.

"Ein Dolch. – A dagger."

Something frightful passed through me. Unlike the other things in the box – the coat, the cigarette case, his wallet – that had brought my father close, I recoiled from the dagger, even from my father.

I watched Mother take the dagger out of its scabbard, afraid, and then relieved when she replaced it and wrapped it in the paper she'd put aside. In the days and weeks that followed, the memory of my father's dagger continued to haunt me. It had exposed something vaguely bad about him, when I had believed him to be only good. Not until I was an adult did I learn that it was a ceremonial dagger of the sort everyone in the *Wehrmacht* was issued according to his rank.

And then, matter-of-factly, as if she were going about an ordinary chore, Mother opened the wardrobe and stashed everything on the bottom shelf, as far out of sight as possible.

"*Also!* – All right!" she said. There was resolve in her voice. She had completed her task. Taking my hand, she led the way out of the bedroom. The day's chores were waiting for her.

4

The only decorative touch in our small Rockensußra bedroom was my father's photograph on the night table. It was his farewell remembrance to his wife and children when he was deployed from the Rhineland to East Prussia, a thousand kilometers from home: his image, postcard size, in a wooden frame that bore Mother's scroll-carved initials. A proud man, a few military medals pinned to his uniform, he gazes into a still-intact future.

I watched Mother as she placed a black ribbon over one corner of my father's photo. "Josef," she said, her voice serious, deeper than usual. It conveyed something decisive, something I didn't understand, not then. Years later, I thought of it as the moment she bid her husband farewell and, more importantly, took charge of her own life and that of their children without him. He had been dead for only two months.

Mother remained quiet for a while, sitting beside me on the bed. Then she told me, in a calm voice, that a black ribbon signified that the person in the photo was dead, like the Köppel's sons. "They lost their boys in the war." Framed snapshots of them in uniforms were displayed on the cupboard shelf in the front room.

Always, when I looked at my father in the photograph, I saw a gentle man looking back at me, his eyes meeting mine. They had the same tender quality that, when Gitta was a little older, became the facial feature that made her resemble him so much. His eyes and his generous mouth, with a slight V-shaped dip in the center of the upper lip. *"Ihrem Vater wie aus dem Gesicht geschnitten.* – Her father's spitting image," Grandmother liked to say, with an uncharacteristic touch of sentimentality. I liked my father's smile in the photo, faint, but so real, it made me smile back at him. I pretended he was alive.

In my young memory, there was no one who had died – other than my father. There were those who had died before I was born – my paternal grandfather, a casualty of World War I; my great-grandmother, who, Grandmother told me "died the hour your Mama was born"; Onkel Willie, Grandmother's favorite brother – but those dead people hadn't ever been real to me. They were like stories from a past that also wasn't real.

So, I came to equate being *dead* with the only reference I had: never coming home again. That's what Mother had said, "Your Papa is dead. He'll never come home again." But the meaning of the word *never* had not yet grown to its full compass in my understanding: everything was open-ended, or could be reversed, or perhaps a mistake had been made.

This kind of childlike speculating allowed me to construct a make-believe world in which a time would come when my father returned to us. That time, in my imagination, was the end of the war. All fighting would come to a stop. The soldiers would go home. My father, too. He would walk up the path from the highway, as had the stranger who'd brought the news of his death.

Yet, there was also a budding sense that I had created a lie. Several years later, in the same way, I began doubting there was a *Christkind*, a Christ Child, who brought gifts on Christmas, and an Easter Bunny, and that fairytales were factual: one moment they had existed, the next moment they did not. The boundaries between childhood magic and objective reality were shifting. I wanted to hold on to fantasy and make-believe but, at the same time, I did not.

"*Dein Papa ist im Himmel.* – Your Papa's in heaven," Mother said when I pressed her to tell me where my father had gone. "Good people go to heaven after they've died."

My image of heaven and God came from holy pictures that Grandmother Neuss – whom Mother pejoratively described as *eine fromme Frau* – a pious woman – kept in her prayer book: a grandfatherly God on a throne floating above billowy clouds, angel choirs in attendance, the same elusive place from which the *Christ Child* descended on Christmas Eve.

"Your Papa always watches you," Mother told me, smiling tenderly, after I'd done something to deserve praise or frowning, after I'd misbehaved. The suggestion that my father was able to see me made him present in a way he hadn't been when he was still alive, away at war. It brought him closer even than the photograph on the nightstand. I imagined him observing me as he peeked down from heaven through the clouds. Wanting to please him, I tried my hardest to behave like the good girl I believed he wanted me to be. But as much as I gave credence to his elusive presence, I was also afraid I was making it up.

Many weeks had passed since Christmas. Still, Christmas was alive as a bright spot in my memory, not yet darkened by the news of my father's death. I wanted to make a drawing for him of that merry time, having been promised by mother that he would come to collect it from the window sill in the middle of the night, when everyone was asleep.

Mother tore a sheet off her writing pad. "Take this. What use is it to me?" Her practice of writing almost daily letters to him had come to an end.

With only a regular pencil – I had no coloring pencils in Rockensußra – the tree in my drawing was a lackluster tree. It had none of the sparkle of the real one that had lit up the front room. I could not duplicate the red of the candles, the yellow of the halos, the silver of the glass ornaments that had mirrored my face and made it look funny. The dress I had worn, standing next to the tree – a pretty dress Mother had made from an old skirt of hers, the soft fabric a light blue, the bodice smocked with dark blue yarn – looked drab in my drawing. It made me feel sad.

Mother opened the bedroom window. Ready for bed, barefoot and in my nightgown, I shivered with excitement and the cold. We looked out into the early night. The air was still and chilly as it touched my face. The inside of my nose smarted with each breath. The evening star hung low in the sky. I placed the folded drawing on the weathered windowsill. On the outside, it read "PAPA," in clumsily written block letters.

Mother tucked me in for the night. "Will Papa really come get it?" I asked in a whisper.

"Of course," Mother whispered back. She sounded so sure.

I fought sleep and I watched the window for as long as I could keep my eyes open, trusting I would see my father float down from the sky.

It was still dark when I woke up early in the morning. I jumped out of bed, dashed to the window, peered through the ice-flowered glass. The drawing was gone.

5

Late in the evening, sounds from the downstairs hallway awakened me. A click from the front door lock falling back into place. Footsteps on the tiled floor. Muffled voices. I climbed out of bed and tiptoed out the bedroom door, which was always left ajar to help ease my fear of the dark and my fear of being left alone. I heard Mother, *"Um Gottes Willen, du bist es! –* Oh my God, it's you!"* followed by a man's hushed response.

I ran down the stairs, feet barely touching the treads, one hand gliding along the banister. A wedge of light came through the open front-room door. It illuminated a narrow strip in the otherwise dark hallway, where the caller stood facing Mother, both of her hands in both of his.

My father. He had come back from the war. I rushed up to him and thrust my arms around his thighs.

"Let me look at you," he said, letting go of Mother's hands and bending down to hug me. A pair of strong arms lifted me up. A face came close to mine. I scanned it in the shadowy light, searching for my father's familiar features. I had not seen him since he'd been home for Gitta's birth, a little more than a year ago, but my memory of him was as keen as his image in the photograph on the upstairs nightstand.

The face before me was that of an old man, gray stubble covering his cheeks and chin, his thinning hair disheveled. I could not find the smartly trimmed collar of the uniform I remembered, only a heavy scarf wrapped around his neck.

Panic struck me. This man wasn't my father. This man was a stranger. Kicking my legs and screaming, I struggled to free myself. After a vain attempt to calm me, the stranger put me back down.

"Du kennst mich nicht? – You don't remember me?"* The man's voice was kind, its lilt rang of home.

"Your Onkel Jean," Mother said.

If I did recognize the visitor then as the man I knew as Onkel Jean, I couldn't yet make the leap from feared stranger to kindly friend. Confused and afraid, I turned to Mother for comfort, but all she said was, "*Stell Dich nicht so an!* – Pull yourself together." I felt ashamed.

Not related by blood, Onkel Jean was an old family friend. He was like a great-uncle to me. My favorite one. His orchard, half a block from our flat back home in Delrath, had been the first place I'd ventured to alone, even before I'd been brave enough to cross the quiet main street and walk to Grandmother's house. Straddling his shoulders, I had picked ripe cherries and peaches and Mirabelle plums from his most prized fruit trees. Holding his hand for safety, I had gingerly petted his goat, whom I'd feared for its unpredictable bucking. Onkel Jean had come for us when air raid sirens had howled us out of sleep. While bombers had streaked closely above and huge light cones from anti-aircraft batteries had searched the night sky, he had carried me, running for shelter to the schoolhouse basement at the end of our street.

Now the three of us were in the front-room in Rockensußra. A dim light illuminated the room. Onkel Jean opened his small suitcase.

"Gifts from your grandmother," he said, expecting, it seemed, I would be consoled.

Mother wiped the tears from my eyes. Onkel Jean coaxed me with gentle words until I finally overcame my shyness. Then he let me help unpack what he had brought for us: a bag of Grandmother's plain and chocolate marbled shortbread; white cotton underwear; smoked ham wrapped in layers of newspaper; red and green apples, their skin shriveled after a long winter in the root cellar; and a flat tin box, forest green, with the trademark of a pelican.

"My coloring pencil set," I exclaimed, in disbelief. I opened it. Like a Christmas wish come true, it contained all the colors, arranged by hues from light to dark. Of varying lengths, the coloring pencils had been neatly sharpened with a penknife.

"It's late," Mother said. "Long past your bedtime."

"I'm not tired," I protested, to no avail.

Onkel Jean, too, agreed: He'd tell me stories tomorrow about *Oma* and *Opa,* my grandparents, and about *Spitz,* the new puppy. With a tight hug and a playful pat on my bottom, he sent me on my way back to bed.

I climbed up the stairs, stalling on each step. When I reached the top, I didn't go to our bedroom. I crouched in the far corner of the landing, knees pulled up to my chin, and eavesdropped on the conversation downstairs.

His voice low, Onkel Jean did most of the talking, most of which was beyond the understanding of the five-year old I was, but pieced together later when I learned more about the events in the final months of the war: about the futile fighting; about the Soviet army moving west; about streams of civilians fleeing from the eastern provinces.

He spoke about the bombing of Dresden by the Allied Forces, its total destruction and the many dead.

"People jumped into the Elbe River to save their lives," I heard him say, "but the river caught on fire, burning them to death." The image I created in my mind those many years ago is still alive in my memory with all its visual horror.

He told Mother then, and told me long after we were back home in Delrath again, how he had traveled to Dresden from our hometown by whatever means available – by train, on foot, on the beds of trucks and horse-drawn wagons – to look for a friend he'd hoped had survived the bombing and the ensuing firestorm. How he'd given up after days of searching through the rubble of the leveled city.

"That's war. Wrongs fought with wrongs," he said, sadly, that evening, and again in his later retelling.

Silence. The conversation had come to an end. I waited for Mother's steps on the stairs, but all I could hear was the wind whipping through the fir trees on the side of the house. Then, after a while, I heard Mother sob, "I beg you. . . Please. . . take us home."

Onkel Jean didn't speak immediately. Perhaps he didn't have an answer. Perhaps he was thinking about how to refuse Mother gently.

Finally, he said, "No. You and your girls are safe here in Rockensußra. The bombings in the west are fierce. Nightly air raids even in our small town."

Mother wouldn't relent, "You can't leave us here, Jean. With Josef dead, nothing else matters anymore – only home."

But he argued that it would be too dangerous for us to attempt traveling now. "I'll come back for you. Soon. I promise."

Lowering his voice to an almost whisper, he said that the war would be over in a matter of weeks. *"Der Führer verspricht noch immer Sieg. Lächerlich!* – The *Führer* still promises victory. Laughable! *Bis auf den letzten Mann werden sie kämpfen.* – The fight will continue until the last man falls."

I imagined Mother still weeping, although if she were weeping, she didn't make a sound.

"Don't repeat any of this to anyone. I warn you. You can't trust a soul," he said.

Then he, too, fell silent.

Shivering with cold, my cheeks red hot, I pulled my nightgown over my knees. I had overheard things I sensed I wasn't supposed to hear and only half understood. I felt frightened and confused, and guilty that I hadn't listened to Mother and gone straight to bed, but now I didn't dare move for fear of making the floorboards creak.

Eventually, I must have fallen asleep. I woke up not knowing where I was, Mother lifting me up in her arms. She touched her hand to my forehead. It felt cool against my skin. Knitting her brows with concern, she said to Onkel Jean, who'd followed her, *"Das Kind fiebert.* – The child's running a temperature."

6

In my recollection, daylight did not return for many days after the fever began. Murky twilight came into the bedroom through the louvered wood shutters. I was covered with itchy red spots from head to toe and burning up. Cocooned in feverish dreams, I was oblivious even of Mother when she sat at my bedside. *"Masern, –* Measles," had been her diagnosis.

With deft hands, she wrapped cold, wet compresses around my chest and calves. I shrank from the initial contact with the icy cold, but as the heat drained from my skin, it felt good.

Wakefulness and sleep merged as a recurring dream beleaguered me: *My father and I walk along the main street back home, on our way to Grandmother's house. I skip next to him, keeping up with his pace. From the meadow we pass, a flock of white geese charges toward us. I reach for my father's hand. The geese are at eye level with me. They snap at my face. I can see into their inner bills, yellow and toothless, and down their gaping throats. Their honking drowns out my screams. My father doesn't hear me.*

I'd come out of sleep, the dream's geese still encircling me, necks stretched to pluck at my bed sheets and face.

But my father, he wouldn't be there. My sobs would summon Mother to my bedside, her presence and the coolness of her hand comforting me.

"Die Gänse. . . – The geese. . . They're here again," I whimpered as I slipped back into the dream. I faintly heard Mother's voice, "They won't get you, my child. Everything's all right." She stroked my cheeks. Still, nothing could wipe away the fear that kept me isolated in my feverish world, at the mercy of a flock of geese.

Onkel Jean had left Rockensußra without my noticing. My recovery from the measles had progressed slowly and tentatively, at first. I spent weeks in bed, the window behind my headboard shuttered. Even after all symptoms disappeared, my health remained fragile, and I stayed cooped up indoors for more weeks.

It was the beginning of April, a fine early spring day.

"You still look so pale. A little sunshine would do you good," Frau Köppel commented. "You've been indoors for too long."

That was all the encouragement Kurtie needed. "Come on. Let's go," he said.

And so, off we went, Kurtie and I, both of us bundled up in warm sweaters. I followed him across the barnyard and out the gate.

"*Schau, die Amis haben das Dorf besetzt.* – Look, the *Amis* occupied the village." "*Die Amis!*" I repeated to demonstrate that I understood the reference. It made us feel adult to call the Americans *Amis,* an abbreviation, more or less, of the German word *Amerikaner.* It was a derogatory, or innocuous, term, depending on the tone and the context in which it was used.

In the big meadow on the hillside next to the highway, a row of tanks stood lined up within easy view. Their barrels pointed in our direction. I dropped back gawking at what looked like the scene of war. Kurtie noticed. "They won't shoot at us," he said authoritatively. Not a soul was around. Just an ominous presence of war. It was curiously quiet.

I trusted Kurtie. He knew about things I didn't know.

But when I heard the sound of footsteps and saw a soldier walking up the path from the highway, I wished I hadn't come along. The soldier's gait looked strained under the weight of two buckets filled with water that was sloshing over the sides. He stopped close to us, put down the buckets. He rubbed his palms together and whistled a sigh of pretend relief. A big, white-toothed smile came over his face. He was chewing on a small white wad of something I didn't recognize. He tipped his cap and spoke animatedly. Neither Kurtie nor I understood. Maybe I knew already that there were people who lived in other countries and spoke in languages other than my own, but I had never heard another language spoken. Shrinking away now, I pushed myself against the brick wall, eyes glued on the soldier. It wasn't from fear that I pulled back, but a kind of confusion: if this was the enemy, his friendly, even silly, behavior muddled my understanding of what an enemy was.

Like the Russians, the Americans were the *Feind,* the enemy, as were the French and the British – the *Alliierten,* the Allies. The Russians had killed my father. The British and Americans dropped bombs on our cities, killing people in their houses. Those were my closest associations.

Sieg, victory, was the promise people spoke about. I had heard Herr Köppel rant about *Deutschlands Endsieg,* Germany's final victory. Onkel Jean had told of a different, a secret, outcome: that the *Wehrmacht* would soon be defeated.

The American soldier seemed so ordinary. His uniform was not unlike my father's. I could tell them apart only by their colors: the soldier's was a khaki color; my father's had been dark green.

I was certain the soldier meant no harm and would do no harm, just as I was certain my father had meant no harm and had done no harm.

The soldier said something, something unintelligible.

"That's English," Kurtie said, the expression on his face one of self-importance. He took a step closer to the soldier, pulling me along by my sweater sleeve, to bolster his courage and present a united front. The soldier stooped down, his hands resting above his knees. *"Verrrshtain?"* he said, rolling his *r* as if he were imitating a dog growling. It was clear enough for us to know that he was asking whether we understood.

His speech made me feel so awkward that I started to giggle. Smiling broadly, he came closer and lifted me in his arms. I leaned back from him stiffly, my gaze fixed on his jaw still moving up and down. The smell of peppermint was on his breath.

He uttered something that sounded like the German *Kuss,* and, turning a clean-shaven cheek toward me, pointed to it. "He wants a kiss," Kurtie said. I turned my face away, but when Kurtie pressured, "Come on, don't be a sissy," I gave the soldier a hasty peck and, still giggling, wriggled myself back down.

The soldier reached into his pants pocket and, with a sleight of hand, produced four slim, paper-wrapped packets. He handed two to me and two to Kurtie, who beamed, whispering, *"Kaugummi.* – Chewing gum."

Mother looked worried when I came back into the house. "Where were you?" she asked. "Out with Kurtie," I said, not eager to tell the whole story, nor to divulge what I held clasped in my fist. "You'll get sick again," she said and then, with that uncanny omniscience of hers, "What's that you have in your hand?"

I showed her the packets of chewing gum. Her face darkening, she demanded to know, "How did you get those?" "A soldier gave them to me for a kiss," I said, half-expecting my spoils would appease her, half-knowing trading a kiss was something wrong. I was not used to Mother raising her voice. But now she spat out, "Don't you ever do that again." She ripped the packets from my hand and flung them into the garbage pail. Shame burned my cheeks.

I had received my two packs of gum and Kurtie his two packs for the favor of a kiss I'd given to a soldier. Mother's admonition – one that made me feel ugly, as it survives in my memory – instilled in me that even a little girl's kiss lacked propriety. I also sensed it could lead to danger of an unspoken kind. Those were the cautionary lessons I learned. It was not within my grasp, then, that perhaps, there was another reason for her disapproval.

That reason didn't become apparent until the following year, when the war was over and we were home again, and even then didn't add up to anything I could fully understand. At Mother's invitation, her friend Anna, widowed early in the war, had lived in our flat with her young son Manfred during the time we spent in Rockensußra. Onkel Jean's niece, Anna had the looks and bearing of a 1930s film star, her blonde hair marcelled, her voice low and raspy.

Mother was appalled to hear the neighbors gossip that an American officer had been Anna's frequent caller. A greasy spot on the wall, just above the living room sofa – caused by the pomade in his hair, Mother suggested disparagingly – was the telltale evidence. *"Wie konnte sie nur?* – How could she?" Mother said. She rubbed away at the stain with a soapy rag. Leaving the flowers on the wallpaper slightly worn and a hint lighter, it served as a reminder of Anna's dalliance with the American, but also something that didn't dawn on me for a long time – that Anna had shown a lack of patriotism as a German woman, fraternizing with the enemy. Likewise, it may have been at the root of my own later reluctance – when I was already away at college in Munich – to seek contact with American military stationed there.

7

The women huddled around the radio. Herr Köppel was pacing the room, his hands clenched behind his back. Ear to the radio speaker, Kurtie had joined the grown-ups listening to the voice coming over the airwaves. I, too, listened, sensing, if nothing else, the weight of the moment, but all that remains in my memory is a man's steady voice. I now know that it was the broadcast of Germany's unconditional surrender.

Herr Köppel switched off the radio. He stomped out of the room, muttering, *"Eine Schande!* – A disgrace!" His work boots thudded in the hallway. A door slammed shut.

The women had grown silent, the expression on their faces was one of relief, as if, what they had been waiting for, had come to pass. The eldest of the daughters, who was the one closest to Mother in age, took my hand and then Mother's hand and put her arms around us. I thought I could hear both women weep.

"The war is over," Mother said, wiping her eyes with the back of her hands.

She stepped to the same window from which, almost exactly four months earlier, I'd seen the uniformed man trudge through the snow. I had never gone near that window again, held back by the superstitious belief that, if I did, worse things would happen.

Now the window was wide open. Cool air and the smell of spring earth swept into the room. It was mid-morning, a sunny day, not a cloud in the sky, not even smoke billowing from the chimneys of the houses in the village. The cherry trees across the highway stood in full white bloom.

I climbed onto the stool below the window, close to Mother where she stood gazing into the distance. I searched to see what held her attention. The highway looked deserted, save a few stray sheep, nibbling on patchy tufts of grass at the roadside.

"We're going home," Mother said, with a determination in her voice and bearing that, if I hadn't known it was good news, would have frightened me.

She lifted me up with a firm grip and sat me on the windowsill, my feet dangling against the stucco of the outside wall. She wrapped her arms around me and, putting her cheek close to mine, pointed into the distance to a place neither of us could see. "All we have to do is follow the sun west."

Going home. It meant sitting on grandmother's lap again; playing with Doris, Sybille and the other children in the neighborhood; picking fruit in Onkel Jean's orchard; the adventure of another journey – that too. Those were the promises of the end of the war.

Mother had talked about *Friedenszeit,* peace time, with longing – a sometimes hopeless, sometimes angry, longing. *Friedenszeit* was of a past long ago, before I was born. Then came *Kriegszeit,* wartime. In my memory, that was all there had ever been; nothing on the other side of it was imaginable. *Friedenszeit* was of a future so far away, was anyone sure it would ever come?

The word itself was imbued with the magic of fairytales. A place, rather than a condition, where only good things happened, and all was fun and games and plenty.

The soldiers would return home from the war. My father, too, perhaps.

8

On most afternoons, a small group of Kurtie's friends got together in the barnyard to kick a ball into a makeshift soccer goal. A day or two after the announcement of the end of the war, they huddled together in a sunny spot at the edge of the meadow. The only girl and younger than the boys by a few years, I eavesdropped from a short distance. They spouted all sorts of ideas about the lost war and things to come. One of them proclaimed that the end of the world was near. But what I remember most is a warning Kurtie voiced. "It's forbidden now to salute *Heil Hitler.* You'll get in deep trouble if you're caught just raising your arm."

"Like how?" one of the other boys taunted, lifting his arm extra high and shouting, *"Heil Hitler!"*

I ached to follow his lead. I felt a twitch in my right arm I could barely resist. Mother had not taught me the Hitler salute. But I had loved imitating my father when he was home on leave. *"Heil Hitler,"* we'd both say, raising our right arms, as we passed people in the street. I'd seen the locals in Rockensußra salute *Heil Hitler,* I'd heard the roar of *Heil Hitler* at rallies broadcast over the radio. Once, I'd asked Mother why she never saluted. She'd said, *"Man muss ja nicht. – It's not mandatory.* And I just won't do it." Then she added, as if she regretted her remark, *"Aber du weißt ja. . . so was darf man nicht laut sagen. –* But you know. . . you mustn't repeat this to anyone."

Kurtie looked around, surreptitiously, and so did all the others, making sure no one had seen or heard. The yard was empty. Only the sound of someone pitching hay came from the barn.

"I wouldn't do that again if I were you," Kurtie said.

The boy stepped forward, daring Kurtie, repeating the same gesture and an even louder *Heil Hitler,* then punching and pushing Kurtie to the ground. Kurtie, who was no coward, regained his footing and charged the boy. Soon the two lay wrestling in the spring grass, while the rest of the boys moved back a few steps, forming a circle and cheering them on. I clapped my hands. "Kurtie, Kurtie," I squealed, but he didn't seem to hear me.

Herr Köppel strode out of the barn. He leaned his pitchfork against the wall and strutted in our direction. His tall frame appeared even more towering, his face dominated by a neatly twisted handle-bar moustache more intimidating.

Feet spread apart, he stood still for a moment, assessing the scuffle, before he pulled the two boys to their feet. *"Du Taugenichts.* – You good-for-nothing," he shouted at Kurtie, but not at the other boy. It wasn't the first time I'd seen Herr Köppel treat his son with undeserved harshness and rage. Now he gave him a mean kick in the buttocks, which sent Kurtie limping and howling like an injured dog.

Grabbing the other boy by the collar and, lowering his face close to the boy's, he said, "You're a ruffian all right, but a coward you're not." There was a pause as he relaxed his grip. His voice weary, he said. "You would've made a fine soldier. But that's all over now." He let go of the boy, who followed the rest of us scrambling off into the meadow.

Herr Köppel commanded the respect owed to a hardworking man who toiled and tilled his fields. But he also commanded absolute obedience and subservience from those around him.

As I remember our arrival in Rockensußra on that balmy evening the previous August, the Köppel family had welcomed us warmly. I'd clung to Mother, hiding my face in the folds of her summer skirt. She'd encouraged me to be polite. *"Sei höflich."* But I'd put my hands behind my back, cringing with discomfort, refusing to shake anyone's hand. The women had been kind, nevertheless, stroking my head. But the old man, he'd grunted, "An ill-mannered girl, eh?"

He treated Mother, I sensed, with the disdain some farming people have for those that don't make their living plowing the fields. More sophisticated in the way we spoke and dressed, we had no legitimate place in his world. And we were outsiders, from the west. He granted Mother, Gitta and me room and board begrudgingly. I think now that, if it hadn't been for Mother's untiring work in the kitchen and around the house, he wouldn't have tolerated our intrusion.

What's more, I was a finicky eater, with a particular distaste for his home-butchered pork sausage. The old man had quickly become wise to my squeamish eating habits.

"You're a spoiled brat," Herr Köppel bellowed one day during our meal of potatoes, cabbage and sausage, after he'd caught me pushing the sausage aside. "If you were one of my own, I'd give you a good spanking."

My chin barely clearing the table, I stared at my plate, eyes welling up with tears and spittle choking my throat. "Eat," Mother said, ashamed of her willful child. She patted me on my back, encouraging me to do as I had been told, and to save us from the old man's wrath. His cruel eyes on me, I forced down every last piece of his detestable *Wurst*.

Luckily, I escaped his attention on most days and got away with leaving the sausage pieces uneaten. Mother let me. She took them off my plate and, on the sly, dropped them in her apron pocket.

Even as I remember Herr Köppel all these years later, the sting of his disapproval of me and my fear of him comes back. I had learned for the first time that not everyone liked me. It had also taught me that I was flawed.

9

Army surplus supplies of the defunct *Wehrmacht* had been trucked to a depository in Rockensußra and made available to the civilian population. The news spread like wildfire. People came from all over the countryside and nearby towns. Many came on foot. Others on bicycles, which they left leaning haphazardly against a low wall surrounding the village green. Some brought handcarts. A few arrived in horse-drawn wagons. Carrying empty suitcases, baskets and rucksacks, a crowd swarmed around the door of the red brick barn next to the Lutheran church. They shoved and elbowed. Everyone wanted to be first. Noisy arguments were left unsettled, with people exchanging angry looks.

It was a crisp morning in late spring. I carried my own little basket in one hand and held on to the handle of Mother's suitcase with the other; we kept to the periphery of the growing crowd that extended onto the dewy grass.

At the first peal of the church bells – at seven a.m., the same time they rang every morning – the massive double doors of the barn swung open. The crowd was set in motion all at once. People moved as a single mass and then, as they reached the entrance, ran into the barn in all directions.

What met the eye were mind-boggling heaps, tall enough to climb, of *Wehrmacht* uniforms, parachutes, blankets, flags, boots. There were towering stacks of typewriters, typing paper, boxes of pencils, fountain pens, erasers, and paperclips.

People grabbed indiscriminately, stuffing their suitcases, baskets, rucksacks. When those were jam-packed, they took bundles of whatever else they could carry.

Mother, too, crammed her suitcase with stuff: a parachute, a blanket, an army coat – mostly items she would later use to make into clothes.

For a while I stood watching. Then I, too, got caught up in the frenzy. I wandered off, passing piles in disarray and people who paid no attention to me. I stopped when I came to a corner with masses of writing paraphernalia.

Everything tempted me. Unsure what I could take, I stalled. A young woman with a red and green kerchief on her head looked at me from where she sat crouched on the ground, filling her own bags. She smiled as she tossed a few pencils into my basket. *"Nimm dir. –* Help yourself," she said. Encouraged now, I began collecting whatever caught my eye: sheets of paper, more pencils, erasers, paperclips, pencil sharpeners, even a bottle of ink.

When I'd filled my basket, I looked around for Mother, expecting to find her next to me and to show her my treasures. She wasn't there. I tried to spot her in her black dress and black pillbox hat. She was nowhere to be seen. I was frantic.

My vision clouded with tears, I stumbled through the fray of strangers. I didn't know where I was headed. I wanted to scream, but all that came out was a whimper.

I ended up near the entrance of the barn, where it was less crowded. Someone took my hand. I heard Kurtie's voice. "Come on, crybaby. You lost your mommy?" he said in a mock-pitying tone.

"Lass mich. – Don't," I sniveled as he dragged me through the village green, up the street and across the highway to the farmhouse. Half-running, half-falling, I looked back over my shoulders. "Mama. Mama," I called.

Once we were inside the house, I ran upstairs, a sense of unlikely hope quickening my step. Perhaps Mother had come home. Perhaps she was waiting for me.

The bedroom was empty, only Gitta was asleep in her crib. I shook her awake, half-expecting that she could tell me where Mother was, or maybe join me in a misfortune that would also be hers. She startled out of sleep and, screaming, pulled herself up on the crib bars.

Gitta was my little sister, but, for the most part, she was a nuisance to me and someone who demanded Mother's attention at my expense. Now, there was comfort in seeing her distressed in the same way I was distressed. It made me feel a sisterly bond with her, for the first time, perhaps.

I stepped to the closed window overlooking the highway. People trudged in both directions. They stooped under their heavy loads. I just stood there. Watching. Waiting. Gitta screaming from her crib. A feeling of separateness and independence from Mother began to calm me, and a belief that I was safe, after all. I became convinced that Mother was the one who was lost, and that I would wait for her until she found her way home.

I don't know how much time had passed when I saw Mother among the thinning stream of people. She was carrying her suitcase in one hand, my basket in the other.

This is where my memory breaks off. I don't recall Mother coming into the bedroom. I don't recall my relief, nor do I recall her scolding me for having left the barn on my own. At the very edge, where the remembered and the unremembered meet, the hint of a realization lingers: Mother had not been lost. Neither had she thought I had been lost. She had taken for granted that I was old enough to find my way home without her.

10

A mass exodus had begun in the summer of 1944. As the Soviet army advanced from the east, an estimated twelve to fourteen million German nationals fled west. They were comprised of whole populations leaving German territories in the east; of German nationals living in areas annexed by the Hitler regime; and of ethnic Germans in eastern European countries. They left voluntarily or through forced expulsion, and relocated to parts of Germany not occupied by the Soviets in a migration that continued until 1950.

Simultaneously, millions of others migrated from their homelands: non-Germans who had been uprooted in Germany and other war-torn countries; European Jews who had survived the Holocaust; gypsies; former Nazis who were fleeing prosecution.

Some of these areas had been seized by Germany before and during the war; others had gone back and forth between Germany and neighboring countries for centuries.

Suddenly, Rockensußra was no longer the sleepy village it had been. The highway that ran through the village filled with a steady stream of people on foot: young and old women, children and old men. There was only a sprinkling of younger men, many of them with limbs missing and on makeshift crutches.

The able-bodied lugged suitcases and overstuffed packs. They pulled handcarts loaded to overflowing. They carried infants and toddlers. Children clung to their mothers' skirts. Some even brought their dead on makeshift hearses, in search of a dignified place to bury them.

Kurtie had seen two dead bodies on a horse-drawn wagon by the churchyard. *"Richtige Tote* – Real dead people," he came running to tell me, gesturing animatedly, as if proclaiming that he'd discovered a treasure. Curiosity got the better of me. I abandoned my solitary game of hopscotch, and followed him to the village green and down a short lane.

A small group of people stood at the open tailgate of the wagon, women crying and men talking quietly among themselves. I stretched tall on my tiptoes. Still, I couldn't see what was on the wagon. Kurtie grabbed me around my waist and lifted me up. There, lying on the bare wood, were two distinctly human forms shaping the burlap that covered the side-by-side bodies from head to toe. Something eerie about those shapes, so separate from the living, frightened me; but I felt fascinated, too.

Kurtie set me back down. *"Siehst du.* – You see," he said. I stood rooted to the spot.

A woman, her eyes red and teary, noticed us. *"Ihr Kinder.* – You children," she said and, with a sideways gesture of her hand, motioned for us to go away.

We took off, fleeing from the presence of death. Running faster than I'd ever run before, I reached the farmyard, Kurtie ahead of me. Our cheeks were flushed from exhaustion, both of us bending over and panting, as if to exorcise what we had seen.

It was midsummer, when it stayed light into the late hours of the evening, and temperatures stayed balmy until early morning. Daily, refugees came to knock on the farmhouse door. They asked to fill their canteens from the well, or for handouts of food, or to seek shelter in the barn at nightfall. Often, they were women with their children and infants. Sitting on the front steps, they would rock their infants to sleep in their arms. Mother and the Köppel sisters would join the women and children with a loaf of bread, sometimes a sausage cut into slices, and a jug of milk or water.

The women would tell their stories, how they had been on the road for many weeks, on foot, for the most part, pointing to their worn-out shoes. Mother would pay close attention; much later, I would realize that she was gathering pointers for our journey back home – a journey that, since the end of the war and even before, had occupied her thinking. She would ask about the trains, whether they were still running? For short stretches, then broken tracks or bombed out railway stations disrupted service, she was told. And food? Nothing you could buy for money, some rations at organized camps, not much otherwise.

The main thing was to stay ahead of the Russians, who were close, they would warn, at most fifty kilometers away. They'd talk in hushed tones of atrocities committed against the German civilian population by the Red Army. "*Entsetzlich!* – Unspeakable! The marauding. And the poor women," a young mother had whispered, whose baby had fallen asleep.

Those horrors, the implications of which went beyond my understanding, were happening far away from where we were. I felt safe in Rockensußra. Nothing bad had ever happened here.

11

A rumble, like thunder, sounded from the east. The summer sky flaunted its most ambitious blue, an occasional cloud pasted above the trees in the wind-still distance. These were not conditions for real thunderstorms, which silenced the songbirds who now went on chirping as if to defy the warning sound of oncoming danger. But the rumble was real. It moved closer and closer.

And after a time, the sight of a long, dark column of tanks came snaking along the highway from the direction of Ebeleben – a nearby town where, once or twice, Mother had gone by bus to buy notions – and Jena, the capital of Thuringia, further east. My chin propped on the white-washed sill of the open window, I watched and listened.

Hurried footsteps came up the stairs. Mother called my name. She burst into the room, Gitta on her arm. Grabbing my wrist, she yanked me away from the window.

"The Russians." Her voice was agitated. She shoved Gitta, first, under the bed into the narrow space between floor and bedsprings, and then me, both of us crying. Once she'd situated us, she crawled in, herself, and draped her arm over us. She was shaking.

"Shh!" Mother said to quiet the two of us. Her hand searched for mine; her lips brushed my neck. I felt reassured despite the fear in her shallow breath.

The thunder and the column of tanks had a name: *The Russians.* What people had whispered about for days and weeks, what they had hoped and prayed could be averted, now it was real.

The rumble of tanks grew louder, came nearer, until it was a roar so deafening it made the floorboards vibrate beneath us and the walls rattle. Then everything fell silent, all at once, without warning.

Voices rang from outside. Shouting voices of men. The clanging of metal against metal, and the thud of the entrance door as it was flung open. Hollow steps on the tile floor in the hallway. Doors slamming. Short, angry utterances and silences that hung in the air, not those that prefigure the end of danger but those that threaten something worse to come.

A cacophony of sounds rose abruptly from the kitchen: boots shuffling, women shrieking, a clattering perhaps of chairs being hurled, and more silence. Unearthly silence, broken by groans, the likes of which I had never heard before, together with rhythmic pounding, over and over. Underneath guttural explosions, a woman's sustained scream, piercing. Silence.

Heavy steps pounded up the stairs, accompanied by shouts coming nearer. Mother put her hand over my mouth, pressing so tightly, I thought, I couldn't breathe. The bedroom door opened and thudded against the wall. Boot steps measured the room, to the small closet, and turning, approached the bed. There they stopped. A shaking went through me. I didn't know whether it was Mother's or my own.

Rough hands dragged first Mother, then me, then Gitta from under the bed. They shoved us into the nook between closet and wall. I took hold of Mother's skirt and pressed the side of my face into the fabric. Gitta's arms reached for Mother. She screamed.

A boot jammed into Mother's belly. She winced. A face pressed itself near to hers. A face contorted and purple with rage.

With this image, my memory closes itself. I don't remember what followed.

And then we were alone again. Maybe nothing was lost in the sequence of things I recall. Maybe only enough time had passed for the soldier to leave the room.

Squatting beside us, Mother took us in her arms.

"It's all right," she said. The tightness in my throat let go to tears. My belly shook in short spasms. Even after the tears had dried, the shaking would not stop. Not for a long time. When it finally did, the soldiers were gone, the tanks had left. Mother took us downstairs. The women were going about their daily chores. No one said anything.

Mother never spoke of the day the Russians came, not then or in later years. I never looked back, nor did I remember what nightmares yanked me out of sleep, that night and many nights after, crying. By morning they were always forgotten.

The event of the Russians coming, as with most events in my early childhood, was shaped by the perceptions of a five-year-old child; by the actual occurrences and by what was insinuated through assumptions and conclusions I drew much later. My recollection of these events was affected also by Mother, who deflected and filtered my experiences. All of these were the elements that created my memory.

My mother put her arms around me at night so I would fall asleep less afraid. She held my hand when I was frightened. She had shielded Gitta and me from the brunt of the war by leaving our hometown when the bombings were at their height. But her own fears, those beyond my understanding, did they not linger in the air, unmentioned?

In the end, my memory becomes muddled. It is no longer my own singular perception. It is infused with the memories of others and the collective history of the time. It is viewed through the lens of subsequent memories that have come to bear on earlier ones.

The significance of the Russians coming to Rockensußra was amplified by what came much later. A memory of Mother and Frau Scheer, our upstairs neighbor back home in Delrath: snippets of an adult conversation, mere intimations beyond my grasp to protect my innocence. I was eight or nine years old. They were speaking, in low tones, of the boy who lived with his mother in the attic room they'd been assigned in our building by the housing authority. Frau Scheer said, "Just look at his Slavic features. The narrow forehead. The high cheekbones. No doubt that boy's the product of the Russian occupation."

"She claims she's a war widow," Mother said.

"That's what she'd rather have us believe," Frau Scheer said. "Do the numbers. That boy was born too late to be a German soldier's child."

I picked up on a disturbing suggestion of disgrace the woman in the attic had suffered, as well as an unspoken accusation of impropriety on her part. I remember feeling sorry for the boy, afterwards, and different from him. He didn't have a father at all. Not even a dead one. Only a mother who had been stigmatized by a misfortune that would not take a clear shape in my mind.

Later, when I was in high school, Dieter Wegener, my classmate and already a budding historian, told me of the more than one hundred thousand rapes perpetrated on German women by Soviet soldiers as the Red Army moved west. "The prerogative and revenge of the victors," he said, in his often cynical way.

Dieter lowered his head to hide the pain in his face as he went on to speak of wartime Berlin, where he had been born, and of his mother – *Mütterchen,* he called her, which translates, not literally but in tone, as *poor little mother.* Knowing the Russians were close, she hid with her sons in a camouflaged enclosure in the basement of their home. When she heard Russian soldiers break down the front door, she pulled a small pistol – with a mother-of-pearl handle, Dieter remembered – from her purse.

"She was ready to sacrifice her own two sons to spare them from witnessing the ultimate disgrace," he said. "I don't know if she would have pulled the trigger or not, if I hadn't pleaded with her."

12

The cherry trees in the neighboring orchard had long shed their blossoms. Green pellets had grown in their place and swelled into deep red fruit. With nothing better to do in the rising heat, three of Kurtie's friends and I, the only girl, lazed in the grassy ditch that ran along the orchard fence and the footpath. Dampness rose from the soil and cooled our bare limbs. The sun had colored our faces a rosy tan. We passed our time pulling grass blades and tossing them idly into the still air.

Stretched out next to me, his head resting on his propped-up elbow, was Theo, the oldest and tallest of the boys. He told tales about the woman who lived in the house behind us. That she was an evil witch. That her husband had run off to the war and, even when the war was over, had not wanted to come back home. That she kept her children locked inside and tortured them. I half-believed his stories, and enjoyed the thrill of goose bumps creeping up my back.

"Let's make blow whistles," Kurtie announced. He was the leader of our little troupe, at least in my adoring eyes. He broke short, pithy stalks off a leafless bush that had not survived winter. He dug out the whitish pulp with a thin stick and blew out the loose pieces that wouldn't budge, his ruddy cheeks ballooning, the veins in his neck swelling. With his folding knife, he cut a triangular slit for an air hole. It barely resembled a proper whistle but, blowing into it, Kurtie was able to produce a single note. Before long, he had fashioned a small line-up of whistles, each giving off a different tone.

The other boys made the same crude whistles with equally deft hands. They had no knives of their own, but Kurtie, warning them not to ruin the blade, let them use his.

For a time, I just watched.

"You make one," Kurtie said, encouraging me, the way a big brother would his little sister. He'd made it look easy enough. I broke off a stalk of my own and, following his instructions, dug and scraped, trying not to perforate the fragile sheath. In the end it split anyway, as did a second, a third and a fourth. I was close to tears.

"You're just a girl," Kurtie said. With a sneer, he threw me one of the whistles he had made.

"Yeah, stupid. Go pick some cherries," said Willie, a stocky boy who liked to single me out with his often cruel teasing. I'd stayed at a safe distance from him, afraid he'd pull my braids, or mimic the way I spoke, which was different from the local dialect.

"Too scared, little girl?" he taunted me, "Nice red, ripe cherries. I dare you to pick some." He smacked his lips and rubbed his belly.

I looked at Kurtie, counting on him to stand up for me. He did. "Lay off her," he said. But the boy kept goading me, "Sissy." "Coward." "Baby."

"It's stealing," I said, emboldened by Kurtie's words trying to stand up for me.

Now the other boys chimed in. Soon they harmonized, singing the same monotonous line, "We want cherries. We want cherries." followed by the same epithets, "Sissy. Coward. Baby."

"I'm not a coward," I said, my own courage taking me by surprise. To prove how brave I could be, I went to the gate and, unlatching it, slipped inside the orchard. I glanced around. No one was near. Protected from easy view, I grabbed a low fruit-bearing branch and tore off a handful of cherries.

Just then, the neighbor woman came bolting down the garden path. She planted herself in front of me and, twisting my ear, yelled, *"Du kleine Diebin!* – You little thief."

The boys hadn't exaggerated: at least in my memory, she resembled a witch, down to a hairy mole on the bottom of her chin and a tattered black smock. Only the proverbial broom was missing. I backed up a step or two, then froze. I glanced over the fence. My playmates had run off. Even Kurtie.

"We don't need the likes of you around here," the woman said. "Go tell your mother to take you back where you came from. There is barely enough food to go around as it is." Venom in her voice, she commanded that I hand over the stolen cherries.

Too ashamed of what I had done, I kept the incident from Mother. I knew I had done something wrong, and I swore I would never steal again. However, without Mother's forgiveness, with which she always restored my sense of virtue - "*Gut' Kind.* Good child," she'd say as her final absolution – the theft of those cherries gained the weight of a cardinal sin. I relived the misadventure at night, and, during the day, avoided going anywhere near the scene of my crime.

What tortured me just as much as my shame was that the woman regarded us as outsiders and intruders and wished us gone from Rockensußra. I believed it would be upsetting to Mother to find this out. And so, I kept it from her.

13

With the signing of the Potsdam Agreement on July 26, 1945, the Allied Forces divided Germany into four zones and carved the capital of Berlin into four sectors. The zones and sectors were named after each of the victors – American, British, French and Soviet – who assumed governing authority.

Thuringia, the area where the village of Rockensußra was located, along with other central German territories initially occupied by the Americans, was ceded to the Soviets as part of what became the *Sowjetische Besatzungszone,* the Soviet Occupation Zone, commonly referred to as *Ostzone,* Eastern Zone.

A Soviet patrolled border – known as the *Oder-Neiße Linie,* defined by the Oder and Neiße Rivers – extended from the Baltic Sea in the north to the Czechoslovakian border in the south. It not only stemmed the passage of refugees between East and West, it sealed off those on one side from the other. Those caught crossing the border were taken into custody. Some, trying to flee, were shot, it was rumored. Exploding land mines took the lives of others.

The newly drawn border ran eighty kilometers west of Rockensußra, placing us in the East, the wrong part of the country, under Soviet control. The border precluded free passage into the West and jeopardized Mother's dream of taking us home. We were trapped.

Mother would lament about her predicament in later years, long after we'd left Rockensußra. "Two small children. A dead husband. Cut off from family and friends. And no one to help. The many nights I lay awake, despairing and without hope."

One late afternoon that early summer, two women, older than Mother, knocked on the farmhouse door. They resembled each other like sisters,

but weren't, both of them olive-skinned with black, curly hair. The taller
one wore a red kerchief in her hair. She caught me glancing at it
curiously. "Would you like it?" she asked. I did, very much so, though I
couldn't bring myself to do anything but shake my head. "Shy girl," she
said. A friendly sparkle lit up her dark eyes as she took off the kerchief
and tied it around my head.

Vague about where they were coming from, and vague about where
they were headed, the two women said they were looking to find people
they had known in Hamburg, before the war. Mother speculated that
our latest callers were gypsies. "Something about them," she said.

I listened and watched furtively as Mother, the two women and the
Köppel sisters gathered in a huddle outside the barn, talking quietly.
Perhaps, Mother saw her opportunity. Perhaps, the women offered their
help. They were familiar with the ways of the road; everything about
them spoke of courage and perseverance; both of them, it happened,
were fluent in Russian – a rare skill that could come in handy crossing
the border. Frau Köppel offered the two women a night's shelter and
some food for the journey. A sweet barter. Mother looked grateful. She
smiled with tears in her eyes.

Mother put Gitta and me to bed earlier than usual that evening.
"We're going home," she said, kissing us goodnight. Before falling
asleep, I could hear the hushed preparations going on below.

It was still dark when Mother roused us the next morning.
Downstairs in the barnyard, Herr Köppel was getting an old handcart
ready that had fallen into disuse. He hammered a few loose slats into
place, and tightened and oiled the wheels. "It'll get you to the border,"
he said. Frau Köppel had packed an extra loaf of bread and a bagful of
apples from the root cellar. "It won't last you long. But it's all we have
to spare."

A young woman approached from the highway, carrying a small
rucksack. She sought out Mother and, shaking her hand, said a shy,
"*Guten Morgen.*" The eighteen-year-old daughter of a neighboring
family, Mother had enlisted her to help on our journey home. Her
payment, it had been agreed, would be Mother's wedding gown.

Herr Köppel deftly stacked our two suitcases and the women's
rucksacks onto the cart, leaving a nook for Gitta to sit securely. "You're a

big girl now. Old enough to walk," Mother said to me. At five years and four months, it boosted my sense of adulthood.

I spotted Kurtie examining the cart with an air of authority, making adjustments to the load. I tapped on his shoulder. He pretended not to notice. Then, without looking at me, he muttered, accusingly, "I know you'll never come back." He turned away brusquely and disappeared inside the house.

Our hasty farewells sounded muffled in the now lifting darkness. "Write us when things are back to normal," Frau Köppel said. We shook hands and waved goodbye to our hosts, and they waved back. Kurtie had come back. He stood there with his hands dug in his pants pockets, shrugging his shoulders to his ears. When I turned around for a last look, he tipped his forehead for a quick goodbye.

We walked ahead of the rising sun, along the highway out of Rockensußra. The shutters on the few houses we passed were still closed. For a while, the sound of hoofs and wheels on the asphalt followed behind us. It was Herr Köppel leading his horse to work in the fields.

There was nothing to dampen my spirits, nothing to forewarn me of the trials that lay ahead. The mild early morning temperature, though a certain harbinger of the heat to come, could not have been more perfect. I skipped and walked alternately, keeping up with the pace of our small party. Gitta, too, looked happy, as she was being pulled along in the cart. I didn't envy her. Not yet.

We walked for hours that first morning. The women talked with each other, at first, then grew quite as time went on. Passing through a hamlet, we took a break, just long enough to eat an apple and drink water from a well. The heat was rising mercilessly. My enthusiasm had long dwindled. I'd grown exhausted and bored. The landscape of rolling hills – with its fields, small wooded areas and the occasional farm along the roadside – stretched into the endless horizon.

Our steps left faint footprints in the heat-softened asphalt. Waves of hot air shimmered above the pavement, creating the illusion of water puddles ahead of us. Like mirages, they receded further the closer we came. As each puddle vanished from sight, I put my hope onto the next one, only to find that it, too, was a deception. For a while, the game distracted me.

The sun had moved to its highest point. The heat and humidity were unrelenting. The still hum of summer rose above the crunching sound that the wheels of the cart made on the asphalt. Even the women walked wearily now. Gitta fell asleep, after some fussing, her neck kinked, her small body slumped over to one side. Mother put her straw hat over Gitta's little face.

I begged Mother to carry me. "You're too heavy," she said and, clutching my hand with a tight grip, pulled me along. Like a stubborn mule, I dug in my heels. I whined, until Mother took pity on me, taking the hat from Gitta's head and putting it on mine. The shade cooled my face for a moment, but when the sweat band slipped down over my face, I whined again, "Please, carry me." At her wits' end, Mother grabbed me under my arms and lifted me onto her shoulders with impatient hands. I felt relief, but none of the delight I remembered, when, play-riding high on her shoulders, taller than anyone in the world, she had pranced under me, and I had squealed and bounced to the rhythm of her step. Now, she had relented only because she could no longer refuse. I knew it would be short-lived. Still, I wished it would not end.

Time dragged on. What most likely were only minutes, felt like hours. Unyielding were the heat, the boredom of putting one step in front of the other, the mounting exhaustion. Then, in the distance, the low drone of an engine broke into the monotony, alarming the women. It grew louder as it drew closer, and a truck quickly caught up with us. We stepped to the side of the road. The women exchanged anxious glances. The truck slowed down and stopped. Hopeful smiles came over the women's faces: this was not a Russian army vehicle, as they had feared, but a local farmer, most likely.

The driver leaned out of the window, "Where are you headed?"

"To the border," the woman, who had given me the kerchief, shouted over the sound of the engine. "Can you help us?"

The man who jumped out of the cab was rugged looking and not given, it seemed, to pleasantries. He motioned us to follow him to the rear of the vehicle and folded down the tailgate. Wasting no time, he threw our possessions, handcart and all, onto the bed of his truck and gave each of us a hand climbing in.

Soon, the clatter of the engine lulled me in and out of sleep as we drove along the highway. I woke up to a stillness, confused at first, where I was or not knowing how much time had passed – though it must have been hours.

"Da ist die Grenze. – That's the border. You might find a place to sleep in the farmhouse yonder," the man said. With a broad sweep of his hand to suggest the immeasurable, he drew our attention to the forested belt some way ahead of us. The trees had swallowed the evening sun, leaving a jagged outline, crimson where the sun touched them. After the day's unbearable heat, it was now limpid and balmy.

A short walk up a dirt road took us to a farmhouse, half-timbered, like most in the region, but manor-like in appearance and size, attesting to the wealth of its occupants. A woman stood in the doorway. Her stout build and majestic posture would have been intimidating, had it not been for her welcoming smile.

"We're crossing into the West," the women said, speaking over each other. "Is there room for us, overnight?"

"You're welcome to stay," the woman said, "Many do. The border's only a stone's throw away."

She showed us to the barn, its huge sliding door wide open to allow the cooling air to enter. "There's plenty of hay to sleep on, blankets too, if you need them, and a glass of milk for the children in the kitchen," she said, with a friendly gesture of her hand.

Mother spread enough hay to mold a hollow for herself, Gitta and me. She covered us lightly with a horse blanket from a small stack and lay down between us. Late evening dusk steeped the barn's interior in a mauve glow. The fragrance of fresh-cut hay tickled the inside of my nose. Prickly shafts scratched my naked legs. I was too exhausted to let any of it bother me.

Drifting off, I asked, *"Gut' Kind, ja?* – Good child, yes?" the way I always did at bedtime, always in the pre-grammatical form of a much younger child. *"Gut' Kind!"* Mother repeated in the same manner of speech, preserving the shared intimacy of our ritual, evening after evening. *"Und jetzt schlaf schön.* – And now sleep tight."

With the distance of years between then and now, I wonder about the accuracy of my memory. Did it compress actual time? The long route on foot, the drive in the truck, other events I might have forgotten, did these, in reality, take days? In my recollection, the road was empty but for our small group. This seems unlikely, given the steady stream of people fleeing west.

I woke up to the sound of the women talking among themselves, as they moved about to put things back in order. It was the hour of the day when darkness and light met. As if by sleight of hand, up-to-then invisible mountains of baled hay stacked all the way to the roof came into view. In a wooden pen adjacent to the barn, pigs squealed as a farmhand poured feed into their troughs.

Outside, the morning air cooled my face, still flushed from yesterday's sun. The night's sleep had washed away all memory of hardship and restored a new sense of adventure.

The kitchen was bustling with activity. The farmer's wife and her helper, both wearing cotton-print aprons, were clearing the long breakfast table as a number of men rose from their chairs and headed outside. A pot of malt coffee, a few slices of bread and two glasses of milk stood waiting for us on the corrugated-metal drain-board next to the kitchen sink.

Our farewell was brief, hushed, like a warning or a premonition.

"Take the trail behind the house. It's safer than the highway," the farmer's wife said in parting.

"Thanks for everything," the women said, shaking her hand. *"Auf Wiedersehen."*

"Alles Gute! – Good luck!"

Leaving behind our handcart, we were ready to take off – Hanna, her small rucksack on her back, offered to carry one of our suitcases; Mother with Gitta on her arm, carried the other suitcase; the two women strapped their overstuffed rucksacks to their backs.

The trail hugged the low contours of the grassy hillocks. After some distance, it ran alongside a shallow creek. The water rippled around large rocks. It radiated in circles where bugs had landed. Otherwise, the water flowed lazily, as if it had not yet awakened to the new day. From the open country we were leaving behind, the early sun cast our shadows in front of us – long-necked and lanky, they always stayed ahead. I tried to step on mine, but it mimicked my movements and outwitted me each time.

Once inside the forest, the two Russian-speaking women took the lead, indicating, as it were, that this was their purview. They walked briskly, setting the pace. Hanna followed with Gitta. I walked fourth in line, just ahead of Mother. We stayed close together. No one spoke.

Protected by overhanging trees, the trail continued close to the meandering creek. Once or twice, we stopped for a brief rest a few steps off the trail and out of view. Hanna and Mother put down the suitcases, rubbed their hands on their hips to soothe their aching palms. Circumspect and attentive, they listened to the sounds of the waking forest. Only the tentative call of birds broke the deep silence.

We walked on and on. As time passed, I became bored and weary.

"*Sind wir bald da?* – Are we almost there?" I asked. My own voice jarred me, as it rang through the quiet of the forest. The two women hushed me, harshly. Putting down her suitcase, Mother took my hand, harshly too, and yanked me near her. Any suggestion of adventure vanished.

Danger was all around us. In the women's now frantic looks. In Mother's sweating palm. My eyes followed the direction of the women's, when I spotted the cause of their alarm: a bicyclist in the far distance, riding toward us along the path through a patch of sunlight. The women scrambled for the wooded area off the path, dragging me along as well as the loads that bore them down.

There was no cover anywhere. No shrubs, not even undergrowth, only the trunks of trees not thick enough even to hide a child. With nowhere to turn, the women slowed down, unsure what to do next. Perhaps they hoped that the bicyclist was a harmless farmer on his way somewhere, though they must have suspected he was a Russian soldier on patrol.

Birds calling, a twig snapping off and falling to the ground, water dribbling over a rock in the creek. No other sounds, and time suspended. Until the even whirring of pedals drew nearer. The women looked at each other, frightened, then trained their sight on the trail that disappeared among the trees. The forest, benign as it had been, now brimmed with danger. I cowered close to Mother, as I too, watched the trail.

Time wore on endlessly. After a long while, the bicycle rider came into range again, pedaling toward us unhurriedly. When he was level with us, he coasted to a stop. A Russian soldier. He looked young, his skin smooth as a boy's, his eyes wide-set and watchful. Swinging one leg over the seat, he dismounted the bicycle. His right hand on his holster, he shouted *"Halt"* in heavily accented German, followed by a terse litany of commands in Russian, to which the two women responded loudly, one talking over the other. I clung to Mother's skirt, as he moved closer to Gitta, who was squirming on Mother's arm.

The soldier snatched Gitta from Mother. Gitta screamed and pounded her little fists on his chest. Hanna opened her mouth to say something, but nothing came. The soldier returned to the trail with Gitta in his arms. He was patting her back. Mother scurried after them, flinging herself at the soldier and talking hysterically as she tried to wrestle Gitta from him.

"Mama, Mama," I cried. She didn't hear me. *"Sei still. –* Be quiet," Hanna whispered and put her hand over my mouth. "Mama, Mama." The words sounded like the unintelligible call of a deaf-mute. Maybe the Russian-speaking women believed that the soldier meant Gitta no harm, or they feared that Mother's outburst jeopardized us even more: they urged her to calm down. She did not heed them. Pummeling his back and tugging at his tunic, she shouted over and over, *"Mein Kind. Mein Kind. –* My child. My child."

Unperturbed, the soldier proceeded to put Gitta on the carrying rack of his bicycle and leaned it against a tree. His mood seemed to shift. His stride combative, he came back for Mother. His strong hands restrained her as if she were a mad woman. He twisted her arms around her back, and held her in place until she stopped resisting.

No one dared to say a word. Even Gitta had turned quiet. Only the sound of the Russian-speaking women tearing Mother's suitcase open and rummaging through it frenziedly could be heard. At last, they pulled out an old *Lebkuchendose,* a ginger snap tin. They waved it at the soldier.

He took it and inspected it suspiciously, then removed the lid. He lifted the tin to his nose and, grinning, took a pleased whiff. It was filled with sausage scraps.

The soldier stashed the tin in the front of his blousy tunic and returned to his bicycle. His face close to Gitta's, he made funny faces and gurgling sounds at her. It made her giggle. He clapped his hands and, turning to Mother, gave her a boastful smile.

Gitta straddling the carrying rack, he pushed his bicycle in the direction from which he had come. With a broad sweep of his arm, he gestured for us to follow.

After crossing the clearing where we had first spotted the soldier, the trail curved away from the creek and climbed up a dandelion-dotted slope. In the distance, a highway snaked along a ridge, the continuation of the same highway we had traveled the day before. The soldier stopped. He cupped his ear, calling attention to the faint revving sound of an engine, then pointed to an army jeep moving north. It looked the size of a toy car from where we stood. The women translated what the soldier said, their tone and demeanor suggesting friendly collusion with him: the Soviet commander was making his morning rounds. We would have to wait until he had completed his patrol. After that, it would be safe to cross the border.

A lively group now, the women all looked at each other triumphantly. They chatted about our good fortune, how the soldier had been swayed by the two women's fluency in Russian, but mostly, by Mother's tin of sausage scraps.

As we walked on in single file, the soldier began humming a melody, his voice soft and melancholy. He took off his visor cap and playfully put it over Gitta's head. Only her chin showed. She was cooing. He tickled her bare neck, and she pulled her shoulders up with delight. I watched their game with envy, wishing I could have a turn on the carrying rack, or sit on the frame between the handlebar and seat. But the soldier didn't offer. Had he never even noticed me?

The trail wound uphill in sweeping curves. A shortcut through flattened summer grass, not much wider than the width of a boot, led to an isolated beech tree towering at the base of the hill. A group of a dozen or so soldiers rested idly in its shade.

As we came closer, the scene froze in my mind like a photograph, merging with one in our family album: *The sports club soccer team back home in Delrath, like these Russian soldiers, sprawling in the grass: my father, their goalkeeper, lies in front of them, his head raised on his elbow. Half-smiling, he looks into the camera.* The Russian soldiers and my father's soccer team, superimposed and inseparable.

The soldiers stirred. They rose and, shouting at us and each other, surveyed our group. Brandishing weapons, three of them elbowed their way in our direction. The women put their arms around each other and huddled around me at their center.

Over the shouts of the men, the soldier who had led us here shouted back. He reached for Mother's tin inside his tunic. The rest of the soldiers moved close, watching him opening it and displaying the contents. Appeased, their hostile demeanor relaxed. They passed the tin around and helped themselves to small handfuls of sausage bits. Smiling at us, they returned to lazing in the grass. It seemed we were safe again.

The women scanned the tree-lined highway on the distant ridge. It stretched across the entire width of the panorama in front of us. No vehicles were in sight. Time passed. Eventually, the commander's jeep could be seen crawling south, on its return patrol: the young soldier, *our Russian,* as the women would later call him, signaled for us to leave. He kissed Gitta on the forehead and handed her back to Mother, a big grin on his face. It was safe for us now.

We walked back to the trail beside the creek, where the trees made us less conspicuous and their shade sheltered us from the worst of the heat. It was only mid-morning, but already the temperature exceeded that of the previous day. The women panted under their loads, their bodies stooped. I dawdled behind, too weary even to cry. Mother noticed. She waited for me to catch up, and taking my hand, pulled me along.

"Just a little longer."

14

The West was on the other side of the highway. The highway marked the border. No giant chain curtain suspended between heaven and earth, as I had imagined, no fences or wire to climb over or duck under – only a road to cross. No change in the landscape: the same trees, the same sun.

Hunched over, we ran across the road that was as ordinary as any other road. On the other side, a heavily used trail through open meadows took us into the West. Ahead of us, the red roofs of a hamlet.

We slowed down just enough to catch our breath, glancing back every so often, as if still sensing danger from behind, an imaginary presence that eyed our backs. We did not stop again until we reached the village.

The grass grew tall in the village green. The divided main street that framed it looked empty. Not a soul about. Only the barking of a dog from afar. Squat houses nestled together, like those in Rockensußra. Their shutters were closed to keep out the midday heat.

The Russian-speaking women fell into each other's arms. Laughing and dancing, they sank into the grass. Their mid-length gathered skirts left their tanned calves exposed. Mother took Gitta and me to the water pump in a grassless patch closer to the street. She swung the handle with even strokes. Tipping our heads, we drank from the stream of cold water. Squealing, we splashed our sweaty faces.

The perils of the morning, the long trek, even the exhaustion, were washed away. Rockensußra was all but forgotten. Only much later, when Mother received the occasional postcard from the Köppel sisters, would I think about Kurtie again and remember our time on the Köppel farm.

This was *the West,* not the wartime West we had left behind during the bombings, when East and West were still one country. Under Western Allied occupation, friendly by all reports, *the West* was a place altogether different from *the East,* now under the yoke of the Soviets. It was a place of *Freiheit,* of freedom and liberty, so the story went. The idea that had formed in my mind was an absence of rules, a place where everyone could do as they pleased. Even children were not told to finish their plates or when to go to bed at night.

Mother unwrapped the rest of the bread Frau Köppel had provided for the journey. She broke it into chunks for everyone to share. A simple repast, it was a celebratory occasion and one of silent gratitude.

My hunger still unsated, I was looking around the commons and the nearby houses when a cherry tree caught my eye in a front yard. Though late in the season, it had not yet been harvested, and was heavy with its dark red crop. I could taste the juicy sweetness on my tongue.

"I'll go pick some cherries," I told Mother, the obvious thing to do, in my mind, in a land of freedom. I was already on my feet, about to run off, when Mother stopped me.

"No," she said, her voice startlingly stern.

"Why not? They're everyone's." It's what my logic told me. *Freiheit* implied sharing what one owned and taking what one needed. After all, we were in the free West now.

"They're not ours to take." Her answer was not at all what I expected or wanted to hear. I felt let down. Had the promises of freedom been false?

Mother caught me by the hem of my dress. She drew me back. She said nothing about the cherries, but took me in her lap. She squeezed me gently and stroked my sweaty hair with her palm.

"Wir haben es geschafft. – We made it." she said. *"Ein tapferes Mädchen warst du. – A brave girl you were."* She smiled through a sadness that was always there. It had come to define her melancholy beauty. It's how I remember Mother through my childhood years.

15

Our journey continued. Stretches in my memory of it are tattered. We were on the road for days. For weeks? "God knows, it was a long time," Mother said when I asked her about it years later, when I had already begun to try to put together the many pieces of our wartime lives into a cohesive whole. "Nothing but hardships. Why would you want to dwell on such a miserable past?" It wasn't a question, but a pronouncement of finality, as was typical for her when she put an end to an unsettling conversation. The same sadness she carried in those early days flitted across her still-beautiful face. But in spite of Mother's reticence, I couldn't let go of that past. I was disturbed by what I had forgotten, as if whatever had happened had been taken away from me.

I don't recall by what means we proceeded from our first stop in the West at the village green, or how long it took to reach a town with a railway station. I don't recall at what juncture the two Russian-speaking women, whose fate had been so closely knitted to ours, left us and went in another direction. "Do you know their names or where they went?" I asked Mother, pressing for clues. "Everybody had only one thing on their mind," Mother deflected, "and that was to get on with their lives."

My memory returns to an overcrowded platform of a bomb-damaged railway station. I was bored, thirsty, fretful and nagged Mother endlessly with the same question, one I knew she couldn't answer: "How long?"

"Stop pestering me," she said.

Sulking, I found a nook to nestle in between our suitcases and Hanna, who had Gitta in her lap. My gaze wandered to the high vaulted roof. Much of its black steel framing was gone. Where the framing remained, the glass panes were opaque with soot and dirt, or without glass, except for splintered borders that created bizarre patterns. Watching clouds drift above the empty spaces, I fell in and out of drowsy sleep.

Occasionally, Mother left to fill my father's wartime canteen with water. Back in Rockensußra, she had removed its green felt and polished the aluminum to a bright shine. Sometimes, she came back with a slice or two of bread. Once, a young mother offered her a peach in return for a fresh diaper she needed for her baby boy. Hanna, Gitta and I shared the fleshy parts, while Mother sucked the stone clean, then broke it open with her teeth and ate the almond-shaped kernel.

Not many trains came. Even fewer stopped. Passenger trains. Freight trains. Any train pulling in enlivened the crowd. Everyone on the platform would get to their feet, all eyes on the long succession of cars either passing through the station or, on rarer occasions, slowing to stop. "Stay close to me," Mother would warn over the loud clatter.

The arriving trains, all of them moving west, were packed solid. The few passengers who disembarked shoved their way through the waiting mass of people. Those, like one solid organism, moved to the edge of the platform. Men and women aggressive enough to push or trample their way through the crowd or fortunate enough to end up where a door opened, would get on. A handful were so brave or desperate, they'd hold on to the rail alongside the door and, when the train departed, traveled on the outside step. Most of them jumped off before the train left the station. Some slipped and fell alongside the tracks. With each departing train, the waiting started all over again.

Discomfort and boredom and impatience slowed down time. Days and nights passed – fewer, most likely, than my memory tells me. The heat and humidity were stifling. Dreariness and apathy subdued the would-be passengers.

It was mid-afternoon. Its steam engine hissing, a freight train came chugging into the station. A hum went through the crowd as everyone rose. Mother took my wrist. The weight and mass of men, women and children pushed us toward an open cargo door. A pair of large hands grabbed me under my arms, shoving me into the freight car. Mother's hand slipped off my wrist. I turned back as she disappeared in a sea of people.

The wooden door fell shut. The train set in motion. I was trapped between grown-ups, who towered over me. Their sticky, damp clothes rubbed against my face. Their weight crushed me. It was dark. The clanging of wheels pounded in my head. There was no air. I struggled to breathe. Mother was gone. Something utterly wild unleashed in my head and limbs, thrashing to free itself. But the thrashing was only inside me. My arms, my legs were paralyzed.

Gitta's muffled screams through a wall of people, Hanna quieting her down. Then Mother's frantic voice. "Step aside. Please." Feet shuffled, bodies shifted. A warm wetness, like something comforting, seeped between my legs and trickled down my thighs. My breath returned. I could smell Mother's scent before the texture of her linen skirt brushed against my skin, and her hand found my face. As utterly lost as I had been only seconds earlier, now I felt safe. Soothed by Mother's touch, soothed by the rhythmic clatter of wheels, I fell asleep, propped up by legs and bellies, my head nestling in Mother's cupped hands.

An ear-piercing sound jolted me into wakefulness. The train braking. Everything shuddered, shifting the mass of passengers backward, then forward and backward again. A loud, unruly commotion arose inside the car. When the train came to a full halt, calm returned.

Heavy rain drops spattered on the metal roof of the freight car. Walking along the track, the conductor shouted, *"Alle aussteigen. –* Off the train, everybody."* He lengthened and separated the words to underscore the urgency of his instructions. People piled off the train, grumbling with discontent.

White zigzag lines tore the black sky apart, in short order discharging a crashing roar. It was pouring. We ran for shelter with the other passengers, under a row of trees paralleling the train tracks. All of us drenched to the skin, we looked up into the sky, anticipating the next spectacle.

"Lightning won't strike when it rains," Grandmother had once told me when, during a thunderstorm, I'd hidden behind the wicker chair where she always sat in her kitchen. *Eichen weichen, Buchen suchen. –* Oaks are lightning's attraction; beeches offer protection, an old proverb instructed.

"Are these beech trees?" I asked no one in particular. It was Hanna who answered, "Yes, they are," she said, "don't be afraid." We were safe, doubly safe, as it were: the rain and the beech trees, both were favorable omens to prevent lightning from striking us.

Yet, the storm came threateningly close. I counted the seconds between lightning and thunder, equaling, as Grandmother had taught me, the distance in kilometers between the storm and where we stood. At first, the two occurred at virtually the same instant. Gradually, the intervals increased while the noise diminished, until only a faint rumble came from far away.

When the rain subsided, it was still and cool. A new crispness had replaced the earlier heat and humidity. The air had been cleansed, even of sound, by the thunderstorm and the rain.

A procession of people set into motion on a path alongside the train, two or three abreast where the path allowed, single file where it narrowed. Everyone moved at the same sluggish pace, except for a few who recklessly stampeded ahead to be the first to see what had happened.

We passed the locomotive and, continuing beside the tracks, reached a slow-moving river and the remnants of a bridge. Its massive framework was torn and contorted. Bent steel girders protruded from the murky water. At the embankment, twisted train tracks jutted over the river. We stayed clear of bomb craters near the sandy shoreline.

I strain to remember what followed, but nothing reveals itself. Instead, a dream from a much later time surfaces: *Mother is wearing a black pleated linen dress. Her light brown hair, waved in the fashion of the forties, frames her ageless face. We are preparing to cross a river. I ask to use her cream-colored camera to document the passage. It has no film in it. Mother offers the camera to black marketeers. "Why?" I ask. "You wouldn't know the meaning of this," she says. Her tone suggests that I am wrong or not entitled to such knowledge.* The dream rolls back to the beginning and starts over.

"Did we see a bomb explode at the river?" I ask her at the time when I had begun piecing my memories together.

"You saw nothing," she replied, "You've always had a fertile imagination."

My mother, throughout her life, remained reluctant to return to her postwar memories, and to the war itself. She kept the answers to my questions – whether linked to the biography of our family or to the greater history of our country – to a minimum, often deflecting my questions altogether.

Was she guided by a desire, perhaps, to continue to protect the child I had been then, or to silence some degree of remorse she carried? Remorse for having thrust her children into danger, even when it was through no fault of her own? Did she want to forget – at first, as she struggled through early widowhood and postwar deprivation; later, in times of returning normalcy, as she began to build a new life? Or was she part of the much larger silence that hung over the German people? On those rare occasions when she did speak about this event or that, it was as if they belonged to another era, one that wasn't truly hers.

Not until the last years of her life did my mother tell some of the stories of the past. Mostly, they were about her growing-up years between the wars. With a nostalgic ring and a knack for the dramatic, she recounted anecdotes of her family history in the town that was still home to her, "the most beautiful place in the world," she once called it. On fewer occasions, she told about the war itself.

Glimpses, too fleeting to hold long enough to bring into focus; bubbles of memories refusing to burst and tell their stories; or just a phantom lead that vanishes in the thicket.

A river. In the white sand at its shoreline, a smooth metal surface reflecting sunlight.

Mother opening a can of white processed cheese with a key-shaped opener during a bumpy ride under the canvas cover of an army truck.

On a bridge in a rainstorm. I am petrified, staring at the fast-moving river water through gaps in the planked pathway.

Waiting somewhere. I am nagging Mother, "When are we leaving?"

Trekking along scorched asphalt highways in an endless line of people. I am thirsty, exhausted.

Watching the clouds travel along the sky.

Walking in the rain. I seek out puddles to step in. Mother says, "Stop it. You'll catch a cold."

Waking at night, panicked, not knowing where I am. Mother saying, "Don't cry. I'm here."

Then I remember. Mother washing and wiping my face with a handkerchief in a train station lavatory. The stench was unbearable, but the itch on my head was worse.

"Stop scratching," Mother said, her voice curt, after too many reminders that had gone unheeded. I listened, until the urge to scratch became so torturous I couldn't stop myself. The harder I tried, the more I itched.

"I can't," I said, as the itch crawled on my head, one way and then another. All I wanted to do was dig my fingernails into my scalp.

"You're full of lice." Mother sat down on the chair next to the wash basins – the chair that, in better times, was reserved for the lavatory attendant to receive coins in return for keeping the toilet seats clean. Mother pulled my head onto her lap. She parted my hair with quick movements, searching for infestations of lice. The sudden stirring prompted them to scurry in all directions. Another itch, and another, and another, and Mother's elbows so firmly planted on my back, I couldn't move, let alone scratch.

Her fingertips pursued the escaping lice. Most got away. The few she was quick enough to catch, she squashed between the nails of her thumbs. It made a clicking sound. A small bloody smear remained, which she dabbed on to her handkerchief. The itch stopped. For a moment. Then it reappeared in yet another spot.

Mother couldn't control the lice population, not on me, nor on Gitta. No matter how many she eliminated, there were always more that hatched from countless nits.

"You've scratched your scalp raw," she said. She trimmed my fingernails short and wound a kerchief tightly around my head. It didn't stop the itching, and it didn't stop me from digging my hands under the kerchief and rubbing my scalp with the blunt tips of my fingers. At her wit's end, Mother let me be.

Another train station. Walls torn apart by bomb fire, collapsed roofs, glass and brick haphazardly piled up, and the drone of human voices.

"How much longer?" I asked.

"We're almost home," Mother said.

I had asked the same impatient question so many times. Always, she had given the same answer in the same exasperated tone, "We're almost home." Still, I kept asking. Just hearing her say so – even as I sensed that she was only humoring me – almost made it true.

This time, something different attended her voice. Something that diminished the sadness in her face. Something that animated her demeanor. "*Köln*. Another twenty-five kilometers, and we'll be home."

We navigated around heaps of debris to the station's main entrance, now nothing but structural remnants of walls and doorways. Mother put her suitcase down, Hanna, Gitta and me at her side. Looking out onto the city's medieval square, reduced to only rubble and empty façades, she gasped. The cathedral's two majestic towers – their intricate architecture ravaged – ascended out of broken masonry; a spire shorn off to a stump; walls gaping with black holes; larger than life-size statues of saints that had once surrounded the main portal strewn on the steps; buttresses torn; cavernous openings where stained glass windows had been.

"Oh, God!" Mother said, "How could You have let this happen?" Her words rang like a prayer.

People shuffled along. Only a few paused to look at the cathedral. Maybe they were numbed by all the devastation they had already witnessed. Maybe days and weeks of travel had made them too weary to absorb the disastrous sight in front of them.

We made our way back into the station. Military personnel funneled the crowd through a checkpoint, where two British servicemen inspected Mother's and Hanna's identification papers. Some people raised loud arguments, which the servicemen ignored. Some were asked to step aside and wait. Most were motioned on with a glance and a nod.

We filed through an open door. A powdery dust and a sickly smell hung in the room. People coughed and gagged. Some fanned their faces with their hands or covered their mouths with handkerchiefs. Gitta coughed and cried at the same time. The back of my throat tickled with each breath. Soon I, too, coughed and whimpered.

The line haltingly moved toward a woman in a red skirt dusted with what looked like flour. She was standing at a small metal table near the far end of the room. Her eyes peering over a piece of cloth tied around her mouth and nose, she administered blasts of white powder to everyone's head from a device resembling a bicycle pump.

Mother lifted me onto a stool in front of the woman. She pressed one hand over my mouth and nose, and shielded my eyes with the other. A few quick puffs from the woman's pump wafted on my hair. My scalp smarted in a thousand places.

"Now, that wasn't so bad," the woman said, in the sing-song intonation of her native Rhineland, and signaled Mother to steady Gitta for her turn.

16

Fighting against the Rhine's strong current, its motor thrumming purposefully, the ferryboat from Himmelgeist, on the eastern side of the river, to Üdesheim on the western side, reached midstream. It rocked in the wake of a barge that was slowly moving around the bend, on its way to a harbor further north or to Holland, where the river divided before flowing into the Atlantic Ocean.

"That I should see the Rhine again!" Mother exclaimed wistfully – as, perhaps, she remembered girlhood summers when she had swum across its powerful waters from shore to shore, or Saturday evenings dancing at *Fährhaus Pitt-Jupp,* the old ferry house. Bent forward now to rest her arms on the ferry's railing, pride gathered in her face at the view of the river and the native countryside she must have held so dear. The wind blew her hair and raised the back of her skirt, exposing her slender black-stockinged calves. She was the most beautiful woman in the world. I wanted to look like her when I grew up.

The distance between ferry and shoreline diminished, bringing closer the broad meadow that, in some years, when the snowmelt in the southern mountains was fast or the rains were heavy, the river claimed.

A snapshot of me taken along the River Rhine in the summer of 1943. My father's favorite, the snapshot had been among his possessions returned from the front: *Mother has combed my curls, tousled by the wind that blows from the Rhine. She has re-pinned the lock on the crown of my head. She has smoothed the bow on my smocked dress. I'm surrounded by tall summer grass, clutching a bunch of Queen Anne's lace, the river flowing behind me.*

It was a favorite of Mother's as well. When, in later years, I'd see it framed on her bureau among other family photos, it sometimes released memories, or fantasies created subsequently, of childhood outings to the river, dreamlike and elusive. *Wildflowers populate the meadow. My father teaches me their names: Butterblume – buttercup, Löwenzahn – dandelion, Disteln – thistles, Wiesenschaumkraut – Queen Anne's lace. The latter, its name unpronounceable to the barely three-year old, is the flower I like best. Its lacy clusters make me think of stars.*

Weeping willows thrived in the damp soil. Their shaggy tresses hung so low they touched the grass. It was said that the ghosts of barge people who had drowned in the river lived in their gnarly burls. If I squinted my eyes, I could see their ghoulish faces in the bark of the trees; at night, they were the shadowy outlines on the ceiling above my bed.

The ferryman slung a heavy rope around the mooring posts and, with each tug at it, brought the ferry closer to the landing ramp. Water lapped the metal where it touched the sand-and-pebble shoreline, forming a frothy scum. He raised the barrier, cautioning his passengers to mind the step. His strong hand gripping my forearm, he helped me make the timid jump over the gap between ferry and ramp.

A cobblestone street, steep enough to contain the rising waters in spring, took us into the river town of Üdesheim. An isolated community with no railway station or industry to be targeted by Allied bombings, it had been spared major destruction. Artillery damage to some of its old brick dwellings was the only evidence that war had struck here, too.

"I'll be back in no time," Mother said, leaving Hanna, Gitta and me to wait for her on the street corner. Pushing her wind-swept hair back from her forehead and smoothing her skirt, she paused at a house a few doors away from us. She stepped back and looked up at the façade, as if to reassure herself she had come to the place she had in mind, or perhaps to gather courage. Then she knocked on the door. Someone let her in.

There was a happy bounce in Mother's step when she reappeared through a gate on the garden side of the house. "I'll be sure to return it soon," she called back to the young woman, who watched her roll a wheelbarrow down the sidewalk.

Mother's suitcases and Hanna's rucksack piled into its paint-worn bed, Mother and Hanna took turns pushing the wheelbarrow as best they could, while the other carried Gitta. Sometimes it tipped this way or that on its single wheel, but somehow the women always managed to right it again.

We followed the main street. Young housewives, spreading bedding to air on upstairs window sills or sweeping the sidewalk, stopped to greet us with a quizzical *"Guten Morgen,"* then resumed their morning chores.

17

Once the town of Üdesheim lay behind us, we passed long stretches of potato and sugar beet fields, farmhands hoeing between the planted rows here and there. Then came the highway. We turned left and continued under the shady canopy of linden trees.

"Not even half hour, and we'll be home," Mother said at the bridge that spanned the short channel between the Rhine and the *Baggerloch,* a lake-size swimming hole. Mother pointed to the sandy beach, where my father had taken pictures of Mother and me, both of us wearing the same style, one-piece bathing suits.

On the river side of the bridge, whirlpools, powerful enough to suck big pieces of flotsam into their vortexes, made it unsafe for swimmers, while a calm current lapped the shoreline of the swimming hole. The loud banter of a group of school-aged boys splashing in the water rang up to the bridge.

The Rhine in back of us, we left the highway for a dirt road. As far as the eye could see, farmland and pastures stretched out in the undulating countryside. The wheat stood tall, ears bending with ripeness, cornflowers casting a bluish tinge. Along the roadside, bright red poppies bobbed gently. Rows of poplars, like tall hedges to protect from the wind, broke up the monotony of the land. In the distance, a church steeple rose above the roofs of a small town. The wind from the river had died down to a light breeze.

"Soon," Mother announced. But though we walked and walked, the cluster of houses that was our destination remained far way. Sometimes it sank from view behind a rolling hill or a line of trees.

Tugging at her skirt, I plagued Mother with another, "How much longer?"

"*Lass mich!* – Don't!" she said. Then, as if to herself, "*Wer weiß, was uns zu Hause erwartet.* – Who knows what awaits us at home."

The clatter of wheels and the tapping of hooves drew near. A horse-drawn cart approached from behind. It came to a slow halt next to us. "By God, you've made it home, Gertrud," the coachman said. He spoke in the dialect of the region.

He jumped down from his seat and looped the horse's reins over a short post on the bed of the cart. He shook Mother's hand with manly vigor and extended a cautious greeting to Hanna.

"My friend Hanna," Mother said quickly, "She helped us across the border." Then he stroked my head and Gitta's. His hands were large and awkward, attesting to years of manual labor. He looked austere, his movements were lumbering in the way of the men of the river country.

Esu a Unglück. – Such a tragedy. . . about Josef," he said in the local vernacular. As an awkward apology to ease Mother's loss, he added, "I'd say close to half of us men who went to war didn't come back."

"Fate's inescapable," Mother said. Her detached manner seemed to tell that she did not wish to dwell on her or anyone else's ill fortune. He seemed to understand, or at least respect, her philosophic response.

He allowed a few moments to pass before he announced, in an upbeat voice, "Your mother and father are alive and well. Your flat's all right, except for a big hole in the wall from artillery fire."

He rearranged the metal milk canisters on the back of the wagon to accommodate our possessions, tipping the wheelbarrow upside down to keep it from sliding. He invited us to squeeze in next to him on the blanket-covered bench in front. Responding to a clucking noise he made with his tongue, the horse tossed its mane and set into an even trot.

One last bend. The yellow signpost on the roadside read, *"Delrath"* and underneath it, *"Kreis Grevenbroich."*

We were home.

Home was a small town halfway between Düsseldorf to the north and Köln, Cologne, to the south, its farmland bordering the Rhine River to the east and the railroad tracks to the west. My mother's family had relocated here from Düsseldorf during World War I, soon after my mother's birth, to establish a trucking and building supply company; my father's family had come from Bremerhaven, a few years prior, when the newly built zinc smeltery outside of town drew workers from other parts of Germany.

The cart slowed down to a bumpy ride up the deserted main street, pavement rife with potholes where explosives had struck. Solid two-story houses, their brick façades darkened brown with age. A few had been damaged by artillery fire; one on the Delrath side of the railway station had been bombed out. Red blooming geraniums spilled from window boxes. The sun stood at high noon.

The horse, obeying the man's tug, veered to the curb and stopped at the corner of Rheinstraße and Schulstraße.

"Here we are," the coachman said.

I remembered the three-story brick building, the concrete steps to the front door, and our upstairs flat with its row of tall windows. Their wooden shutters were closed. At the far end of the wall was a hole, large enough for an adult to crawl through. It was tightly stuffed with straw to keep the weather out.

Mother gasped.

The man commanded the horse to resume its trot. Less than five minutes later, the cart pulled over again. On the left side of the street was Grandmother and Grandfather's house, larger than most in the neighborhood. I glanced up to the very top of its side gable, where rusted forged-iron numbers were bracketed to the wall: 1881, the year it had been built.

Mother opened the unlocked front door. We stepped inside. The hallway looked the way I remembered: a brown-and-white checkered tile floor, deep green tile wainscoting, a polished brass chandelier suspended from the ceiling. It was cool and dim here. We passed the front rooms on both sides, and the staircase in the center. The door to the kitchen on the left was wide open. Sunlight streamed through the windows overlooking the courtyard.

Grandmother was sitting where she always sat, in her wicker armchair against the far wall, the cooking stove on one side, a work table on the other. Her posture poised and commanding, it was from this spot that she ruled her household.

As a younger woman, Grandmother had been stricken by a severe inflammation of the hip joint that had shortened her left leg by nine centimeters. A lifelong contorting limp had resulted. "It was God's punishment," she'd once told me, "and I don't even believe in Him," she'd added in the same breath. When I'd asked what she had done, all she'd said was, "You just be sure you're always a good girl."

Grandmother never left the confines of her property. Disregarding convention in a primarily Catholic town, she didn't attend Mass on Sundays, nor funerals. Later I would realize that, if it was her disbelieving nature that kept her out of church, it was the vanity of a once beautiful woman, now crippled, that made her shun the outside world.

We stood in the doorway of the kitchen, Mother holding one of Gitta's hands and one of mine, Hanna behind us. We waited for some sign from Grandmother. She didn't move. Or speak. She just looked at us. Then, a tenderness came over her face as she raised herself out of the armchair and, thrusting her large body forward, hobbled halfway across the room. There she remained standing, torso bent, arms spread wide open.

I ran to plunge into Grandmother's embrace. She pressed my face into the softness of her ample breasts and let me breathe the fresh smell of her starched smock. It ended all too soon with Gitta's tugging for her turn.

"*Ihr armen Kinder.* – You poor children," she said.

Grandmother straightened her torso enough to clasp Mother's face between both hands and pressed a kiss on Mother's forehead. "If there is a God, He must've heard me," she said. Turning to Hanna, she gave her a welcoming handshake. "You must all be hungry and tired."

Grandmother limped back to her armchair, Gitta and I scampering after her. She lifted me onto one knee, Gitta onto the other. Softly, she began humming a nursery song.

A summer ago, we had come to say goodbye to Grandmother on our way to take the train to Rockensußra. She'd stood in the open front door, erect, equalizing the disparate lengths of her legs by pointing the foot of her shorter leg so the tip of her shoe would touch the concrete step, putting all her weight on her good leg. One hand propped on her hip to maintain her balance, she'd waved us goodbye with the other. Her eyes had shone with tears.

Grandmother's tears had perplexed me then. They'd been at odds with her always self-possessed temperament and incongruous with my expectation of adventure ahead. How excited, how proud I'd been! The timid little girl, who had just recently found the courage to walk to Grandmother's on her own, had grown into a big girl now.

Turning back and waving to Grandmother, I had sung the nursery song she was now humming: *Hänschen klein / ging allein / In die weite Welt hinein. / Stock und Hut / Steht ihm gut, / ist gar wohlgemut. Doch die Mutter weinet sehr, hat ja nun kein Hänschen mehr.* . . Little Hänschen / he has gone / out into the world alone. / Staff in hand, a hat to suit / he is a happy chap. / But his mother cries a lot / now she has no Hänschen got. . .

A year later, humming the melody and tapping her foot to the song's simple rhythm, was Grandmother, too, remembering that day?

PART TWO

The Post-War Years
1945 – 1956

18

We resumed life in our small town of Delrath. Grandfather came to fix the hole in the bedroom wall of our flat. He found enough good bricks in the rubble of the bombed-out house at the train station, and fitted them into place. The new brick and mortar, lighter in color than the undamaged parts of the original façade, remained visible as a lasting scar.

In the rural areas, such as Delrath, the aftereffects of the war were not nearly as severe as they were in the cities. Rationed food, not enough to survive on, could be supplemented with homegrown fruits and vegetables on land not available in urban areas.

Grandfather's garden yielded enough potatoes, legumes and greens for all of us. Onkel Jean brought fruit from his orchard by basketfuls. On warm summer days, Mother and Grandmother would sit in the breezeway of my grandparents' house, shelling fresh peas and French-cutting string beans to preserve in mason jars. They shredded white cabbage, pickling it in wooden vats to make sauerkraut. They canned summer fruit.

Grandmother raised chickens for eggs. Every year, Grandfather fattened a hog with potato peels and odd food scraps from the kitchen. Then the butcher came to slaughter the hog, and an inspector to examine the meat for trichinosis. A whole day was devoted to preparing sausages. Some of them Grandmother would give to her neighbors. Portions of the meat went to the butcher and the inspector. The rest was stored in a makeshift smokehouse that formerly had been a bedroom.

Mother bartered for food, with legitimate goods at first; later, when she had access to American coffee and cigarettes through her sister, Irma, who was employed by the US Forces, she traded on the black market.

With my father's Olympia typewriter strapped onto the rack of her bicycle on one occasion, his Leica camera on another, or whatever possessions of value she knew were desirable, she rode to farmers in outlying areas, trading her goods for a small sack of flour or a chunk of bacon. She would come home pleased with her spoils, and contemptuous of the farmers who, she claimed, were getting rich off the backs of a hungry population.

Untargeted by Allied bombings, rural areas had suffered less destruction resulting in a housing shortage. That would come later, when more refugees from East Germany flooded the West. In Delrath, the house next to the train station had been the only one hit. It would never be rebuilt.

Although I owned just one change of clothes, not counting my Sunday best, and one pair of shoes, I didn't feel we were poor. As I outgrew my clothes, Mother sewed new ones for me from garments of hers; Gitta wore my hand-me-downs.

If it hadn't been for Gitta catching pneumonia and Grandfather driving us to the hospital in the neighboring town of Dormagen, the rest of 1945 and continuing into 1946 would have passed without disruption. I spent mornings in our preschool – the converted front room and walled-in backyard of a house next to the old chapel. Afternoons I played alone or with playmates in Onkel Jean's orchard when the weather permitted and in our flat when it was too cold or it rained.

As it was, Gitta came down with a cough and a fever at the beginning of spring. After several days, none of Mother's home remedies brought Gitta's temperature down; her breath became more shallow and wheezing.

"*Komm.* – Come along," Mother said, calling me away from playing with my doll. It was early evening.

"Where are we going?" I asked. No answer came. Carrying Gitta in her arms, Mother bolted down the stairs and up the street to Grandmother's. I kept up with her, running as fast as I could.

Grandmother touched Gitta's forehead. "You'd better get that child to the hospital, or you'll lose her." Gitta looked lifeless, as if she were already dead.

"Let's go," my grandfather said, hurrying out the door, heading for the barn. He started his truck, barely giving us enough time to get into the cab, and backed it through the courtyard and into the street.

We drove down Rheinstraße at a speed not fast enough for Mother, who urged Grandfather to hasten, but too fast for the condition of the pavement. The vehicle lurched and bumped along.

Just after we made the turn onto the main highway, I saw the constable in the middle of the intersection. I said nothing. Neither did Mother, if indeed she, too, had noticed him. Grandfather apparently had not, as he certainly failed to follow the constable's gestures to pull over. He drove on with undiminished speed.

The swinging door to the children's ward fell shut behind the nun who, after one quick look at Gitta, gathered Gitta's limp body into her arms and whisked her off. Despite Mother's protestations, we were instructed to leave by another nun. "Those are the rules," she said, lips tightening, "Come back during visiting hours tomorrow." Barely out of the sister's earshot, Mother said, *Die nennen sich die Barmherzige Schwestern.* – They call themselves Good Samaritan Sisters, but despots is what they really are."

There was no alternative but to drive home. After we pulled into the courtyard, Grandfather was the first to see the constable waiting inside the open gate.

"What does that old Nazi want?" he said, under his breath, slamming the truck door behind him.

The constable came marching up to Grandfather. A bully of a man, short and stout, he grabbed Grandfather's arms and forced handcuffs over his wrists.

Grandmother came hobbling through the back door. "You take those contraptions off my husband," she said. Mother, too, protested, demanding to know why the constable was here in the first place. Grandfather said nothing.

"Curfew violation." The irritation in the constable's reply suggested something more, something perhaps even ominous and hostile.

Mother pleaded with the constable. She tried to explain that her little girl was near death, that she had to get her to the Dormagen hospital in a hurry. Her words fell on deaf ears.

Grandfather was hauled off to jail.

Leading the way, Grandmother limped back into kitchen. She lowered herself into her armchair next to the cooking stove. Her breathing seemed agitated. Mother, hands covering her face, broke down crying hysterically. No one noticed that I, too, was crying.

"Gertrud, control yourself," Grandmother said to Mother, "Worse things have happened." Without pause, she continued, "Didn't I warned him again and again that his fancy communist ideas would come back to haunt him, once Hitler and his henchmen were gone. But no, he'd rather be ostracized as an outsider. And now this."

Over time, I would be able to create a fuller picture of my grandparents' political past. Grandmother had supported the Hitler regime in the beginning. Lifting the country out of economic disaster had been a good thing, she would say, as had been the lessening of crime. In postwar times, when it was unpopular to do so, when everybody claimed they had known nothing about anything, she nevertheless admitted that, ill-guided as it had been, she'd held Nazi convictions early on.

"True," she said the evening of Grandfather's arrest, "He never spoke up in any public way against the Nazis. But they knew. Especially that pompous ass of a constable. Denazification or not, a Nazi is what the man was and still is."

It was bad enough that Grandfather's construction supply company had been shunned under the Nazis; but unlike others in town, he had not been called to appear at the Allied Control Council to clear his name from Nazi involvement and be reeducated to democratic ways.

I didn't make a clear connection then, but gradually I would understand that, back in a position of small-time power, the constable was getting even with Grandfather for never having joined the Nazi ranks and, afterwards, having been spared the humiliating denazification process. "After all, those old Nazi big shots were put through the wringer," Grandmother said.

Since the evening of Grandfather's arrest, Grandmother and Mother looked preoccupied, paying little attention to me or Gitta. They talked quietly among themselves. Every day, Mother took the train to Neuss, two stations to the north. The nearest city to Delrath, it was also where the nearest prison was located. There, in what I pictured as a black building with barred windows, Mother went to visit Grandfather.

When Grandfather hadn't been released after what seemed like a very long time, she went to the courthouse to plead with the authorities on his behalf. A date for a court trial was set, but when the day came, the trial was postponed to a later date and then a later date again, while Grandfather remained incarcerated. Grandmother insisted it was nothing but harassment.

Gitta did not die. After two weeks, Mother brought her home, in a basket attached to the handle bars of Mother's bicycle. Grandmother baked an apple tart to celebrate. She brewed *real* coffee from her meager rations, instead of the usual *Malzkaffee*, made of ground roasted malt. For Gitta – who looked thinner now – and for me, Grandmother made a concoction of water and beet syrup, which she called lemonade. It was a happy day. The worries over Grandfather were temporarily forgotten.

Grandfather had been in prison for over four weeks, when Mother and Grandmother hatched a clever plan to bribe the judge: they packed a basket of foodstuff Mother took to the court. In a private meeting with the judge, she explained what she thought were the reasons for the constable's motives for Grandfather's arrest. The judge lent her a sympathetic ear.

That same day, Mother brought Grandfather home with her. Of slight stature by nature, he now appeared gaunt. His unshaved cheeks looked sallow, his eyes wary behind his wire-rimmed spectacles. Even to my eyes, young as I was, his faced looked like the face of a defeated man. "It's over," he'd say, shrugging off his experience.

His arrest and time served in prison had only deepened my grandfather's sympathies for the underdog and the working man. Three years later, when the democratic government of West Germany, the *Bundesrepublik Deutschland,* BRD for short, was established, he would announce that he wasn't going to vote. "How can you trust any government, after what happened the last time around?"

Grandmother wasn't going to vote either, but for a different reason.

Determined to remain housebound, there were very few occasions important enough to rouse her broken body from her confinement. The election of a new government was not among them.

19

Mother bartered a mahogany desk that had been part of our sitting room furnishings for a pair of high top leather shoes for me, custom made by an Italian master shoemaker in Stürzelberg, the neighboring town at the bend of the river. They were brown lace-ups, a size too large, to allow for my growing feet.

For a few sausages from Grandmother's smokehouse, Mother's cousin Anne traded two meters of dark blue yardage, better suited for a man's coat than the dress Mother intended to sew for me.

I grumbled about the many tedious fittings. I grumbled even more about the fabric, its dreary color and scratchy texture.

"You want to look like a pauper on your first day in school?" she said, accusingly. Then her tone softened as she promised to accent the dress with an embroidered apron to be worn over a dress. She got a linen sheet from the closet and, within a few days' time, transformed it into the prettiest garment I ever owned. It had gathered pockets on the front and stitched scallops of yellow daisies with orange centers on the bodice and above the hemline.

The *Volksschule Delrath,* the local primary school, was a block away from our flat up Schulstraße. A three-story, red-brick building with large windows, its basement had served as the town's only air raid shelter during the war.

I counted the days leading up to my first day of school in April of 1946. Spring, traditionally, marks the beginning of the school year in Germany. I had turned six the month before. I packed and repacked the leather satchel Grandmother had ordered from a traveling salesman. It was a surprise gift, as was the money she gave me to buy a slate tablet, a sponge to wipe it clean, slate pencils in a wooden pencil box with a sliding top, and a primer – all of which I purchased at *Kreuter's* grocery store.

I woke up before dawn. A clear sky promised a fine spring day. As I dressed in front of Mother's three-way mirror, she made last minute adjustments to my outfit. I endured her routine, but shook my head defiantly when she braided my medium-length, blonde hair in a wreath all around my head.

"I won't go to school with a halo," I said.

"You'll look special," Mother said.

I didn't want to look *special*. I didn't want to draw attention to myself with a hairstyle that I knew would be fancier than anyone else's and risk being ridiculed by my classmates. But no amount of pleading or angry tears changed Mother's mind. She prevailed; the halo stayed. It survives in the photograph the school photographer took that morning. My satchel strapped to my back and holding the traditional sweet-filled cardboard cone first graders were given on enrollment day, I look into the camera with an embarrassed frown. A slate tablet, propped up next to me, read: *Mein erster Schultag. 1946* – My first day in school. 1946.

Public school instruction had been suspended during the final war years and had not been resumed until 1945. This lapse accounted for the age discrepancy of two, even three years, in my class of about forty boys and girls. At barely six, I was among the youngest.

Fräulein Reiners was the first-grade teacher. She wore her salt-and-pepper hair pulled back into a bun at the nape of her neck, like Grandmother, but looked even older. She had a reputation for being strict. Not as strict as Fräulein Hölscher, the second-grade teacher, whose swats and famously nasty cheek twists kept even the most unruly boys in line.

I could count comfortably to twenty, haltingly beyond that. I could write the alphabet in cursive upper and lower cases, as well as my first and last names. More than anything, I wanted to learn to read. It mystified me, the way a short string of letters, when decoded, revealed a word, and that, in sequence, words told stories. I believed it took a trick of magic to unlock meaning from letters. All morning, I waited for Fräulein Reiners to tell us how it was done.

Instead, she had us count from one to ten in unison over and over, and wrote 1 + 1 = 2 and 2 + 2 = 4 on the blackboard during our first session.

After recess, she demonstrated the lower-case *i* on the blackboard, making much ado about its proper slant and exact placement of the dot. She instructed us to copy her perfectly executed example on our tablets. It seemed easy at first. With repetition, my *i's* became more uneven in size, slant and space between them, and the chalky slate lines got smudged. When she dismissed class early that day, Fräulein Reiners gave us our first homework assignment: we were to fill the lined side of our tablets with rows of lower case *i's*.

Counting from one to ten in unison and copying lower case i's were the rudimentary beginnings of our first-grade learning; Fräulein Reiners' swift, burning swats to the palms of our hands were as important as the lesson. Their memory, too, has lasted through the years. At the slightest provocation – talking, fidgeting, or staring out the window – Fräulein Reiners would call attention to the disruption, her voice stern though never raised. She would punish the wrongdoer individually or, if she couldn't identify an instigator, she would instruct all of us to rise and shuffle up the aisle in single file, right arms extended from the elbow. We would receive her blows, flinching involuntarily at the impending whoosh of her wooden ruler descending on our open palms.

It was unreasonable discipline, sanctioned by the unquestioned authority and capricious power vested in our teachers. Moreover, Fräulein Reiners' discipline was unfair. She lessened her blows to the palms of the smart students whom she favored and the ones whose parents sent along baskets of eggs, fresh baked bread and fruit. *Smartness* bore a stigma in the eyes of all of us but the smart students. So did baskets of foodstuff only the better-off parents could afford. Suspect in those days of postwar shortages, they were regarded as offerings in exchange for leniency and grade-inflated report cards. They offended our incipient sense of fairness.

At almost eight, Hubert Ingermann was one of the older boys in class. Though smart, he was not one of Fräulein Reiners' favorites. He was a wiry boy, with thick lashes framing his steady blue eyes and sharp-cut features. It seems to me now that he had a mind that was shrewd rather than brainy. He wasn't rowdy exactly, or bullying, as many of the boys were, but there was a toughness about him. He was a defiant boy: he strutted, head high, his back swayed. He despised compliance even at the risk of corporal punishment and was among the few who took it without flinching. For that reason alone, he was not one of Fräulein Reiners' favorites.

"Teacher's pet," Hubert Ingermann mumbled under his breath during seat assignment, when Fräulein Reiners called my name, waving her ruler to the center aisle seat, first row. The smart students sat in the first row. The smart students who gave her no trouble, that is. Or the not-so-smart students who brought her food baskets. Hubert was assigned an outside seat in the second row. Sitting down, he jammed his satchel onto the shelf beneath the desktop. It didn't go unnoticed. Fräulein Reiners strutted to his seat and twisted his ear.

Hubert Ingermann's accusation that I was a teacher's pet upset me. It kept me away from him during recess. I worried that he might torment me for some elusive wrong: I half believed that, somehow, I was guilty of having ingratiated myself to Fräulein Reiners; that being a teacher's favorite depended more on behavior than just smartness. The line between the two seemed smudged.

It was during recess, a few weeks after the school year had begun. Hubert Ingermann was leaning against the stubby post at the bottom of the dozen or so steps from the schoolhouse into the schoolyard. I spied him from the top landing. Afraid he was indeed waiting for me, I looked the other way. I heard gravel crunch under his feet, then the sharp clack of his shoe as he shot a small rock up into the air. It came flying my way in a low arc, missing me by a few inches – he'd probably planned it that way – before it landed in a rain puddle in the schoolyard with a plop and a splash.

I eased my way down the stairs, close to the banister on the side away from him. He started up in my direction, arms swinging a nonchalant beat. He stopped, his face right up against mine.

"You're not going anywhere, girl."

He spoke in *Plattdeutsch,* or *Rheinisch,* the Low German dialect indigenous to the Rhine region. Used mainly by the mostly rural, and generally less-educated people who were native to the region, it often was the only form of German they spoke with ease. Standard High German was the language of the more educated, and of the refugees from the East – although many of them had their own native way of speaking, as well. High German was the standard language of instruction in schools, of church proceedings and of official dealings. Being able to speak it well was a mark of a person's social standing. But it was considered elitist by many of the local people.

But the Rhenish dialect was part of the land, as was the river that gave the region its name. It was part of the endless wheat fields, the hamlets crouching around low-steepled churches. It came from the souls of the inhabitants of the land, a pious and somber people, given to hard work and brooding. And it was a part of me, too. I knew how to sound it out in my mind, I could feel it inside me, but without speaking it at home, my tongue was unaccustomed and unwilling to set it free, not even in that endearing way Mother had of blending High German with the Rhenish dialect in her conversations with neighbors.

"*Was willst Du?* – What do you want?" I asked in High German, indignation and a pretense of fearlessness in my question.

"*Isch heeß Hubert Ignatius Ingermann.* – I am Hubert Ignatius Ingermann," he said puffing his chest and, as before, addressing me in the dialect. He emphasized his odd middle name, as if it were a special distinction. "*Hüür misch jood zo, Mädsche, isch well disch wat saare.* – Listen to me, girl. I have something to say to you."

Dredging up courage, I repeated my question, "What do you want?"

"*Do Anjewwer, all we do schwaadst, do glövst wal, dat do wat besseres wörst.* – You show-off, the way you talk, you think you're better than us."

Goaded by his belligerence, I wanted to prove that I, too, could speak his stupid, primitive dialect. I heard my response in its native intonation as it assembled in my mind; I felt the words forming, physically, in my throat. It was meant as a comeback, to set him straight. *Loss misch in Roh.*

But what I spilled out was, "*Lass mich in Ruhe.* – Leave me alone." I said it in High German. It sounded timid, not in the least showing guts, as had been my design.

These were not the words I had composed in my mind. Those words had disappeared, suddenly.

He mocked my reply, whining and coloring it with affected High German speech, *"Lass mich in Ruhe."* He laughed. It was a fake laugh. Then he turned away.

"Eenjebildet Koh. – Conceited cow," he said in the dialect, and laughed again, in the same fake way.

At the end of recess, the principal sounded his high-pitched whistle. We stopped our games and made our way to the bottom of the staircase. We lined up in twos and by grades, boys and girls separated. While we were waiting for our signal to enter the schoolhouse, I counted the pockets in the brick wall, dug by shell fragments in wartime skirmishes. The girl behind me fidgeted with my apron strap, undoing the tidy bow Mother had tied in the morning.

"Grade one," the principal shouted. We moved, slowly and in orderly fashion, first the boys, followed by the girls, up the stairs, through the gaping double door, and down the unlit hallway.

Sunlight flooded the classroom. I sat down in my assigned seat in the first row, still unnerved by the boy's insult. The chatter of first-graders ebbed as Fräulein Reiners entered. The class stood up, awaiting Fräulein Reiners' *"Guten Morgen."*

In my memory, on the same day that Hubert Ingermann called me *eenjebildet Koh,* I made up my mind with all the confidence I could muster that I would transfer out of our local school as soon as the system permitted. In retrospect, I realize that one event may have preceded the other, but the insult and the resolve loomed so large that they dwarfed everything else in my memory of that time.

Four years later, I passed the required exam to enter secondary school in Dormagen, a train stop south of Delrath.

20

Grandmother, although she never left her house, was kept informed about everything that went on in our town. Neighborhood women who stopped in for a chat, itinerant merchants who offered their wares, Rosmarie, the young woman in charge of the cleaning – they all brought the town's news and gossip into her kitchen. Grandmother knew who was pregnant or had delivered a child; who had died and what illness had taken them; she knew who was getting married to whom and had an opinion on whether or not they were a good match. And, she had a compelling interest in keeping track of eligible bachelors, specifically those who would make suitable matches for Mother.

"Gertrud, it's been almost two years. Your black clothes aren't going to bring Josef back," Grandmother said. "Besides, people will start wondering what's gotten into you."

Mother relented, though not all at once. Initially, she embellished her black blouses with white, lacy collars. Only gradually did she bring her regular clothes to the front of the wardrobe. When she let me, I watched her try them on and look at herself in the mirror, loosening her chignon-gathered hair so it would curl around her temples, turning coyly for a side view of her slender self. She would smile shyly, pleased at her reflection.

"Never mind that he is balding and almost twice your age, Schönewald is in a position to take good care of you and your children," Grandmother said about the rich merchant who had called on her to make his intentions known. "You must learn to be practical." Her advice may not have been welcome, but in the end Mother never went against Grandmother's wishes. She stood her ground for as long as she could. Then the wealthy Schönewald, almost twice her age, became a regular visitor to our flat.

I peer into a fogged glass jar, which I have chanced upon in Mother's bedroom closet. Inside the jar, I see my mother, dwarfed to the size of a thumb, her face blank and ghostly white. She is staggering through a lush miniature garden. She has been wounded in ways that are not visible. I want to wave to her, but my arms feel leaden. I open my mouth to scream, but I have lost my speech. Then I know: my mother will die.

I woke up, still caught in the dream.

Mother was asleep in the bed next to mine, her face turned away. Her even breathing set my mind to rest. It had only been a dream.

I crept out of bed. I tiptoed to the verandah. Outside, it was gray, chilly, dead quiet. I went over to the glass jar in which I had set up a caterpillar experiment with clumps of clover, dandelions and bare twigs. I caught sight of the green, wormy captive humping its ugly body up a leaf. A putrid stench rose from the jar.

I took the jar and, holding my breath, carried it down the stairs, through the washhouse and into the garden. I walked along the dirt path dividing the vegetable beds, ignoring the pain of scattered pebbles digging into the soles of my bare feet. I pulled the mesh-wire covering off the jar's opening and dropped my experiment into the rhubarb patch, jar and all.

I kept the dream secret from Mother. Nor did I tell her about the abandoned caterpillar project. I believed dreams were of my own making, that I fabricated their stories in my sleep. I felt horrified, and ashamed, that I had cast Mother as a helpless captive, so much like the creature I'd kept in the jar. I also believed that relating the dream to her would make it come true.

It was unbearable to consider Mother dying, now, or later, or ever. Nonetheless, a shift occurred in my perception of her. Before the dream, she had been perfect and could do no wrong; now, my love for her was no longer as trusting as it had been.

A sickening feeling lingered for days afterwards. I harbored suspicions that I was unable to identify, relating to something outside of what I knew. I observed Mother to see what was different about her and to glean information from what she said, often in her veiled conversations with Frau Scheer, our upstairs neighbor and Mother's confidante.

Mother put Gitta into her crib and then tucked me in for the night.

"*Gut' Kind, ja?*" I said, not knowing it would be the last time I asked our nightly question.

"*Ja, gut' Kind,*" Mother said.

A prayer-like ritual, it had always given me the assurance that I had been a "good child." Her blessing was only perfunctory that evening. She dismissed me with a hasty kiss on the cheek and left the room more hurriedly than was her custom. She did not leave the light on or the door ajar. I protested, but she only snapped at me from behind the closed door. "You're old enough to sleep without the light on and the door wide open."

Stifling anger and an unarticulated sense of betrayal, I sat up in bed, cheeks burning and my heart beating so loudly I could hear nothing else.

After a time, an unfamiliar calm washed over me. A calm that signified – it struck me then – that I was leaving something of myself behind. I was seven years old.

A burst of laughter awoke me late that night. Not the laughter of good times, but a kind of laughter unaccustomed to my ears: a giggling mixed with high-pitched squeals and coarse grunting.

Driven by jealous misgivings, I left my bed and stole into the hallway. I cracked the living room door open and peered inside: Mother and the balding merchant were on the sofa, his face buried in the crook of her neck, his skull staring at me, sweat-beaded and hairless but for a narrow fringe at the base of his head. Mother's skirt had been pushed up to her thighs. Her body was squirming to free itself from the grip of his hand between her legs.

I ran from the door. What I had seen was real, it was forbidden, and it was nameless.

I pulled my featherbed over my head. It muffled my screams.

I woke up the next morning into a world different from the one I had known. I twisted my mind into forgetting what I had witnessed the previous evening. But like the dream of mother trapped in the glass jar, it clung to me like a nasty secret, neither fully remembered nor forgotten.

21

"It's as sturdy as any air raid shelter. The only one I'd ever trust," Grandmother said of the cellar that spanned the entire width and breath of the house. "And you won't starve in it, to boot," she added, laughing at her own joke. At a time of postwar scarcity and rationing, Grandmother was proud of all that her cellar supplied for her family's survival.

The shelves with jars of preserved vegetables and fruits in the root cellar would dwindle in late winter and early spring; one had to dip deeper into the vats for scoops of sauerkraut or butter. The coals and briquettes would diminish to almost nothing, and the potatoes would grow white shoots and become soft to the touch.

But in early summer and into fall, Grandfather and Onkel Jean would bring baskets of ripe vegetables and fruits into Grandmother's kitchen. Mother and Grandmother would preserve them in jars and replenish the cellar shelves; piles of potatoes and apples would appear in the bins, thus making the cellar an inexhaustible source upon which we relied for sustenance.

A door opposite a clothes rack in the hallway opened to a staircase into the root cellar. At the bottom of the staircase were two enormous bins. In ordinary times, Grandfather dumped wheelbarrow loads of coal and briquette down the chutes until the bins were filled to the brim. In the lean, post-war years, only the officially allocated amount, barely enough to keep the kitchen stove going, would tumble down in a pathetically thin stream. In an alcove at the end of the cellar farthest away from the staircase, was a stack of old-fashioned three-piece mattresses. Mocking earnestness, Grandmother dismissed Mother's suggestion to get rid of those musty dust catchers.

"They're in nobody's way" , Grandmother said, "They served us well during the bombings and, if the mice don't chew them up first, heaven knows, they'll come in handy if the world goes crazy again." I took her words seriously. They bolstered my hope that, even if the end of the world were to come, as some of the town's religious fanatics prophesied, we would survive in Grandmother's cellar.

While the idea of the cellar as a source of plenty and safety was reassuring, it was also a dark, cavernous place isolated from the rest of the house, and fear-inspiring. On occasion, when the door had been left ajar, I would stand at the top of the stairs and look down into the depths, wildly afraid and, at the same time, possessed by a desire to brave the cellar's unexplored mysteries.

That opportunity came one day, when Grandmother instructed me to fetch a scoop of butter from the butter vat in the cellar. Never before had she sent me into the cellar. I didn't want to go. I also didn't want to disobey Grandmother or act like a little girl. After all, I was seven years old.

Fighting my dread, I took the butter dish and headed from the kitchen across the hall and to the basement door. I turned the large key that was always in the keyhole. The door creaked open. I stretched to reach the switch that turned on a light deep in the bowels of the cellar, a light I couldn't even see from the doorway. The wooden stair treads, dipping at their centers from decades of wear, were steep and narrow. I put my feet sideways on each tread and felt my way along by placing my hand on the rough cement wall. Slowly and cautiously at first, by the light that slanted through the open door, then racing to the bottom part of the staircase.

A single, low-wattage light bulb hung from a cord from the ceiling behind a partition. The bulb dangled above my head. It spread a yellow cone of light, making a circle on the packed dirt floor. I dashed into that circle. The light's power, I believed, protected me from my own fear; gradually, the light identified what was within its sphere – an empty bucket, a coal shovel, not much else. Darkness obfuscated what was outside its periphery. Gathering courage, my eyes penetrated the cone's imaginary border and scanned the immediate area beyond the light. What at first glance seemed ominous configurations of the gleaming eyes of horned devils, slowly shaped themselves into harmless jars of Grandmother's preserves lining the shelves. I made out the pickling barrels, the butter vat, the potato crate and, as I expanded my view to include the far side, the sectioned mattresses. A thick film of dust covered everything.

I stepped out of the circle of light, heartened, now, that I could make other, at first-glance scary things harmless by identifying them. With each step, the barrier between the known and the unknown moved further away.

I held my gaze on the darkest places in the far corners, even more menacing than the rest. What had been unnamed and, thus, unnamable, revealed itself: cobwebs suspended from the shelves and ceiling; thick dust balls in the spaces between barrels; a crumpled rag in the shadows. That was all. Nothing that could harm me.

I straightened my shoulders and stood tall. The light seemed different, brighter and more encompassing than before. An utter silence isolated me from the muffled sounds of dishes clattering in the kitchen. A distinct odor filled my nose. It was the smell of the earth: damp, fertile, cool, musty, more pungent than the freshly turned soil in Grandfather's vegetable garden.

I flared my nostrils and expanded my chest to let the cellar air flow into my lungs. I held my breath until the inside of my skull tingled. At the threshold of lightheadedness, I exhaled. And then greedily inhaled again. I did this until all of me felt permeated with that air, and there was no longer a separation between the cellar and me.

I heard Grandmother calling my name. Remembering suddenly why I'd come into the cellar, I scooped butter from the vat into the dish I was still carrying.

After that day, I revisited the cellar often, when Grandmother asked me to fetch a jar of beans or peaches for a meal or to lug up a scuttle of coal to feed the kitchen stove. Sometimes, I went down for no reason other than to feel traces of the old fear and experience the unknown opening up.

Until the afternoon when Grandfather locked the cellar door, taking out the key, and Grandmother warned Gitta and me to not ever go near the cellar again.

The Laues were among the millions of *Flüchtlinge*, refugees, who had fled eastern Germany. A few dozen had come to Delrath, where they had been assigned quarters in homes throughout town by the housing authority that had been put in place to alleviate the post-war housing shortage. The Laues and their two teenage sons had moved into the street-facing rooms on the second story of my grandparents' house: the room that had been Grandmother and Grandfather's bedroom, and two smaller rooms that had been the rooms of my uncles – Onkel Ernst, still held prisoner-of-war in Siberia, and Onkel Gottfried, missing in action after the battle of Stalingrad.

Grandfather didn't seem to mind the inconvenience of emptying a rarely used sitting room adjacent to the kitchen and of sleeping downstairs. He willingly moved the spare furniture from the sitting room into the barn.

"This house is too big for us anyway," Grandmother said. "Besides, it saves me from hobbling up and down those stairs," she added, making light of the situation.

There was an unspoken rift separating the native population from the *Flüchtlinge,* as they were referred to in those days and years later, still, even after they had long established themselves in the community. Both the term and the rift remained. Intruding on a way of life already compromised by the war, they were not universally received with open arms. They were strangers to the locals, many of whom had never traveled beyond the boundaries of Delrath and the adjacent towns.

Uprooted in their native cities and villages in the East, the refugees had left with little more than the clothes on their backs, perhaps a few family photographs and memories they deemed of value in the packs they carried. They had fled the war-torn regions they called home, made their long journeys through war-torn country, only to find themselves at destinations that, too, were war-torn. They had to rely on public assistance and on the kindness of others that wasn't always forthcoming.

They spoke the harsher sounding vernaculars of eastern Germany, unfamiliar to the Rhenish ear. With few exceptions, they were of Protestant faith, in a Catholic community, where going to Church and observing Catholic ways was central to life.

The adults treated one another with guarded friendliness and silent resentment. The children, on the other hand, were oblivious to such reservations, happy for every new playmate who joined the small neighborhood groups. Maybe some of the children would pick on the refugee children for this or that – a game they didn't know how to play or an outfit they wore that seemed peculiar – but soon the differences began to blend into local customs, or disappear, or just go unnoticed.

The Laues had been expelled from their native *Schlesien*, Silesia, where Herr Laue had been the caretaker of an estate. He was a reticent man, not given to niceties. He walked with a stoop, his eyes trained on the ground in front of him. Jobless during the initial months, Herr Laue spent much of the day busying himself in Grandfather's workshop. Eventually, he would find a job in the local zinc smeltery.

In my memory, Frau Laue always carried a water bucket and mop. Not a shy woman, she occasionally stopped at the open kitchen door for a chat with Grandmother. I don't recall the names of either of their two sons, though I do remember their shy and unsocial demeanor. When we crossed paths in the hallway or in the street, they would lower their eyes or turn their heads and look away.

The day Grandmother declared the root cellar off limits began as a beautiful summer morning. Before the events of the afternoon unfolded, a spectacular mountain of clouds had begun gathering beyond the railroad tracks, and by dusk, lightning flashed in the sky. That, anyway, is how it has been preserved in my memory.

I recollect Mother at the kitchen sink, eyebrows knitted, lips pressed together tightly. Gitta was hiding under her apron. I heard the unmistakable sound of Grandmother thumping up the staircase to the second story and, soon after, snatches of accusations and an adolescent, balking, "No, I didn't." Then, an exchange of harsh words between the boy's mother, insisting, "He's a good boy. He wouldn't do that," and Grandmother, raising her voice, "I won't have this. Not in my house."

The expression on Mother's face deepened as she, too, listened to the argument upstairs. She pulled Gitta closer to her, then looked at me.

"Hat er dich auch angefasst? – Did he touch you, also?" she asked in a tone that implied he had. The word *anfassen*, touch, suddenly lost its

regular meaning and hinted at something darker, more suggestive, something *adult* that was bad.

"No," I said.

She persisted, as if she knew something and were trying to catch me in a lie.

"No," I insisted, "No, he didn't."

The uneven galumph of Grandmother coming back down the stairs echoed in the tiled hallway. Hands at both sides of her waist, which helped propel her heavy body forward at a faster speed, she hobbled the length of the kitchen. Sitting down in her wicker armchair, straight and tall as the ruling mistress of the house, she summoned Gitta and me to her side. She lifted Gitta's chin, then mine, and instructed us never to set foot in the cellar again. *"Habt ihr das gehört?* – Did you hear me?" she said, emphasizing the urgency of her point.

Did I have some half-formed understanding, at barely eight years old, of what Grandmother was implying, or did I guard myself against actual knowledge, feigning ignorance to keep the child-world I inhabited intact? I asked my grandmother, simply, "Why not?"

"It just isn't a good place for little girls. That's all," she said, making it clear that the subject was closed.

All the root cellar had been for me – its bounty, my conquered fears, the smell of the earth filling my lungs – from that day on, was lost. Now the cellar became something else for me: the place where I suspected I'd seen something, and perhaps did see something: the sense that something bad had occurred in the cellar began to form in my mind. It was the image of the cellar staircase, halfway down the steps, four-year-old Gitta pinned against the cement wall, the younger of the Laue brothers, fifteen years old at most, reaching under her skirt.

Grandmother had been dead for fifty years when she appeared in a dream: *Like a large guardian angel, she hovers over me as I walk down into the cellar of her house. The stairs have a fresh coat of paint, a glossy forest green. It's dark, except for shafts of light entering from the courtyard through an iron grate. My eyes strain to recognize the surroundings, no longer familiar. Grandmother holds a desk lamp. Its warm, yellow light begins to illuminate the immediate area. She places it on a small antique writing table. "You'll need this if you're going to write down here," she says.*

22

Doris' father had also been killed in the war. While this was a circumstance we shared, and might have united us, it separated us instead. We never talked about our dead fathers, as that would have been tantamount to admitting our families were flawed. Nor did we talk about her mother's new husband, nor about my mother's gentleman friend. We shared a pretense that neither stepfather nor suitor existed.

Our mothers didn't seek each other's company beyond the casual exchanges that go along with being good neighbors. Unspoken, mutual recrimination was the reason. Even as a child, their cold demeanor and hints of disapproval toward each other did not escape me. My mother suggested that Doris' mother, in order to preserve her moral and social integrity, had married the first man who had come along after the war. That he turned out to be neither a good provider nor to have much love for Doris and her younger brother only fueled Mother's argument that he was not a sensible choice. Doris' mother, in turn, disapproved of my mother who, after indulging in an excessively long mourning period, now regularly entertained a suitor twice her age.

I have no memory at all of Doris playing at our flat, and only one of me in their kitchen, when I felt embarrassed and vaguely diminished by a remark Doris' mother made. It could have been something like, "If it's true what they say, then you, too, will soon have a new father."

Although Doris and I were both in the second grade, and her family lived in the flat across from ours, we played together only occasionally. A particular adventure with Doris that has stayed with me, unshakably, takes me back to a spring day in the barn.

For want of anything better to do, Doris and I, on that particular afternoon, made our way down Rheinstraße to my grandparents' house. "Let's play hide and seek in the barn," I suggested. Built of the same age-darkened brick as the main house, it spread the width of the courtyard on the far side, separating the meadow and the garden behind it.

The barn housed last summer's bales of straw. Some towered so high they touched the beamed ceiling of the roof, others were piled in squat stacks. They created a multi-layered labyrinth, in which it was easy to lose one's bearings or one's footing.

I had no trouble finding Doris, a stranger to the barn, in the obvious hiding places she chose, whereas I, familiar with every nook and cranny, made it tough for her to find me. For a time, I enjoyed winning. But after many long waits crouching in tight crevices while Doris looked for me in all the wrong places, I became bored. In the end, Doris began to pout with frustration, and we abandoned the game.

We ambled aimlessly to the other side of the barn, kicking up loose straw, unsure what to do next. That's when we encountered a grouping of five or six black, round objects close to the wall, the largest the size of a tennis ball.

"Hey, let's play soccer," I said, less from enthusiasm than a lack of more exciting ideas, and bent down to pick up one of the balls. Just then, what had been a motionless object, quickened to the touch of my hand. I let go, shrieking, as the rest of them began to stir as well. Long spines bristled straight up from each of them. Doris and I both jumped back and, in utter disgust, watched the little troupe set out in a slow stampede.

"Hedgehogs," we screeched, and bolted into the front seat of the carriage parked at the rear entrance. Our fright felt at once blown all out of proportion and tantalizing. These little creatures could do us no harm, but fleeing from them gave us a sense of having escaped imminent danger. I shuddered with squeamish delight and wiped my palms on Doris' dress to get rid of all traces of hedgehog. She protested, slapping my hands. Giggling wildly, we clung on to each other while we rocked back and forth on the upholstered seat.

We tore off our clothes in a frenzy, both of us shivering in the early spring cold. Arms by her side, thighs pressed together, Doris stretched out stiffly on the dark green velvet. Neither of us spoke. I picked up a straw from the carriage floor. I touched her flat chest with one end of it and made-believe I was listening to her heartbeat through the other. Her lips quivered. Gooseflesh covered her pale skin.

An unfamiliar sensation rushed through me. It was answered by shame: not the kind of shame that came with an ordinary misdeed, but something of Biblical magnitude. It was drowned out by a throbbing between my thighs, in a place I had never touched or tried to look at, nor did I know its name.

I trailed the straw gently over Doris' round child-belly to the nameless place. I drew small circles on the smooth mound. I feathered it with the straw. A fluttering below my stomach pulsed with a rhythm of its own. I pulled the straw up and down the mound, a little lower each time, until it penetrated, if barely, the shallow cleft. Doris giggled.

"You're tickling me," she said, her body now squirming and twisting away.

We reversed roles. Lying on my back, nude, I now submitted to Doris' exploration. The unnamed frenzy, which only moments ago had swept me to an unnamed edge, suddenly drained from me. Remorse brought me to my senses. As if Doris, too, had come to her senses, she stopped.

We drew our clothes on in a mad rush. We fled from the barn.

Doris and I didn't speak, then or later, about what happened that afternoon. Our silence kept it hidden, even between the two of us. I hoped Doris would forget the thing that wouldn't leave my mind.

In the evening that followed, Mother prepared my bath, as was her custom. With coal still rationed and the building's central hot water system not yet back in operation, she heated pots of water on the kitchen stove. She carried them one by one into the bathroom, filling the tub and adding cold water from the faucet.

"Get undressed," Mother said.

Held back by a new kind of shyness, I turned away from her and took off my clothes. She didn't comment on my changed demeanor but lifted me playfully into the tub. The warm water covering me to my waist, I pulled my knees to my chest. She ran the palm of her hand over the knobs of my vertebrae.

"I don't want you touching me," I said.

"What's gotten into you?"

"Just don't touch me."

I flung my arms to keep her from coming closer. She looked at me aghast. Grabbing my forearms, she held them in place until I submitted to what had always been our ritual: she washed my face. She wet my hair and, in the absence of shampoo after the war, rubbed soap into it. Globs of foam oozed down my forehead.

"Cover your eyes," she instructed, pouring pitchers full of water over my head.

I got to my feet, as she gestured I should. "You're so thin," she said, washing my chest. *"Man kann deine Rippen zählen. –* I can count your ribs."

With brisk strokes, Mother scrubbed between my legs, then my bottom, thighs and calves. I lifted my feet for her to wash. It tickled.

"All done," she said and slapped my wet bottom teasingly. It made a splashing sound. "A quick rinse, and you'll be squeaky clean again."

"I want to die," I said, hatefully.

I couldn't forgive myself for what had happened in the barn. I wanted to be born again and given a second chance.

I didn't want to confide in Mother, but it made me angry that she was oblivious to my difficulty. I waited for her to ask why I wanted to die.

She didn't ask. She said, "What a silly thing to say."

I burst into tears. "You don't know anything."

Perhaps Mother saw my confusion about my body and, feeling helpless, turned a blind eye. At any rate, I made up my mind then and there, in the bath, that she couldn't be counted on in things that mattered. Another rift opened up. Like the rift that had opened between us on the night of the balding merchant, this rift would never close again.

I was alone with my troubled thoughts. I was also alone when I tried to make sense of what we were learning in our twice-a-week catechism class.

Sitting behind the teacher's desk in a class of Catholic second graders, Pastor Steinbach, taught us the story of Genesis. He came to the part about Adam and Eve's nakedness, and how their nakedness had led to the expulsion from paradise. The word *nakedness* made a few of the boys giggle. It made my palms sweat, remembering what Doris and I had done in the barn.

I'd always known that nakedness was bad, that looking at nakedness and touching nakedness, even one's own, was a sin. I'd never seen Mother naked, or my father, when he was still alive. I'd seen Gitta naked when she was very little. But that was different.

Pastor Steinbach, in a tone that was urgent, as if cautioning us, went on to explain that Adam and Eve's nakedness had been the reason why, henceforth, mankind would be born into original sin and be mortal. Baptism, he said, exonerated us from original sin and restored our purity. Probably, I wouldn't have known what *purity* was or how to preserve it, had it not been for that afternoon of Doris and me nude on the front seat of the carriage.

We learned the Ten Commandments by heart. The sixth one, "Thou shalt be chaste," was the only one the pastor didn't comment on. For as long as I could remember, I'd had some inkling of what it meant. I didn't know what sex was, nor was it a word I had ever heard. Babies, I still believed, were brought by the stork; on the other hand, the idea of chastity had been deeply inculcated in me, somehow, whether by Mother or Pastor Steinbach's religious instruction or something innately familiar. Mother may have said, "Don't touch there," or "Don't ask me that," when I queried about certain body parts.

However, by the time I was seven, what had been inklings and speculations had begun to take she shape of uneasy knowledge. Spying on Mother and the balding merchant, I had witnessed the forbidden; the root cellar, once a sacred place, had been defiled by the forbidden; and, worst of all, I myself had stepped into the forbidden with Doris in the barn.

The fear of having fallen into God's disfavor weighed on me.

Whether to appease God or whether I wanted to please Fräulein Reiners, who rewarded Mass attendance with holy pictures, I started going to church every morning.

It was not unheard of in those days to attend Mass daily. While the pews on the women's side typically were well filled, the pews on the men's side remained empty, except for a handful of mainly old men. I was among a smattering of boys and girls in the front pews reserved for children.

Mother was perplexed by my *übertriebene Frömmigkeit,* my exaggerated piety, as she labeled it. A Catholic in name only, and contemptuous of all religion, she didn't go to church, except for Midnight Mass on Christmas Eve. But she sent me every Sunday and Gitta, as well, when she was old enough. My father, on the other hand, had been a strict Catholic. He'd been an altar boy as a youngster and had sung in the church choir as a young man, Mother had told me, even though, she sometimes jested, he couldn't carry a tune.

Mother tolerated my newly-found enthusiasm, sometimes even poking her head into my room when I'd overslept. "If you want to go to church, you'd better get out of bed," she'd say.

Most days, I made it to my assigned seat in the third pew just as Mass was about to begin. Two white-smocked altar boys entered first, one swinging the censer, the other shaking the chimes. Vestured in his white everyday cotton robe, Pastor Steinbach shuffled in after them. His large, hairless hands were folded over his chest, his gaze, fixed on his fingertips. As the short procession made its final turn to the altar, the pastor, without the slightest movement of his head, sneaked a sideways glance at his congregation.

Leading the prayer was a high school boy, the organist's son and the pastor's hope for the new generation of clergy. He was pale and handsome in a studious way, and always wore a dark crew-neck sweater under a dark sports jacket, approximating the priestly look without the white collar. He, too, attended every Mass.

Several years later, the rumor that he was marrying a girl who was expecting his child would take the town by surprise. Denounced as a hypocrite, he would be relieved of his church duties.

But now the boy's voice, barely past breaking, guided us through hymns and prayers with the innocence and fervor of a saint while, at the altar, Pastor Steinbach and his altar boys mumbled Latin phrases back and forth.

Fräulein Reiners kept an eye on the girls from where she knelt in the last row of the girls' section on the left. Her vigilance assured our good behavior. Most of us didn't dare glance at our neighbors, let alone whisper. The bolder ones exchanged holy pictures under cover of the pews.

Following cues that spread invisibly and instantly among the worshippers, we rose to our feet or knelt on the wooden knee benches in unison. We prayed and sang hymns. We stood during the reading from The Gospel, sat for Pastor Steinbach's notoriously boring sermons.

The Mass dragged on, at long last culminating in the Eucharist. His glance turned upward to the high-vaulted ceiling, Pastor Steinbach raised the Holy Host above his head. His softly mumbled *Pax Domini* alternated with the sound of the Sanctus bells. Wafts of incense curled in the shafts of morning light streaming through stained glass windows.

As predictably as the ceremony unfolded at the altar, each morning I'd feel the blood draining from my face, and I'd break out in a cold sweat. Everything around me would whirl in a haze. The statue of the Holy Virgin on the pedestal in the transept looked as if she might topple. My hands and arms, suddenly heavy, would drop to my side. The girl next to me would tug at my sleeve. "Go outside," she'd whisper.

I'd stumble to the end of the pew and manage a lopsided sign of the cross. Knees buckling, hands weakly folded, I'd stagger down the aisle to the main portal.

Pushing against it with my shoulder, it would ease open with a long squeak. Once outside, I'd lean against the brick-and-mortar wall, its coolness soaking into my skin, the crisp morning air filling my nostrils.

Eyes closed, I'd wait until the ground under my feet felt solid again, and all signs of lightheadedness had vanished. The spell would be over.

A few of the women would turn their heads as I made my way back to my seat. I could feel their chastising stare on my back after I'd passed them.

"What do you expect when you go to Mass on an empty stomach?" Mother said when I told her about my daily episodes. Her argument, while reasonable, wasn't what I believed. I was certain God was punishing or, worse, rejecting me.

At the end of most weeks, Fräulein Reiners rewarded me with an extra holy picture for record attendance.

"If you keep up your fanatic churchgoing, you'll end up in a nunnery," Mother said, unwittingly planting the idea to become a nun when I grew up. Little did she realize that what she saw as a punishing fate for being overly pious became the romantic fantasy of a seven-year old with a bad conscience.

Even if I didn't break the Sixth Commandment again, as I had vowed not to do, I had concluded that sins were an inevitable part of our human existence. Sometimes they popped up as small lies, cheating in a game, fighting with Gitta, or not listening to Mother.

Nuns, on the other hand, were pure. Reclusive convent life separated and safeguarded them from our sinful world. Betrothed to Christ, nuns wore a gold band on their ring fingers, symbolizing the holy union. Even their black habits and veils, distinguishing them from ordinary women, added to the idealized image I had of them.

I kept my thoughts from Mother, for good reason. Her distaste for the Catholic Church, in general, was exceeded only by her hatred of nuns. She had attended a prestigious convent school as a young girl. When her parents had fallen on hard times in the twenties and been habitually late paying her monthly tuition, the nuns had shown their true character as hypocrites and worse, Mother said.

"The way they dressed me down in front of the whole class! It was outright sadistic." No child of hers was going to be submitted to the rule of nuns.

On the other hand, my father's mother, Grandmother Neuss – we called her that because she lived in Neuss – would have been pleased. She might have even encouraged me. A reclusive widow since her husband's death from complications of WWI injuries, she lived in a spartanly furnished, third-story flat in Neuss.

I was fond of Grandmother Neuss, and she was fond of me. Once I was eight years old and ready to take the train by myself, I'd spend Easter breaks with her. I'd spend hours looking out the back window of her flat, my elbows propped on a pillow on the wooden sill, watching children play in the courtyard next door. How I longed to join their fun! But Grandmother Neuss wouldn't hear of it. She was an anxious woman. She feared for my safety, and wouldn't let me leave her flat without her.

Armed with sandwiches and sliced apples for picnic lunches, she'd take me to the playgrounds in the *Stadtgarten,* the city park, and the *Rosengarten,* a park with vast beds of roses. Early evenings, we'd attend devotions in the *Marienkirche,* St. Mary's church, in her neighborhood.

A devotee of the Virgin Mary, after whom Grandmother Neuss had been named, she'd teach me hymns in the Virgin's honor from her inexhaustible repertoire. Next to her bed was an altar, replete with a carved Madonna, votive candles and sprigs of evergreen.

My Delrath grandmother, not in the habit of mincing words, once said to Mother loud enough for me to hear, "Your mother-in-law has deluded herself into believing she is the Holy Virgin reincarnated, and if you don't watch out she'll turn your daughter into a religious fanatic as well."

Cousin Maria had crimson lips. Her large brown eyes were set deeply, eyelids slanting downward at the temple sides. This and her pure white complexion gave her the appearance of a young saint. Maria had lost both of her parents, her father to pneumonia early in the war; her mother, a few years later, to an aneurism caused by an abscessed wisdom tooth. Grandmother Neuss was godmother to both of us. While she made it her task to take us each under her religious wing, she paid special attention to poor Maria.

It was hard for me to look at Maria without being reminded that she was an orphan. I kept watch for signs of grief in all she said and did. The screen of pity, through which I saw her, kept us at an uneasy distance. I thought of her religious zeal, greater than even mine, in terms of her losses.

Not long after her mother's death, cousin Maria spent the summer with us in Delrath. Both of us were nine that year; our birthdays were a day apart – a difference that put me, as the older, in the role of incontestable leader.

The neighborhood children weren't quick to include strangers. They ridiculed Maria's regional intonation, different from ours, despite the relative proximity of her hometown in the Siegerland, a mountainous area two train hours southeast of Delrath.

A non-swimmer, Maria had been instructed by Grandmother Neuss not to go to the swimming hole, ruling out my favorite place to spend warm summer days. Neither did she know how to ride a bicycle. When I criticized an angel she had drawn, saying its head looked like a skull, she cried and never wanted to draw again. Playing Mass was an obvious choice for the two of us, and a game we returned to with fervor.

We assembled a makeshift altar on Mother's dressing table. An oak crucifix with a silver Jesus and adjustable candle brackets – Grandmother Neuss' engagement present to my parents – served as the centerpiece. Long banished to the bottom shelf of the hall closet, its faint silhouette was still visible on the bedroom wallpaper.

We collected potted ferns from the window sills and placed them on either side of the crucifix. We draped napkins over a bowl of bread crusts cut into circles and over Mother's prized antique silver goblet, filled with water instead of wine. Our prayer books did duty as Bible and Roman Missal.

We were priests, but we dressed up as nuns. We half-covered our foreheads and framed our faces with starched napkins folded to approximate wimpled cornettes. We wore blankets over our heads and shoulders, loosely tied at the waist with belts from Mother's closet.

We approached the altar from an improvised vestry behind the draperies.

Extemporizing the Mass ceremony, we went through elaborate motions of spreading our arms, bowing, kneeling, making the sign of the cross, all of which we accompanied with snatches we pretended to read from the Roman Missal: *Domino vobiscum. . . Et cum spiritu tuo. . . Kyrie eleison. . . Christi eleison. . . Oh, oh, oh, oh ete missa est,* and a lot of la-la-la's to fill in the gaps.

Maria read a passage from the Gospel and I, as the more articulate one, delivered the sermon. We enacted the changing of our pretend wine into the blood of Christ and of bread into his flesh with dramatic piety, our eyes alternately fixed on a point on the ceiling and cast to the floor. We took turns kneeling in front of each other to receive the bread-crust hosts on our tongues and then sang fragments of the *Gloria Dei* in pseudo mystical states.

At the final blessing of the congregation, a sudden change would come over us. Released from our trance, we rushed madly to take off our habits and dismantle the altar, just as though we were afraid we might get caught at our game. It was more than the idea of Mother surprising us. She might have shown her disapproval, saying, "What in heaven's name are you two doing?" or frowned at us in her inimical way.

No, it was something vaguely but deeply disquieting. Our reenactment, which was an innocent game and testimony to our young faith, wasn't altogether seemly. Mother's censure would've been one thing; partaking in Communion, the holiest of holy, when we hadn't even gone through First Communion, was another.

"Do you think you'll become a nun when you grow up?" I asked Maria after celebrating one of our many Masses.

"No," she said, without hesitation.

"Why not?"

"Nuns can't marry," she said. "How about you?"

Her answer surprised me, as did my own sudden change of mind. "No way. They can't read Mass."

"Worse, nuns get their hair chopped off," Maria said, as she ran her hands down her pitch-black, waist-long braids.

23

When a limousine pulled up at Grandmother's house and a uniformed chauffeur unloaded a trunk full of boxes the size of milk crates, it brought the neighborhood children swarming around the vehicle. Twice as long as any car that had ever passed through Delrath, the limousine's gray body was polished to a shine, and reflected the children's faces.

They threw furtive looks at the chauffeur, covering their mouths with their hands and giggling. The chauffeur was a young man with dark brown skin and a white, toothy smile. He didn't seem to mind the attention he was getting. None of us had ever seen someone of a skin color so different from our own.

Whatever impression this unlikely scene made on me, I didn't want to show it. I acted as if neither limousine, nor packages, nor *Neger* chauffeur were anything extraordinary.

Tante Irma had made arrangements to have the boxes delivered to Grandmother's house from Frankfurt, where she lived. She was Mother's younger sister and my favorite aunt – beautiful, sophisticated, glamorous. With an elegant flair, she would wave her mottled tortoiseshell cigarette holder as she smoked her cigarettes. Judged by our standards, she was wealthy. The difference between the two sisters was striking. Mother, reserved by comparison, was largely overshadowed by Tanta Irma's outgoing nature. However, what she lacked in the kind of worldliness her sister possessed, she made up for with a beauty that was genteel, almost shy.

Tante Irma had long before left the small-town life of her growing-up years in Delrath. In the late 1930s, she had made a career in Frankfurt, first in the administration of the *Schauspielhaus,* the city theater, whose director she had married and divorced. Later she worked in radio.

After the war, Tante Irma was hired by the *Amerikaner,* the colloquial reference to the American Occupational Forces. Vague about the work she did – I secretly imagined she was a spy – she described herself as a *Verbindungsperson,* a liaison between the Americans and the Germans.

Living on an army base in Frankfurt, she had access to the PX, and was able to buy foodstuff and other merchandise that was rationed or generally unavailable to the German populace. Her superior, Colonel Friedeberg – whose family doted on her in many ways – provided the chauffeured limousine that pulled up at Grandmother's door with a delivery every few months.

"Wie wär's mit 'ner Tasse Kaffee? – How about a cup of coffee?" Grandmother suggested to the young American chauffeur near the end of his first visit. He probably didn't understand a word of what she was saying, but he sat down at the kitchen table anyway. They talked, each in their own language. They gestured and laughed and carried on. They understood one another, somehow – or, if they didn't, it didn't seem to matter to either one.

It intrigued me to hear a language spoken that wasn't my own, although it sounded more like a seamless jumble than individual words strung together to form sentences and convey meaning. It perplexed me that anyone could be fluent in such a language, and that anyone would be able to understand it.

My eyes were glued to the chauffeur. His dark skin made me think of the pictures I'd seen of near-naked people in the jungles of Africa – which I assumed was his homeland. I was surprised and disappointed when Grandmother later told me that the chauffeur was an American and that, in America, *Neger* used to be bought and sold by wealthy farm owners and kept as slaves.

His skin color, his tightly curled hair, his broad nose and full lips all fascinated me. But it was the whiteness of his palms, incongruous with his otherwise dark skin, and the fact that I, too, had white palms that struck me most. It made the difference between him and me less mystifying. He noticed how his palms caught my attention, and stretched out his open hand to show me, or for me to touch. Shyness got the better of me. I looked away.

When he stood up to leave, he gave a mannered salute, then said, *"Auf Wiedersehen!* and goodbye."

The American chauffeur had spoken one word in German and then the same word in English. I was able to see the parallel: there were direct word equivalents from language to language. It was a discovery that thrilled me.

"What's all the commotion I've heard about?" Mother asked when she arrived in Grandmother's kitchen later that afternoon. Excited to tell her about the limousine and the *Neger* chauffeur, Gitta and I talked over each other, showing her the boxes that he had delivered.

"Our Irma," Grandmother chimed in. "She has a heart of gold."

Mother moved the first box on the table and opened the flaps. Gitta, standing on a chair, and I, tall enough to reach, unpacked the contents:

Cans and jars with illustrated labels provided clues as to what was inside – pineapples, mushrooms, orange marmalade, fruit salad, all novel to us. Bars of *Hershey* chocolate. A box of *Corn Flakes* with a cartoonish red rooster. Curious, Grandmother poured out handfuls for all of us to try.

"I wouldn't know what it is, but it sure tastes good," she said.

She also opened a jar of peanut butter, not something one would find in the local grocery store. Its smell nauseated me. Its brown color, I decided, proved that it was real butter gone bad. No amount of coaxing could get me to try a spoonful.

A second box was full of baking goods, from bags of flour and sugar to baking soda and egg powder; a third box, less interesting to Gitta and me, contained cartons of *Lux* soap flakes, laundry powder and bars of *Ivory* soap in blue and white wrappers.

"Not that one," Grandmother said, raising her hand to stop us from unpacking the next box. "And not a word about it to anyone."

That box, I knew, was chockfull of cartons of *Chesterfield* cigarettes and cans of *Maxwell House* coffee.

It wasn't exactly a secret that Mother was involved in the black market, and that cigarettes and coffee served as unofficial currency in the post-war economy; but I don't recall anybody ever talking about it.

Neither did I have a clear idea about what the *black market* entailed. I must have heard the words "black market" when the grown-ups were talking quietly, and I must have understood, somehow, that this activity was illegal. I envisioned mysterious meetings in city alleys, where black marketeers, hooded and disguised, gathered. I imagined Mother went to meet them under cover of night to sell or trade her goods. I had heard rumors about raids and confiscation.

After I accidentally discovered a cache of Tante Irma's American cigarettes and coffee stashed on the bottom shelf of the sitting room cabinet, I wrongly suspected that the trading took place right here in our flat. It never crossed my mind that Mother actually traveled with her wares in a basket on the back of her bicycle, bartering for food with farmers in surrounding areas.

One final box remained, the largest, but lightest in weight. Mother had saved it for last. She took it upon herself to unpack it, promising that a surprise for Gitta and me was inside.

Mother sorted an armload of girls' clothing by size, the smaller ones for the four-year-old Gitta, the larger ones for me, now eight – dresses, skirts, blouses, all hand-me-downs from the Friedeberg daughters. They were *American clothes,* so very different from the plain, post-war clothes we wore, I instantly decided I wasn't going to like them.

"I'm not going to wear these frilly things," I protested.

Pretending not to have heard me, Mother held up a dress in a flower print. Made of a puckered fabric, of a kind I had never seen, it was baby blue and baby pink, my least favorite colors. Fussy lace bordered its neckline and puffy sleeves. The skirt, with its layers of staggered ruffles, looked more like a gown for a dance than a school dress.

On Mother's insistence, I tried it on, anyway. As she stepped back to evaluate my appearance, an admiring smile came over her face.

"You're going to be the best dressed girl in the whole school."

"I don't want to be," I said, as I imagined the other children gawking at me.

Mother responded with the most devastating weapon in her arsenal, worse than a slap. Her face set, she closed her eyes. When she opened them again after a few, very long seconds, her look was one of deep disappointment in me. A seldom delivered punishment, it had never failed, not up to that moment.

Shoulders slumping, arms dangling, I planted myself in front of Mother. I wanted her to see just how absurd I looked in the American dress.

"You're an ungrateful girl," she said, in a last effort to shame me.

Grandmother intervened. "Let her wear her old rags, if that's what she wants."

Grandmother was siding with me! But was she really? Wasn't she also agreeing with Mother?

I was torn for a brief moment, then stood my ground: "Yes, I'd rather wear my old rags than be seen in this stupid outfit."

On rare Sundays, Tante Irma herself showed up on Grandmother's doorstep, unannounced, for short visits. She'd arrive on the train with her son, Jochen, loaded down with a suitcase full of gifts. A towheaded toddler not quite three years old, Jochen was a quiet boy. He seemed to like being off in a corner, by himself, pushing a toy car in circles and mimicking the sound of an engine.

Tante Irma took great pleasure in the generosity she was able to afford. The things she brought were different from the things we knew. They had an expensive, city-type look: embossed, personalized stationery; Belgian chocolates in fancy boxes; linen-covered books; sometimes a fashionable skirt or blouse for Mother.

We'd all gather around Grandmother's kitchen table, indulging in the fancy baked goods Tante Irma had brought, along with real coffee for the adults and cocoa for the children. Too soon, she'd announce that it was time to leave, and Grandmother would urge her to make her visits more frequent.

After her goodbyes, I'd walk Tante Irma and Jochen to the train. I was fond of Jochen, and proud to be Tante Irma's niece. On parting, she'd sometimes slide a few banknotes into my hand.

"Don't tell anyone," she'd say, winking.

The day Tante Irma arrived at Grandmother's with cousin Jochen and two heavy suitcases, one with Jochen's clothes, the other with his toys, mother and daughter talked for a long time.

When it was time to catch the train, Tante Irma hugged Jochen goodbye and, leaving him on Grandmother's lap, slipped out the door quickly. Jochen cried pitifully, his nose snotty, tears rolling down his cheeks.

"Poor little boy," Grandmother sighed, and rocked him for as long as it took to calm him down. "You stay with me until your mamma can take you home again."

Jochen was the youngest of the three grandchildren born during Grandmother's lifetime. He would soon become her favorite. I didn't mind Grandmother doting on him more than she did on me, but I remember envying him the red scooter the chauffeur delivered on one of his visits.

I was intrigued by the toys Tante Irma sent for Jochen. They were expensive and sophisticated compared with the simple toys we had. My favorite was an Erector Set. Jochen and I would follow diagrams, assembling metal pieces with nuts and bolts, adding wheels and gears, for as long as it would take to complete a particular contraption. A crane we built, again and again, was our big pride and joy.

Grandmother would raise Jochen until she suffered her first stroke, seven years later, when Jochen was nine years old. By that time, Tante Irma would have established a thriving, but all-consuming, business with the help of a generous loan from Colonel Friedeberg, her former boss at the American base.

She would come to fetch Jochen and take him away to her new home in Krefeld, thirty kilometers to the north. A nanny would take care of him there.

24

I answered the rap on the front door of our flat. The town's chief gendarme towered in front of me.

"I'm here for your mother," he said, tipping the peak of his cap. Though his words were menacing, he delivered them with an impish smile. Still, I was sure this was a raid to confiscate black market goods, and he had come for no other reason than to arrest Mother.

I could've said that Mother wasn't home. But she was.

The chief gendarme followed me down the hall into the kitchen. The thudding sound of his boots echoed on the wood floor. Mother put her knitting into the work basket. She rose from her chair. A puzzled look appeared on her face when she saw who the caller was. She glanced at me, then at Gitta, who'd stopped playing with her blocks, then at the door. I took the hint, grabbed Gitta by the hand, and left.

For a moment, I hesitated behind the closed door, fighting the impulse to eavesdrop, then raced to Grandmother's house. I bolted into the kitchen and, breathlessly, blurted out what I thought was happening. Grandmother listened.

"Don't you worry. Your mother won't go to prison," she said, with enough confidence to set my mind at ease. Half angry, half disgusted, she muttered, barely loud enough for me to hear, "That small-town opportunist is there for something else."

Grandmother was right. Mother didn't go to prison. She would also prove right about the chief gendarme's intention, puzzling as her remark had been.

Back at home, I asked Mother why the gendarme had stopped by. "He just came to say hello," she said. An unaccustomed smile came to her eyes. It roused questions of my own, fueled, perhaps, by what Grandmother had said: did he like Mother in a certain way?

When he returned a day or two later and regularly after that, my questions were answered. But unlike the balding merchant – long gone by this time – I was glad to see the chief gendarme. Unlike the merchant, the gendarme was the embodiment of a man after every woman's heart. Of tall and muscular build, his full head of hair slicked back to accent his ruggedly handsome face, his presence radiated self-confidence. His voice and manner could be serious one minute, playful the next. And he sported a policeman's uniform.

Soon Mother started calling him by his first name, Lutz. It made me uneasy when he paid the kind of attention to her that didn't include me – for example, when he spoke to her quietly, so I couldn't hear him. At the same time, I sensed that he was fond of me, also.

"Schönen, guten Tag, junge Dame." he greeted me when he came to the door. *Junge Dame,* young lady. No one had ever spoken to me like that. It made my eight-year-old self feel special and adult. Sitting on the sofa, one of Mother's black market cigarettes in the corner of his mouth, he'd hand me a box of matches with a playful tilt of his head. Flattered, I would strike a match and light his cigarette. He showed interest in what I was learning at school and which books I was reading. He complimented me on how I looked. "You're just as pretty as your mother."

The chief gendarme treated me in ways I yearned for, but had no idea I was missing. I had no concrete memories of my father's presence, nor did I have thoughts of what his role might have been as I grew up. If I hoped the chief gendarme would take my father's place, I didn't know it. I liked the way he talked to me as if I were someone worth talking to. I enjoyed the good-natured banter he encouraged, the smiles he seemed to have just for me.

Weeks had gone by since his first visit. It was the first warm day of spring, cloudless and buzzing with the promise of summer. Time to get the deck chairs from the basement and set them up on the verandah outside the kitchen. I carried the leg rests, the chief gendarme carried the folded chairs. Mother dusted them off and sighed that the faded red-and-green striped canvas would have to do for another season.

I changed into a pair of white rib-knit cotton underpants. None of the girls in Delrath had bathing suits, and tops were not common for girls our age. I settled back in the deck chair nearest the French doors off the kitchen. Mother had opened them wide to let in the fresh, warm air. The chief gendarme moved his chair at an angle to mine. He was wearing black boxer shorts.

The late morning sun had already risen above the neighboring roof. Mother watered her planters of red geraniums, in full bloom already, and picked off a few dead leaves. "Don't stay out too long. The sun is treacherous this time of year," she warned. Her summer dress brushed my naked legs as she left for the kitchen to prepare our noon meal.

I pressed my eyes shut and followed the flickering display of tiny specks behind my eyelids. I wondered about their nature, whether they were real or an illusion. When I opened my eyes, I searched the sky for the stars it had swallowed at daybreak and would not release until dusk. I stared into the sun, a yellow sphere at first, and watched its color change to white, then black, its outline vibrating in a huge canopy of milky blue. It looked as if the sky were the earth's ceiling that separated us from the rest of the universe, and that the light of the universe flooded through the circular hole to illuminate our planet.

"Sun-gazing makes you blind." The chief gendarme's words startled me out of my reverie.

"It doesn't," I said, although, of course, I'd heard it said.

Eyes still wide open, I turned away from the sun. I saw nothing in the darkness that was all around me. It lasted no longer than a minute, as I knew it would. Gradually, recognizable forms began to reemerge: the flowers and leaves of the geraniums sketched against the sky, their edges translucent; the mortar-and-brick pattern of the short wall that enclosed the verandah.

I turned toward the chief gendarme. Eyes closed, the back of his head nestling in the triangle of his muscular arms crossed above his head, he looked asleep.

My gaze moved to his smooth chest, glistening in the heat and, drifting down to his shorts, came to the outline of a taut bulge, flesh exposed where it had raised the loose fabric. I diverted my eyes quickly, to undo what I had seen.

The chief gendarme's deck chair creaked in its hinges. I remained still. Eyelids closed to a slit, I could see him rise to his feet. A shadow traveled over my body. I sank deeper into the cotton sling of my deck chair. Turning my face to the sky, I opened my eyes as wide as I could into the midday sun. Its glare forced tears down my temples.

"What on earth are you doing?" Mother's raised voice jolted me. It was coming from the doorway. "Don't you know that looking into the sun can blind you?"

"I don't care," I said, afraid only that she might have caught me looking where I shouldn't have looked.

I wanted to believe that Mother was unsuspecting. I also wanted to believe that the chief gendarme did not know what I had glimpsed. I wanted it to remain a secret, one I tried to keep concealed from myself, as well. And so, I did not reflect upon it. In some half-cognizant way, I had liked his attention, even what I thought I had witnessed on the verandah, improper as I knew it was. Something illicit, mysterious and secret, something that must never be acknowledged, had entered the relationship between us that spring day on the verandah. It had lost its innocence.

In my memory, Mother's dalliance with the chief gendarme was short-lived. Even after it was long over, I welcomed the occasional chance encounter – both of us waiting for a train to pass at the railroad crossing, or when he waved, riding past me on his bicycle.

"How's my favorite young lady?" he'd say, in a tone so winning and redolent of the past, my cheeks flushed. I would respond with a shy smile. Raising his hand to his policeman's cap, he'd salute smartly.

"Remember me to your mother," he'd say. Perhaps, I only imagined a touch of sadness in his voice.

25

Frau Scheer, our upstairs neighbor, was older than Mother and younger than Grandmother. She believed in occult mysteries and knew how to read Tarot cards, palms and tea leaves. This raised suspicions among the neighborhood women that she was a Gypsy, and among the children that she was a sorceress.

Frau Scheer was Mother's friend and confidante. The two would sit at each other's kitchen tables, drink black coffee and talk about important matters or consult the Tarot. Frau Scheer would spread out a deck of cards and answer Mother's questions about what the future would bring.

Irmgard was Frau Scheer's twenty-year-old daughter, a fun-loving free spirit who knew how to draw my mother out of her post-war shell. Irmgard coaxed her to come along to Saturday night dances, when dances were getting popular again, and join in weekend gatherings that Irmgard organized. She looked nothing like her mother, whose pitch-black hair and keen features did indeed call up the stereotypical image of a Gypsy fortune-teller. Irmgard was tall and slender, with freckles on her nose and windblown curly hair the color of chestnuts touched by the sun.

Irmgard played the piano masterfully, her long fingers hammering or caressing the keys, according to the mood of the music. Her mother more than once said that, if it hadn't been for Hitler, her daughter would have followed a career as a concert pianist. She always said this with pride as well as an undertone of bitterness and accusation. It sounded as if she were setting herself apart from her listeners, intimating that they were to blame for Hitler, and she, as someone born in France, was not. Irmgard would mock her, feigning a French accent her mother did not have, *"Mais oui,* my daughter has a talent for playing the piano." Then she'd curtsy and, putting on theatrical airs, pretend to wait for applause.

At nighttime, the sound of her music flowed from the Scheer's flat above ours. I listened to it in my bed, eyes closed. I favored the melancholic pieces, when the room seemed to swell with a bittersweetness that mirrored my own often doleful spirits.

At gatherings, Irmgard played folk music on the accordion, her torso swaying with the rhythm of her arms opening and closing the bellows, her fingers nimbly traveling over the keyboard. The gaiety in her clear voice animated the crowd to sing along.

It took all the charm of the much younger Irmgard to convince Mother, in her mid-thirties then, to embark on a trip to the Bavarian Alps. Few people traveled for pleasure in those days, when it was still difficult for most to keep themselves and their children fed and clothed.

By nature, Mother found it easier to grapple with the hardships of life rather than pursue its limited joys. She meted out happiness for herself, and also for her children, keeping pleasure within reason lest the blows of fate intervene. "Plan all you want," she'd say with a shrug, "fate lies in wait at every turn, ready to dash your hopes." It would anger me, even then, when she'd attempt to keep my dreams small. Speaking about her holiday with Irmgard in later years, the carefreeness of those days seemed eroded by her sense that it was undeserved. Always, she would emphasize that it had been Irmgard's wild idea.

Grandmother made no bones about her disapproval. "You don't have to travel to the end of the world to find someone to marry you," she said, "What kind of man are you looking for, anyway? Good looks and charm don't put food on the table." She reminded Mother that the wealthy Schönewald, balding as he was, had been a perfectly acceptable choice. How foolish and shortsighted she had been to drive him away with her chilly indifference!

If it was painful to see Mother leave, there is no trace of it in my memory. I remember the two women getting on the train – Mother carrying the small leather suitcase that had first accompanied her on her honeymoon, which had gotten badly scuffed on our journey back from Rockensußra; Irmgard in a gauzy print dress, wearing a big straw hat.

Frau Scheer took care of Gitta, who was not happy with the arrangement. Now five years old, Gitta was intimidated not so much by

Frau Scheer's appearance as her stern disposition – so much so that she'd often run way, mostly to the train station, where she had last seen Mother getting on the train.

Frau Scheer would call me away from jumping rope or playing catch in the street. "Go find Gitta." Her voice was both angry and anxious.

Sure enough, I'd find my little sister curled up asleep in the entryway to the ticket office. I'd drag her back to Frau Scheer's flat. She'd scream all the way.

I was lucky enough to stay at Grandmother's house during Mother's absence. I slept in an upstairs bedroom that overlooked the courtyard. Sparsely furnished, it was cold and damp even in warm weather. Moisture had lifted patches of wallpaper underneath the window where the bed stood. It had left the wall blotched with mildew already turning a spotty black. The pillow and featherbed smelled musty, like the room itself. Here, I spent rainy afternoons and late nights reading an illustrated version of *Little Women,* enthralled by the stories of these young American girls whose lives I romanticized and envied.

Some nights, the hoot of an owl rang hollow through the courtyard. It was said to be an omen of death if it came on three successive nights. Grandmother said that you couldn't always believe these superstitions; they were true sometimes, other times they were not. To be safe, I made-believe that if Spitz, the watchdog, barked in response to the hooting – which he always did – it would neutralize the omen.

In the absence of explicit rules in Grandmother's household, I spent my after-school time as I pleased. Grandmother didn't ask me to account for where I had been or whom I had played with. She did not send me off to bed at the strike of seven, Gitta's and my bedtime under Mother's rule. At meals, she didn't badger me to finish up my plate or to help with the dishes afterwards. My one chore, expected though undeclared, was brushing her long gray hair in the morning, then braiding and twisting it into a bun at the nape of her neck. I loved inhaling its fragrance, a mixture of plain soap and the smells in her kitchen.

"On vacation in the Alps," I proudly told anyone who asked where my mother was. It had the ring of faraway places, like Istanbul, Biarritz,

New York, the North Sea.

Everything about the Alps was unfathomable. Their magnitude exceeded anything I could envision. Just as I was unable to picture a body of water without a far shore in sight, I could not imagine a landscape without horizons, where the eye couldn't sweep across unending fields of wheat and rye. What I conjured up in my mind were craggy rock formations as formidable and mysterious as the words that described the landscape: ravines, glaciers, summits of eternal snow.

As well as serene images: valleys, alpine pastures, replete with grazing cows and quaint cabins, mountain lakes, edelweiss. Would Mother bring back a sprig of that exotic flower, native only to the Alps? She did, and she attached it to the frame that held my father's photo, the same one that had been on our nightstand in Rockensußra. It was now on a curio shelf among gifts my father had given to her, and a Hummel figurine of a boy playing the horn. My father had brought back the figurine for me on one of his leaves. It's the only surviving memento I have of him.

Also unfathomable was the notion that, somewhere high in those same faraway Alps, a trickle of water from a small crevice swelled to become the majestic Rhine that flowed past our town.

After less than two weeks, Mother and Irmgard's vacation was suddenly interrupted, when the West German currency reform, following an Allied plan, was put into place. The announcement was made over the radio. Two days later, on June 20, 1948, the old, grossly inflated German Reichsmark became almost worthless. It was replaced by the newly printed Deutschmark, at a ratio of 10: 1. Disorienting, at first, it was as if everything had become inexpensive and more affordable. A liter of milk that used to cost 1 RM, now cost 10 Pfennig, a tenth of the earlier price.

Mother and Irmgard were fortunate to make it back to Delrath quickly, or else would have gone penniless during the first round of the reform. As it was, the day they arrived was the day everyone lined up at the town hall to collect their allotment of 40 Deutschmarks per family member – the equivalent of 10 US Dollars at the time. A month later, there would be 20 Deutschmarks more. The old Reichsmark money was collected at bank-like agencies and, through an application process, disbursed at the established exchange rate.

"Didn't I tell you your *Alpentour* was a hare-brained idea?" Grandmother said when the two women showed up in her kitchen so much sooner than planned. Faces sun-colored and exuberant, nothing could dampen their spirits. They recounted their adventures hiking on mountain trails and swimming in icy lakes. They left out how they had danced through the nights. Those stories Mother didn't share with me, or with anyone, until she was an old woman remembering the follies of her younger years.

26

Time rolled on in an orderly fashion. It was divided into weekdays, which included Saturdays, when the adults worked and the children went to school, and Sundays, when most everyone attended Mass and observed a day without labor. There was comfort in the gradual shift from season to season, with religious holidays and feasts punctuating the year.

I didn't question whether it had always been this way. My wartime experiences had long receded into memory. Our post-war way of life was the only way of life I really knew. The adults spoke only rarely of the past. When they did, their accounts were parts of their own stories or of the larger history, with little bearing on my life. If, before and during the war, there had been rallies or marches through our town, if there had been crowds lining the streets cheering and shouting the Hitler salute, no one spoke about it now. Even the isolated bits of disturbing, now forgotten, knowledge that I sometimes gleaned listening to adult conversations didn't create a picture of a world that had gone mad. Perhaps because that world was too difficult, too frightening, too incriminating a world to talk about.

Occasionally, something unpredictable happened to disrupt the certainty and order in the passage of time; or a memorable occasion highlighted the day-in, day-out regularity of our lives.

One day, a hearse rattled down the main street, followed by a handful of mourners.

"What happened?" I asked Mother.

"Frau Becker. They're taking her to the cemetery."

The news unsettled me. For as long as I could remember, death had never come to Delrath. Death happened in faraway places, like my father's death, on the battlefield, like the corpses Kurtie had taken me to see in Rockensußra, or in stories people told. But never here.

I had known Frau Becker by sight. I'd seen her walking down the hill on her way to the store, a wicker basket hooked on her arm. Her face was dappled with warts, her eyes small and wide-set. Short, as short as the dwarf who did cartwheels for coins at the annual fair in Neuss, her head was disproportionately large and her legs bowed. I was oddly fascinated by her misshapen form. I wanted to both look at her and look away. *"Guten Tag,"* I would call as we passed each other on opposite sides of the street. She would wave, grinning in a childlike way that made me feel ill at ease.

"Why did she die?" I wanted to know.

"People like her don't live long," Mother replied.

"Did she have children?"

"No."

"Because she was . . ." I stopped myself short of saying "a dwarf?"

Mother went on reluctantly, "Before and during the war, they made sure people like her and her husband didn't have children." She didn't specify who "they" were; she never specified who they were, when she spoke of the Nazis. Her voice was matter-of-fact, perhaps to disguise what she really thought or knew about eugenics as it had been practiced under Hitler, perhaps to protect me from such knowledge.

None of this would occur to me until, in later years, I became aware of the concept of *Rassenreinheit,* race purity – part of the national socialist ideology of the Aryan master race.

Driven by a macabre desire to see with my own eyes where death had intruded, I walked up the hill. I stopped in front of the house where I knew Frau Becker and her husband had lived in converted attic rooms. A black mourning veil hung stiffly from the front door of the two-story brick house. The curtains of the upstairs windows were drawn shut. There was no one close by. I stood there, under a bare chestnut tree, alone and unmoving. Before long, I felt a slight motion behind me. I stiffened my shoulders. Death was making its presence known. I could feel it, even as it pursued me bolting back down the hill.

A month later, I watched the hearse pass again. Frau Becker's husband had died – of a broken heart, people said.

Then there were the joyful events that lifted us out of our ordinary existence. A young father proudly carrying his newborn to church on a Sunday morning, while his wife stayed at home, still confined after the birth. Family and friends would gather around the baptismal fountain, tears in their eyes, as Pastor Steinbach poured holy water from a silver pitcher over the screaming infant's head and mumbled words of salvation.

May and June were wedding months. Most brides and grooms made their way to church on foot; some were taken in a white carriage, drawn by two white horses. Either way, well-wishers would stand in their doors, waving, and a string of children would follow the young couple. The bride wearing the same wedding gown that had been her mother's before her, the groom in a borrowed black suit. The day after, the gown was laundered and ironed once again and retired in the bedroom closet for a younger sister or cousin. Yesterday's bride and groom moved into the main downstairs living quarters of the family home, to take over the bakery or the old farm, while the parents retired to the upstairs rooms.

And there was First Communion Day, following the Sunday after Easter. It was a turning point in our young lives at a time when religion was a dominant thread in the social fabric. It was as important an event as any other holy day.

Pastor Steinbach led twice-a-week preparations in Catechism throughout the forty days of Lent, from Ash Wednesday to Easter and the week after.

As boredom set in during his monotone lessons, I absentmindedly followed the movements of his pasty hands and watched the puckered cleft in his chin twitch when he reprimanded disruptive behavior. Or I daydreamt about the new, grown-up version of myself I would soon become. First Communion would initiate me into full membership in the Church, allowing me to participate in the Mystery of Christ. I would become His bride, one with Him. I would go to confession. All my sins would be forgiven. No longer would I sit in the smaller children's pews closest to the altar, but in the taller ones in the women's section.

On the final days of preparation, Pastor Steinbach guided us through endless enactments of the First Communion ritual. We rehearsed how to approach the altar, how to kneel on the Communion bench, how to receive the Holy Host and how to return to our seats, in prayer. When he pronounced us ready for our First Communion, the smile of a saint illuminated his face.

In the expansive silence, characteristic only of churches, every sound seemed pronounced – the closing of the portal, footsteps to and from the confessional box, a boy clearing his throat. Twilight filled the high spaces. Waiting in a pew, I rehearsed my list of sins, until my turn came.

I knelt on the confessional bench. A velvet curtain, nap worn at the folds by the shoulders of the many penitents before me, shielded me from view. I closed my eyes in the near darkness. The inside of my mouth felt sticky. I whispered my sins through the latticework behind which Pastor Steinbach sat in a tight cubicle: "I disobeyed my mother." "I was envious." "I quarreled with my sister." "I lied." And, rushing through the final, most egregious, sin, "I-got-nude-with-a-neighbor-girl-we-touched-each-other."

A soft rustling came from the other side of the latticework. I could feel Pastor Steinbach's warm breath as he muttered brief words about respecting one's elders and the importance of chastity. He pronounced God's forgiveness of my transgressions and asked that, for penance, I recite the rosary once. Gesturing the Sign of the Cross, he said, "In the name of the Father, the Son and the Holy Spirit. Amen."

At the Marian altar, I knelt on the prayer stool. The Virgin seemed to gaze at me benevolently. I took Mother's First Communion rosary from its pouch. Rubbing the silver cross, I said the Apostles' Creed. Then, sliding my fingers from pearl to pearl, I rattled off the Lord's Prayer three times, and the five sets of ten Hail Marys, each separated by a larger pearl for the Lord's Prayer.

Absolved of my sins, I skipped along the gravel path outside the church. If ever I had doubted that Pastor Steinbach had the power to intercede with God on my behalf, a rush of bliss through every part of me was proof that he did.

By the time I came to the end of the church grounds, elation and gratitude gave way to a new sensation. The street was empty of people.

The houses I passed, the sidewalk under my feet, everything was different. Less tangible and remote. Hail Mary prayer fragments rose to my mind: *voll der Gnade,* full of Grace . . . *Frucht deines Leibes, Jesus* . . . fruit of your womb, Jesus. I said them over and over rapidly until, after many repetitions, they lapsed into meaningless sounds, then into silence.

I looked up, into the dying daylight. The evening star shone over the roofs, its short rays etched in the flawlessly clear sky. Something vast enveloped me. Something larger than myself. I would not have been able to describe the sense I had of the infiniteness of the universe and the silence within myself as one and the same.

"Finally," Mother greeted me when I opened the kitchen door. The table was set with bread and cold cuts. I sat down without a word.

"Cheer up. You're acting as if this were your last meal before the execution," Mother said in a teasing, yet biting manner.

There was nothing she could have said to penetrate the wall that insulated me from her and from everything around me. I didn't respond, but kept picking at the food on my plate. Shifting to a tone of authority and reason, she said, "Eat something. You have a long fast ahead of you." Her eyes rested on me for a long moment, before she sighed a resigned, "Reason is lost on you."

I woke up to Gitta howling fragments of hymns from the kitchen. Mother had already laid out my First Communion clothes, the first step in preparing for the ritual of dressing me. It didn't seem to bother her that she had long drifted from the Church. My First Communion Day was – as Gitta's would be four years later – as important an occasion for her as it was for me and as integral a part of growing up in our small-town as even a wedding would be.

Mother went about her task quietly, methodically. It seemed odd, at first, to think that she would dress me. She hadn't done so in years. But as she became engrossed in her part of the ritual I, too, abandoned myself to it. Not just a simple act of dressing and being dressed, it entailed something larger. Mother, I felt, was a helper in ushering me into a place of detachment from the ordinary, in preparation for what was to come. She was with me – and I was utterly alone. If there were sounds, I didn't hear them. I was blind to everything around me.

I stood naked before Mother. She slid the white ribbon-laced chemise over my head and guided my arms through the armholes, then pulled it down to cover my chest and hips. She gathered the lengths of the white stockings with her fingers. Slipping them over my feet and up my legs one by one, she fastened them to the garter belts that dangled from the chemise's hem. She held the panties for me to step into and pulled them up to my waist.

Made of a soft, ivory-colored jacquard fabric, the dress had a gathered skirt with a pleasing, below-the-knee length. She put it on me and tied the wide ribbon belt into a floppy bow. A ruffle that hugged the neckline and curved down the front bodice created the illusion of a separate bolero jacket. That was the detail I loved most. She slipped over my feet a pair of black patent leather shoes and tied the laces, completing the ensemble.

Next, I sat down on a stool. Mother brushed and combed my hair. Satisfied that it was smooth, she began curling it with a curling iron she had borrowed from the hair salon. She wound each strand tightly around the heated rod, and, after holding it firmly in place until my scalp began to smart, released it with a downward tug. She repeated this as many times as it took to create a row of vertical corkscrew ringlets around the base of my head. Reserved for young girls on festive occasions, the style was known as *Schillerlocken,* an allusion to the hairstyle of Friedrich Schiller, the 18th century German poet and playwright. Mother looked pleased with her handiwork.

Last came the accoutrements: a white wreath of starched fabric roses that Mother placed on the crown of my head, tucking in the few stray hairs the curling iron had missed. A three-leafed lace ornament, representing the Trinity, that she pinned over my heart. And a silver necklace, its pendant a cross with a mounting of cabochon turquoise beads. Tante Irma had brought it back from a trip to the Vatican. It had been blessed by Pope Pius XII.

Mother took my hand and led me to the mirror. She stopped when both of our reflections were in full view. Her head tilted slightly, she looked at me with a smile. *"Was für ein schönes Mädchen*! – What a beautiful girl."

The last lingering peals came from the bell tower. I took my place in the pews on the girls' side. I stared blankly into the high space before me, registered nothing – though my memory, or what I later re-imagined, brings back images of splendor. White and purplish blue hydrangeas flanked the steps ascending to the altar. Elegant arrangements of long-stemmed white lilies and asparagus fern adorned both sides of the tabernacle. Sprigs of white lilac were strewn at the hem of the Holy Virgin's gown. The flickering lights of dozens of candles set the crucifix in the apse aglow.

The church was steeped in an otherworldliness, neither entirely strange nor familiar, and awash with a soft sound, like that from a seashell pressed against the ear. I stood alone, oblivious of all the other girls in their white First Communion dresses, oblivious of Mother darting looks in my direction, alternately proud and anxious, oblivious of Grandmother Neuss and Gitta somewhere in the women's section. Of Grandfather, too, who stood behind the men's pews – having set aside his atheist convictions for the day, but not far enough aside to join the believers in the pews. Grandmother stood by her abiding refusal to go to church. Although I'd wanted her there for my First Communion, I admired her principled stand.

The Mass unfolded, leading to its most sacred crescendo: the simultaneous ringing from the bell tower and the piercing sound of the Sanctus bells the altar boys shook with zeal. With his back turned to the congregation, Pastor Steinbach's violet vestment – lavishly embroidered with gold filament – took the shape of an arcane symbol as he raised his arms above his head to offer the Sacred Chalice. Then, lowering the chalice to his heart with one hand and holding the Holy Host between the thumb and forefinger of the other hand, he turned toward the congregation.

He nodded. It was the signal for the First Communicants to file into the aisle.

Hands held in prayer, eyes cast to the tips of my fingers, I joined the column of girls that formed as, one by one, we exited the pews. We walked to the altar in even steps, and knelt at the women's side of the Communion bench.

Pastor Steinbach administered the Holy Sacrament, first to the boys, then to the girls. The mumble of his blessings grew more audible as my turn approached and I was able to discern the movement of his hands out of the corners of my eyes. At long last, he stood in front of me. I opened my mouth wide, as the pastor took the Holy Host from the paten. He raised it imperceptibly, as if to show it to God, and, placing it on my tongue, spoke his barely intelligible *Pax Domini.*

By the time I got back to the pew, the wafer had lost its firm, round shape and turned into a sticky lump. Still, as prescribed by the ritual, I attempted to swallow it whole, but neither would it move nor would my throat open. Instead, it attached itself to the roof of my mouth and stayed lodged there. Panicked, I felt an urge to cough, or worse. Just then, my tongue curled up on its own accord and, twisting and turning, scraped up the lump. It inched down my dry throat.

Back at our flat, neighborhood children dropped in to bring potted plants and First Communion greeting cards on their parents' behalf. The kitchen – with Mother in charge and Frau Scheer and Grandmother Neuss helping – was abuzz with the preparation of Mother's favorite dishes from *Dr. Ötkers Kochbuch,* the standard cookbook of the time: hot beef broth with diced celeriac root and semolina dumplings; the main course of garnished veal roast, parsley potatoes and white asparagus from Grandmother's root cellar, accompanied by a side dish of Belgian endive salad; and finally, a creamy vanilla pudding topped with raspberry sauce for dessert.

Grandmother, the grandmother who lived locally, made her entry with cousin Jochen in tow. They'd come in a hired limousine, the same limousine which, on a warm Indian summer day six years later, after Grandmother had suffered her first stroke, would take us on a trip to the place where she'd been born.

Grandfather wanted no part of the limousine. He walked the short distance to our flat. But he did not begrudge Grandmother's extravagance. He respected the pride of his once beautiful wife and her reluctance to show herself to the town as a hobbling cripple.

Grandmother looked stylish in her shirtdress, black, as were all her clothes. She wore custom-made, lace-up shoes for the occasion, one with a platform sole to balance her contorted posture. She did not look like a woman who lived a housebound life, but presented herself with proud grandeur. Gitta's baptism, most likely, had been the last time she had made an exception to her self-imposed confinement and now, five years later, my First Communion. She noticed my pleasure.

"Your First Communion isn't just any day," she said, "And if I'm not dead and buried by the time your wedding comes around, you can count on another visit."

The table was set with Mother's best china, a cream-colored service with gold trim along its scalloped edges. My father's engagement present to her, she only brought it out on Sundays and special occasions. The white damask tablecloth had been starched and ironed to a sheen.

I sat at the head of the table. A garland of white fabric flowers surrounded my place setting. Uncontested matriarch of the family, Grandmother sat at the opposite side. Grandmother Neuss, because she was my godmother, and Grandfather, because he was my godfather, were to the right and left of me, respectively. Next to them came Gitta and Jochen on one side, Mother and Onkel Jean on the other.

Grandmother draped her napkin over her large bosom. *"Guten Appetit"* 'she said, signaling that the meal was about to begin. She found herself overruled by Grandmother Neuss, who began incanting a blessing – which my other grandmother endured with a sigh.

A few other guests came for four o'clock coffee and cake. "Congratulations on your First Communion," my friends Uli Bauer and Sybille Rapior said, shaking hands with me, their demeanor formal to observe the solemnity of the occasion. I answered the door for Fräulein Reiners – soon to be my fourth-grade teacher – who lived in the flat down the hall from us. She handed me a potted, crepe-paper-wrapped hydrangea, greeting me with an out-of-character smile. It may have been the first and only smile I'd ever seen on her face. The last guest to arrive was Tante Irma. She'd come in on the train from Frankfurt. When she breezed into the room, all eyes turned to her. Jochen rushed into his mother's arms, squealing with delight. Grandmother glanced at her daughter reproachfully. "Well, our Irma has finally made it."

"Wo ist denn unser Kommunionskind? – Where is our first Communion child?" Tante Irma called out, waving a beautifully

packaged gift in my direction. I was happy. It made me feel special that she had traveled a long distance to be here on the day of my First Communion.

The table had been extended to capacity with additional leaves. It took an extra tablecloth to cover it, and Mother mixed her good china with her everyday ware. Once the guests were seated, Mother offered pastries she had prepared during the preceding week: *Schwarzwälder Kirsch,* a fluffy chocolate cake with preserved black cherries and whipped cream; a layered butter cream cake, elaborately decorated with swirls of frosting, and a plain pound cake.

"I know which one's your favorite," Mother said and served me an extra large slice of *Schwarzwälder Kirsch.*

By five o'clock, the plates were empty. The conversation was at a lull.

"Come on, Gertrud, pour some more coffee and let our First Communion girl open her gifts," Grandmother said, a touch of impatience in her voice.

All eyes on me, I opened the presents everyone had brought. I enjoyed being celebrated, while, at the same time, I felt uneasy being the center of attention.

"To start your hope chest," Tante Irma said, as I unwrapped her gift of a set of ornate Sterling dessert forks and servers.

Mother's present was a velvet lined leather case with a *Mont Blanc* mechanical pencil and a fountain pen. They had been my father's. Mother had gotten them engraved with my name in gold lettering.

Grandmother Neuss, always secretive, reached into her handbag underneath her chair and dug out a small kid leather pouch. "It's gone through generations of women in your father's family," she said. "Take good care of it." It was a rosary, its mother-of-pearl beads rubbed shiny with use.

There was a First Communion card from Grandmother and Grandfather of Dürer's praying hands; inside were a few smoothed-out bank notes. "For a new bicycle," Grandmother said.

An autograph book from Sybille. A pair of amethyst earrings from Uli, the greengrocer's daughter. Uli was my favorite of the neighborhood girls.

Frau Scheer gave me a fancy box of chocolates.

The guests had said their goodbyes. The table had been vacated but not yet cleared, the gifts in a careless pile; the room had lost its festive aura. Ribbons of cigarette smoke trailed close to the ceiling. Mother drew the lace curtains open. I looked out into the beginning twilight. The day was taking its slow leave.

A dark, brooding mood got hold of me. The joyous events of First Communion, and the festivities that had followed, were overshadowed by a sense that I had been let down, that I had not been brought closer to Christ. It amounted to the same realization that had haunted me at other times: that everything was in vain.

I pulled the flower wreath from my head. The *Schillerlocken,* relaxed under the day's weight, looked unkempt. Everything appeared lackluster, my white dress smudged, my shoes scuffed. Unnoticed, I slipped from the flat.

Mother found me sitting at the base of the old pear tree, whose huge crown shaded Onkel Jean's house. Knees pulled to my chin, I was sobbing.

"Himmel hoch jauchzend, zu Tode betrübt. – On top of the world, or in the depth of despair," she said, citing the famous Goethe line, commonly used in the vernacular to describe a drastic mood swing, often derisively. I said nothing, but stared into last year's crushed grass, threads of tears and snot dripping and clinging to the brown blades.

"You'll get grass stains on your dress," Mother said. When I still didn't respond, she took my head between both her hands. I could hear my ears ringing against her palms. For a defiant moment, I met her eyes, then turned my gaze away from her.

"Was ist mit Dir? – What's wrong with you?"

"Nichts. – Nothing."

"Then why are you crying?"

"You wouldn't understand," I said, "You never do."

Even if I had known how to put it into words, this sense of letdown, of emptiness and futility, I would not have wanted to confide in her. I shook myself free from her grip.

"*Was ist?*" Her clipped phrasing made it clear that she felt entitled to an explanation. I stayed silent. Then, shifting her tone to encourage trust and convey that, no matter what was troubling me, I could come to her for an answer, she said softly, "You can tell me." I wanted to believe her, even though I knew it would be a mistake.

Still, I took Mother's bait, less in hope of an answer than to expose her ignorance and show my own superiority. I said, "Tell me, then! Why are we here on this earth?"

Mother wiped my face with a crumpled lace handkerchief she pulled from the inside of her sleeve. The frown on her face dissolved into an expression of bewilderment.

"You should be playing with your friends instead of asking grandiose questions," she said.

She had expected to hear something truly tragic, and what had come out of my mouth, in her eyes, was nothing but an idle concern.

"I hate everything," I said with so much anger and venom I thought she might slap me. I blamed her for failing to have an answer to the question of the meaning of life she herself had never asked. While the concept itself, most likely, was still outside of my understanding, I had asked the question. It had been my first inkling that there was a realm outside of ordinary existence. Mother, I realized, had no access to that world. It made us different from one another. That difference was the real and, as it would turn out, permanent gulf between us. I ducked to protect myself from her. But she did not slap me.

"I am speechless," she said. She put her handkerchief back up into her sleeve.

Neither of us spoke for a time. Then, she said, "Let's go home. You can't sit here forever."

I went back to Mass the next Sunday and all the Sundays that followed. But I no longer went because I felt called. I went out of duty and convention. Sunday mornings, Mother made sure I got out of bed on time. When Gitta started school the following spring, and her church-going days began, Mother sent us off together, with me as reluctant chaperone.

I participated in the Communion Sacrament without an

expectation of Divine Mystery. It all became part of the ordinary. If I had been disillusioned, it faded away. I no longer asked the question I had asked of Mother. It, too, had been swallowed by the ordinary, so that I could feel whole again. Nevertheless, a sense of loss and estrangement from Mother never left me.

27

"Where are you going?" my playmates would call after me, when I'd wander off from a game of hopscotch or a game of cards in the courtyard.

"Nowhere," I'd reply. Something vaguely disturbing had taken hold of me. A listlessness and a sense that our play was futile and without real purpose, reminiscent of the despair I had felt the afternoon of my First Communion. It would begin with something that was nothing more than a mood swing; but before long, a physical sensation of emptiness, bordering on queasiness, would spread below my ribs.

"*Spielverderber!* – Spoilsport!" my friends would grumble and resume their play without me.

Skirting Spitz, the dog Grandfather kept chained down at the barn entrance, I'd make my way across the straw-strewn floor to the rear gate. A Dutch door in need of repair, its hinges squeaked as I lifted and dragged the lower half open just wide enough to duck and squeeze through.

The view of a large meadow, which we called the *große Wiese*, lay before me. It was untended, except for once or twice a summer, when Grandfather cut the tall grass. He swung a scythe like that of the *Sensenmann*, the Reaper – an image that had fascinated me in a book of medieval woodcuts, as everything did that had to do with death.

The meadow had once been the undisputed habitat of a small flock of geese. They'd charge at anything that moved, thin necks thrusting forward, spitting out their venomous cackle. When I was little, Grandfather had carried me across the meadow, my legs curled up in terror, but I'd felt safe in his arms. Over time, the geese had been slaughtered one by one and roasted for holiday meals; their feathers and down had been used to stuff pillows.

An imaginary barrier made me hesitate at the threshold between barn and meadow, where the ghosts of the geese still stood guard. I fixed my gaze on a point low in the sky, and crossed bravely into the territory that, long ago, the geese had defended. It was as if I had broken a spell. Freed from the bullying of the geese, my spirits lifted; my limbs felt light and nimble. I didn't know what it was I had escaped, but I did know I wanted to be here. All that was behind the barn, held a promise, a promise of something I couldn't have named either.

In a depression near the neighbor's wall, ground water bubbled up from the sandy soil. It filled a pond the size of the shadow cast by the old walnut tree that towered at its slimy edge. I picked up pebbles from the gutter along the barn wall and skipped them on the surface of the pond. I felt powerful, destroying the reflection of the tree, and I watched its image recreate itself as the ripples calmed. I poked around the edges with a stick, squeamishly excited at the thought of uncovering worms, maybe even a water snake or a toad.

Ordinary sounds – my playmates' laughter, the din of household goings-on, the occasional neighing of a horse in a nearby corral – died away. New sounds came to life: a breath of wind in the tall grass; a humming; a gentle plop on the water. The air had an edge of crispness. Colors were more intense here, as if a recent rain had washed everything clean.

I lay in the meadow where the grass grew tallest, the dampness of the earth cooling me. Sometimes a blade of grass or a stray ant tickled my bare limbs, and a few insects danced above my face. I watched the clouds travel over the sun. I saw the moon, pale and barely visible, rise inexplicably along its daytime arc.

After a time, when boredom set in, I'd follow a new impulse. Leaving my hollow in the grass, I'd scramble up a mound of dry rubble where the meadow ended and a chain link fence ran the width of the property. I'd slip-slide down the other side of the mound, along an overgrown runoff, now dry. There, out of ordinary sight, was a hole in the fence. Large enough to crawl through, it was my secret access into the garden, the lushest orchard imaginable.

So dense was the foliage that sunlight touched the ground only after the leaves had fallen in late autumn. Here, fruit trees and berry bushes grew wild and in no particular arrangement. A velvety layer of green moss covered the weather side of the trunks. The dark ground was always damp, alive with earwigs, centipedes, sow bugs – whose bustle I keenly watched. In the hollows, where it was coolest, nettles proliferated, unchecked. Weeds and isolated clumps of grass sprouted freely. Rank shoots grew from tree trunks and gnarly burls. A fairytale-like place, I imagined only I could enter it.

Songbirds chirping back and forth, echoing each other's melodies, accentuated the silence. I found their nests hidden in berry bushes and precariously wedged between the forked branches of fruit trees. I was tempted to touch the spotted miniature eggs inside them, but fought the impulse.

Grandfather had once told me that mother birds abandon their unhatched eggs, even their young, if they've been touched by human hands. "How do they know?" I'd asked. "They've learned to be afraid of us and recognize the scent we leave behind," he'd answered. His warning had made me sad as I'd gathered, for the first time, perhaps, that humans intentionally do harm.

Some afternoons, I'd see Grandfather walking along the path in the vegetable garden adjacent to the orchard, dragging a water hose to rows of staked legumes or to the potato patch bordering the boxwood hedge where the wheat fields began. Or I would hear a crunching sound as he forced his spade into the defiant soil, followed by a succession of quick taps to loosen and smooth another clod of earth he'd turned. Grandfather appeared oblivious to my presence, even when I was in full view, up in a tree or roaming in the meadow. Or, did I have the power to make myself invisible?

Short summer downpours left the orchard drenched, giving off new fragrances: the musty smell of soil; the tang of wet grass. Large sparkling drops of water clung to the leaves and fruit. The warm earth, cooled by the rain, released a fine steam.

The meadow and the orchard invited unbounded reverie. Here, I fancied myself a budding biologist. Following ants on their trail, observing how they touched one another, antennae to antennae, I speculated that they were exchanging messages, maybe communicating in a language humans couldn't hear. I witnessed a monarch butterfly free itself from a cocoon underneath a leaf and take its first, tentative flight. I counted the feet of a dead centipede, thirty altogether – a disappointingly smaller number than a thousand, which the German *Tausendfüßler* implied.

Other times, I fancied myself a future archeologist, looking for objects in the shallow trench along the neighbor's wall, finding worn shards of green and clear glass that had been washed to the surface of the soil through the years. What if they were of Roman origin, not just pieces of old beer bottles? The Romans, I had learned in school, had conquered this region almost two thousand years ago. Remnants of their fortifications survived in nearby Neuss. Grandmother Neuss had taken me to walk through the *Obertor,* the medieval gatehouse to the city, and told me that the *Novesia* chocolate, manufactured in Neuss, was named after the Roman garrison, *Novaesium,* that had been there.

I realize now that I vested the orchard with the attributes of a secret paradise: with abundance, with peacetime and living forever. I daydreamed about my father here, that he was alive and would come home again; about my mother, that she would never die, nor would my grandparents, who were old already, and whose passing I often dwelled on.

Sometimes the sudden approach of fighter planes would disrupt my daydreaming. I would hear, then see them coming from the fields behind grandfather's garden, without warning. One moment, they weren't there; the next moment, they were. Pitch-black silhouettes racing across the sky at ominous speed, they would fly so low it looked as if they might graze the roof of the barn. Five or six of them in tight and precise formations. Their deafening noise caused the air to quiver and the ground to shake. A remembered fear that they were harbingers of war would rush over me. Covering my ears and crunching my eyes shut, I would remind myself that these were American planes engaged in training maneuvers. "They're showing us who won the war, as if we didn't know already," Grandmother had once said when we watched them streak above the courtyard. They would disappear as quickly as they had appeared. A restlessness would stay in the orchard long after they were gone.

A dream I had in the 1990s, when I was already preparing to chronicle the years of my growing up, returned me to the meadow: *The walnut tree is gone; the pond has been covered with rubble and dirt. Along a dilapidated fence between meadow and orchard is a row of espalier trees. My grandfather has pruned and trained them. They are laden with nectarines and gooseberries. My grandfather explains that the nectarine is a hybrid of peach and apricot, that nectarines hadn't yet been developed when I was a child, and that gooseberries do not grow on trees. He is wrapped in an unbleached linen shroud, and carries a second shroud draped over his arm. A woman, elegant and younger than my grandfather, accompanies him. She is carrying a notebook. She asks, "Why the second shroud?" He doesn't respond. She says, "You brought it for me?" Evading an answer, he now addresses me, "You take after your mother. People say her sixth sense brought Onkel Jean's and Grandmother's secret to light."*

Waking up from the dream, it felt as if my grandfather had given me permission to tell Grandmother's and Onkel Jean's story.

28

A blustery spring day toward the end of my first year of secondary school. I was eleven. During mid-morning recess, two hundred students were milling around in the schoolyard. I was alone, facing the brick-and-wrought-iron wall on the street side. From behind me, I could hear the crunching sound of footsteps on the gravel coming nearer. They were determined steps, not the bouncing steps of children at play. They stopped close to me, so close the air around me stirred.

"Who was that speaking to you?" The voice was Dr. Kirchfeld's, our history teacher. I turned to face him, heat rising to my neck and face. I looked down at my toes, unable to come up with an answer.

"I asked you who that man was," he said.

"No one in particular."

He placed his index finger firmly under my chin and tilted my head up. "You will tell me who that man was."

"A friend of my mother's," I replied, inaudibly, afraid that even the half-truth might expose what I could not bring myself to say.

"Speak up."

Cornered by his relentless query, I said, *"Der Bekannte meiner Mutter.* – My mother's acquaintance," a term, in the vernacular, euphemistically used to describe a boyfriend or lover. It also implied that there was no prospect or intent of marriage.

"And what exactly did your mother's acquaintance say to you?" he continued, emphasizing the word 'acquaintance' pointedly.

"Nothing. . . He only said. . . hello."

His eyes remained fixed on my face. He seemed to ponder what to ask next. His lips parted to form what I dreaded would be another, even more invasive question. But the words didn't come. Instead, he lifted his eyebrows and walked away.

Worse than Mother's private life having been exposed was the fact that I had been the one to divulge what I wanted no one to know.

I ran into the girls' restroom and slammed the door shut. I shook my head from side to side. My braids whipped across my face. When I stopped, the walls swayed, my stomach twisted and wrenched behind my navel. A painful lump settled in my stomach, the same lump that settled in my stomach most evenings, ever since Mother's acquaintance had arrived at our flat.

I rushed into a stall. I bent over the lavatory and stuck my finger down my throat. A succession of quick jerks moved my stomach up and down. Tears flooded my vision. A sour taste gushed into my mouth. Threads of spittle dribbled into the porcelain bowl.

The school bell rang hollow through the tiled restroom. I wiped my chin with the back of my hand and, digging my knuckles into my eyes, rubbed them dry. I pulled up my knee socks and smoothed my skirt. As I headed out, I caught a glimpse of myself in the mirror. "Go away. I hate you. I even hate your name," I hissed.

The man who had spoken to me over the schoolyard wall had been living with us since the previous autumn. When he arrived at our door with a small suitcase, Mother introduced him as our *Untermieter,* our lodger. The arrangement would be temporary, Mother said.

At the same time that I wanted to believe that he was a lodger, I sensed it was a cover. I was alert to anything that would confirm my suspicion and expose him as my mother's live-in suitor.

The lodger had drifted into town from a ship that had taken anchor at a small port along the Rhine. Mother had met him at a Saturday night dance. The arrangement, not uncommon in the post-war years and reluctantly condoned, was called *Onkelehe,* which literally translates as "uncle marriage." War widows, especially those with children, rather than jeopardize their government pensions through re-marriage, lived with their partners without legalizing the union. The children called their quasi stepfathers *Onkel,* hence the term *Onkelehe;* the women referred to them as *Bekannter,* acquaintance.

My dislike for our lodger was instant, almost as if it had preceded his arrival. Nothing could win me over. Not his jovial manner or the small gifts with which he tried to ingratiate himself to Gitta and me. Everything about him irritated me: his accented speech that identified him as non-native to the Rhineland; his looks, handsome by any standard but my own skewed judgment; his self-confident demeanor, arrogant to my mind. His name, too: *Ferdinand.* Neither odd nor uncommon, it would never lose its disagreeable ring, not even in later years, after he had long left our lives. He went by *Fredie,* a nickname so embarrassingly juvenile to my ear, I couldn't bring myself to utter it, let alone call him *Onkel Fredie.*

At first, I ignored Fredie when I could, and was rude to him when I couldn't. When it became obvious that he was firmly entrenched in our lives, and there was nothing I could do about it, I learned to avoid him. At best, I treated him with reasonable civility, occasionally even with goodwill, as when I asked him to write a remembrance in my autograph book. I begrudgingly credited him for talent as an artist, but resented it when a portrait, drawn in pencil, he'd done of Mother ended up framed on the living room wall.

If my dislike of Fredie was unfounded in realistic terms, his age, younger than Mother by more years than she would admit – twelve by my calculation – made their relationship an ill match, not only in my eyes but in everyone else's, I was sure. Grandmother called Fredie "a worthless free-loader," who wouldn't be able to provide for a wife and children in the best of times, and predicted that he would leave Mother for a younger woman, anyway.

But Mother made excuses for him. "As a career navy man, what options does he have in this economy but to take on any kind of work that comes up?" "Unskilled work," Grandmother interjected. "Fredie is a fine artist," Mother said, expecting, perhaps, that this would appease Grandmother. "A starving artist?" Grandmother responded. Her disdain for Fredie was matched only by my disdain.

"You don't appreciate all the nice things he does for you," Mother would say, annoyed with me for my rude behavior and rash judgments of him. It was true, occasionally Fredie came back from the city with a paper bag full of oranges, considered exotic at the time, or a bar of

Novesia chocolate. For Christmas, he built a toy grocery store for Gitta and me. No matter how tempting, I made it a point to snub his favors, calculated, as I suspected they were, to win me over.

"That's just it," I'd argue, "I don't want him to do anything for me – but leave."

I was jealous, when *jealous* wasn't yet part of my vocabulary. I was afraid of losing my mother, although I wasn't aware of it. I felt the moral and societal shame that Fredie had brought on us, even though I wouldn't have known how to say it. But I did entertain the fleeting thought, irrational even to the child I was, that my mother and Fredie's relationship amounted to a betrayal of my dead father. I didn't know, of course, that I was trying to cover my misery and rationalize my hostility and bitterness with Fredie's shortcomings, imagined or real. He was unsuitable to be Mother's husband and unsuitable to be our stepfather. That was all there was to it.

I did not have an ally in Gitta, who was going on six at the time Fredie entered our lives. To her, he was not the intruder I saw when he came through the door. Gitta welcomed the small favors I rejected and enjoyed the playful attention I resented.

There was an occasion that could have turned things around, one evening when Fredie came back from Cologne. He sat down at the kitchen table where Gitta and I were playing *Mensch Aergere Dich Nicht,* our favorite board game, similar to the American Parcheesi.

Fredie scooped up our dice playfully, and placed a wad of crunched-up newspaper on the table.

He recounted how he'd been hired that morning to oversee a crew remove the rubble of a bombed-out building. How his men had shoveled a load on to a truck when what he'd first thought was an exposed shard of china had caught his eye. He'd climbed on top of the mound and scraped away the dirt surrounding it.

"Look," he said, pointing at the wadded-up newspaper. "See what's in it. It's yours."

"I don't want it," I said and pushed it away from me.

"Dummes Mädchen! – Silly girl!"

Perhaps it was the tenderness in his tone, exposing my own rude behavior, that made me change my mind. Perhaps it was the presence of Mother who'd left her soup pot simmering on the cooking stove, and now was looking on. Perhaps it was plain greed. I took the wad and unwrapped it. The newspaper rustled.

Nestled inside was a blue-and-white porcelain figurine of a Dutch boy in ankle length trousers and clogs. He was playing a flute. There was a sharp, ragged edge where a small piece of the flute had broken off.

So beautiful was the figurine, I coveted it. But how could I accept a gift from this man who I despised more than anyone in the world?

"Find someone else to give it to," I said.

Mother looked at me aghast. She raised her hand angrily. "You should be ashamed of yourself."

"It's you who should be ashamed of yourself. . ."

Tears running down my cheeks, I flung at her the words I knew would sting the most, "You're old enough to be his mother."

"I didn't know you were capable of such viciousness."

I felt an impulse to strike Mother and throw myself at her.

"I can't stand him. I never will."

I felt caught in what I knew was irrational behavior and, at the same time, unbearable pain. I bolted out of the kitchen, flinging the door shut behind me.

At school and at play, I banished Fredie from my thoughts. He didn't exist. I never talked about him to any of my friends, neither did anyone ever ask about him. Sybille could have been the exception, but wasn't. Like me, she had an uncle; but the two of us avoided the topic of our home lives altogether, both of us aware of what they were.

When evening came around, I fantasized that Fredie would not come back after work in the city. But he always did. I would recognize the beat of his footsteps skipping up the staircase and bouncing down the hall. The door lock clicking shut would dash my last bit of wishful thinking. Before he opened the door to our flat, my stomach would tighten into a painful lump.

I would drop into a gloomy frame of mind, consumed with antagonistic feelings toward Fredie – his looks I didn't like, his name I liked even less, his jovial manner, how off-putting it was to me. I was unable to shake those feelings. It would make me cringe to witness affection between Mother and Fredie. I would read things unspeakable into a simple kiss on the cheek, bringing back the memory of the balding merchant. Any evidence of happiness Mother displayed – her hand stroking his, a smile only meant for him – escalated my unhappiness.

I look back with regret, thinking of Fredie, whose love for Mother helped Mother emerge from her shell of widowhood, and who went as far as trying to endear himself to her children for her sake.

Looking for something to do one afternoon, I stopped in on a small crowd of girls my age standing outside the grocery store around the corner from our flat. I saw Christa R. approaching. Christa lived on the other side of town. She hardly ever came to our neighborhood and, when she did, it was to cause trouble. She had been my classmate in elementary school, the only girl who had dared defy Fräulein Reiners' authority and who had not flinched when slapped on the palm of her hand with Fräulein Reiners' ruler. She had a perpetually runny nose and raw patches of skin on her upper lip.

Christa pushed into the center of the group, hands on hips, chewing on the end of one her pigtails.

"Want to know how babies are made?" she said, with a little laugh. No one answered. Squinting her eyes, she assessed her audience and scanned the upstairs windows for accidental listeners. She leaned in and, in a low, raspy voice, gave us the description of something so unimaginably vulgar we all squirmed with disgust. Then she looked at us with a challenging lift of her chin.

A smug grin appeared on her face. "What do you think of that?" she said. "God strike me dead, if this isn't the truth." She started dribbling a ball she'd grabbed from one of the other girls. She strutted across the street, and, without a glance back, threw the ball in our direction.

At eleven, going on twelve, my idea about where babies came from had evolved from the stork to the more credible claim that God planted a seed in a mother's belly. Even though I had nothing tangible with which to replace the seed story, I'd come to suspect that it, too, was something of a tale that adults put over on children. Among my friends, the subject wasn't talked about and, for the most part, I did not dwell on it. When I did, it took me to the edge of feeling sordid and thinking of Mother being alone with Fredie. While Christa R's version was nasty beyond description, the fact that it involved a mother and a father's secret parts made me suspect that it had some truth to it.

I ran home. Mother and Frau Scheer were chatting over afternoon coffee at the kitchen table.

"I know how babies are made," I said, combatively, breaking into their conversation.

Mother gave me one of her hooded-eyes looks.

"What you did to have me is despicable." I was shaking.

"What on earth has gotten into you?" she said.

"I wish I'd never been born."

Mother got up from the table. Before I could duck to protect myself, she struck my face with her palm, the first and only time she ever raised her hand against me. A hot pain stung my cheek.

I fled from the room. I went to find my autograph book in the bottom cabinet of my nightstand. I leafed to Fredie's entry on the back page, where, in his exacting cursive hand, he had written: "Life teaches me. / It teaches me as long as I live. / It still teaches me. / Otto von Bismarck"

I ripped out the page and crumpled it into a small ball.

I threw myself on to the sofa and dug my face into Mother's needlepoint pillow.

That night, I dreamed about my father:

He staggers through the front door of our flat. His uniform riddled with bullets and covered with snow. A dagger in a black sheath dangles from his waist. He has no face.

Disturbing as the dream was, it created the expectation that my father would come home again. Was it not plausible that he hadn't been killed, that he had been wounded and survived? That he had been taken captive by the Soviets and now, after six years, had been released from one of the many still existing prisoner-of-war camps in Siberia? Just as Grandmother still held hope that Gottfried, her oldest son, and Ernst, her youngest, would return home one day.

I told Mother about the dream, leaving out the gory parts.

"It's just a dream," she said. "Your father's gone for good."

"Maybe he isn't. Maybe he will come back." It angered me that she had so little faith.

"He won't. He's dead and buried on some battlefield."

I wasn't ready to give up. "What if my dream is true?"

"Nonsense. Your dream is a dream and won't bring him back."

"I'll go find him when I grow up."

29

I could always count on Mother being there when I came home after school. "How was school?" she'd greet me, lunch waiting on the table. The day that she wasn't there stands out as a cruel memory.

I pressed the front door handle down, once, twice. The door wouldn't open. I rammed my weight against the wooden panel. Nothing budged. I called for Mother. There was no answer.

Footsteps came thumping down the staircase from the third story. They weren't Mother's buoyant steps. I felt a kind of uneasiness, like a misgiving, when I saw it was Frau Scheer.

"Where's my mother?" I said, and without waiting for an answer, said it again, louder and more frantic, as if blaming Frau Scheer for Mother's absence. "Where's my mother?"

"Don't make a spectacle of yourself," she said. Then, speaking more kindly, "She'll be gone for a few days. You'll stay with me; Gitta will stay at your grandparents' house."

"What happened?" I asked, frightened, for I felt certain that something was terribly wrong.

"I'm telling you, she'll be back."

There is nothing in my memory to tell me how many days passed. Maybe it was only a few. Maybe it was weeks. I remember sleeping in the attic bedroom of Frau Scheer's flat, a skylight looking out on a starry sky. I remember running down the hallway at night, breathless and petrified of the dark. I remember Fredie talking to Frau Scheer, and the queasiness I felt in the pit of my stomach, eavesdropping on their veiled exchange. I remember suspecting that whatever had taken Mother away had something to do with Fredie, that it was his fault. I remember the unchecked hate it spurred for him, and the hate for Mother I stopped myself just short of feeling.

And I remember coming home from school one day to find Mother lying on the sofa, a blanket tucked under her chin. A smile flitted over her face. She looked pale, with dark circles under her eyes. I followed the weak tapping gesture of her hand and sat down at the edge of the sofa. The weight of days or weeks of uncertainty lifted.

"Where have you been?" I asked.

Her eyes fell shut. I waited for an answer, but none came. I looked into her face, fascinated, at first, by its absolute stillness, until a horrid fear that she was dead jolted me.

"Mother!" My voice was barely audible.

But then I felt her hand on my thigh. *"Ach, frag mich nicht. –* Oh, don't ask me."

For weeks after, Mother spent her days resting on the sofa. It was a cold, wet summer: I remember the wind whipping through the trees outside the windows and the rain beating against the glass, and Mother asking me to shut the door because she felt chilly. She spoke very little and never laughed. I didn't want to let her out of my sight. Often Gitta and I crunched together in the same armchair, doing homework on our laps. Frau Scheer did the chores around the flat, and cooked our meals. Most afternoons, she pulled a chair close to Mother and talked to her quietly. Sometimes Irmgard joined them. Her cheerful presence lifted Mother's spirits as she sang from her repertoire of folk songs. Mother listened with her eyes closed and, for short bars, hummed along weakly. Early evenings, her face brightened at the sound of the same bouncing steps coming up the stairs that brought hate back into my belly.

Mother didn't tell me where she had been those days or weeks, nor what had been wrong with her. Perhaps I never asked again after that first time. Perhaps I was too naïve, still, to recognize the defining moment that could have triggered the knowing. "Has it stopped?" Frau Scheer had asked Mother one day, and I'd flashed on the blood splotches I'd seen on the sheet. Or another time, when I lifted the lid off a bucket behind the bathroom door and saw a blood-soaked heap of cloth pads. Horrified, I'd raced out the door, and following the tug of my steps and a nameless hunch, had climbed up the stairs into the drying attic.

The louvered window on the gable wall let in sheets of sunlight, alive with specks of dust lazily floating in the air. Everywhere else a brooding dusk hung. Stretched from one side of the attic to the other were three or four clotheslines. They sagged with the weight of freshly washed laundry, heavy with moisture. I parted the sheets and towels, breathing in their fresh scent. When I reached the line closest to the back wall, I looked up. I saw a long row of elongated cotton pads neatly hung from their narrowing straps on one end while matching straps dangled down from the other. I scanned them for telltale evidence I neither knew to expect nor wanted to find. On some, the outer layers had worn threadbare. All had been washed white as snow.

I returned to the attic many times, always furtively, always drawn by some dark urge. Each time, I found what I had come for. Found the elongated pads hung on the back-most clothesline. Gradually, their numbers dwindled. And as they did, Mother regained her strength. She resumed her housework and rested less. Color returned to her cheeks. Her movements became brisk again.

In her old age, the summer before she died, we talked about the two or three years Fredie had lived with us. She recalled her unwanted pregnancy, and the back-alley abortion that had gone wrong; how the nursing staff at the Dormagen hospital, all Catholic nuns, had left her waiting until she'd almost bled to death.

Compassion for Mother swept over me and, at the same time, a horrible suspicion. I said, "Frau Scheer had nothing to do with the abortion. Tell me she didn't."

"It wasn't her fault."

That's as much as she would say.

During that same conversation, she recounted that, not long ago, more than forty years after her affair with Fredie had ended, she'd wanted to know his whereabouts. Through a chain of contacts, she'd been able to track him down to an East German town on the Baltic Sea.

"The sea was in his blood. Even when was he here, it kept calling him. I always knew . . ." She stopped, as if she'd said too much already, more than she'd wanted me to know. He had left her, it struck me. She had not ended the relationship, as I'd always assumed.

She looked lost in her thoughts, remembering, maybe, how it had ended between them. In that moment, the woman I had never seen as anything but my mother, became a woman with a life apart from her children, with longings and disappointments of her own. It was a painful letting-go for me, but I also felt as though I were setting her free.

"We wrote a few letters back and forth. Then I stopped. What was there to say? Our lives had gone in different directions."

"I made things hard for you and him, didn't I?" I said.

"You were only a child." She looked past me, into the early evening light coming through the window. I looked into her face and saw the vestige of something seductively feminine in her eyes, the look that Fredie had captured in the portrait he'd drawn of her so long ago. She'd taken it off the wall once he was no longer with us.

When Gitta and I settled my mother's estate and divided her personal belongings, I looked for the figurine of the little Dutch boy and for Fredie's drawing of Mother. I found the figurine and took it. I did not find the portrait.

30

In the summer months of 1952 the polio epidemic swept through Germany. The public swimming pools in the cities were closed as a precautionary measure. When that didn't curb the spread of the disease, classes in schools were suspended. In the densely populated areas, the number of children infected by the virus kept rising, whereas rural regions, such as ours, remained unaffected. Not that the epidemic wasn't talked about in town, for it was. The women, chatting in line at the bakery or the butcher, had their various opinions about it – most said that we had nothing to worry about; others said, God knows, worse things had happened and would. "It's the second plague," one woman said.

With our regular July-into-August summer vacation extended for weeks and then weeks again, time seemed endless. Day in, day out, the swimmers among us took off on our bicycles, picnic baskets swinging from the handlebars, and headed for the local swimming hole. It wasn't off limits. Not yet.

Manmade in the 1930s, the *Baggerloch,* as it was known in those days, had been dredged to supply sand and gravel for the construction of the autobahn system, begun during the Weimar Republic and vastly expanded under Hitler. It was large enough for informal rowing competitions and for small yachts to take anchor – evidence of new wealth in the economy of the post-war boom, and occasion for us to marvel from afar. In the shape of a T, the larger of its two arms connected to the Rhine.

A few of us children, Sybille and I included, would arrive early, before the heat had risen, and stake out a stretch of beach along the western shore, closest to Delrath. We'd spread our towels on the sand and stash our baskets in the dense shrubbery to keep our sandwiches and drinks cool. We rubbed our bodies with *Nivea* cream and laid out to tan when the sun was at its hottest.

Only the strongest swimmers attempted to cross the swimming hole's daunting diagonal. Most stayed close to shore. Sometimes, I swam into the deep waters alongside Sybille. When I'd wear out, she'd let me hold on to her shoulders, and we'd continue in tandem.

The eastern bay opened to the Rhine. Only the occasional, foolhardy boy dared jump off the bridge into the river current, returning, breathlessly, with reports of whirlpools that had sucked him down into rapidly spinning centers.

The news spread quickly from house to house, when a girl two doors up from Grandmother's came down with a case of polio. She was put in an iron lung to keep her alive. Fear went through the town.

Mother had a worried look on her face when Gitta and I came home after a day at the *Baggerloch*. We had each been there with our respective friends. We didn't mingle. Mother asked whether we had ever played with the girl, whose name was Christine and who was a year behind Gitta. We hadn't, we assured her.

"Touch your chin to your chest," she instructed us.

"Why?" we asked, as both of us lowered our heads.

Mother exhaled. The frown line between her eyes relaxed. "A stiff neck is the first symptom."

The epidemic had made its mysterious leap into our town. Whether for good reason or just because it was a body of water, the *Baggerloch* was blamed and closed, although the girl didn't know how to swim and had never been there.

It was as if demons had taken possession of it. I came to shun even the narrow trail through the heather that circled the shoreline. Looking down over the bridge at the Rhine River, I saw with my own eyes how the silvery waters had gone a brooding gray, and heard with my own ears a foreboding rustle in the bushes along the steep banks.

Fishermen could be seen sitting at the eastern bay's shore, where perch came to breed in protected pools. If I strained my eyes, I could make out a fishing line swaying in the light breeze, and fish flapping in buckets kept cool at the shallow edge. We had always stayed clear of the fishermen, who claimed these waters for themselves. If, accidentally or to taunt them, we'd trespassed into their territory, they'd chase us away with angry curses or pebbles flung in our direction.

Deserted now, except by the fishermen who added to its desolate appearance, the *Baggerloch* had become a phantom of the happy place it had been. I felt an ache in my chest, similar to the one I would experience many years later, an ache for my native country left behind and lost to me.

The temperatures had risen to record highs. Windows and shutters were kept closed after the cool early morning hours, to keep out the worst of the heat. Days of unchanging weather made the air in the darkened rooms stagnant and unbearable. With the midsummer sun setting late in the evening and twilight extending past eleven o'clock, the short nights brought little relief. I'd toss and turn in my bed, never falling into more than a fitful sleep.

It had not rained in more than two months. People said it was the worst drought they could remember. There would be a famine, some alarmists predicted. There were those who talked about rainmakers with otherworldly powers; others talked about cloud seeding, which had been in the news as an American discovery to induce rainfall.

Our little neighborhood group of girls always knew where to find one another. There weren't that many places, and none were far apart: the windowless wall on the driveway side of our building, smooth and high enough for bouncing off balls; the sidewalk in front of the fenced-in vegetable garden adjacent to the pub, where centuries of foot traffic had packed the dirt down, making it perfect for rolling marbles; the yard behind the greengrocer, ideal for playing catch or hide-and-seek; Grandmother's courtyard; Onkel Jean's orchard. Or we gathered in the weather-protected entryway to our building, where the memory of that afternoon began.

One by one, the usual group of girls gathered there after lunch on that particular day. Heat-weary and bored, we plopped onto the cool stone steps: Sybille from across the street; Doris, whose family hadn't moved yet from their flat across from ours; Hanni, thrilled the

Baggerloch was closed, since, as a non-swimmer, her mother hadn't allowed her to go there in the first place; Uli from next door; and me.

When we could think of nothing to do, we dawdled down the street. Aimlessly. Listlessly. We stopped outside the schoolyard wall, where a row of linden trees cast speckled shade on the sidewalk, enough to cut the sun's glare but too little to mitigate the brutal heat.

We were in our white cotton underpants. They doubled as shorts or swimwear on hot summer days. We wore no tops. We weren't expected to. At the age of 12, we still had the bodies of children.

Taking turns, we tight-roped back and forth on a shoulder-high section of brick wall. It ended at the school gate on one side and a boxwood hedge where the principal's property began on the other. But the heat soon exhausted us. Doris fell into the hedge, half-intentionally, when she lost her balance, and remained there giggling until we heard the reprimanding voice of the principal's wife.

Uli and Hanni went to sit down on the curb. Their shoulders slouching over their knees, they began doodling circles and lines in the bone-dry dirt with small sticks. Following Sybille's lead, Doris and I perched on the edge of the wall, legs dangling down. If we were waiting for a break in our boredom, it was already on its way.

"Watch out. . . trouble," said Doris, and pointed in the direction of two boys, the Schmeling twins, ambling up the road. One short, the other tall, they were a couple of years older than we. They were passing Grandfather's potato field on one side and a hilly meadow on the other, a kind of no-man's-land that separated our part, the old part, of town from the *Siedlung,* a development, built between the two world wars.

The two boys came closer. There was a bad-news swagger in their bare-foot walk. We looked the other way with staged aloofness, thinking it would keep them moving past us. But it didn't work. Instead, it seemed to provoke them.

They stopped at the schoolyard gate, just steps from where we were. They sent high arcs of spit flying into the street.

"Bet you sissies can't do that," the taller of them said.

"So?" said Sybille. She was the oldest in our group. She was the biggest, too.

"Shut your mouth, girl," he said.

The shorter one now took the lead. Menacingly, he said, "Listen up. You know the girl with the polio. Lives at your end of town. Any of you just looked at her, you'll get it. Probably die."

He touched his chin to his chest. "Can you do that?"

We all did. We all passed.

"Actually, it means nothing. It's in your bones already. You just wait."

"Let's give these little virgins some real stuff," the taller and meaner one said. He proceeded to tell crude jokes, whose punch lines went over my head but whose vulgar language, just because I was listening to it, made me feel as though I had done something wrong.

"Why don't you two just go away," I said. My own brazenness startled me.

"You heard what she said, the little bitch?" the shorter one said.

They stuck their heads together, snickering and whispering. Then they positioned themselves right in front of me, legs apart, hands deep in their shorts pockets.

They looked me up and down. Waving his index finger, the taller one directed me to get off the wall. I looked around at the other girls. Sybille and Doris were staring at the ground. Hanni and Uli kept drawing circles in the dirt. I was on my own. I squirmed my way off the wall, scraping the backs of my bare thighs on the rough edge of the brick.

"What do you want from me?" I said, in a show of bravery I didn't possess.

"You got little knockers swelling on your chest," he said, cupping his hands over his own naked chest.

The two burst into sinister laughter. Their faces came close, so close they almost touched mine.

"Let's go," the shorter one said and grimaced smugly. They stumbled away, bumping into each other and clapping their hands.

Neither I nor the other girls said a word. Everything was how it had been before the Schmeling boys appeared: five bored girls whiling away a hot summer afternoon.

But it really wasn't the same. My temples throbbed. The corners of my eyes were teary. I hated the boys – and blamed myself. They had looked at me in a way no one had ever looked at me before. I wanted to flee. I wanted to hide the nakedness of my chest, which from that day on I would never again leave uncovered. But I stayed sitting on the brick wall, my legs swinging up and down just a little faster.

31

I find Gisela sitting in a windowless room in the center of her childhood home. I'm an older woman; she's still the thirteen-year-old I knew in school. I clasp her head with both my hands and, moving close, look into her face. It is startlingly white, as is the color of her pageboy-styled hair. I search for the mole beneath her left eyebrow. It is still there.

In an old photo as well as in my memory, that is how I would recognize Gisela: by the mole, prominently noticeable, though not detracting in the least, from her beauty. That is how I would recognize the adult, even now, if I were to chance upon her: I have looked for her on my visits home, on her old street, at the train station, in shops. That's how, even in a crowd, I would find her – searching for her mole.

Back then, Gisela's hair was a medium brown, not at all the striking white of the dream. She wore it braided, the way we all did. The brown of her eyes matched the brown of her hair. No matter how much I probe my memory for more, everything else about her appearance remains featureless.

At school, she excelled in all subjects and was at the top of the class. Already in those early days, her mind was set on becoming a medical doctor.

Oddly, one of the things about her I have not forgotten is her birthday, September 1, 1939, the actual day on which the Second World War broke out. She must have told me that.

Gisela lived in a stately, two-story home halfway between the Dormagen train station and the school we both attended. Surrounded by a wrought-iron fence, the house stood on the corner of a beech-lined street and an unpaved road that ran through sugar beet fields. Green and rust-colored ivy covered the stucco walls, all the way up to the gabled roof where new growth nuzzled under the eaves. The houses on my street looked dwarfed and impoverished by comparison. Gisela's house was a mansion, where rooms had fancy names, some of which I had only run across in books: *music room, library, gentlemen's study, reception parlor, scullery.*

Her family was the ideal family: a mother, a father and three children – two girls and a boy. Gisela was the eldest.

Gisela was my best friend, from the time I entered secondary school at age ten to when I was thirteen. Or was it that I wanted her to be my best friend?

Every morning on my way to school, I rang the bell at the iron gate of her house. Her younger brother, Oliver, a chubby boy with a jolly face, would stick his head out of his upstairs bedroom window and call out, "She's on her way."

I'd hear the back door close. I'd see her make the turn from behind the house, down the gravel path to the gate, carrying a well-worn leather school bag, a hand-me-down from her father's university days. We'd shake hands, as was the custom. No sooner had the gate fallen shut than the two of us would dive into conversations. They were of the headier variety, conversation about the books we read, even about grammar and classical music, rather than gossip about the girls in our class. That's how we were together.

I have a clear memory of her mother: the way she dressed in plain shirtwaist dresses, accentuating her generous hips; the warm smile with which she welcomed me when, on some Fridays, she'd asked me to stay for lunch. "You must be hungry," she'd say, and sit down with us at the dining table, while a uniformed maid served the meal. She knew to say things that put me at ease: "What a pretty smock you are wearing." Or: "Tell me about your English test." While she was inquisitive, she never asked questions that might embarrass me: *Your mother, does she have an acquaintance?* Or: *Wouldn't you like to have a stepfather?*

I remember Gisela's father too. More elegant than his wife, he was a tall man, handsome in a studious way, who always dressed in a suit and tie. A chemist, he held a high-level position with the local Bayer plant, the largest company in the area, where most of my classmates' fathers were also employed. Gentle though he was around his family, he conveyed an air of authority and sophistication.

In Gisela's father, I saw the ideal of a father and of a man: caring for his family, successful in the world. I would have wanted my father, had he lived, to be just like him.

Gisela's father never showed anything but kindness toward me. Still, I suffered some discomfort around him, as I did around all fathers. His presence as a father emphasized the absence of a father in my life. But unlike other fathers, he ignited a longing in me: around him, I discovered what it was I did not have, what it was I was missing, not just that something was absent.

When, on occasion, Gisela's father was at home, he'd set up a projector and a screen in his upstairs study. An amateur nature photographer, he'd show us tray upon tray of slides, mostly of flowers, insects and landscapes, predominantly of the Odenwald, a low mountainous area in southwest Germany, ancestral home of the *Ruf* family.

I watched the parade of photos and listened to his commentary and explanations. I imagined taking photos myself and putting them in albums, the way *my* father had. I recalled the camera that could've been mine, if Mother hadn't traded it on the black market, "for a song," as she'd say with some anger and regret. Now a new camera was a luxury out of our family's reach.

A perfect day for gardening. It was early spring, cool, windy, with only a few clouds in the sky. Gisela and her siblings each had a small plot of their own in the expansive area behind the house. I looked on as they turned the soil to prepare for seeding and planting. Why couldn't I have a patch like theirs, in Onkel Jean's orchard or in Grandfather's vegetable garden? The idea had never occurred to me before.

Gisela's father tapped me on the shoulder. "Come along. I'll show you our rock garden."

I followed him to the western end of the property. Walking along the meandering paths, he explained how a desert ecology can be sustained even in a wet climate, such as ours.

"What we have here is sandy soil, which is porous, the kind that cacti and succulents prefer. The ground slopes toward the west, allowing for optimal sun exposure, kind of what you see in the wine-growing areas." Pointing to the various specimens, he called out their names.

Though his attention pleased me, I was afraid that he did not see me as his children's equal, that I counted less than Gisela and her siblings, who were raised in a conventional family – a family superior in status to mine.

Later that same afternoon, all of us were sitting around the dining table for hot chocolate and home-made apple tart, when Gisela's father turned to me, "Gisela tells me that your father was killed in the war."

"Yes," I said. "Toward the end. Christmas 1944."

"Do you know where?"

"In Kurland."

"I'm sorry for you and your family."

He waited for a moment, before he said, *"Ein Verbrechen* – A crime."

I didn't know how to respond or whether I was even supposed to respond. So I said nothing.

At the end of the afternoon, Gisela took me to the gate to say goodbye.

"Your father, he wasn't in the war?" I asked her.

"A lung ailment saved him from being drafted." Then, to offer a further explanation, she said, "And anyway, he was opposed to the war and to the regime. Not publicly though – that would have been too great a risk."

I was struck, all at once and for the first time, by the thought that there was more to the war than what I knew, that there was something disturbing about the nature of the war itself and about those who had fought in it.

For the most part, nobody spoke about the war. My knowledge of the war was limited to my own experiences. Those I kept intact as a child's memory, unquestioned. But there had been clues – things I may have heard people say or allude to, such as Mother remarking that the war had been a 'senseless war' – that could have begun the questioning earlier, but they had not. The world I lived in was an unexamined world.

Now, an insinuation that would remain unexplored for several more years had seeped into my mind: that the war may have been a wrongful war, and that those who had fought in it may have committed a wrongful act. I felt a hint of humiliation on my father's behalf and, already, a first small inkling of personal implication as my father's daughter. I pushed these unpleasant warnings away, without giving them substance or words; but having had a glimpse, I could never completely dismiss them.

Shifting course, I thought about how lucky I would have been, if my father, like Gisela's father, had suffered from a physical impairment which, ironically, might have saved his life. Gitta and I would have a father. He would hold an important position in the company where, already, he'd been on track for a promising career before he enlisted. Mother would not be a widow. How different our lives would be. How unfair, I thought, and in a moment of envy, wished Gisela's fate and mine were reversed.

A case of bronchitis, accompanied by a high fever, had kept me confined to bed and out of school for over a week, when Gisela, quite unexpectedly, came to visit on a Sunday afternoon. I heard Fredie answering the doorbell, and Gisela asking for me. I cringed, afraid that the secret I kept so closely guarded about Mother's "acquaintance" had been exposed. I wished she had not come.

"Who was the man who answered the door?" she asked, standing at the foot of my bed. It might have been an innocent question and not the trap I surmised. I felt caught. Still, I lied. "Oh, just somebody."

I could not admit to Gisela that the man who had answered the door was my Mother's *acquaintance.* I was even less prepared to admit that he lived with us in our flat. Worse still, I feared that she knew the truth before she asked the question, and that she would tell her mother, who had sent along a home-baked lemon cake to wish me a speedy recovery.

Gisela and I never spoke about her visit that Sunday afternoon, nor did she ever broach the question again. I wanted to be her best friend, but couldn't ignore that I was hiding something important from her. Best friends, I believed, didn't keep secrets from one another. They told each other everything. But the shame I carried about Fredie was greater than my commitment to our friendship.

On the outside, nothing changed: as before, I rang the bell at her gate each morning; we walked to school together; we sat next to each other in class; I continued visiting her home on some Fridays; Gisela never came to see me at our flat again.

Gisela transferred to a school in Cologne at the end of our third year of secondary school, when we were both thirteen. I tried everything to persuade her to stay, but her parents, she said, insisted that she attend an academically more rigorous school.

Her seat next to mine in the classroom remained vacant for only a day or two, but the ache of her absence did not go away. When I passed her house in the morning and again in the afternoon, the loss of her often felt unbearable.

Weeks or months passed before I saw Gisela again. Then, one afternoon on my way to the train station, I spotted her, the mole under her left eyebrow visible even from across the street. She was in the company of new friends. I took a few steps in her direction. Her posture stiffened. An expression of reserve came over her face. I paused for a moment, not knowing what to do or say. Gisela took the initiative.

"*Guten Tag,*" she said and nodded to me.

"*Guten Tag,*" I said. I wasn't sure whether she heard me. She had already returned to chatting with the other girls

It was the last time I ran into Gisela. Once Gisela started attending a more prestigious school, the social difference that had always been there between her circumstances and my own opened into a rift.

After that day, the ache for Gisela was gone. Whenever thoughts of her came to my mind, I rejected them. I made it a point not to take note of her house when I passed it on my way to and from school.

More months passed. It was well into the next school year. Approaching Gisela's house one morning, something oddly different caught my attention. I turned to look: the green and rust-colored ivy had been torn off the façade, exposing gray stucco and a web of dirty veins and claw-like prints where the ivy vines had been. The curtains were gone. The house appeared uninhabited, the garden unattended. What I saw no longer resembled the mansion it had been. It looked rather ordinary. Even shabby.

32

It was the convention, unspoken and rarely broken: girls age thirteen and younger wore their uncut hair braided. Except to trim split ends, no scissors had ever touched mine. I had two shoulder-length pigtails, which I sometimes wound around and pinned on top of my head, like a tiara. A few of my classmates had thick braids that came down to their waists.

Once past their thirteenth birthday, most of the girls had their hair cut chin length and permed into wavy curls; the few who didn't wore ponytails.

The way we wore our hair was the visible sign of where we belonged in the hierarchy of age. That, and the length of our skirts: above the knees for the younger girls, below them for the older ones.

The girl I'll call Hilda was the one exception among my classmates. At thirteen, she wore her long, blonde mane draped over her shoulders and down her back. She pranced along the school corridors, secure in her developing body, arching her plucked eyebrows and pouting her Vaseline-wet lips. Most of us other girls treated Hilda as an outsider and regarded her with a sense of moral superiority. We excluded her from our little in-groups. None of us would have admitted to feeling envious of so much hair, so much nerve, and so much attention from the boys. But we had plenty to talk about after some upper-grade girls said that they had seen Hilda and a boy from another school necking in the bushes at the *Baggerloch*.

The plan to have my hair cut seemed to come out of the blue – as out of the blue as my first menstrual period a few months later. I had turned thirteen in March. Now it was June. It took no struggle to make up my mind, as it did for some girls, whose hair was long and thick. They agonized over it, until, one morning, they'd present themselves to their little circle of classmates with grown-up hairstyles. My hair, scraggly by my own description, was nothing to be proud of. Once the idea struck me to have it cut off, nothing could've stopped me.

It had happened like this: one Saturday after school, I sat down in front of Mother's three-way mirror. I undid my braids. I brushed and combed. Before long, I was overtaken by the desire to look different from the way I looked. I tucked my hair under, to approximate a bob. I viewed myself from all sides. I loosely arranged it in waves and curls framing my face, like Vivian Leigh or Marlene Dietrich, whose pictures, along with those of other film stars, I had cut out of magazines and collected in a folder. When I braided my hair again, I knew it was for the last time.

Envisioning a new, glamorous self so different from the plain, childlike image I had of the girl I was, I rode my bicycle at top speed to Renate Schwalke's home seven kilometers away. She lived with her family in the coach house of Kloster Knechtsteden, a 12th century monastery, where her father was resident artist and restorer of the basilica frescos.

Renate had replaced Gisela as my best friend. The boys and some of the girls called her "Blackie" because of her pitch-black hair. She wanted them to call me "Blondie", but no one ever did. Two years older than I, she already wore her hair short, with an s-shaped curl slicked down over her right temple.

I stormed into her house, out of breath. "I'm going to get my hair cut."

She looked at me, her dark eyes beaming. "When?"

"Today. And permed too."

I raced back home. I made the same definitive statement to Mother as I had made to Renate. "I'm going to get my hair cut."

Mother looked up from ironing a blouse, the first from a small folded stack in her laundry basket.

She knitted her brows in disbelief, "What for heaven's sake got into your head?"

"I'm going to get my hair cut," I repeated, this time more slowly and with greater emphasis.

Mother stood her ground. "No," she said.

"All the other girls have had theirs cut."

"You are not all the other girls."

"But my braids are so deplorable."

"If you took better care of your hair, brushed it a hundred strokes a day -"

"I want it cut off."

"A girl your age should wear her hair braided."

Her sense of propriety unnerved me. "Whose rule is that?"

"It's just not befitting," she said, skirting the question.

I was too angry to cry.

Even if I didn't fully realize the implications of Mother's refusal, I sensed that she was determined to keep me a little girl for a while longer. I was equally determined to become a grown-up.

Realizing, perhaps, that she could not stop the inevitable, Mother opened her palms in a weak gesture of giving up. She resumed her ironing.

Minutes later, with money from my savings clutched in my hand, I ran down the street, past Onkel Jean's orchard and the old school house. I got to the hair salon at the bottom of the sledding hill, just as Herr Kollenbroich, the owner, was lowering the roll-down doors to lock up for the day. It was six o'clock.

"You'll have to come back some other time," he said.

"Couldn't you do it now? Please!" I said.

"I'm sorry. It's past closing. And anyway, it would take us until midnight."

Without a convincing argument, I pleaded with even greater urgency. "Please. Today."

"I could get fined for staying open beyond mandatory closing hours," he said, in a last bid to talk sense into me. But something more than even my determination had been set into motion. Just like Mother, who couldn't stop the inevitable, Herr Kollenbroich, too, relented.

"All right then," he said, "as long as your mother knows where you are."

He turned the lights back on and led me to the far station, separated from the only other station by a pink-on-white, polka-dotted plastic curtain.

I sat down in the chrome and leather-covered chair. Herr Kollenbroich put a plastic wrap around me. It matched the curtain, except that the color scheme was reversed. Herr Kollenbroich stood behind me, his hands placed on my shoulders. He leaned forward until his face appeared in the mirror next to mine, not a face with striking features, but pleasing. After a day's work in the salon, his straight, blonde hair looked as freshly combed as it would have in the morning. His smile put me at ease.

"What's my young lady's pleasure?"

I reached vaguely toward the back of my head, my hands cupped to indicate the curled fullness I envisioned.

"No *Meckiefrisur* for you!" he said, with a wink I didn't quite know how to interpret.

A hairstyle, very different from those of the women idols in popular culture, had come into fashion. The style called for uniformly short hair not unlike the quills of a hedgehog called Meckie – the *Steiff* brand stuffed toy it had been named after. Mainly younger women seemed to favor it, while Mother and her contemporaries didn't follow the trend. Theirs remained as it had always been: hair swept upward from the face and worn high over the forehead, wavy and curled on the back of the head. Thinking about the *Meckiefrisur* now, it appears to have been a reaction against the feminine image of women in the post-war culture when many women, thanks to a shortage of men, had to take on the role of breadwinner.

I shook my head, laughing, "No."

Putting my gestured description into words, he said, "Wavy curls? That should suit you well."

He ran his hands down the length of my braids. "So you really want these pretty things cut off?"

I nodded.

"Okay then." He proceeded to open and close his scissors over my pigtails. It made a crunching sound.

"Will you save them?" He held them up, one in each hand. "Most girls keep them as mementos, or have them put on their dolls." He allowed a moment for me to consider.

I shook my head. He shrugged his shoulders and dropped them into the waste bin. With a barely audible thud, they landed on top of the day's accumulation of cut hair.

He took another pair of scissors, daintier than the ones he had used to sever my braids and, with nimble motions, snipped at the uneven length of hair to give it a bobbed shape.

"Now, let's shampoo."

My head bent low over the wash basin, a terrycloth towel pressed tightly over my eyes, I could hear and feel the sound of water dousing my hair. Soapy bubbles began to pop under his shampooing hands. He rinsed and towel-dried my hair. He dragged his comb through it to smooth out any last tangles.

Strand after strand, he put my hair in metal rollers, securing them with rubber bands, until my entire head was snugly covered.

"Any of them hurt?" he asked.

"No," I said. It was easier to lie and endure the sting of two or three around my face that were so tight I could feel the skin pulling away from my scalp.

He left the station to mix the permanent wave solution in a small bowl. Coming back, he brushed it over the rollers, careful not to miss a single one. Its distinct, obnoxious odor enveloped me.

"This will take a while," he said, leaving. A door opened and closed.

An unreasonably long time of waiting passed. Horror stories about permanents gone wrong had circulated among my classmates. Panic rushed to my head in a wave of heat. Herr Kollenbroich had forgotten I was here. The glamorized image I'd created of myself was replaced by one of a frizzy disaster, and a fear that my hair would fall out, gobs of it.

At long last, Herr Kollenbroich reappeared. "That should do it," he said. He began to unwind the rollers with deft fingers, leaving my whole head covered with little ringlets, too tight to relieve my apprehension.

After another shampoo and thorough rinse, he put my wet hair in a second round of rollers, an assortment of sizes, larger than the first.

"Time to go under the dryer," Herr Kollenbroich said. "About twenty minutes."

Once or twice he came to lift the bonnet. He undid a roller to check whether my hair was dry.

It seemed endless but, finally, I was in the chair again. My face looked flushed, my ears red from the heat. Herr Kollenbroich took out the rollers. Large, smooth curls covered my head. He brushed them out and fluffed my hair, shaping it with a large-toothed comb. For a final touch, he pressed waves into place with his fingers. He looked at me in the mirror, pleased.

"*Fertig.* – We're done," he said, holding a hand mirror in back of my head, moving it from side to side and up and down. I had watched him go through the same motions after doing Mother's hair: she had parted her lips ever so slightly and tilted her head, nodding with approval. I looked into the mirror, blindly. Afraid to see the changed image of myself, I saw nothing.

"*Schön,*" Herr Kollenbroich said. He took the plastic wrap off my shoulders.

"A cut and perm. That will be twenty Marks."

I counted out the money, four Five-Deutsche-Mark notes and handed them to him. They were damp after hours of holding them in the palm of my hand.

We bid each other goodnight. It was nearly ten o'clock. Walking back up the hill, I could hear the rumble of his wooden roll-down doors closing. A strong night wind tousled my curls. I brushed my hands through them. I touched the back of my neck, jarred by its nakedness and the finality of what I had done.

The flat was dark. I tiptoed to bed and slipped under the featherbed, mindful not to wake Gitta next to me. The residual odor of the permanent wave solution surrounding me, I fell into a restless sleep of fragmented dreams.

At daybreak, I slipped out the front door. I ran my hands over my hair. I lifted the back to accentuate its fullness. The wind of the night before had quieted down. The limpid air hinted at early summer warmth.

I headed for Onkel Jean's house. He lived alone in the house he'd built in the middle of the orchard. He'd be up at this early hour, for that was how he lived, following the rhythms of the natural world, "keeping the same hours as the sun," he liked to say. I found him standing at the kitchen window, in dark blue overalls and wooden clogs. Hands in his pockets, his gaze skimmed the tops of the fruit trees into the unmeasurable sky.

"Look, Onkel Jean," I said from the doorway, too impatient to wait for him to notice my presence. He turned, surprise registering on his face. He was unshaven. His thinning hair looked ruffled.

With an unsure smile, I twirled around once, like an awkward ballerina. He narrowed his eyes as he appraised me, then drew a circle with his forefinger, indicating he wanted me to twirl again. I became light-headed by the motion and with regret. What if I looked cheap with my waves and curls, like Hilda with her long, blonde hair?

When I came to face Onkel Jean again, his expression shifted to a melancholy smile. He walked over to me, his clogs thudding on the concrete floor. He stroked my head with his palm.

"You're a young woman now," he said.

He remained standing there, lost in thought, perhaps, or wondering what to say next. But he said nothing.

He paid no notice as I walked deeper into the hallway. I stopped in front of the wall mirror across a mounted coat rack, overloaded with overalls and hats. Early sunlight streamed through the door. I looked at my image tentatively. Recognizing the young woman Onkel Jean had seen, I angled my head as if posing for a photograph. Parted on one side, my blonde hair framed my face with rippling waves and curls.

The church bells started to ring for early Sunday Mass. Onkel Jean came up from behind me and put his arm around my shoulders. We walked out into the orchard, side by side, both of us silent, along the brick path and around to the front of the house to where the old pear tree stood.

There he remained standing, while I continued down the path toward the street and the church. I felt his eyes following me, my hair bouncing with each light-footed step. I wanted to turn and look at him one last time, but fought the impulse. I was long out of his sight when I opened the church portal. But I still felt him watching me.

"You're a young woman now," I repeated to myself.

Onkel Jean had given a name to my new identity. All day long I reveled in the self I had become. Only yesterday, I had run and played like a child, my short pleated skirt flapping. Today, in a skirt pulled below my waist so its hem touched below my knees, I paced my walk like the adult women – already familiar to myself in my new guise. I was different from how I had been yesterday: there were no words, just intimations – my braids, absent now, no longer marking me as the child I had been.

True to the early morning signs, the day turned glorious. The women of the town opened the upstairs windows and put their featherbeds over the ledges to air. The men were in the gardens, loosening the soil around the still tender bean stalks and rows of root vegetables. The old people sat outdoors, taking in the sunshine and watching the younger ones pass by. The neighborhood children played games of hopscotch on the sidewalks or tag until, cheeks flushed from exertion, they sank into the damp meadows, ready to think up something else to do. That was the kind of small-town day it was.

I walked along the streets in our neighborhood, and in the *Siedlung*, too, where I rarely went. I wanted to be seen. I wanted to present my new, grown-up self to the townspeople. "You got your hair cut," the children said, and many of the adults as well. I felt as though they were applauding me. I went to see to Sybille, Hanni and Doris, who had already made the big leap and had their braids cut off; and to see Uli, younger than I by a year, who looked at me with a mixture of admiration and envy.

I returned home midmorning. A place setting was still waiting for the breakfast I had missed. Mother did not ask where I had been. She assessed my new hairstyle with a critical eye.

"So. . . you got what you wanted?" she asked, rhetorically.

Early in the afternoon, I went to see Grandmother. She was in her wicker armchair in the summer kitchen, across the breezeway from the main house. Something quizzical came over her face. "Well!" she said, "Don't you look just like your mother?"

Gitta and Cousin Jochen sat at her feet on the cool concrete floor, playing *Mensch Ärgere Dich Nicht*. They both took diabolic pleasure in kicking each other's game pieces off the board. Gitta looked up at me. A nine-year-old tomboy with short pigtails, she grimaced and rolled her eyes at me. Snickering, she swayed her shoulders and chest provocatively.

"*Ei! Ei!* – Oh! Oh!" she said.

The balmy air of afternoon chilled as the sun dipped behind the small forest of dwarfed oaks west of town. That's where, on a rare Sunday afternoon when we'd taken a walk, Mother had put her hands over my eyes as a naked man disappeared into the thicket. Afterwards, she had told me not to go there again. Sometimes I'd gone anyway. As I did that early evening, for it was there I wanted to end my day – alone in the small, forbidden forest, no longer a child.

I took the trail deep into the woods, exploring over-grown paths that ended in the thicket or in sudden ditches. When at last I came to the clearing at its center, dusk had fallen. The hush of early evening disquieted me. I ran back through the woods and down the dirt road into town. Where it intersected with the main street, Onkel Jean's older brother approached from the opposite direction, his walking stick tapping the sidewalk. He stopped in front of me.

"Onkel Jean is dead," he said.

33

The door to our flat was unlocked, but no one was home. I bolted back downstairs, and raced up the street to Onkel Jean's orchard, forgetting the adult walk I'd practiced all day. It was nearly dark. I slowed down under the old pear tree. Something inhospitable and unearthly made me hesitate.

Keeping clear of the front door, I walked around to the side of the house, and paused at the sitting room window. The shutters were open, allowing a view into the interior. An overhead lamp spread dim light on three figures. They were bent over Onkel Jean's desk, their backs turned to the window.

A fourth figure approached through the doorway from the dark kitchen, paused for a moment, then moved into the dim light of the room. I saw that it was Mother.

"Where's your respect for the dead?" she said. Her voice trembled with outrage. "His body isn't cold yet and you're rummaging through his papers!"

The figures dropped what they were doing. Their faces turned to the light. I recognized Onkel Jean's younger brother, his wife and their eldest daughter Agnes – who was Mother's good friend. A brief argument followed; I heard the sound of voices talking over voices, although I couldn't make out the words being spoken.

Presently, the back door opened and fell shut. Footsteps on the brick walk echoed in the darkness. They came nearer. My shoulders hunched, I waited, half-expecting Onkel Jean to appear from around the corner.

But it wasn't Onkel Jean. It was only Mother, appearing out of the shadows.

"Come on," she said. She grabbed my hand and yanked me away from the window. I could feel her rage. "Where's Gitta?"

A whimpering came from the washhouse, and then a howling, more woeful than anything I'd ever heard. Then Gitta came running toward us, and buried her face in Mother's skirt.

"Onkel Jean," she screamed and sobbed and didn't stop all the way home.

Later, I would learn that Gitta had gone to see Onkel Jean late in the afternoon. He'd been on the sofa in his sitting room. Short of breath and barely able to speak, he'd asked her to fetch our mother. In her adult years, when Gitta spoke about that day, she added, "I was the last person to see him alive." Something uncharacteristically boastful resonated in her tone, implying it was a special distinction, something that no one else shared.

Even then, when we were already adults, it kindled a trace of envy in me. Gitta's last encounter with Onkel Jean made mine less significant. His final words to me, *You're a young woman now* – a blessing so significant in my young life – didn't measure up to the part Gitta had played in his final moments.

Mother never missed an opportunity to tell the story of what had happened once she'd come to Onkel Jean's. Always, she began with the same turn of phrase, one that I thought was odd and old-fashioned.

"Ich hab' ihm beim Sterben geholfen. – I helped him die." It emphasized the importance of her role in his passing, something resembling a midwife to death.

"He ripped his shirt open. He gasped for air. Like a drowning man. His lips had turned blue." Each time she described this, her delivery was immediate, as if she were reliving the event, bringing it into the present for her listener.

"It was his angina," she said, touching her own heart, "I held him in my arms. He fought hard with death. He wouldn't let go." She'd pause, and in that pause, it seemed, she wanted to give him another moment to live.

That pause in her description always had the same shuddering effect on me, for I knew verbatim the words that would follow:

"A rattle came from his chest and a gurgling, so unearthly, I knew it was over. After that, his weight collapsed into my lap."

In her retelling, she'd look down, as if to meet his face. "I pressed his eyes shut. Then I sat with him, alone, until I felt his body lose its warmth."

The morning after Onkel Jean had died, my own sobbing woke me out of a dream. Its single image followed me into wakefulness: *The fruit trees in Onkel Jean's orchard are charred. Row upon row, their skeleton branches fingering the sky.*

So real was the devastation in the dream, I couldn't shake it off, not on my way to school nor sitting through classes. Always, it came back.

I wanted to see with my own eyes that the dream had only been a dream, and headed to the orchard before even going home after school. Nothing looked different, but nothing looked the same, either. It was as though I were seeing the fruit trees and the meadows with an altered gaze, or through the eyes of the dream: not actually charred, but separated and surreal. The June sun, summerlike the previous day, lay hidden behind a solid layer of gray. No wind to gather the clouds, to release the sun, or the rain. A stillness hung in the trees.

Like someone trespassing, or afraid to move into harm's way, I paused where a row of sour cherry trees behind the washhouse sheltered me from view. Onkel Jean's German Spitz slunk near me, his fluffy, curled tail pulled between his legs. Now and then, he made small whining sounds or rubbed his wet snout against my calves. "Shh!" I said, stroking his head.

I circled the house, at a safe distance at first, then drew nearer. I quickened my step past the front door, where a black mourning veil had been draped over the door knocker. It swayed gently in the breeze. Almost running as I passed it, I threw a quick glance at the sitting room window on the side of the house. It was now shuttered.

A last turn took me to the backdoor where a transparent pane in the intricate pattern of the stained glass window permitted a view into the interior hallway. Hesitant, yet unable to control the urge, I peered inside. Laid out in an open wood coffin was Onkel Jean's body, his broad hands folded over a buttoned-up suit jacket, his face locked in a sleeping smile. I bolted from the window, from the house, from the orchard, pursued by what I had seen, already stuck fast in my memory.

I had found what I had come for, without having known I'd come for it – to find Onkel Jean, but also to blur the line between life and death. Onkel Jean was dead. And he was still here, in his house, on this earth.

Two black-draped horses drew the hearse down the main street. The tapping of hooves and grinding of wheels merged with the shuffling sound of the mourners. Onkel Jean's family – his brothers and their wives, nieces, nephews and their children – walked directly behind the hearse. The men in their black suits, carrying wreaths of evergreen, the women in veiled hats and mourning clothes. Observing a polite distance, our family followed – Grandfather, Tante Irma with cousin Jochen, Onkel Ernst, Mother with Gitta and me. Behind us, in twos and threes, came a long line of people, who had known Onkel Jean, and many who had not, but made it their business to attend every funeral.

The procession was nearing Grandmother's house. Dressed in mourning clothes, Grandmother was waiting in the open doorway. She stood tall, her seldom used ebony cane supporting her heavy body. With the bearing of a matriarchal queen, she held her head high, composed in her unveiled sorrow, braving the many glances in her direction.

Before the funeral Mass, I'd gone to see Grandmother. I followed her as she hobbled to a remote corner of the courtyard where a group of lilac bushes stood in bloom.

"He planted these when we were still young," she said.

Grandmother looked drawn, perhaps from weeping. Strands of hair had come undone from her twisted bun and curled around her sagging cheeks. Her crippled body bent, she cut a half a dozen stems of lilac. One by one, she placed them in my arms. Then, as if it were an afterthought, she snipped two sprigs of white climbing roses from a nearby vine.

Back at a table in the breezeway, she pulled a few leaves off the lilac stems and snapped the thorns off the roses. She arranged two bouquets of lilac, each with a white rose, and tied them with flax twine from her pocket.

"You and Gitta put these on his coffin for me," she said.

Six men carried the coffin through the old section of the graveyard, along a gravel path shaded by chestnut trees. Life-size granite statues of guardian angels, turned a sooty gray over time, looked down benevolently on their charges beneath the earth in manicured graves. It was quiet but for the crunching steps of mourners on the gravel.

The men lowered the coffin into the freshly dug grave. They took off their top hats and, holding them to their chests, joined their wives and children.

It began as a sniveling, at first, then a scream came from behind. Heads turned as Tante Irma pushed through the crowd. Pastor Steinbach raised his palms to stop her from coming nearer. She shoved him out of her way with flailing arms. Her feet at the very edge of the grave, it looked as if she were about to throw herself onto the coffin.

"Why?. . . Why. . . did nobody tell me he was my father?"

A murmuring went through the assembly.

Mother came rushing to the gravesite. She put her arm around her younger sister's shoulders. "Calm down, Irmchen," she said.

The crowd turned quiet. Pastor Steinbach delivered the eulogy. He praised Onkel Jean for having been a God-fearing man and a pillar of the community.

Concluding the burial prayer, he mumbled, "Earth to earth, ashes to ashes," as he pitched three spades of soil onto the casket.

Starting with Onkel Jean's family, the mourners filed past. Spadeful after spadeful of earth thudded on top of the coffin. Mother held Gitta's hand and mine, until it was our turn. *"Tschüss, Jean.* – Bye, Jean," Mother said quietly. First Gitta, then I, each tossed a bouquet of purple lilacs with a single sprig of white roses into the grave.

What had been suspected and rumored in the town for more than thirty years, came finally into light with Onkel Jean's passing. It was as if he had wanted it that way. As if, upon his death, he had wanted to say: *This is how it was.*

Mother made the discovery that began the actual unraveling. She went to Onkel Jean's house the morning after he had died.

"I opened the cellar door and walked down the steps. God only knows why," she said afterwards, to explain what, inexplicably, had prompted her to go into the cellar. At the bottom of the staircase, tucked behind a loose brick in the wall, she'd uncovered a copy of Onkel Jean's will, neatly rolled up. Grandfather called it her uncanny sense and, while Onkel Jean had wanted the truth to be known, it appeared, Grandfather probably would have preferred if none of it had ever been revealed.

The will designated Mother's younger siblings, Irma and Ernst, as heirs of Onkel Jean's substantial estate. Onkel Jean's brothers contested the will, but lost the case in a drawn-out court battle.

In the coming days, Mother would recount more of the particulars that had transpired. On the morning of the funeral, she had told her sister, Irma, what she had come to intuit for many years: that Irma and Ernst were not Grandfather's biological children but the progeny of an extramarital love affair between Grandmother and Onkel Jean. Reading the will the day after Onkel Jean had died, an uneasy fog had lifted from her childhood memories of certain exchanges between their mother and Onkel Jean as well as later conversations she'd overheard between them. They had made her feel oddly uneasy, but their significance had eluded her until she read the will.

According to Mother, the two sisters had looked at themselves in the mirror side by side. For the first time that morning, they noticed Tante Irma's strong physical resemblance to Onkel Jean – the slight flare of the nostrils, the wide-set eyes, the shortsightedness that ran in his family but not in Grandfather's.

Tante Irma is supposed to have asked Grandmother on the day of the funeral whether it was true that Onkel Jean was her birthfather. Grandmother is supposed to have said, "How dare you ask!. . . Have I not been punished enough with an illness that made a cripple of me?"

Asked the same question that day by Tante Irma, Grandfather claimed not to have known of his wife's indiscretion, nor that he had raised two children of another man's blood. "Luise is a good woman," he'd said, defiantly. But he did threaten that, unless Irma and Ernst shared their windfall inheritance with their older sister, my mother, he would change his will in favor of her as his sole heir.

The estate was settled the following year. According to my grandfather's wishes and because of the goodwill of Irma and Ernst, we moved from our flat on the corner into Onkel Jean's house, halfway down the block.

The pear tree was the first of the fruit trees to be felled. It was a sad day for Gitta and me. We'd both swung from its lower branches. Gitta, more daring than I, had climbed way up into the crown, picking the odd pear in the near barren tree. After it was cut down, we counted a hundred and seven rings in the trunk, recording its age. An unsettling nakedness now exposed the house. Soon, Mother had its weathered brick façade resurfaced with a coating of eggshell colored stucco, like many of the older homes in the neighborhood. In the thriving post-war economy, it was a renewal and, at the same time, a distancing from what was old and past. A straight gravel driveway replaced the time-trenched foot paths that wound to the front door from all directions. Over the years, the fruit trees – too old or sick to bear – were cut down, their roots yanked from the ground. They made room for brick-bordered flower beds, a vegetable garden and lawns. A lone cherry tree in a prominent place behind the house was spared. "Onkel Jean's pride," Mother said of it. It continued to bear its ample yield for all the years I remember.

These would be the early steps in a project Mother undertook to transform a plain house in an orchard to a suburban home on immaculately maintained grounds. It would take Mother most of her lifetime to complete.

Even under the weight of scandal, Grandmother did not relinquish her role at the hub of her world. From her wicker chair next to the cooking stove, she continued to rule her household. She ran things in the way she always had. She doted on her grandchildren with generous treats and her permissive love. Women stopped in for gossip. Tradesmen brought their deliveries. She kept silent when Grandfather took up with the young woman who did the housework. No one would have guessed that her spirit was broken.

How I loved Grandmother! Her courage and her pride. Even the silence with which she protected Onkel Jean and their love affair. She gave no reasons, no excuses. She did not apologize. She never tried to defend herself, neither in the court of her family nor in the court of the town.

She stood by what she had done. Unflinchingly, she had come to the front door of her house to wish Onkel Jean farewell. That was the gesture I admired most. I became her silent ally. I responded to her complex nature – it provided comfort for my own.

34

A sea of early green wheat streaked past the train, interspersed with the flickering shadows cast by occasional rows of poplars, then a farmhouse not far from the tracks. The clatter of train wheels reverberated in my head, exacerbating the question that was tormenting me: would my face ever be right again?

The clatter intensified when the train rumbled into the city, where soot-stained brick buildings close to the tracks reflected and amplified the sound. Their proximity darkened the window, now mirroring my face. It was distorted, the corner of the left side of my mouth turned down, my left eyelid drooping.

It had been that way since the day before. A sagging sensation across the left side of my face and a numbness had distracted me during class all morning. It was awkward to speak or chew or smile. I looked at myself in the girl's bathroom mirror. My left eye didn't blink. Raising my brow, the left side of my forehead remained motionless while the other frowned. I tried to whistle. Only a soundless stream of air escaped from my lopsided, pursed lips.

One of the boys, the most annoying tease in our class, poked fun at me when he saw me during recess. "What's with that twisted face of yours?" he said. But most of my classmates made no mention of it.

"Good gracious, you must have gotten caught in a draft," Grandmother said, when I stopped by at her house after school. If she was concerned, she had masked it, quickly adding, "You better take that crooked smile to the doctor."

Before I ate my lunch, before even going home to show Mother, I went to Dr. Siepe's office a few doors from Grandmother's house.

"That's something for Dr. M to look at. The nerve specialist in

Neuss," he said.

"Will it go away?" I asked, already convinced that it was permanent.

"He'll figure something out."

When he handed me the referral slip, I looked for the good-natured glint in his eyes that was his trademark. It wasn't there.

Mother showed greater concern than Grandmother had. She looked alarmed when I came home after my visit with Dr. Siepe, and consulted her medical book.

"I can't find anything," she said, nervously. "It must be something rare, especially for a thirteen-year old. I want you to go see that nerve specialist right away."

I decided to count my steps from the station ticket taker's gate to Dr. M's office. If I arrived on an even number, I would be cured; if I arrived on an odd number, my condition would be permanent. It was more than a game or a distraction; it was a way to influence fate and affect the certainty of a bad outcome,

1, 2, 3, 4, 5, I began, and walked up the main shopping street. It was easy to keep track of the numbers at first, but when I reached double and then triple digits, it required every bit of concentration.

At the corner with the milliner's shop where Mother bought her hats, I took a shortcut across the farmers' market on the *Quirinus Münster Platz,* the basilica square, where the vendors were taking down their canvas covers for the day. I walked down a windy cobblestone alley, past shop windows displaying all manner of religious mementos, from carved crucifixes and rosaries to statuaries of saints and scale replicas of the basilica, the city's landmark. I came to where it dead-ended at the *Markt,* a busy street, next to the concert hall – still called the *Zeughaus,* after its medieval use as an arsenal. On the other side was a long row of attached, three-story buildings.

"3,597, 3,597, 3,597," I repeated rapidly as I stopped for an opening in the traffic. But it didn't let up. Cars continued to whoosh by. It took a long time of impatient waiting, until I found the courage to cross to the center, stopping there until I could make a quick run to the sidewalk on the other side.

I walked past two or three buildings in the direction of the city hall, and came to *Markt 33,* the address on the referral slip. A white enamel sign on the wall next to the entrance door read: *Dr. med. Walter M, Nervenarzt;* the then current term for neurologist, which literally translates to *nerve doctor.* Listed below that were the office hours in the mornings and afternoons, and the words *Alle Kassen,* insurance accepted.

3,597 – I remembered with a jolt. But that was on the other side of the street. I had forgotten to count. It was a bad omen.

I opened and closed the heavy front door to *Markt* 33. An open door at the end of a tunnel-like corridor led into a good-size room, where a number of men and women – all of them older – sat waiting in wooden chairs along the walls. A low wattage floor lamp dimly illuminated one corner. Filtered light came through a tall frosted glass window, obscuring the view to the street but for the shadowy shapes of cars streaking by.

I sat down in the only empty seat. I took stock of all the other patients as I tried to memorize their faces, so I would not miss my turn. Next to me was a side table with an array of magazines, their covers hidden under drab brown dust jackets. I leafed through several, but the thought of my appointment with Dr. M kept me distracted.

Everyone sat stiffly in their chairs, except for one man who, at brief intervals, jerked his head and let out small, high-pitched barks. No one took notice of anyone else, not even of the barking man whose bizarre behavior fascinated me. I gawked at him, looking away sheepishly when it seemed that his fixed gaze turned toward me.

After only a few minutes, Dr. M appeared in the inner office doorway and nodded to the departing patient. Of slender build and medium height, Dr. M was wearing a white coat. He kept his hand on the polished brass handle as he scanned the room. "Next patient, please," he said. I felt his eyes on me for a brief moment.

A woman with a floral headscarf, double-knotted under her chin, got up. She noisily collected her belongings and followed him into the consultation room. Muffled sounds came from behind the closed door. Then, after another door fell shut, it was quiet again but for the barking hiccups of the jerking man.

Not long after, Dr. M appeared again, and then again and again, as he released the previous patient and asked the next one in.

More people arrived at intervals. Over an hour must have passed. Everyone who had been there before me had been seen. It was my turn.

"Next patient, please," Dr. M said in the same calm voice.

The room we entered – an ante-room, as seemed – was cramped with all manner of medical apparatus along the walls. A large black-leather-covered table stood in the center. A strong antiseptic odor permeated the air. Minimal light came through a partially shuttered window.

Dr. M ushered me into an adjoining room. Here, sunlight spilled in through tall windows, covered with tightly gathered muslin curtains. French doors opened into a lush, walled-in garden. Everything in the room looked fastidiously organized; everything seemed to have its place. The desk was spare with only a blotter and a gray metal box, its lid open. A stack of index cards was inside. Against the wall stood a weighing scale and, next to it, a contraption, not unlike a dental chair, with numerous attachments.

Dr. M turned to face me. "You've come to see me on such a gorgeous day. I bet you'd rather be at the swimming hole with friends," he said. "That's where my sons are, twins about your age."

"Yes," I answered. I was feeling awkward.

Dr. M said nothing about my crooked face, as if he hadn't noticed.

He sat down in a swivel chair behind his desk. Unscrewing the top of his fountain pen, he asked for my personal data – name, date of birth, address, what kind of insurance coverage I had. My voice trembled as I gave him the information. He recorded it on a large index card in his neatly scripted hand, together with the date of my visit, the first in a series of two every week over the next nine months. On all subsequent visits, he would add another notation.

Dr. M placed his hand lightly on my shoulder, guiding me to the seat that was part of the apparatus against the wall.

"Let's see," he said as he sat down on a tall stool facing me. He focused on my face from behind metal-rimmed spectacles, whose bridge had worn an indentation into his finely chiseled nose.

He instructed me to attempt various facial movements. "Purse your lips." "Close your eyes." "Raise your brows." "Smile." "Scrunch up your face as tightly as you can." None of which I was able to perform without my face twisting hopelessly out of kilter.

"Now wink at me, one eye at a time." Dr. M's tone changed to playful. The idea of winking at him made me giggle. Demonstrating, he blinked one eye, then the other.

"I can't," I said. Still giggling, I covered the lower part of my face with one hand. He took my wrist and, giving it a friendly squeeze, put it on my lap, as if to reassure me that I didn't need to hide or, perhaps, that things were not as bad as I thought.

He leaned back, his expression serious, though not alarmed. "What you have is Bell's palsy, an inflammation of the nerves that causes a paralysis of the muscles in one side of your face." Sunlight sparkled on the lenses of his glasses, preventing me from seeing his eyes. "Not the kind of thing one would expect in a thirteen-year-old, but we'll fix it, over time." Dr. M stroked my head.

I felt reassured. Dr. M had proved wrong the gloomy forecast of my superstitious scheme of counting steps. He would cure me.

Treatment began the same day, a procedure which involved what Dr. M described as *electrical shock stimulus.* The term itself was daunting enough. But even when, after repeated visits, I knew what to expect, I dreaded each application, just as I did the first one.

Sitting in the same seat every visit and holding a metal device in my left hand, I fought the reflex to pull away as Dr. M placed a wet implement on my face. It sent an electric impulse through my body. Sometimes, he seemed satisfied with the intensity of the spastic motion it produced; other times, he adjusted the controls up or down. Waiting for the next discharge, I'd stiffen up and hold my breath.

"It won't be long," he tried to comfort me, dabbing the left side of my face systematically. Afterwards, he dabbed my cheek and forehead with a hand towel.

"Well done, my girl," he'd say at the end of each session, patting my back to underscore his praise.

Nevertheless, I looked forward to my appointments on Tuesday and Thursday afternoons. A few weeks into the treatment, there were visible signs of improvement, worth the discomfort I had to endure. I liked the easy manner in which Dr. M related to me. I believed that I mattered to him. After most visits, he took time for conversation. He asked questions about school. Did I have any favorite subjects? Or did I excel in all of them?

Sometimes, he showed me illustrations in medical books and explained the functions of the human brain and nervous system.

"Have you ever thought of becoming a doctor?" he once asked.

"My school doesn't offer Latin," I said.

"What a shame! That of course is a prerequisite."

I felt honored, even flattered, when he spoke about his personal life: his student years at the University of Tübingen where he received his medical degree; that he was divorced; how, at 49, he still felt passionate about fast cars.

"If we can work it out, I'll take you for a ride in my Porsche," he once promised.

He asked about my father. "What kind of work did he do?"

"He was department head at *Rheinland,*" I answered.

"A fine insurance company," he said, "The oldest and most renowned in the area."

He asked about Mother. "Hasn't she found a good stepfather for you yet?"

"No." I hoped he wouldn't pursue the subject.

"And your sister, is she as pretty as you?" His question made me blush and cover my crooked mouth.

On my way home, I sometimes daydreamed about Dr. M marrying Mother. How I would have liked him to be my stepfather!

The visits always took the same course: first the treatment, then time spent talking. It changed one day, after perhaps two months of regular appointments, when he didn't start up a conversation.

His tone was serious when he said, "We need to do a physical examination."

He instructed me to take off my clothes behind a folding screen. "Everything, except for your underwear and socks."

"Step on the scale," he said after I emerged undressed, my arms crossed over my chest. He slid the counterweight increment by increment, until the level hung in perfect balance. He noted my weight on the index card. He measured my height, noting it as well.

I felt self-conscious standing naked in the room, but Dr. M's kind smile put me at ease. I watched him position the ivory-colored earpieces of his stethoscope in his ears. He rubbed the sound disk in the palm of his hand. "It'll be a bit cold," he said, placing it on my chest just below the collarbone. Goose bumps rose on my skin and vanished again. I stood facing the windows, at a sideways angle to Dr. M, who sat on the corner of his desk.

Almost grazing the windowpanes were leaves from a large philodendron bush. Delicately hued moss clung to the cement filled grooves of the brick wall, atop which clear and green colored glass shards caught the end-of-summer light here and there.

"Inhale deeply," Dr. M said. I felt my chest rise and, at the periphery of my vision, could see the small mounds of my developing breasts.

"Now hold your breath," he said. After a few seconds of listening to my heartbeat, he asked me to exhale. Repeating his instructions, he moved the sound disc, no longer cold to the touch, all over my chest, my upper back, then over my chest again.

Dr. M removed the tips of the stethoscope from his ears and rested the flexible tubes around his neck. The sound disc dangled on the front of his buttoned-up, white coat. His voice sounded as if coming from a distance. "Did you know you have a heart murmur?" he asked.

"No, I didn't," I said.

I avoided meeting his eyes.

It had been a hot day, and it was still balmy when I got home late in the afternoon. I found Mother sitting on the back terrace, an empty coffee cup on the small table next to her chair. She put her embroidery on her lap and scrutinized my face to assess the progress.

"It's getting there," she said, pleased.

I told her about the examination.

"You're seeing him for a paralysis. Why would he check your heart?" she asked. An expression, probing and accusing at the same time, flitted over her face. It rekindled the unease I had felt in Dr. M's office.

"I have a heart murmur," I said, welcoming the opportunity to change her focus.

"*Wie könnte das sein?* – How could that be?" She was not expecting an answer, not from me. Visibly agitated, she rushed upstairs. She came back with a medical book she kept in the drawer of her bedside table. Her hands leafed nervously through the pages, until she found the passage she was looking for.

Mother looked up, her composure regained. She closed the book with a sense of victory.

"It's pretty common. Not much to worry about," she said.

I believed her.

I had escaped Mother's further query. I reassured myself that nothing improper had occurred in Dr. M's consultation room. All he had done was examine my heart.

What happened during my next appointment set the precedent for every appointment thereafter. Following the treatment, Dr. M instructed me to undress behind the folding screen, then step on the weighing scales.

He noted my weight on the index card, then replaced his fountain pen in the breast pocket of his white coat. He sat on the corner of his desk, and, taking me by both arms, positioned me at a sideways angle to himself, the garden in my line of vision. He rubbed the sound disc of the stethoscope in his palm. He placed it on my chest and, moving it around methodically, listened to my heartbeat. He told me when to breathe in, when to hold my breath, and when to breathe out, just as he had during the initial examination.

Pausing, he removed the stethoscope and his spectacles, folded them neatly and placed them on top of the index card on the desk – the silent prelude to what came next. He pressed me against his inner thigh. I could feel the tensed muscles of his legs. He waited briefly, then began kneading my small breasts with the tips of his fingers. Slowly. Tenderly. My arms hung limply from the shoulder joints. My eyes fixed on a point outside the French doors, on a brick in the garden wall, a single leaf, or a cloud drifting past in the sky. I could hear Dr. M's breathing and the ticking of his watch marking the unbearably slow passage of time, and a silence whooshing in my ears as he lowered his face to my chest. I felt his breath, warm on my skin, before his tongue touched the soft-pink around the tips of my breasts. He took my hand and laid it near the top of his inner thigh. It lay weightlessly on his starched, white coat.

It was over. I stepped behind the folding screen to put my clothes back on. I warded off any misgivings before acknowledging what they were, except for a sensation of revulsion and shame that would not leave. When I returned, fully dressed, my legs felt heavy, as if I were walking up a catwalk with a crowd watching.

A smile registered on Dr. M's tanned face. It was caring, reassuring, and almost succeeded at putting my mind at ease, but for some imperceptible gnawing behind my navel.

Just as I accepted the discomfort of electrical charges jolting my body, I submitted to Dr. M's fondling as inseparable from his otherwise fatherly demonstrations of kindness. I never faulted him for his advances, at the same time that I knew that what he was doing was wrong. Although I dreaded them, I believed that I was a party to an intimacy to which I contributed. I felt ashamed. I decided that he was responding to the seductive nature of my budding womanhood. There were boys in my class who had crushes on me. That was different. I had noticed, too, the looks I would occasionally draw from some adult men. Those would embarrass me.

My own shame compelled me to secrecy. Dr. M did not have to suggest it. He never did. He could count on me.

I left my encounters with Dr. M closeted in the consultation room. I dissociated from them. Once I stepped outside, I did not think about them. I kept my appointments faithfully. My recovery continued to progress.

When I showed Mother a bottle of *Delial* suntan lotion that Dr. M had given to me, I had not anticipated a worrisome, let alone accusatory, response.

"Why would your doctor give you an expensive bottle of suntan lotion? And why would you accept such a gift?" she asked, her voice leaving no doubt that this was a serious breach.

My impulse to show her his gift had been innocent enough. I had wanted her to know that I was special to Dr. M. I had not realized it could be used to construe that something outside of the ordinary doctor-patient relationship was occurring.

I met her suggestion of impropriety with indignation, "What's wrong with it?"

"Is anything inappropriate going on?" she countered, as if her question didn't require further explanation.

"No," I said. My answer, although a lie, carried the weight of a truth, even to myself.

Mother wanted to believe me. She dropped the subject.

Not long after my 14th birthday in the spring of the following year, I went to Dr. M's office for my final appointment. It, too, took place in the accustomed order: treatment, examination, and the inevitable fondling.

After I'd gotten dressed, he asked me to step in front of the mirror that hung above the washbasin. He stepped behind me. Too shy to look in the mirror, I lowered my gaze. He clasped my head between both his hands and raised it, so my eyes would meet both of our reflections in the mirror. I laughed and, out of habit to hide my crooked mouth, covered it. He pulled my hand away, just as he had done during the initial visit.

"You don't have to do that any longer," he said, "Show me your beautiful smile."

At the door, he patted my cheek, the one that had been paralyzed. "Come back to see me. I'll be here any time you need me."

I walked out through the crowded waiting room. I let the entrance door fall in its lock and stepped on to the sidewalk.

It was drizzling. Cars whooshed past me on the slick pavement. A fine spray of rain moistened my face and hair. I took a circuitous route to the train station, idling along the busy main street and stopping to look at window displays. I bought a small bag of roasted almonds from an outdoor vendor. I munched on them until every last one was gone. Then it was so late that I was in danger of missing my train.

I presented my train ticket at the gate. I ran to the end of the tunnel and up the stairs to Platform 5, taking two and three steps at a time. The stationmaster's whistle blew for the five o'clock train to leave. The locomotive let out a steaming hiss as it started to pull away slowly. Running along the train, I jumped onto a door step and opened the door.

35

The number of students in our class – twenty-two girls and twenty boys – remained constant, for the most part, from year to year.

In our third year, Gisela transferred to another high school; two boys and one girl transferred back into their former primary school, when they couldn't keep up with the academic standards of the secondary school.

One boy died of a brain tumor. I recall his sickly, pale complexion and large, deep-set eyes, but not his name.

Irmgard Holtz left Germany at the beginning of our third year, when her family emigrated to America. Her stepfather – her biological father had been killed in the war – had taken a position as a scientist with a chemical company in Pittsburgh, Pennsylvania. Irmgard's family home had been bombed during the war. In the ensuing fire, Irmgard had suffered burn injuries that had left the right side of her face and neck badly scarred. She tried to hide her disfigurement, with a scarf, with her hand covering it, or by keeping her head turned a certain way, always presenting her pretty side.

After she'd left, she sent letters to our class with rhapsodic descriptions of life in America. Most families, she reported, owned not just one, but two cars, and there was a television set in every living room – a luxury still years away for us, in Germany.

At thirteen, Irmgard was in her final year of American junior high school before she would start high school in the autumn. It was the same progression for all students, she wrote, regardless of level of performance. There were no entrance exams for students in the US, as there were in the German system, which consisted of two separate tracks after four years of primary school. German students then either continued in the primary school system for another four years –

followed by apprenticeships in the trades – or they transferred into six- or eight-year secondary schools – tracks that would lead toward the professions and higher education.

In one letter, Irmgard boasted that boys and girls went out "on dates" – a term for which there wasn't even a German equivalent – and that many "went steady" – unthinkable in an environment that discouraged boys and girls from spending time together outside of the classroom

As time went on, a foreignness crept into the language in her letters. Often, an English word slipped into her accounts, or she fell into odd-sounding syntax. Eventually, the letters stopped coming at all.

I sometimes thought about Irmgard in a foreign country, among people whose sense of home and history she did not share. The idea of being surrounded by a language that, at least initially, she did not speak, except in its most rudimentary form, created a sense of loneliness, of being out of place. I would feel the same ache, then, that I would feel years later, when I myself had emigrated to America.

I didn't know, then, that even after formally learning English myself – studying it first in high school, then in college, and, later, speaking it daily while living in England and in America for decades – the gaps I would experience in both languages, English and German, would remain for me an ache and the source of a conflict too deep to reconcile. I would never be able to embrace the English language fully and, at the same time, I would suffer the partial loss of my mother tongue. It would be as if I had been robbed of what was *home* to my most profound experience, the German language – a loss that I would feel deeper than having left behind the familiar, physical place where I was born and raised. Nothing else defined my Germanness more than the language I so loved.

New students transferring into our school were just as rare as students leaving. Dieter Wegener and his younger brother Wolfgang were the first. They appeared in our chemistry class, unannounced, on a day in the early summer in our third year. Shorter than Wolfgang, who had the build of an athlete and would become the top player of the boys' soccer team, Dieter had the look of a dreamer. Neither of them were shy by nature, and would soon find their place among our classmates.

I hadn't spoken to either one of them when, after recess within just days of their arrival, I noticed Dieter edging his way next to me in the crowded hallway. All of us were pushing and shoving to hang our jackets on a row of hooks outside the basement classroom.

"*Ich mag dich.* – I like you," he said, his head lowered and cocked ever so slightly, a mannerism I would learn was characteristic of him.

The chatter of forty or so teenagers in the low-ceilinged hallway almost smothered his words.

Nobody had ever been this forward with me. The color in my face rising, I pretended that I had not heard him and turned away. None of the class was paying attention, not to his brazen remark or to my self-conscious blushing.

Dismissive as I tried to be of Dieter's audacity, his words went on tumbling through my mind, even after I was in my seat, and Herr Paschek had begun his discussion of chemical formulae.

Dieter was standing outside the schoolyard gate after our last class that day. I passed him with studied indifference, swinging my school bag ever so slightly.

"I'll walk with you to the train station," he said, ignoring, or misconstruing, my show of snubbing him.

"No, you won't."

I kept on walking. So did Dieter, right next to me, my school bag between us.

Neither my standoffishness nor my curt replies to anything he asked seemed to thwart his determination to engage me in conversation.

Nor did my behavior deter him from walking to the station with me that day, the next day and the next day and the next day.

Over time, I was persuaded by his intelligence, his interest in culture and history that far exceeded mine. He challenged my mind. I reasoned that our friendship was what in those days was called *platonic* – not romantic – and therefore above suspicion.

Growing up in a city had made Dieter more sophisticated than those of us who were raised in a provincial environment. At fifteen, he was one of the oldest students in our class and more than two years my senior.

His family had been bombed out in Berlin. They had fled to the West after the war and settled south of us, in Marburg, where they lived for several years. Then the promise of a better job for his father had brought them to the Rhineland.

Dieter's passion was classical music. There wasn't a composition, from Bach to Beethoven to Wagner, that he couldn't identify. Even more impressive was his ability to hum just about everything in the classical repertoire. It had been his childhood dream to become a conductor.

"History is okay, too. Maybe that will be my future," he once told me, explaining how the war had interrupted his early aspirations. Dieter's parents realized his musical talent, but in the post-war struggle to reestablish themselves, a piano and piano lessons were beyond their means. "But," Dieter elaborated, "playing the piano is essential for a conductor. You have to start early, and it's too late now."

"What was your father's rank in the war?" Dieter asked me. It was the day that World War II had been the short lesson in our history class. Dr. Kirchfeld had skimmed the period of the Third Reich, encapsulating it in three sentences, just as he had in previous years: "In 1933, Adolf Hitler came into power. On September 1st, 1939, World War II broke out. It ended in Germany's capitulation on May 8th, 1945."

The brevity of the lesson made it seem less significant than all the other wars in German history Dr. Kirchfeld had discussed at length. Likewise, an apparent lack of relevance placed the war into an obscure era, and created a distance between it and the present. It was almost as if it had never happened.

Dieter and I had barely left the school grounds, when Dieter asked the question. It perplexed me. The military ranks of our fathers or the war, for that matter, had never been topics of discussion among any of us. The war had receded into history. It no longer seemed to impact our immediate lives. Its aftermath had become all but invisible. Our eyes had grown accustomed to pockets of ruins, like the rubble left overgrown near the Delrath train station and other such eyesores in the cities. Shortages had become a thing of the past. What would become known as *das deutscheWirtschaftswunder,* the German economic miracle, was already in full swing. In conversation, personal events were often referred to as having occurred "during the war" or "before the war" or "after the war," with nearly the same significance as B. C. and A. D. My father barely had a presence in my thoughts, except when something triggered the memory of his loss.

"*Er war Unteroffizier in der Infanterie.* – He was a sergeant in the Infantry," I said.

Perhaps, Dieter's question was not one to which he really wanted or expected an answer; perhaps it was only meant to make a provocative statement, something he delighted in doing.

"They were all complicit in the system, no matter what their ranks. Every one of them. Our mothers, too." he said.

I was shocked by the outrageousness of his indictment.

"That's just not so," I said.

At the same time that I contradicted him, I sensed that here was a plausible explanation for the pervasive silence around the war. I realized, then, that I had taken that silence for granted and had even perpetuated it: never once had it occurred to me to query Mother or my grandparents about it, or to raise my hand in our history class to ask further questions.

I fell silent. We were passing Gisela's old house, still unoccupied, it appeared. I remembered that it was there, when her father had spoken about the war, that I had felt first inklings of its wrongfulness. I'd left all unease about it behind, then. Now it had come back to haunt me.

Dieter said, "Why do you think they don't teach us about the war or about the time leading up to it?" He paused, as if waiting for my answer. Then he answered it himself, "Because our teachers, like everyone else, were part of the system. Think of it – it was mandatory for educators to join the Party if they wanted to keep their jobs. Even if they weren't committed Nazis. But believe me, most of them were."

I felt a surge of rage and a desire to speak up against such generalization. I wanted to defend my own mother and father. "You don't know that," I said.

"There's no doubt about it," he said, with a tone of finality.

Still, fighting to win the argument and, by winning it, have the last word, I said, "I'd say it's because the text books covering those

times haven't been written yet." I thought of myself as very smart at
that moment.

To my surprise, Dieter agreed, "You're right. But that's not all."

He put his index finger on my lips. His tone as provocative as
his gesture, he said, "It is the history of the Third Reich that has yet
to be written."

Dieter and his brother had been at our school for over a year. The
friendship between Dieter and me grew, even though our time together
outside of the classroom did not extend beyond walking to the train
station in the afternoon. Sometimes, other commuter students joined us
on our walks, but mostly, it was just the two of us.

Filing through the Dormagen ticket taker's gate one morning, I felt a tug
at my sleeve, and Dieter slipping an envelope into my hand.

"I wrote to you," he said.

I didn't open Dieter's letter until the middle of math class later in
the day, when, demonstrating algebraic equations on the blackboard,
Fräulein Plönis' back was turned to the class.

An das Mädchen mit den grünen Augen! – To the girl with the green
eyes! the letter began. It told of our encounters, starting with him as the
new boy at our school the previous spring; how he had come calling at
my house just a few weeks earlier, unannounced, and presented my
mother with a bouquet of flowers; our walks to the train station; Herr
Erdmann, the principal, and a known ex-Nazi, chastising us when we
were caught talking at a street corner. Dieter's facts mostly matched how
I, too, recalled our experiences together, until it came to his version of
what had happened on a recent Sunday afternoon. Four of us, Renate
with Heinz Wilhelm Orfgen, who was her unrequited heartthrob, and
Dieter with me had gone to see *The Rose Tattoo* at the Dormagen movie
theater. It was true, Dieter had sat next to me. But it infuriated me to
read that, in his telling, we had held hands; in reality, I had pulled away
as soon as I felt his sweaty palm on my wrist.

I shoved the letter into my math notebook. I stared at the numbers
and symbols on the blackboard and heard Fräulein Plönis' distant
explanations. *To the girl with the green eyes!* The words swirled through

my head. I felt flattered. My vanity had been stroked. But I felt shabby, too, for I knew I would never feel the same for Dieter. We went for *types* in those days, and Dieter's bookish looks were a far cry from those of the dimple-chinned O. W. Fischer, my film idol since I'd seen him in *Tausend rote Rosen blüh'n,* its English title *A Thousand Red Roses Bloom,* the year before. Although I'd suspected from the day Dieter approached me in the hallway, that he had a romantic interest in me, I made believe that, if I didn't respond likewise and treated him as just the friend he was in my eyes, it would go away or didn't exist. Now I was in a bind, asking myself whether I'd led him on by not having discouraged him enough.

I avoided Dieter as we changed classrooms and during recess in the schoolyard that day. Our walk to the station after school seemed to go on forever. We spoke very little. Neither of us broached the subject of the letter. I was sure that he was waiting for a reaction from me. I didn't have one, at least not one that I was eager to voice.

By the time we arrived at the station, the unease and the silence between us had grown unbearable. Our train was still a few minutes away. We walked behind the ticket office and sat down next to each other in a damp patch of grass, a good distance between us.

"Will you answer my letter?" Dieter asked.

"No."

"Why not," he persisted.

"I can't."

Then, in that forward manner that was typical of him, he said, *"Aber du magst mich doch auch, oder?* – But you like me, too, don't you?"

I didn't know how to say it any other way, or didn't try. I simply spilled out what I felt. "As a platonic friend, yes. . . In other ways, no."

He turned away from me. We remained sitting in the grass for another moment, both of us silent. Dieter was the first to get up. He extended his hand and pulled me to my feet. I avoided looking at him. My hands smoothed the back of my damp coat. I was waiting for something, something Dieter might say, or something I might say, to mend things. But what I had said remained suspended between us. It couldn't be taken back. It couldn't be changed. Not even the rumbling sound of the train pulling into the station could obliterate it.

Sitting across from each other at the open window of the

compartment, curtains flapping in the cross-draught, Dieter said, "I like you anyway."

Decades later, Dieter and I reminisced about those early years of our friendship. "Your response to that love letter I wrote to you was devastating. Such a blow to my budding manhood," he said, "I remember it word for word."

I cringed, remembering it, also.

"How cruel it must have sounded."

"Even now, it still stings," he said.

"Though in retrospect, wouldn't you say, that was the moment our friendship truly began?" I was hoping he would agree that the end justified the means.

"I felt one way. You felt another. It's still that way – and it doesn't matter."

36

Most of the girls in our class liked arias. Many had a repertoire and could sing the first one or two stanzas from famous operas and operettas. We favored those with romantic storylines. Like popular songs, arias were part of the culture. We'd heard our mothers and grandmothers sing them. We'd heard them on the radio. None of our classmates, however, except for Dieter and his brother, had ever actually been to the opera. When the announcement was made that our class would attend a matinée performance of Mozart's *Die Zauberflöte, The Magic Flute,* it was received with resounding applause, mainly by the girls.

During the weeks before the much-anticipated event, Herr Richter, our music teacher – a meek little man who looked like the step-ladder librarian in the Carl Spitzweg painting – introduced us to the opera. He discussed the structure of Mozart's score and led us through the story of the libretto. We memorized the texts of the major arias and some of the choral pieces as well. Those with the best voices were asked to sing solo in front of the class. I was not one of them.

But I did participate in the discussion about what to wear for the occasion. We all agreed that long dresses, traditionally associated with the opera, would be too formal for an afternoon fieldtrip and, anyway, would look pretentious on teenagers. A few argued in favor of combinations of black-and-white, which was a kind of dress code for attending live theater in those days. We all wanted to look fashionable.

Mother suggested her cream-colored silk blouse, just slightly large on me, and her light brown suede clutch. I settled for the idea, as it came with the promise of shopping for a new skirt and shoes in Cologne.

We took the train to Cologne and walked past the *Dom,* the cathedral, up *Hohe Straße.* In the display window of one of the first boutiques we came to, I spied a flared skirt on a mannequin. "Let's go try it on," Mother said. A bell rang softly as we opened the door, alerting

the saleswoman. She showed us the skirt in my size. It was made of a
fine wool fabric, green plaid on light gray, with large sewn-on pockets.
Mother quibbled that it was too casual for the opera, but relented when
I argued that it was versatile. At Salamander, a shoe shop known for its
solid quality, we selected a pair of brown flats with button-down straps
that matched Mother's clutch. I never tired of either skirt or shoes. They
remained favorites until I outgrew them.

Mother looked at me impishly. "Close your eyes," she said, and,
taking my hand playfully, took me to a lingerie shop next door to
Salamander. I was thrilled when I realized that she was going to buy a
pair of silk stockings for me, my first.

Before taking the late afternoon train home, we stopped at *Café
Reichard*, with its magnificent view of the Cathedral. At fourteen, I was
of coffee-drinking age, and, like Mother, ordered a small pot, along with
Schwarzwälder Kirschtorte, a pastry something like Black Forest Cake,
from the bakery display case.

A chartered bus took us to the city of Reydt, Herr Richter chaperoning
us. We assembled on the steps of the columned, neo-classical opera
house, along with busloads of students from surrounding areas, then
filed into the elegant mahogany paneled, red-carpeted foyer.

The girls, putting on grown-up airs, clutched their pocketbooks
under their arms. They checked the seams on their silk stockings,
alternately stretching one leg, then the other, craning their necks to see
whether they had gone crooked or runs had crawled up their legs. The
boys, in their dark suits, strutted about. A few of them mingled with the
girls and, sensing their insecurity, teased them mercilessly.

The auditorium buzzed with hundreds of high school students chatting
and laughing, competing with a cacophony of instruments tuning up.

The noise ebbed, when the conductor entered. Facing the
auditorium from his podium, he bowed ceremoniously. He turned to
the orchestra, raised his baton and held it for a moment. A last giggle
here and there, the sound of a few throats clearing. Then, it was as if we
had all stopped breathing. When the conductor gave the signal to begin,
the space swelled with the vast music of the overture.

The burgundy velvet curtain parted. It billowed lazily as it swished across the stage floor. An imposing landscape opened up: craggy rocks, trees, mountains reaching into the distance in an illusion of space. The story of Tamino and Papageno's trials and their initiation into the temple of wisdom unfolded. I was bewitched by Papageno, the colorful bird catcher, whose feathered costume evoked both man and bird, cunning and naïve.

As each aria ascended to another crest, the words and melody touched their memorized counterparts inside me, so that every note and every word felt as if they had originated in me.

The mountains parted and the Queen of the Night strode into the scene. Of imposing stature, she wore a flowing, black costume, the flared hem of which swirled around her feet in a wide circle. Long, star-studded spikes radiated from her headdress and terminated in a halo-like ring. Her bosom heaved and her long fingers spread theatrically. Her voice woeful, she pleaded with Pamino to bring her comfort, then became enraged as she addressed Zarastro, the high priest, who had abducted her daughter.

I was irresistibly drawn to her majestic self-possession, how she commanded attention and dominated the stage. I followed the agile runs and leaps and trills of her soprano voice in my own throat, as it were. I wanted to hear her sing forever. I wanted to become the woman she was. Even when she was unveiled as revengeful and evil, I sympathized with her. At the same time, I sensed that I should take the side of Zarastro. Symbolizing good, he was the priest of light, but was he not also the abductor of Pamina, daughter of the Queen of the Night? When, in the final scene, good vindicated evil and the Queen of the Night was destroyed by thunder and lightning, I was caught in a strange tug of feelings.

The curtain closed. There was wild applause, gathering momentum with shouts of bravo as the performers took their bows. The shift in realities, from a fictional world to the immediacy of the moment, rescued me from my conflicted feelings.

In a discussion on the bus ride home, I argued that the Queen of the Night's rage and her vengefulness, even her deceit, were defensible, for she had acted out of a mother's love for her child. Aligning herself with sinister forces, she had pursued a noble goal: the rescue of her daughter. But misgivings continued to plague me: the Queen of the Night had touched something inexplicably dark inside me. The line between good and evil, so sharply drawn in my own thinking, had been blurred with complexity and contradiction I was unable to reconcile.

Dieter caught up with a group of us girls on the way back to the bus. He was humming the melody to Tamino's aria, *Dies Bildnis ist bezaubernd schön* – How sweet, how fair this likeness is. "That's the most popular one," he said, "But the best one is this." He pulled his chin back and puffed out the sides of his neck. A thick lock of his ash blonde hair fell across his forehead, giving him the look of the proverbial artist. Deepening his voice to a strained sounding bass, he sang, *"In diesen heil'gen Hallen, kennt man die Rache nicht,* – Within these holy portals, revenge remains unknown." He stopped at the end of the first measure and bowed. *"Encore, encore,"* a chorus of girls shouted and applauded mockingly. With a theatrical sweep of his arm, he said, "Your turn, ladies." No one took him up on his challenge.

37

"Feigling! Feigling! – Coward! Coward!" Renate and I chanted in unison. We rang our bicycle bells furiously. We wanted to embarrass the boy who was riding in our direction.

He circled around us once, then a second time. Dragging one foot on the asphalt, he slowed down until he came to a standstill. Renate and I gave each other victorious glances.

There wasn't a soul in sight, not even the odd farm vehicle. The country road stretched in a straight line to the horizon, where a cluster of houses nestled around a steepled church. Not far from us, an oak tree towered over a granite crucifix, pock-marked with time. It had been erected in memory of a young farmer who, in that very spot, had been struck dead by a lightning bolt at the turn of the century.

There was no indication of a thunderstorm brewing today. Sunlight sparkled on the spokes of our bicycle wheels.

Putting on manly airs, the boy lifted his chin.

"Meaning what?" he said.

"Just what we said. You're a coward." Renate spoke for both of us. Pointing at me, she said, "You come all the way from Nievenheim and ride past her house every day – but are too gutless to talk to her." Renate saucily lifted an eyebrow in my direction.

The boy looked caught. After a split second, he recovered his composure with a sly smile.

"Want to race?" he asked.

We took the challenge. Renate and I jumped on our bicycles and charged ahead, before the boy could finish his ready-steady-go signal. Our shoulders almost touching the handlebars, we pedaled at top speed.

We were in the lead. From behind, I could hear the whirring of the boy's bicycle wheels. Soon, I saw him out of the corner of my eye. There was a teasing tug at my carrier rack and another, harder one, at the seat, slowing me down. He pulled up next to me.

"I'll beat you," he called out, and streaked past.

Before long, a humbling distance separated Renate and me from the boy. At the road sign designating *Straberg,* the village ahead of us, he got off his bicycle. When we caught up with him, out of breath and with crimson cheeks, he was sitting in the sun-speckled shade of a quince tree, his sun-burnt arms crossed over his knees. A broad grin revealed his irregularly spaced teeth, the one distraction in his handsome face.

"Angeber! – Show-off!" I said.

The following morning, I saw the boy standing outside the ticket taker's gate, suspiciously early for his train to Neuss, where, I knew, he attended a Catholic boys' school. I leaned my school bag against the white, slatted fence, close enough for him to notice me, far enough to make it look casual. He approached me, as I hoped he would.

"G'ten Morgen," he said, and so did I. Striking a casual stance, he put one hand in his shorts pocket.

"You want to meet at the Nievenheim cemetery gate? Four o'clock this afternoon?"

I couldn't think of anything to say that wouldn't appear eager. Just in order to say something, I asked, "Renate, too?"

"Just you. Rain or shine," he said, to what must have sounded like an eager response, after all.

The best looking boy around, he was tall and well built, with a young man's downy facial hair, almost ready to shave. His good looks were a mixture of studious and athletic. He had to be smart – smarter than the boys in my school – to attend the *Quirinus Gymnasium* for boys. Priding itself on its 700-year history, with an alumni of distinguished men, it was the only high school in our region at which ancient Hebrew and Greek were taught in addition to Latin and modern foreign languages.

Nievenheim was on the other side of the train station. It shared its town hall and cemetery with Delrath. I left home early, before it was even three-thirty, taking my bicycle. It was drizzling. I rode around Nievenheim aimlessly, until, at long last, it was four o'clock. At the schoolhouse, I turned right, passed a few low-slung houses, then stopped at the boxwood hedge enclosing the cemetery. The pedestrian walk was empty, all the way to where the fields began at the end of the road. An old man, sitting rigidly on his bicycle, rode through the gate. A bouquet of spring flowers dangled from his handlebars.

Just then, the boy came bicycling out of an alley near the schoolhouse at full speed. He laughed, and teasingly stopped just short of colliding with me.

"Let's go to my house," he said.

We took our bicycles across the street to a two-story brick duplex, and left them leaning against the side wall. When he held the unlocked back door open, I stepped inside, ignoring all qualms that it might not be seemly to accept the boy's invitation. We walked down a windowless hallway, until, off to the right, a door led into a sitting room. Heavy, dark furnishings gave the room a somber ambiance. Rows of leather-bound volumes lined mahogany bookcases along one wall. Needlepoint pillows leaned stiffly on a sofa and overstuffed chairs. Where the almost room-sized Persian carpet did not cover the floor, the wood gleamed as if to defy the lack of sunlight. A floor-to-ceiling curtain of intricately patterned lace rippled in the light breeze.

The boy lifted the lid of the upright piano that stood behind the door, and sat down on the piano bench.

"I'll play something for you," he said.

The boy shuffled through a stack of sheet music and placed *Für Elise* on the music rack. I rested my elbows on the piano, the way I'd seen film divas do in the movies. But I felt self-conscious, and brought them down again, lacing my fingers in front of me.

His slender hands resting on the keyboard, the boy closed his eyes. After a moment, he began letting his fingers run over the keys, and the melody of Beethoven's music – delicate, dancelike, and agitated, in turns – filled the air. I wanted to be absorbed by it, but the sentiment of his gesture preoccupied me. I wondered if people walking past on the street might ask for whom the boy was playing? The idea pleased me. When the piece ended with its gentle repetitions, the boy laid his hands on his thighs.

"Beethoven dedicated this bagatelle to a woman, whose name may not even have been Elise, but Therese, transcribed incorrectly in an early version. Though no one knows for sure," he said.

Afterwards, we rode our bicycles along dirt roads through the fields on the far side of the cemetery. We talked about our schools, the subjects we liked, and the fact that, at fifteen, he was a year ahead of me. We talked about our siblings – his younger brother, my younger sister. He asked about my future plans. Really, I didn't have any, yet. Just to say something, I said the first thing that came to my mind, "I might go into languages," while he sounded so certain about pursuing a career in a combination of pedagogy and theology.

"There was never a question," he said. "Besides, my father was a school principal. . . in Gohr. He died last winter."

"Oh, I didn't know," I said. "I'm sorry."

"Your father, I hear, was killed in the war?"

I was reluctant to talk about my father – plagued by my own still tenuous condemnations of the war and those who had participated in it. I also sensed that to have died in the war was less respectable than having died an ordinary death.

"Yes," I said. "Near the end. Christmas – 1944."

We parted at the train station, on his side of the tracks. We shook hands to say goodbye. The boy asked, *"Sehen wir uns morgen?* – Will we see each other tomorrow?" That's what he would always say, always at the train station, on his side of tracks, which was as far as he went to take me home.

In the evening, I locked myself in my room and began the journal I would keep until the day the boy and I kissed for the first time, nine months later. On the cover page I wrote in flowery letters: *Für Dich.* – For you. The first sentence read, *We found each other.* I did not reveal the boy's name, not then, not later, and I won't reveal it now.

Through the summer of 1954 that had just begun, the autumn and winter that followed, and into early spring, we met at pre-arranged locations: at a bend on the way to the bombed-out windmill; in a lane along the Nievenheim church grounds after his violin lessons, his violin case strapped to the bicycle rack; on the back steps of the station building when the weather was fair; inside the waiting area when it rained or on sub-zero winter days; where a service road took us into the forest at the far end of Nievenheim.

I was unfamiliar with the woodlands west of us that were the boy's stomping grounds. Intimidated by their vastness, I'd only skirted the perimeters. I kept to the open country, the swimming hole, and the banks of the Rhine, where I knew my way.

I trusted the boy when he took me deep into the labyrinth of dirt roads and overgrown trails. Together, we climbed atop hunting lookouts. He taught me how to wait for deer to appear in the clearings below and watch them sniff the air for danger. The boy explained how, depending on the direction the wind carried our scent, the deer would either sprint away or graze unfazed in the undergrowth.

We spoke little as we walked our bicycles among the giant oaks and beeches. Sometimes, the boy motioned with his head to alert me to things he'd seen or heard: a rabbit scurrying into a hole; a hawk diving for its prey; an unexplained rustling in the undergrowth; a spider web caught in a ray of sunlight; a slug on the trail, revolting to my eye, a creature of beauty to him; grasses washed over in the clear water of a running stream.

Once, he said, "Even if there is no god – and I have been taught to believe there is – the divine manifests through nature. You could say, God is nature. Nature is God."

"That's how my mother rationalizes staying away from church," I said, "But you, as a future theologian, how can you say such a thing?"

Unperturbed by my criticism, he said, "It doesn't require great intelligence or dogma, not even prayer, to experience the miracle of nature. It's so immediate."

I was taken by his idea, and regarded Mother's excuse more forgivingly, though I couldn't think of a good response. It had been drizzling. He looked at me and grasped my face between his hands. He tilted my head to the sky, and his, too. "Feel that?" he said.

When sometimes his hand brushed mine, I wished it were a signal of his affection, though I suspected it was only a coincidence. The afternoon he actually put his arm around my waist and left it there, a wave of tingling passed through my body.

Walking silently along a dirt road through fields of beets, close to harvest, we each kept to our own thoughts, mine of delicious reverie, his, I hoped, were the same. We came to the overgrown ruins of the bombed-out windmill, and sat down on the remnants of a brick wall.

"What are you thinking?" I said into a silence that had grown unbearably large when, most likely, not more than a minute had passed.

Looking off toward the train station, visible under the heavy crowns of chestnut trees, he said, "It was a fluke that the windmill got struck. Actually, the Americans were aiming at the station. They missed by no more than 200 meters."

At that moment, the American bombers were of no consequence to me. I felt let down. I questioned the boy's feelings for me, even though, after that day, he always put his arm around my waist when no one was in sight.

On an afternoon in autumn later that year, the boy seemed reserved in a way I had not seen before. He didn't look at me when, rather quietly, he said, "Let's go walk along the train tracks."

We went down an access road, passed the abandoned stationmaster's house, walked beside a shady ditch full of weeds. We were long out of range of being seen from the main street, but the boy did not put his arm around my waist.

Staring at the ground in front of him, he said, "Is it true what they say about your grandmother. . . and your mother?"

This was not a question I had expected. It left no doubt what he was asking. I felt caught, my secret, exposed. I lost, all at once, all sense of the image I'd carried of myself, which did not include what the boy was alluding to. In its place rose a different view of myself – one, I suddenly realized, everyone had of me, for it really was no secret: I was the daughter and granddaughter of women who did not lead respectable lives. My grandmother, who'd had a life-long love affair with Onkel Jean; my mother, who had lived with a man, unmarried, and recently had taken a new lover.

Always, I had felt incomplete because of the father I didn't have. Now, for the first time, I saw myself as an outcast.

Maybe the boy noticed my discomfort. Still, he asked, "Why

doesn't your mother get married?"

"She would lose her war widow's pension," I said, repeating what Mother gave as her reason.

Where the road dead-ended at the brick manufacturing plant we turned back. A freight train rolled by on the near side of the tracks. Its roar filled the silence. The boy put his arm around me. I pulled away.

At the station, we shook hands. "Will we see each other tomorrow?" the boy said.

Perhaps the boy brushed off what he knew about Mother's and Grandmother's lives being so far outside the pious norms of his own mother's. Perhaps he regretted the uneasiness he had caused me. He never spoke about any of it again. We continued meeting at the same places we always had, even through the worst of the winter that followed. We bundled up and trudged through the snow or, on insufferably cold or wet days, sat side by side on a bench inside the train station.

Spring came. A day in late March. We rode our bicycles into the forest. We stopped in a sparse clearing. In the deep shade of bordering trees and undergrowth, small patches of snow had not yet melted. We found a dry place to sit in a hollow of winter-withered grass. The forest smelled of moist earth coming alive after long frosts and snow. A pale sun warmed our faces. Not a breeze moved the air. Not the call of a bird or a broken-off twig falling to the ground impinged on the silence.

The boy wrapped his arms around me. His face almost touched mine. He put his lips on my lips. They felt thin and smooth. I closed my eyes. I could smell the sweat on his face. When he pushed his tongue into my mouth, it felt soft and wet. The taste of the sun mingled in our mouths. I counted his kisses. There were seven. When he released me from his embrace, the air cooled my wet lips.

On our ride home, the boy and I withdrew into separate silences different from the stillness of the forest that had enveloped us. The inside of my mouth felt dry. My cheeks burned. His kisses still tingled on my lips. An awareness plagued me of having transgressed into adulthood before its time. The same thoughts, I assumed, were troubling him.

At the train station crossing, the boy looked away from me. On parting, he did not say what he'd always said, *Sehen wir uns morgen?*

Mother lifted her eyes from the book she was reading, a coffee cup on the small table next to her. She had a quizzical look, as if she knew what I had done, or could see the evidence on my lips, or the smudge of damp earth on my light blue skirt.

"Where were you all afternoon?" she said.

"Just out bicycle riding." My answer satisfied her.

Alone in my room, I sobbed. I opened my small *For You* journal and wrote in it for the last time: *We kissed. We crossed a boundary and took a first step into where we were not meant to go. We gambled away our love. I should have stopped us. Why didn't I? Now, there is no return.*

38

One day after school, Grandmother's chair in the kitchen was empty. For as long as I could remember, Grandmother had always been there when I came to see her, always sitting in her wicker chair next to the cooking stove. The fear that she had died smothered all thoughts of any other alternative. I called her name. There was no answer.

At last, I heard the faint sound of a man's voice. I followed it to the end of the hallway. It was coming from the sitting room. I flung the door open, and saw Grandmother leaning over the credenza, elbows resting on its marble top, head tilted toward the radio. Her large body appeared shrunk, the disparate lengths of her legs more pronounced in her bent-over stance. Seeing her this way, a painful realization come over me as, for the first time, I acknowledged to myself that Grandmother was the cripple people said she was.

She looked up and placed her index finger over her lips. The look in her eyes was both intense and impatient. A deep red flush blotched her cheeks and neck. She moved her head closer to the radio, until her left ear touched the coarse cloth covering the speaker.

An announcer was reading off a litany of names in alphabetical order. Family names, followed by first names – men's first names, all of them.

"Our soldiers. The Russians released them. Gottfried –" She broke off mid-sentence. Her words were hurriedly whispered, as if she wanted to fit them into the pause between names and not miss a single one.

Gottfried was Mother's eldest brother by three years, Grandmother's favorite son, so I gathered from the tenderness with which she told stories about him. In my memory, Onkel Gottfried was only a name and the image of a broad shouldered groom, a rose in his lapel, posing stiffly in a wedding portrait that Grandmother kept in a cigar box.

Gottfried had been drafted into the *Wehrmacht* before I was born. An infantryman, he had been deployed to the Soviet front, and had later fought in the Battle of Stalingrad. The word *Stalingrad* had an ominous ring, designating not the city after which the battle was named, but the battle itself. The bloodiest battle of all time. Hundreds of thousands on both sides had been killed under the most adverse weather conditions in the winter of 1942. By all accounts, it had been the turning point of the war. Like the word *Dresden,* which symbolized the Allied firebombing of that city and the death of tens of thousands, so *Stalingrad* was another horrific episode in the collective history.

No one in our family, least of all Grandmother, spoke openly about their hope that Gottfried might return home, except for Tante Grete, his childless wife. Tante Grete came to visit Grandmother on some Sunday afternoons. Over coffee and cake, she'd sit weeping at Grandmother's kitchen table. There had been no news from her husband since before Stalingrad, in February of 1942. But there had been no notification of his death, either. Without that proof, Gottfried's official designation was *vermisst,* missing in action.

To his wife, he was alive: on his way west; lost in the tundra, perhaps; held prisoner of war somewhere in Siberia. Grandmother urged her to be realistic. The young woman would shake her head willfully, like a child not getting her way.

"My Gottfried is alive. I will wait for him – until the day I die," she'd say, defying Grandmother and defying fate.

More than a decade had passed since the war's end. Konrad Adenauer had been elected the first Chancellor of the post-war democratic government at its inception in 1949. During a recent visit to Moscow, he had negotiated the release of all German prisoners of war still held in Soviet labor camps. Originally estimated at 90,000, by 1955 their number had dwindled to less than 10,000. The rest had been freed earlier – Gottfried's younger brother Ernst among them – or had perished of exhaustion, illness and starvation. That afternoon, while Grandmother had her ear to the radio, the names of the remaining nearly 10,000 soldiers were made public.

I tiptoed over and stood next to Grandmother. Like her, I rested my elbows on the credenza top. Name after name rang into the room, each one delivered with the same somber emphasis, separated by a moment's pause.

While *missing in action* implied a fate unknown – neither dead nor alive – suddenly there was more than just the faint prospect that Gottfried would return, but also the possible end to whatever comfort uncertainty and hope had lent.

The chain of names starting with *F* was longer, it seemed, than any of the lists beginning with the previous letters. The announcer was coming close to the place where his name, *Feinendegen, Gottfried,* belonged in the alphabetical sequence. Grandmother took my hand. She squeezed it lightly, as if to suggest that, rallying our hopes, Gottfried stood a better chance.

I followed the announcer attentively, though I began to lose my bearings when, after the shared first letter, *F,* the second and then the third were identical in a series of names: *Fechinger, Kornelius – Fechler, Josef – Fedderson, Manfred – Feinberg, Rudolf – Feininger, Wilhelm – Feldhausen, Georg – Feller, Hans. . .* The names lapsed into a fast-moving jumble.

Then it hit me: *Feinendegen, Gottfried* had been passed over. The place where his name would have been in the alphabet had come and gone. Grandmother's hand went limp as she let go of mine. She did not move or speak. Keeping her ear pressed to the speaker, she continued to listen, as though she weren't going to give up – not until the last soldier had been given his due, his moment.

The announcer had come to the *K's,* almost halfway through the alphabet. *"Kellermann, Heinrich – Kemlich, Otto . . ."* Ernst, Grandmother's youngest son, burst into the room, too late to have heard his brother's name, had it been among those broadcast. Home for his afternoon break from delivering building materials for the family business, he was not prepared to find the table empty and his mother away from the kitchen.

"There's nothing to eat in this house," he said, voice raised, fists clenched.

I moved closer to Grandmother. I was afraid of Onkel Ernst and his

unpredictable temper. I stayed away from him as much as I could. I had
seen him strike Gitta for no reason.

Ernst looked at Grandmother, then at the radio.

"Turn that damn thing off, Mother. He's dead," he said.

Grandmother straightened her body.

"How dare you! Have you forgotten that I waited three long years
for a sign of life from you?"

Ernst had been called to serve in the *Wehrmacht* at the tail end of the
war. Like Gottfried, he had been deployed to the Soviet front. He had
been seventeen.

"Nothing but cannon fodder. These boys didn't even know how to
pull a trigger," Grandfather said when he talked about Hitler's desperate
end-of-war tactics. "They should have taken old men like me, instead of
wasting our youth."

After the war, when neither Gottfried nor Ernst had returned home,
Grandmother waited for news from them. Every day she had been
disappointed; every day she had renewed her hope.

Two and a half years later, in the early autumn of 1947, a letter
arrived from Ernst. It had been posted in Friedland, a German transition
camp in *Niedersachsen,* Lower Saxony. In a few hastily scribbled words,
Ernst wrote that he had been released from a Siberian camp and would
soon be on a transport home.

On the day of Ernst's arrival and the arrival of three other
Heimkehrer, returning prisoners of war, Grandmother waited in the
open front door, just as she would for Onkel Jean's funeral procession six
years later. Grandfather stood on one side of the door; Gitta, Mother
and I stood on the other. Leaning against the wall of the house, the heat-
saturated brick warmed our backs. Most of the town emerged from their
houses to welcome the four men. People lined the main street or walked
in the direction of the train station. Many waved at us.
"Congratulations," they called out.

There was loud cheering wherever the men passed. A pitiful lot,
dirty and emaciated, they wore broad smiles on their faces. One of them
left the group and shuffled toward us. In tattered clothes, rags and
newspaper tied around his feet for shoes, a grimy piece of cloth covering

his right eye.

"*Ernst. Mein Sohn,*" Grandmother said. Her voice sounded stifled, tears flowed freely down her cheeks.

She reached for her son, awkwardly maintaining her balance with his help. They clung to each other. When he pulled away, ungainly and shy, Grandmother looked into his face. She put her hand over his covered eye.

"That's why they let you go," she said.

Ernst's face now was strained, fierce. His glass eye appeared larger than his good eye and blank, the way it always did. He stormed out of the sitting room, slamming the door shut.

"God help him," Grandmother said, almost to herself. "That war has made an angry man of him."

Grandmother and I returned to listening to the radio, both of us, I sensed, realizing how futile it was.

As time passed, what had been names gradually became inarticulate babble, monotonous and muffled, like sounds filtering into the space between waking and sleeping. I remembered the dream I'd had of my father some years ago. He hadn't been killed but wounded, and had come home. He'd been faceless in the dream.

"My father. He could come back, couldn't he?" I asked Grandmother.

For a sweet moment, I imagined her lilting voice, "*Ja, dein Papa. Warum nicht?* – Yes, your Papa. Why not?"

The reality was different. She said, "No, my child. Don't hope for the impossible."

Still, we listened more attentively through the names starting with S. I took Grandmother's hand, as she had taken mine earlier, to bolster hope.

"*Schorendorf, Erich – Schotringer, Heinz – Schotten, Walter – Schultze, Gerhard – Schultze, Anton – Schumacher, Erich – Schunder, Paul – Schuppmann, Karl. . .*"

My father's name, *Josef Schupp,* had not been read.

The shapes of sunlight on the carpet had shrunk and then disappeared altogether as the afternoon progressed into evening. It was dark when Grandmother turned off the radio. Hands on both hips, she hobbled back into the kitchen and sat in her chair next to the stove.

"We'll have a Mass read, for Onkel Gottfried and for your father, too." she said. "You'll go tell the pastor." There was neither resignation nor defeat in her demeanor, only mournful acceptance.

The name of every returning prisoner of war had been announced. All over Germany, there would be jubilant mothers and fathers, brothers and sisters, relatives and friends rejoined with their beloveds; there would be many thousands more whose losses, after years of waiting and uncertainty, had become final, and whose true mourning would now begin.

39

The lunch dishes washed and dried, the help left for the day. Grandfather, never one to linger in the kitchen, put on his vest and took off for the vegetable garden, to set poles for his runner beans and to put seeds in the ground. Ernst could be heard shifting gears as he drove his truck out through the gate. Gitta had filled a bowl with table scraps to take to Spitz. He was yapping from across the courtyard. We were alone in the kitchen, Grandmother and I.

Grandmother dug into her apron pocket. "For you," she said, and handed me a 100-Mark banknote. "I want you to go buy a good camera for your birthday. If you take after your father, you'll be the family chronicler."

Surprised and grateful, I gave Grandmother a kiss on her cheek.

I wasted no time. It was an early spring day, a week before my 15th birthday. Fighting a headwind, I bicycled to the camera shop in Dormagen. I took the shortest route, a narrow dirt path along the railroad tracks, then past our school and to an arcade on the main shopping street.

Months earlier, when I dreamed of owning a camera, I had set my sights on a particular one in the window display. It was expensive and came with a genuine leather case and adjustable strap. At the time, the possibility of actually owning it was just a fanciful wish.

The very same camera, along with its leather case, was still in the window. The price tag read *DM 95,00*. I smoothed my windblown hair, tucked my blouse haphazardly into my skirt, and pulled up my knee socks. Grandmother's banknote clutched in my palm, I entered the small, narrow shop.

Putting on the airs of someone used to engaging in transactions of this magnitude, I approached the clerk behind the counter. Shoulders straightened, head lifted high, I rattled off my prepared, one-sentence speech.

"I would like to purchase the *Agfa Isolette* with the leather case that's in the window."

The clerk nodded deferentially as if, indeed, I were an important customer. Excusing himself, he left. When he came back, he placed the camera and case on a suede-covered pad.

"Agfa is a fine brand. This camera will last you a lifetime," he said, and included a roll of film in the purchase price.

My new acquisition clamped to my carrier rack, I rode back to Grandmother's house, at a reasonable speed now. Occasionally, my hand reached back to feel the smooth brown leather, attended each time by a wave of anxiety, and relieved each time to find my precious cargo undisturbed.

Views I had seen a thousand times before, I now scanned with a different eye. Unexpected images took shape: the straight-as-an-arrow bundle of cables, running parallel to the train tracks, how they narrowed in the distance; tufts of cloud, how they stuck to the tall chimney of the brick-manufacturing plant; a clump of trees in the barren landscape of late winter, how it stirred up a new sense of desolation. I imagined them frozen as black-and-white images, within scalloped, cream-colored borders.

A portrait of my grandparents would be my first photo. For its location, I decided on the Dutch door on the pond side of the barn.

Grandmother hobbled behind Grandfather across the courtyard. Her step was sprightly, both hands placed on her broad hips, which gave her arms the appearance of wings propelling her forward. Tied to the barn door jamb, Spitz – sometimes vicious, sometimes affectionate, always unpredictable, except in his devotion to Grandmother – bounded toward her until his collar tightened around his neck, raising him on his hind legs. Excited barking turned into a choking rasp, while his tail went on wagging. Grandmother stroked the lift of his neck, coaxing him to sit like the well-trained dog he wasn't. Strings of spittle drooled from the corners of his mouth as he licked her hand in gratitude.

Straightening her corpulent body, Grandmother, now 65 years old, rested her right arm on the ledge of the closed, lower half of the Dutch door. Unselfconsciously posing for the camera, her face revealed an interior view of herself. Her thinning hair, pulled back into a sloppy bun, bared the fleshy features of her face. Her still-full lips recalled the sensuality of youth. There was a sad but steady gaze in her dark brown eyes. Later, I would cry, seeing her captured in the photo that way. It impressed itself in my memory, the only vivid image I carried of her after she was gone.

Grandfather positioned himself to her left. A slender man, of less imposing stature than Grandmother, and sporting a carefully trimmed mustache and a beret, he held his head slightly tilted to the side, the way he did when he compensated for his loss of hearing. He looked serious from behind his wire-rimmed glasses.

I paced off three meters, the distance recommended in the instruction booklet. I took pains to frame my grandparents within the opening of the upper part of the door. I pressed the shutter release. A fleeting darkness eclipsed my view. Then, for a jarring moment, I thought I saw Grandmother's image shifting to look like the negative of a photograph – light becoming dark, dark becoming light.

I lowered the camera and let it dangle from its leather strap around my neck. I hesitated to even glance at Grandmother. When I did, she looked no different from how she always looked. But in my heart, I feared that she was marked to die.

Grandmother raised her head toward the cloud-gathering sky. In her Rhenish lilt, always a comfort to my ears, she said, "It's going to rain before nightfall."

Following her lead, Grandfather, too, looked into the sky. "Nothing like a good sprinkle after a day's sowing."

I wanted to blot out the image I had seen and the irrational message I imagined it carried. But they remained present. They wedged themselves between me and Grandmother as something over which I had no control. I caught myself scrutinizing her for changes in appearance and demeanor that might reveal clues. Often, I felt a painful sense of separation. We already belonged to different worlds. Sometimes I imagined her wicker chair in the kitchen empty.

Until Onkel Jean's death less than three years prior, I had clung to the illusion that life was forever. My father's death had no real place in my reckoning of this: and so it was Onkel Jean's death that had been the lesson that no one was immortal. The first in my grandparents' generation to die, he had become the one ushering all the others out of life. Through him, they had lost their immortality. As time passed, I had thought of Onkel Jean less and less often. Eventually, he had slipped unnoticed even from my evening prayer. But occasionally, inexplicably, his memory burst into my thoughts. It was always accompanied by a feeling of hopelessness that robbed life of all meaning. It replicated, in some way, the disappointment that turned into despair after my First Communion, when I saw nothing but futility in everything.

An event that had happened at a time in my childhood when death was still ungraspable, my father's death was only hearsay, or a story. It lay shrouded on the other side of a curtain that divided my childhood into two parts: before my father died and after he died. Everything that came before seemed made-up or augmented by what I had been told or seen in photographs. Only what came after seemed real to me.

In mid-autumn of the same year I got my first camera, the year I turned fifteen and not long after the day of the return of the ten thousand prisoners of war, Grandmother suffered her first stroke. It left the crippled side of her body noticeably paralyzed. Her mind and speech remained intact.

Dr. Siepe stopped by Grandmother's house and made the diagnosis. Obesity and untreated high blood pressure were to blame. He prescribed a medication he assured Grandmother would help prevent a recurrence. He said goodbye with the usual twinkle in his eyes and told Grandmother to take good care of herself.

Grandmother seemed to take her condition in stride. "Don't start fussing over me," she said to her husband and to Mother, who suggested that she lose some weight. "I'm just fine."

"We're going to Lobberich for the day," she said, once she felt sufficiently recovered. "Even if it's the last thing I do in this life."

Lobberich was the town where she had been born in 1888. A

county seat, it was situated near the Dutch border about sixty kilometers northeast of Delrath. Grandmother had not been back to her hometown in thirty-five years. "That cursed leg of mine has kept me housebound all this time," she said, making light of her condition.

On the day of the trip, with Mother helping and Grandfather looking on powerlessly, Grandmother strained to lower her heavy, partially immobilized body into the passenger seat of the hired limousine. Her breathing was belabored; still, she appeared unflappable. Once she was comfortable, she smoothed her black shirt dress – the same one she'd worn on my First Communion day. Earlier, Mother had arranged Grandmother's hair over a donut-shaped wire curler, creating a bun of impressive size. All of us, Mother, Gitta and I, wore our best outfits. Even Grandfather had put on a suit and tie. He carried a hat in one hand.

I felt heavy inside. I dwelled on the significance of this outing, which had to be on everyone's mind. Although maybe not on eleven-year old Gitta's, at least not in a visible way. She kept bouncing up and down in the folding seat behind the driver. Mother scolded her, telling her to sit still and enjoy the countryside. I stared out the window, watching the pavement streak past in alternating patterns of sunlight and shade. The driver, Herr Kreuter, was whistling the melody to *Lily Marlene*.

"Aren't you getting tired of that old war song?" Grandmother asked after his fourth time through it.

"It was a good song then, and it's still a good song," Herr Kreuter said, and turned quiet.

An uneasy silence followed, until Grandmother began to reminisce about her growing-up years in Lobberich. She spoke about her brother, a schoolteacher, poet and painter, the last child to be born and the only boy in a family of seven siblings. Serving as a young officer in World War I, he'd died of a ruptured appendix that had been misdiagnosed. She spoke of her first suitor, a young man from a town across the Dutch border, how he'd courted her at the local dance on Saturday nights. "He spoke only broken German. I didn't speak any Dutch. But we danced the night away." She paused, wondering, perhaps, whether to go on. "Afterwards, at the Breyller See, he pointed up to the moon and down at its reflection in the water." She paused again, before she said, "I can still hear his voice as he professed his love to me. It sounded so funny. It made us both laugh. . . But all that's a lifetime ago." The unguarded display of so much longing and pleasure made me love her even more.

Tante Maria, Grandmother's younger sister, was waiting on the steps of their childhood home, wearing a pretty, black silk dress appointed with lace ruffles. In the thirty-five years Grandmother's crippled leg had kept her from venturing outside of her own environment, Tante Maria, as well as the other sisters, had occasionally paid Grandmother visits in Delrath.

"Dear God," she said, when she saw the difficulty Grandmother had getting out of the car even with help, and was no longer able to walk on her own.

The two sisters fell into each other's arms, but only embraced for a moment. Grandmother released herself brusquely and, wiping off her sister's tears, said, "Don't cry, Sister. I'm not dead yet."

The table was set in the shade of the arbor behind the house. Tight clusters of small grapes, not yet ripened to their purplish blue of later autumn, hung from the climbing vines. Tidy paths led through a rose garden on one side and an ample vegetable patch on the other. A paint-chipped garden gnome stood amid a group of potted red geraniums on the back stoop. In the faint breeze, changing shapes of light and dark played on the crocheted tablecloth, and the flower-painted china, and the silverware.

Tante Maria placed a large plum tart in the center of the table, its halved pieces of fruit arranged in a spiraling pattern.

At the sight of the tart, Grandmother's face lit up.

"Our mother's recipe and her mother's before that. I'd forgotten all about it," she said, "It has the thinnest crust and sweetest fruit you'll ever want to taste."

Her mother on her mind, Grandmother told the family story I'd heard her tell before: my mother, her first child, had been born just hours after her own mother had died. *"Eine stirbt, damit eine andere leben kann.* – One dies, so another can live," she'd always say. Always, it would make me feel odd and sad.

"I don't know about angels and ghosts," she continued. "But I know as sure as I'm sitting here that my mother's soul hovered near me during the labor." She reached to touch Mother's shoulder. "I swear she left her mark on my little girl. Same raspberry speck on Gertrud's left shoulder that was on hers, too."

"I can believe it. If anyone could trick death, it would have been our mother," Tante Maria said. Striking a serious tone, she added, "She had faith in the Lord, Luise. Which should be an example to you."

Pointing to her crippled leg and speaking with a sternness that allowed no further discussion, Grandmother said, "I haven't been a believer for half my life. And I'm not going to start in my dying days."

In that moment, I came to suspect that not only did Grandmother think of her crippled leg as a punishment by a god she didn't believe in – as she had once told me – it had also been what cost her her faith.

The sun was at just past mid-heaven and the day was already cooling, when we climbed out of the limousine at the Breyller See, on the outskirts of Lobberich. A light breeze had come up, warm as on a summer day. A few rowboats, tied to a dock, were gently bobbing on the water.

"Plenty of time for a leisurely jaunt," the boatman said, offering us his best boat, one with a fresh coat of green paint.

Gitta and I climbed into the hull, positioning ourselves on either side. The boat wobbled precipitously when the boatman, from the ramp, and Mother, from inside the boat, maneuvered Grandmother onto the middle seat. Grandfather was the last one to lower himself onto the only remaining seat.

He took charge of the rowing. With broad, even strokes, he steered the boat away from the dock. It glided smoothly across the lake.

"Take us to the water lilies, Döres." Short for Theodor, *Döres* was her term of endearment for her husband. "There used to be a large patch of them in the far bay."

The boat slid close enough to glance the broad, heart-shaped leaves at the edge of the water lilies. Grandmother leaned over the side of the boat. It caused a startling tilt. She cupped a flower in her hand and let it slip back into the water.

Grandfather let the oars rest in the oarlocks. Our boat rocked gently. We drifted away from the water lilies, into the glow of the setting sun. Sitting in the bottom of the boat, I rested my chin on the narrow ledge and dipped my hand into the tepid water. A wavy reflection of my face formed itself.

"Did he pick a water lily for you?" I asked, remembering Grandmother's Dutch suitor of her youth. As though the answer were to be discovered in the water, I let my eyes drift along the smooth swell next to the boat, where they met Grandmother's face, mirrored not far from my own.

Grandfather, at that moment, dipped the oars back into the lake, fracturing her reflection. As the ripples flattened, I saw it again, darkness and lightness reversed, the way I had seen it through the camera lens.

January 28 – a few months away – leapt into my thoughts, not in the way words sometimes do, and not as an image, either, but like something seen and not seen, heard and not heard. With it came a strange feeling of certainty that Grandmother would die on that day.

"Water lilies don't bloom in the spring," she said. It seemed that hours had passed since I had asked the question.

Grandmother had her second stroke on a Sunday morning in November, only weeks after our visit to Lobberich. Dr. Siepe said that the third stroke, mostly likely, would take her.

"They come in threes. That seems to be the pattern," he offered, all of us gathered outside the closed bedroom door.

Severely paralyzed now, Grandmother was barely able to move her crippled leg and arm on the left side. Still, she rejected any suggestion of a wheelchair, and insisted on dragging herself – with Grandfather's support – from her bed to an upholstered armchair next to the window in the sitting room and back to her bed. She had not surrendered her regal bearing. When she smiled, though her face was twisted now, it was without excuses and beyond vanity.

The stroke had distorted Grandmother's face. The lower eyelid on her left side drooped, exposing the small red veins of the inner eyelid. Her left cheek sagged, as did her mouth on the same side. It was unsettling to look at. Yet, I was driven by a morbid impulse to scrutinize it, recalling my own crooked face from a few years back. Grandmother slurred her words. With a handkerchief in her good hand, she daubed the drooling side of her mouth between sentences.

I felt suspended between my premonition of Grandmother's death and ordinary reality: taken with the idea of seeing into the future, at the same time, I dismissed it as an absurd fantasy. Caught between the two, I believed I had to choose between Grandmother's life and my premonition.

Christmas passed. It was well into January. The sitting room was shrouded in the twilight of afternoon in the deep of winter. Grandmother was sitting in her usual chair by the window, asleep it seemed.

At the sound of my footsteps, Grandmother lifted her eyelids slowly. There was great effort in her voice when she said, "Oh, it's only you," as if she had expected someone else. I pulled up a chair across from her and stroked her hand.

"Grandmother, will you recite a ballad for me?" The cruelty of my own words startled me. Grandmother closed her eyes again, by way of saying, "How could I, in this predicament?" Then, appearing to reconsider, she clasped the armrest with her good hand and, bearing down on it, slightly straightened her slumped body.

She lifted her head with a touch of drama. *"Erlkönig. – Erlking."*

Her speech halting and drawling, her face grimacing with exertion, she began to recite Goethe's poem, *"Wer reitet so spät durch Nacht und Wind? / Es ist der Vater mit seinem Kind.* – O who rides by night through the woodland so wild? / It is the fond father embracing his child."

It was unbearable to witness the strain in her face and voice. I wished I had never asked her to do this. I wanted her to stop. I wanted to flee. But I remained seated in my chair, observing her with odd fascination.

"O father, see yonder! see yonder! he says; / 'My boy, upon what dost thou fearfully gaze? / 'tis the Erlking with his crown and his shroud. ' / 'No, my son, it is a dark . . .'"

Grandmother's voice trailed off. Her body swayed to the rhythm of the poem she no longer spoke. Her face was still, except for a quivering under her spider-veined eyelids.

Soon, her lips began to move again, mouthing the words, soundlessly at first, then in thick, guttural gasps. White spittle stuck to her mouth, lathering in the corners. A babble came forth, intelligible only because I had heard her recite these lines so many times before: "But clasped to his bosom, the infant was dead." Grandmother sank back into the chair.

Grief mingled with compassion for Grandmother and the thought of which I could not rid myself, not then or later, that her dying would be tantamount to her never having lived at all.

"Go. . . Do your homework," Grandmother said.

Webs of tears on her lashes, she looked at me. In that look, I thought I saw that she recognized my anguish, and that she knew I wanted to be alone when I cried for her.

I made it a habit on my way home from school to peer through the sitting room window of Grandmother's house, where she spent most of the day sitting in her chair. I'd wave and, if she hadn't nodded off, she'd wave back with her good arm. On most days, I'd go inside to say hello.

Grandmother's chair was empty on the afternoon of Friday, the 27th of January. An awful chill came over me and, as on our boat outing on the Breyller See, the troubling foreknowledge of her death flashed through my mind. I could not reconcile the two, and beseeched the God I no longer believed in to prove me wrong.

Grandmother had suffered her third stroke and been taken to the hospital. She died alone, early in the morning of the 28th of January, 1956.

After the doctor called to say she'd passed away, Grandfather said to Mother, "Let's bring her home, Gertrud."

"*Vater* . . . " She was unable to say more.

For three days, Grandmother lay in an open coffin in the center of the sitting room. Only Grandfather went in to sit with her.

At the funeral, people said it was the coldest day in the town's memory.

40

At the beginning of the new school year of 1955, Fräulein Köhne took over as the new German and English teacher. Like the other two women teachers at our school, she was unmarried; unlike them, she was young and did not fit the stereotypical image of the spinster teacher.

Fräulein Bock, the girls' homeroom and physical education teacher, was a petulant woman with questionable teaching skills, a deficit for which she compensated by exerting her authority. Fräulein Plönes was our mathematics and French teacher. Her competence was above reproach, acknowledged even by those who failed her classes. We maliciously conjectured that she had secret fantasies about algebraic formulae and French grammar, but had never heard of French kissing and certainly never indulged in it. We were convinced that both teachers were virgins for life.

Fräulein Köhne brought a new sophistication to the classroom. She wore her dark blonde hair loosely curled in the city style of the fifties. She had Marlene Dietrich's plucked-and-arched eyebrows. Her lips were sultry and sensual, a sign, in our minds, that she had compromised her virginity.

Fräulein Köhne dressed in slightly below-the-knees pleated skirts and Merino wool sweaters, accented with silk kerchiefs around her neck. All of us fashion-deprived girls envied her elegant wardrobe. There was a bounce in her walk. She was worldly, seductive. The boys had crushes on her.

I wanted to imitate her look, but no matter how much I practiced, my lips refused to match Fräulein Köhne's sensuality. I was reasonably successful in training my eyebrows to curve in an arch similar to hers – and Marlene's – by dabbing them with castor oil at night and brushing them along the desired line.

Fräulein Köhne would sit on the edge of the teacher's desk, one nylon-stockinged leg crossed over the other, her heeled pumps accentuating the slender lines of her calves. Fräulein Bock and Fräulein Plönes, on the other hand, would stand in front of class in teacher-perfect posture, or march back and forth between the blackboard on one side and the supplies cabinet on the other, as if marking their territory. They wore the kind of shoes we, too, were condemned to wear: sensible, lace-up walking shoes, medium brown, to go with everything in both their and our limited and dated wardrobes.

We welcomed Fräulein Köhne's less formal approach to teaching, which stood in contrast to that of all the other teachers. She didn't rule by wielding the disciplinarian's whip, yet she commanded our respect. She had us memorize fewer passages from Goethe, Schiller and other luminaries in German literature than our previous teacher. Instead, we wrote compositions on the bargain Goethe's *Faust* struck with *Mephistopheles* and on Kafka's allegorical use of language in *Metamorphosis*. It suited me. I lacked the patience for memorizing, but, with Fräulein Köhne's direction, I did excel at exploring literary themes.

That year's term paper for Fräulein Köhne's English class was to write a synopsis and interpretation of an English or American novel of our choice. I selected *The Old Man and the Sea*. It was short, straightforward prose, the language easy, compared to Virginia Woolf's *Mrs. Dalloway*, which I had also sampled in the school library.

Returning the graded paper, Fräulein Köhne said, "You have a talent for languages. A language-related career would be a good fit for you." Her statement stunned me: teachers marked spelling and punctuation errors and, at the end of a paper, noted numbered grades, from 1 to 5, or their language equivalent, from *Excellent* to *Failed*. They did not make verbal comments; they did not offer praise. My report cards typically were a mixture of *Excellent* and *Good* evaluations and two consistent *Satisfactory* evaluations in Fräulein Bock's physical education and home economics classes. While I wasn't particularly passionate about any subject, I managed to stay near the top of the class. The notion of any talent I might have had eluded me altogether. In fact, Mother remarked on my lack of talent every time she signed my report card, "You have your father's athletic ungainliness, and absolutely no talent when it comes to practical matters." These practical matters, to her mind, included everything from sewing on a button to keeping my room tidy. I never told her so, but these were not talents I wished I had.

Late spring drizzle misted the tall windows in the classroom, obscuring the view of the trees, already in full leaf, and allowing only dismal light to enter. It was the first class of the morning.

Following procedure, we rose from our seats when Fräulein Köhne entered the classroom.

"*Guten Morgen,*" she said.

"*Guten Morgen,*" we responded, in unison.

"*Setzen.* – Sit down."

She took roll. Then, sitting on the corner of the teacher's desk, she introduced the topic for the day.

"As we continue with our timeline of German literature, I would like us to look at a selection of wartime writings from a non-historical perspective. We will examine works written during and after World War I that are defined by personal idealism and love of country while wrestling with the moral conflicts they present."

Fräulein Köhne picked a book from the small stack next to her on the desk. The title, in large Gothic font, spelled out *Im Westen Nichts Neues* – All Quiet on the Western Front. In her brief introduction, she mentioned the author, Erich Maria Remarque, and that the book had been published in 1928. Because of its pacifist point of view and implicit condemnation of war, it had been censored by the Nazis and destroyed in the book burning purges of the 1930s.

She leafed to the last page and read the final passage out loud to the class. It began, *Er fiel im Oktober 1918, an einem Tage, der so ruhig und still war an der ganzen Front, daß der Heeresbericht sich nur auf einen Satz beschränkte, im Westen sei nichts Neues zu melden.* – He fell in October 1918, on a day that was so still and quiet on the whole front, that the army report confined itself to the single sentence: All quiet on the Western Front. The passages concluded, he had fallen forward and lay on the earth as though sleeping. Turning him over one saw that he could not have suffered long; his face had an expression of calm, as though almost glad the end had come. "

She closed the book, and read the comment written at the bottom of the cover," *Remarques Buch ist das Denkmal unserer unbekannten Soldaten von allen Toten geschrieben.* It translates, "Remarque's book is a memorial for our unknown soldiers, written by all those who died."

"I recommend it for your reading list."

She wrote the book's title and author on the blackboard. When she turned to face the classroom again, her demeanor was visibly changed. All teacherly comportment gone, she had a distant, almost pained, expression in her eyes. Still, none of us was prepared to hear what followed. In a voice strained, less assured than usual, Fräulein Köhne recounted in broad strokes the story of her failed love: during the war, she had been engaged to a fellow student at her university in Marburg. Weeks before German capitulation, he had been conscripted into the *Wehrmacht*. He had been killed in battle a few days before the war ended. Whatever else she said after that has not survived in my memory.

Only my reflections have endured. How my image of Fräulein Köhne shifted from quintessential teacher to a woman who had loved and suffered. I created a picture of her fiancé, a tall, dashing young man with a bent for philosophy – most likely because it met my own ideal of a man, not because Fräulein Köhne had described him that way. She never said so, but I was left with the impression that marrying another man was tantamount to betraying her dead fiancé, an attitude resonating with a romantic idealism I secretly espoused.

Fräulein Köhne's revelation became the topic of heated discussions after class. Not only had she broken every teacher's rule of keeping personal matters out of the classroom, she had divulged a piece of her past more private than anything we could have imagined. We applauded her courage, then moved to gossipy speculations about her love life – or, as we assumed, the absence of it. Even though I related to her loss personally, I joined in the general view that her sacrifice was sentimental and, if not that, was an excuse for not being able to find a suitable match in the post-war scarcity of marriageable men.

That afternoon, I found Remarque's book in Mother's bookcase. My father's name was finely printed on the flyleaf. It pleased me that he had owned pacifist literature, even though he would join the German *Wehrmacht* as a volunteer. I've sometimes thought that this discovery planted in my own mind the seed for exonerating my father from greater crimes.

As I leafed through the book, I chanced upon vivid descriptions of battle scenes, too disturbing to read. I never returned to it, nor did I overcome my deep-seated unwillingness to read other war novels, not even as an adult.

Fräulein Köhne resumed the topic of World War I literature in our German class the following day. She presented excerpts from the novella *Der Wanderer zwischen beiden Welten* – The Wanderer Between The Two Worlds. Written by Walter Flex, who ultimately became a war casualty himself, it was an account of the brutal fighting on the Eastern Front during World War I. It recounts the soul-searching dialogue between the first person narrator and his comrade, a lieutenant and theology student, whose death he witnesses. While Fräulein Köhne lifted antiwar elements from its pages, during Hitler times, it had been used to serve the Nazi's ideological purposes, on the basis of the two lieutenants' idealism and love of nation.

When she recited one of the poems in Walter Flex's book, *Wildgänse rauschen durch die Nacht* – Wild geese fly whooshing through the night – the loss of her fiancé resounded in her mournful delivery, calling up my own loss, as well. I would later learn that it had been read at the announcement of Hitler's death.

Drenched in romantic idealism, the poem seems to accept death as the ultimate fulfillment of a soldier's life. The first stanza ends with the line, *Die Welt ist voller Morden.* – The world is full of murder. Equating the birds' migratory journey with the movement of armies, it asks rhetorically, *Fahrt ihr nach Süden übers Meer / Was ist aus uns geworden!* – When you fly south across the sea / What fate has come upon us! The poem concludes in defeat with honor, *Und fahr'n wir ohne Wiederkehr, / Rauscht uns im Herbst ein Amen!* – When to war we go and don't turn back, / Autumn roars an Amen. Fräulein Köhne held her breath on the *Amen.* Her pause did not convey agreement with the literal translation of Amen as "so be it," nor with the glorification of a soldier's ultimate sacrifice. It conveyed sorrow, prayer. As it lingered in the room, the dead – Fräulein Köhne's fiancé, my father, the fathers and uncles of many others in the classroom – seemed to have returned from the other world.

It was so quiet, I thought I could hear Fräulein Köhne's breath. She put down the slim volume and, without commenting further, opened another book to a page with a poem she had chosen. I remember neither the title of the book itself nor the title of the poem. I do remember the text of the first stanza.

Her voice pleading, as if on behalf of the voice in the poem, she read: *"Ich bin es, Mutter! / Nein, rühr mich nicht an. / Tu so als schläfst du, / damit es den Mann, / der da im Bette neben dir liegt, / nicht stört.* – I am here, Mother! / No, do not touch me. / Pretend you are asleep, / so the man who lies in your bed next to you / will not be disturbed."

I stared at the dull sky outside the classroom, trying to dispel the images evoked by the poem. Making a leap from the poem's intended meaning – the apparition of a fallen son coming home to comfort his mother – I imagined the ghost of a husband returning to indict his wife. She had allowed another man to take his place in their bed. And suddenly, I saw what, unacknowledged, had been troubling me all along: my mother had betrayed my father and disgraced his name. He had been relegated to an only faint presence, and his name was rarely spoken.

I wept. I covered my eyes with both hands, so no one would see my tears and I wept for my dead father – for the first time. For the first time, too, I wept out of my own grief. The grief that was my father's legacy.

The click-clack of Fräulein Köhne's pumps drew nearer. Stopping next to my desk, she asked, "What is it?"

I shook my head.

"Would you like to step outside to compose yourself?"

I shook my head again. It was painful enough that Fräulein Köhne witnessed my distress. It would be torturous to get up from my seat and make my way to the classroom door, all eyes on me.

I kept my face covered, until the feelings had numbed and the tears subsided.

After the bell, Fräulein Köhne asked me to stay. She didn't speak, at first, as she appeared to search for the right words or to allow me to gather myself. Muffled chatter and laughter came from the

schoolyard, in contrast to the hush in the classroom. I felt alone –
and closer to the dead.

"Did someone die?" she finally said.

I started weeping all over again.

Just a few months earlier, Grandmother had died. I had only
recently stopped wearing the black band over my jacket sleeve, as an
outward symbol of mourning. But this wasn't about Grandmother.

It was about the feelings my father had left in me, something
broken that hadn't been mended and never would be: the loss of him, its
finality, rather than the lesser experience of his absence, which had been
my reality. Mother had denied my loss, and Gitta's. His death had been
her loss; it had made *her* a widow. It had ruined the future *she* would
have had. Never had she acknowledged to Gitta and me that his death
had made *us* fatherless. Never, that his death had been our loss as well.
Never had she said, "My poor children. You lost your father."

"Mein Vater. . . In the war," I said.

"I'm very sorry. I didn't know." Fräulein Köhne spoke quietly.
She looked at me. "I understand."

41

It was spring, 1955, the beginning of our fifth year in secondary school. Herr Paschek, the principal, introduced Peter Conze as a new student in our class, and invited him to say a few words about his background. Forty-one pairs of eyes were ready to assess him. To most of us fifteen- to seventeen-year-olds, this would have been mortifying. But Peter held his head up, defiantly proud, creating a perspective that exaggerated his high cheekbones and the slant of his greenish eyes. He told the class that he'd been born in Saxony; that his family had fled to a town near Berlin at the end of the war; that they'd left the communist East Germany for the democratic West Germany, in search of a better job for his father, and because his parents were at odds with the communist ideology.

Asked about the school curriculum there, he said, "Much of it is like yours, except for foreign languages and religious instruction. I learned Russian from the time I was six. English and French are offered as electives at some schools, but they weren't at mine. Secular philosophy takes the place of religious instruction."

"Thank you, Conze" Herr Paschek said.

A rumble went through the room.

"Ruhe," Herr Paschek silenced the class.

Peter was assigned a seat in the last row on the boys' side, in the same row as Dieter and Lothar Srotzki.

I shoved a note to Renate who sat next to me. *Here comes trouble – smart, tough, good-looking.* I had underlined the latter.

"Really?" ' she whispered and rolled her eyes. She imitated his way of speaking, "His Saxon accent is enough to make me gag." Peter had obviously failed to impress Renate. She had eyes for Heinz Wilhelm Orfgen, a middling student, tall, blonde and athletic. Her scheming for his attention had borne no fruit.

"Once a communist, always a communist," Dieter said on our way to the train station, his hostility barely veiled.

Dieter's dogmatic assessment of Peter annoyed me. "You tend to exaggerate and forget that Peter's family rejected the system," I said. Somewhat wickedly, I added, "Or is this about intellectual rivalry?" For it was evident, after only a day at our school, that Peter was very bright.

As if my accusation had been utterly unfounded and therefore not worth acknowledging, Dieter continued with his line of thought, "Debate him on communism. He'll beat you hands down. He'll have all the arguments they've been pounding into his head since Kindergarten. It's like discussing religion with a Jehovah's Witness. You can't win."

We would soon discover that, indeed, Peter was a debater *par excellence.* He could not be outmatched. Dieter belittled his ability, equating it to an acquired skill. I ascribed it to superior intelligence. Peter always espoused unconventional ideas, while most of us defended the status quo. He broke through the boundaries of the kind of thinking we had been born and lulled into.

In the years immediately following the war and into the early sixties, there had been a steady exodus from the East into the West. East Germans, disgruntled with living and employment conditions at home, crossed the border into West Germany illegally. They were readily absorbed into the booming economy. To staunch the drain of qualified workers, professionals and artists, East Germany fortified the 1,400 kilometer border – stretching from the Baltic Sea in the north to the Czechoslovakian border in the south – with barbed wire and strategically placed checkpoints. In August of 1962, the Berlin Wall was built, separating East Berlin from West Berlin, further obstructing free movement.

A number of students in our class had been part of the original wave of refugees from the East to the West during and soon after the war. Peter, who had been raised under East German rule, was an exception.

For some time after our own escape from East Germany in 1945, Mother and the Köppel sisters had exchanged letters, from time to time.

In this way, we had news about goings-on and conditions in
Rockensußra. As their plight seemed worse compared to ours, Mother
regularly sent packages of Gitta's and my outgrown clothing to them, as
well as what she could spare of her own.

While many left East Germany, for political or for economic
reasons, others had no thought or intention of leaving. It was home to
them, as it was for the Köppels, or they had come to embrace
communist thinking.

The media portrayed the divide between East Germany and
West Germany as deeply carved, pitching Soviet, i. e. communist,
values against American, i. e. capitalist, values. Echoing the tension
between the two governments of the divided Germany – the
constitution of West Germany did not recognize East German as a
state – we pitched our freedoms against what we thought of as their
subjugation. Our feelings toward East Germans were colored by
condescension and a competitive spirit, as theirs were toward us. We
talked about East Germans as imprisoned in their way of life, even
their thinking, and definitely as less well off. Along with the
prevailing thought, we argued that splitting Germany into halves
had been a cruel and unfair settlement between the victors of WWII,
but we accepted it as a permanent condition. "Not in our lifetime,"
we used to say, "will Germany reunite."

However, I for one, was intrigued by Peter's across-the-border
origin. It soon became obvious that he brought with him an otherness
he would never quite shed.

Five of us had gathered in the downstairs hallway, a popular meeting
place during recess on rainy days. Renate, Lothar, who was class
president, and I were sitting on the bottom steps of the staircase, while
Peter and Dieter, taking charge of our discussion, stood in front of us.
We were sipping *Kakao,* chocolate milk, supplied by the school, and
eating sandwiches our mothers had prepared.

A lively debate started about communism versus capitalism. Peter
spoke against what he called our outdated class system as a device to
preserve power for the elite, and argued for an egalitarian society.

Lothar, almost handsome but for the angularity of his face and a nose some of us thought had been broken in a fight, smiled dismissively.

"Nothing but control of the population," he said, in his quiet and pointed manner.

"Capitalism is a system of inherent inequalities," Peter argued, in the tone of someone who has all the right answers and with the bearing of the leader he would become in his adult life as a union organizer.

No one came up with a cogent counterargument.

Renate, shifting course, said, "I'm glad we're free to determine our lives and free to say what we think. That's what counts to me."

Dieter chimed in, "Yes. Free speech. Self-determination. Market economy. What does the communist East offer instead? A prison term for speaking up against Ulbricht, your towing-the-official-line leader? Poverty?"

"Perhaps, you're overrating some of this. If it weren't for your American Marshall Plan, where would the West German economy be?" Peter countered.

I didn't know whether he had a point or not, and was happy when the argument shifted to another topic.

Without so much as in introduction, but with a provocative tone in his voice, Peter posed, "Religious instruction has no place in public schools."

To all of us, it had never even been a question.

"Why shouldn't it?" someone asked.

"Because it's a private matter," Peter said, "in which the state should have no say."

He expounded his contempt for Catholicism and Protestantism, the two denominations represented at our school – outside of one or two *Freidenker,* freethinkers. Summing up his opinion about religion, he declared, "Anyway, God is dead."

"You East Germans read too much Nietzsche and Marx," Dieter said in a tone so combative that it left no doubt that he was Peter's declared rival.

Peter ignored him. "Atheism is the one rational, and therefore valid, position."

The term *atheism* sent shivers up my spine. I was appalled at Peter's audacity. "How can you have the gall to negate any religious traditions?

Some of them go back thousands of years."

"Simple," he said, looking at me directly, "Forget about your sentimentality and, more importantly, your fears. Even your very own Freud was an atheist. Take the side of logic and you'll see there is not and never will be proof of your bearded, grandfatherly God up in heaven. And if you believe at all in the theory of evolution, as a reasonable person does, you will have to reject any notion of Divinity."

I had been put in my place and silenced. Peter did make sense. His logic and reason appealed to me. It forced me to wrestle with my own ambivalence about God and religion. Disillusionment had corrupted my faith. I no longer prayed, nor did I feel called to anything religious. The presence of God, if I'd ever experienced it, eluded me. Yet, I sat through Mass every single Sunday. What kind of hypocrite was I? Peter's unwavering convictions made me realize that, submerged in the comfort of our small-town community, I was unwilling to risk being ostracized as an outsider if I acted truly according to my doubts.

On the first Sunday of Advent – a few weeks after the discussion about God – I dressed for Mass in my new, very smart-looking coat – gray wool fabric, mid-calf length, a Peter Pan collar – and a matching gray hat in the style of the twenties. I stood in the kitchen doorway to say goodbye to Mother, my First Communion prayer book clasped in my kid-leather-gloved hand.

"Take Gitta with you," Mother reminded me.

To my own bewilderment, I said, "I am not going to Mass." I heard the finality in my voice. It had come out of nowhere. It jarred me.

Mother looked at me, aghast. "What has come over you?"

"I'm not going to Mass. Not today. Or ever. With or without Gitta."

Mother opened her mouth to say something. I beat her to it. *"Spar dir die Worte.* – Don't waste your breath," I said, and left her standing at the kitchen table.

It was recess. Renate and I were walking up and down the schoolyard alley that the upper-grade girls claimed for themselves. We were walking arm in arm, the way best friends did to demonstrate their closeness.

"First impressions are always right," Renate said in reference to her assessment of Peter. "I haven't changed my mind about him. He may be brilliant, but he is callous and arrogant, and if you ask me, his looks are debatable."

After her harsh criticism, I wasn't about to confide in her that I was infatuated with him, nor was I going to ask her advice about my timid advances that, so far, had remained fruitless.

"I'm only intrigued by his mind," I said.

Unwittingly, it was Dieter who aided my cause. His competitiveness with Peter had lapsed into outright animosity. On our way to and from school, he was eager to spill every shred of malicious gossip he knew about Peter. Under the guise of casual conversation, it was obvious, he aimed to diminish Peter in my eyes. For me, it was an opportunity to gather information about him. In this way, I knew of Peter's movements and whereabouts after school. Whether he was in love – he was not, but thought a girl named Gisela, with a giggly laugh, who sat two desks away from me, was the prettiest. Peter hadn't said much about me – only that I was intelligent, nothing else, which was a blow to my ego, even though I suspected that Dieter wasn't beyond omitting information he didn't want me to have.

My encounters with Peter appeared accidental. In actuality, I orchestrated them. We ran into each other on the way to the stationery store, only because Dieter had told me that was where Peter was headed. We were at the swimming pool after school at the same time, only because I knew of his plans through Dieter.

If Peter caught on to my scheming, he didn't show it. With his always inscrutable smile, he'd strike up a friendly conversation, or egg me on about anything that came to his mind, or he'd treat me with indifference, reminding me, it seemed, that I was nobody special, just one of the girls.

Once he brought up Dieter. "If anyone has a chance with you, I bet it's Dieter."

"How would you know?" I said. His suggestion made me uncomfortable. I rushed to defend my *platonic* relationship with Dieter.

"We're just friends."

"That's not what it looks like."

"You're not always right, Peter, even when you think you are." I felt I was losing ground, which was how it generally went with him.

"Inseparable, the way you walk together day in, day out. I bet you hold hands when no one's around." There was ridicule in how he said this.

I was determined not to let him have the last word. All I could find to say was, "You're so . . ."

"Look at this one for your scrap book," Renate said with a wicked snicker. She pointed to one in a dozen or so snapshots – taken at school activities – from which we were choosing and ordering duplicates. The photo was of Peter and Fräulein Köhne. Close in height, the blackboard behind, they were facing each other. Fräulein Köhne's index finger on her cheek, her eyes directed into nowhere, she looked as if she were considering an argument Peter had posed.

There was no denying Peter's good looks. He was handsome, without question, no matter what Renate said. His chiseled profile, lean build, confident posture. He was manly.

"See what I mean?" Renate said, "Arrogance personified."

"Don't worry, it's not going in my scrapbook," I said. I still hadn't told her that I had a crush on Peter. I never would.

The day on which we received the small stacks of photos we had ordered, Peter caught up with me in the hallway during recess.

"I want to give this to you," he said.

He passed me the very snapshot of himself and Fräulein Köhne that Renate had teased me about. He looked at me in a way I didn't dare interpret.

"Why don't you write your name on it, to remind me who this is," I said, deliberately cheeky, and handed it back to him.

He blushed, to my surprise and satisfaction, the only time I'd ever seen him flustered. He pulled a three-color ballpoint pen from his breast pocket and set it to the red ink position. He took my hand and spreading it open, placed the photo in my palm. Holding it in place, he wrote in large cursive letters, *Ich liebe Dich* – I love you. *Peter.* Then he took off without another word.

I leaned against the wall, deliriously happy, as I watched him walk along the corridor and make the turn to the staircase.

Thus began a tentative romance between us that I kept a secret – from Renate, who was my best friend, from Dieter, even from my journal. Once or twice Peter and I did our homework together at his family's modest, upstairs flat in Straberg. At afterschool gatherings, we sat near each other, but never together. We hardly exchanged looks, but I was aware of his proximity and, I knew, he was of mine. Sometimes we went for walks on the dykes of the Rhine. Our conversations were always thought-provoking. I never won an argument, and I didn't mind.

"The dirt road just this side of the forest and the railroad tracks, have you been there?" Peter said as we both unlocked our bicycles after the last class of the day.

"I haven't," I said, thrilled he asked, and eager to join him.

We rode along tree-lined streets in residential neighborhoods. Where fields began, the asphalt ended abruptly. We were on a dirt road, empty but for a tractor in the distance. We navigated around the pools of water that yesterday's downpour had left in the ruts and potholes. The sharp wind chased what was left of the clouds across the stark blue sky of early spring. The first green of wheat and rye blanketed the dark, crumbly earth.

Peter slowed down on his bicycle. Dismounting it, he let the wheels slide into the shallow ditch along the roadside. I, too, stopped. With chivalry that surprised me, he took my bicycle and laid it on top of his.

He pointed to the railroad tracks where they crossed the fields and, beyond, where the outline of the forest was etched along the wide horizon.

"That's the view I wanted to show you," he said. "A perfect intersection of nature and technology."

We stood next to each other, both of us looking into this sweeping Rhenish landscape that was native to me, while, until recently, foreign to him.

He turned to face me, and in an abrupt change of mood, intoned, "What is love?" Mock-theatrically, his arm stretched in the grand gesture of an orator. "Some say love is illusion."

"And what do you think? Or is this just more of your cynical rhetoric?" I asked.

He laughed with a small, embarrassed cough. I was pleased to have caught him off-guard.

Still, his mention of love delighted me. As I waited for him to respond, the sharp wind grazed my face. It whistled in my ears.

Like in a dream or in the movies I had seen, Peter put his arms lightly around me. He asked me to look into his eyes.

"They're the same green as yours," he said.

I saw my reflection in his pupils and, behind it, the sky. He leaned toward me, and pulling me closer, kissed my lips.

The following morning, most of the distance from the train station behind us, Dieter and I were crossing the old market place. I was only half-listening to Dieter's tales. Until he talked, casually, as if in passing, about what the boys had said about the girls in our class over a few beers the evening before. One by one, he went through their assessments of each one of us. I found out who was after whom, while desperately wanting to know what they said about me. Dieter took his time. He reported on just about every girl of even marginal popularity and ended with a pause long enough for me to think that I had been overlooked in the discussion – that I didn't count.

The gate to the schoolyard was only a stone's throw away. Students were filing in from all directions. Dieter had still said nothing about me. Then, he slowed his pace and, off-handedly, said, "Most of them agreed you're an okay girl, smart, too. A couple of them called you aloof. Hard to get, is what they meant." I relaxed. It was a rating I could live with.

He lowered his gaze, as he often did when he had something provocative to say. With a tone of objectivity to underline that this wasn't malicious talk, but something he was reluctant to impart, though something that I should know about, he said, "Only Peter. . . He talked big. . . He made a bet."

Dieter inserted another of his cruel pauses.

I couldn't imagine what a bet might entail but, considering how long Dieter took to get to the point, suspected it would be troublesome.

"A bet about you. . . They all accepted it." There was animus in Dieter's delivery, together with a hint of satisfaction.

He waited, baiting me. Finally, he said, "It was for a keg of beer."

"A keg of beer? For what?"

"Peter bet that he could win you over, make you his girl. . . he'd win a keg of beer from the other boys, if he won. He'd pay with a keg of beer, if he lost."

A wave of disgust rushed over me. I felt demeaned and shabby.

What Dieter, Renate, everyone in our class thought about him, in that instant, I realized, I'd wanted to overlook: that Peter was callous, arrogant, cruel.

"He'll lose," I said.

I wished I could've felt thankful to Dieter, for had he not, in his own way, tried to protect me from Peter? I wasn't. I was angry. Dieter hadn't spoken up for me. He'd gone along with the bet, together with the other boys. If it had been his secret hope to win me over for himself, he'd made a bad calculation.

Peter caught up with me walking to my desk before our first period. As I felt his presence near me, the memory of the day before erupted: *Peter leans toward me, pulls me closer.* Here, I changed the memory, in order to preserve my integrity, utterly convinced, now and forever, that it was the truth: *I turn my head away, extricate myself from his embrace. "No," I say.*

Peter tugged at my sweater sleeve.

"This afternoon? At the War Memorial?" he whispered, as his face grazed my hair.

I didn't miss a beat. *"Versuch's mit 'ner anderen. –* Try someone else," I said.

PART THREE

Breaking Away
1956 – 1994

42

I graduated secondary school in Dormagen in the spring of 1956, and continued at a commercial college in Neuss. I was sixteen.

On my first day taking the train from Delrath to Neuss, I eyed Karin K from a distance on the station platform. I was struck by her enviably well-groomed appearance – her blonde hair fashionably cut in a bob, the refined features of her face, her fashionable tartan skirt and twin sweater set, even her finely-trimmed schoolbag that stood out as elegant. I looked away when she turned in my direction. Although I was as guilty of ignoring her as she was guilty of ignoring me, I secretly accused her of being a snob. Still, I was drawn to her. On the fourth or fifth morning, we ended up in the same train compartment – by mutual design, as we admitted to each other later. Halfway to our destination, we struck up a conversation, both of us thrilled to learn we were entering the same class in the same college. From that moment on, we became inseparable friends.

People said we looked like sisters. It flattered me, since I thought of myself as plain next to Karin. She'd been raised in Düsseldorf, 25 kilometers north of Delrath on the east side of the Rhine. Her family had recently moved to Delrath, where they had rented a flat in the second story of Herr Kollenbroich's hair salon. I associated Karin's sophistication with living in a large city. Not only was her bearing different from those of us who'd been raised in small towns, her language was refined, without a trace of a regional accent, a mark of what I thought of as good breeding. Karin's taste in literature was exotic. While I was reading the German language writers of the early twentieth century and post-war years – Thomas Mann, Franz Kafka, Hermann Hesse, Heinrich Böll – she had discovered Sartre, Camus, Simone de Beauvoir. Karin smoked cigarettes.

Eager to discard the ways of my conventional upbringing, I imitated

Karin. I began using the same green colored ink she used, instead of the standard royal blue. I looped my m's and n's in the same affected, upside-down manner as she did. I cut off my permanent-waved curls to match her straight bob. I began smoking *Stuyvesant* brand cigarettes. I devoured *The Second Sex*. Listening to her rudimentary ideas on existentialism, I, too, became a prophet of doom: life was meaningless, godless and absurd. We were quasi-atheists who declared that we were caught in a state of existential *angst*.

Mother disapproved of Karin and of our budding friendship. After I challenged yet another of her digs at Karin – this time that she had the airs of an impostor – she said, "I have nothing against your new friend. She just isn't the right kind of influence for you." Not calling Karin by her name was a sure sign that she harbored objections.

Mother's criticisms tended to be indirect: her dislikes often misplaced. As it turned out, it was Karin's family background she disapproved of and, by a circuitous connection, the recently established *Bundeswehr*, the Federal Armed Forces, and with even less rationale, the now defunct *Wehrmacht*.

"There's talk that your friend's stepfather enlisted in the *Bundeswehr*. As a major. I don't suppose it's a coincidence that that was his rank in the *Wehrmacht*," she said.

She had a point: despite stated policy barring former *Wehrmacht* officers from serving the *Bundeswehr*, Karin's stepfather, among many others, had been accepted into the *Bundeswehr*. In a majority of instances, wartime ranks were restored.

"We don't need the *Bundeswehr* in the first place," Mother said. "Didn't the *Wehrmacht* get us into enough trouble?"

"What does any of this have to do with Karin?" I said, annoyed at her unreasonable comparison.

"Please!" Mother said, "Your friend's family is all about status! What else would warrant their display of self-importance?"

"But Karin's a pacifist," I said, deflecting her remark, "She's as much against the new *Bundeswehr* as I am."

"Say what you want," Mother responded, "They're opportunists and social climbers. They benefited under Hitler, and they're benefiting now."

I ignored Mother's criticism, which did not extend to the fact that Karin's mother was noticeably older than her husband. Karin and I remained best friends. I didn't care for Karin's stepfather either. It wasn't just because of his affiliation with the *Bundeswehr*. He resembled Fredie, Mother's former lover: the poster-boy ideal of the German male in the Thirties – tall, blonde and young – that certain "Aryan" look idealized in Hitler's Germany, that I loathed instinctually. Fredie had long been out of our lives by this time, but was no less despicable in my memory.

After school, Karin and I sometimes stopped in at *Café Calvis*. We'd sit at our favorite table in an alcove, drinking black coffee and smoking cigarettes.

One afternoon, we exchanged war stories. I told her how I had witnessed a bomb fall one early summer day in 1944, at the height of the Allied air raids in the Rhineland. It had stayed with me as a grim memory. I was a four-year-old, alone on the verandah of our Delrath flat, rocking my doll to sleep.

"I heard the telltale sound of bombers. I looked up and saw a plane flying just above the power lines. I trailed it with my eyes, then saw a cone-shaped object plummet from its belly. I'd never seen a bomb before but knew instantly that's what it was."

Here, I stopped my account, but for an instant, I relived the terror I had felt. Coming straight at our house, the bomb would hit us, I was sure. There was an unearthly hiss, immediately followed by the deafening sound of an explosion. The tile floor beneath me shook, and the air around me vibrated. I squeezed my eyes shut and waited, the doll still in my arms. A calmness soothed my limbs, and a silence lulled me. I was sure that I was dead. Time passed in which nothing happened, only a sense, as real as anything I had ever experienced, that I was no longer alive. Then a dog barked, then another, and another. Mother called my name. She came rushing onto the verandah, Gitta in her arms. She knelt down and squeezed me and my doll to her chest.

"Mein Gott," she said.

To Karin, I said, "The bomb hit a house at the train station. No one died. But my mother feared for our safety. Soon after, we evacuated to a small village in Thüringen."

Karin was unimpressed with my one-bomb story. Blowing out a long stream of white smoke, she said, "I saw showers of bombs drop on my neighborhood in Düsseldorf. It looked like giant black hail released from airplanes streaking across the sky." She said she had seen the streets ablaze and buildings crumble. She had seen a small boy blown apart after he'd picked up a grenade while he was searching for his playthings in the rubble of his bombed-out family home. She'd seen heaps of corpses; her arm swept a high arc to indicate their size. "The dead stared at you, their eyes wide open. Legs and arms strewn randomly, reaching for something. My mother pulled me away so I wouldn't see, but I saw it all anyway."

"The war was so much worse for people like you living in cities," I said, not sure that I could fully trust the harrowing descriptions of the scenes Karin said she had witnessed. I only knew a few facts and figures: the bombings of Dresden with upwards of 25,000 people dead, of Berlin, Hamburg, Cologne – and those bombed abroad by the German *Luftwaffe,* most famously, the London Blitz. I had seen firsthand the ruins of the Cologne cathedral. I hadn't witnessed the kind of destruction that Karin said she had. I knew, too, about Hiroshima and Nagasaki. But in our small town of Delrath, only the house at the train station had been struck, and I hadn't actually seen the dead.

Karin introduced me to a sophisticated life I had only imagined or had only regarded enviously from afar. "Let's go to Düsseldorf," she proposed when, occasionally, school let out early. We would take the streetcar from Neuss across the bridge over the Rhine to the big city she knew so well. We strolled along the *Königsallee,* nicknamed *Kö* by the locals. A chestnut-tree-bordered canal ran along its center. Sculptures of mythological figures flanked the iron bridges. Lined with high-end boutiques and cafés, it catered to a *nouveau riche* clientele.

Skipping classes one morning, we had breakfast at the Breidenbacher Hof, the city's most exclusive hotel. We put on the airs of the privileged class and ordered coffee and croissants, the least expensive items on the menu.

Saturday evenings, we hung out at the New Orleans Club, among trendy young people, and listened to Dixieland Jazz.

We watched Fellini's *La Strada* at the Düsseldorf cinema, both of us castigating Giullietta Masina's character for her enslavement to a man, something, we declared, we would never tolerate. The only other visit to a real cinema had been with Mother, when she had taken me to see *Das Lied von Bernadette,* also in Düsseldorf. Apart from that, I'd often gone to Sunday afternoon screenings at the local bowling alley, where the standard fare were American westerns and postwar German and Austrian *Heimatfilme* – noted for their idyllic settings, sentimental themes and simplistic morality.

Catching the train home at the end of the day, we'd upgrade our student tickets to first-class fare with what little money we hadn't spent. We'd sink into the dark green velvet-upholstered seats alongside a handful of men dressed in business suits and ties. We blew cigarette smoke into the stale air.

All public schools offered separate classes in Catholic and Protestant Religious Studies. We were assigned to one or the other, according to our denomination. Karin, who had been born into a Lutheran family, attended Protestant Religious Studies, I attended Catholic Religious Studies.

A new teacher had replaced the old pastor in Karin's class. She touted his progressive teaching style and casual demeanor. "You must come to his class," she said, adding mock-breathlessly, "He's young and dazzlingly good-looking to boot." I was easily persuaded. I skipped my final class of the day in Catholic Religious Studies and sat in on hers during the same time slot.

At that time, I was still lacking the convictions of the full-fledged atheist I wanted to be. Protestantism seemed like a less radical alternative. Karin, nominally Lutheran, had praised it as a more contemporary and liberal expression of Christianity. "None of your Catholic pomp, for one," she'd said, a criticism with which I couldn't argue.

"He'll make a convert of you," Karin said, as we sat down in the front row of the classroom.

The man who took his seat on the edge of the teacher's desk bore no resemblance to any of the other male teachers. They dressed in suits and

ties, even on the hottest days. He wore a cable-knit sweater and
corduroy slacks. He was good-looking in a leading-man way, a rugged
version of Lawrence Olivier, who was both Karin's heartthrob and mine,
since we'd seen him in *Hamlet*. The teacher also had wavy, medium
blonde hair, a touch too long for the times, which added to his non-
conformist appeal.

He looked unflustered by the chatter and restlessness of the two
dozen or more students. As if he didn't mind letting an eternity pass,
he waited, until it was so quiet that not the squeaking of a single
chair could be heard. He held the silence, scanning the classroom,
meeting everyone's eyes in a moment of recognition. Only then did
he begin to speak.

"We'll suspend our regular curriculum for today." An approving
rumble went through the room. It subsided abruptly when he raised
his hand.

He spoke slowly at first, his diction precise and unfaltering. The
words sounded prepared. "Tonight, on October 1, the stage adaptation
of the *Diary of Anne Frank* will open simultaneously in seven cities all
over this country." As he continued, his speech gained urgency, "It is an
important moment in post-National Socialist history, for it will remind
us Germans of the most horrific aspect of our history. It will conceivably
mark the beginning of the end of the silence around it."

We were nearing the close of 1956, eleven and a half years since the
war had ended. Never before had I heard the name of *Anne Frank*. I had
no inkling of the silence he was talking about – at least not then.

He proceeded to tell the brief outline of Anne Frank and her
family's story: persecuted as Jews who had emigrated to Holland from
Germany, Anne, her parents and sister went into hiding in an
Amsterdam garret in 1942. After two years and a month they were
discovered and deported by the German Gestapo. He told us that Anne
had left behind a diary, first published as a book in 1947, now adapted
into a play.

"Anne died in a concentration camp. She was sixteen. Of her family,
only her father survived."

Here the teacher paused briefly – perhaps, to honor Anne's fate;
perhaps, to give us a moment alone with her. But he must also have

known that, what he was going to say next, would be like dropping an even bigger kind of bomb on a roomful of unsuspecting teenagers.

"There were six million like her, Jews, German Jews, European Jews, who all suffered the same fate – annihilation in concentration camps, at the hands of Germany."

Again, the teacher went silent. He got off the corner of the desk where he had been sitting and, taking a few steps closer to the front row, looked out into a classroom of stunned students. No one stirred. So explosive, so unbelievable, was his revelation, my immediate response was one of numbness, speechlessness and, then, a sensation of being strung between two irreconcilable realities – the benign world I knew and a nameless world, a dark world.

After a pause, so long and so painful, it seemed that the silence would last forever, the teacher continued. "What I am about to tell you, most, if not all of you, will not have heard before."

He remained standing. Then he delivered piece after piece of excruciating detail that summed up the history of the *Judenverfolgung,* the persecution of the Jews, against the background of the Third Reich. He spoke without notes. Although his presentation was compelling, his voice was neither detached nor passionate, as if he wanted all of us to absorb the unfathomable in our own, personal way.

Adolf Hitler . . . *Nationalsozialismus …Antisemitismus* . . . exclusion of Jews from the professions and the arts . . . *'Juden verboten'* . . . *'Juden raus'* . . . ghettos . . . the Nuremberg racial laws . . . November 9, 1938, *Kristallnacht,* shattered glass, burning synagogues, Jews being murdered . . . *Judenstern,* the yellow Star of David . . . Gestapo… deportation . . . Warsaw uprising . . . *SS* . . . concentration camps . . . death camps . . . Adolf Eichmann . . . forced labor . . . atrocities . . . starvation . . . *Selektion* . . . extermination . . . gas chambers . . . *Zyklon B* . . . Auschwitz . . . Buchenwald . . . Dachau . . . Sobibor . . . Bergen-Belsen . . . Treblinka . . . *Endlösung,* final solution – the systematic, government-instituted annihilation of six million Jews and others deemed undesirable.

Intermittent clicking came from the radiators under the windows. Otherwise, it was unnaturally silent in a classroom of students prone to shifting in their seats, leafing through books, clearing their throats. It was as if I were listening to a disembodied voice spelling out ever more staggering dimensions of horror.

I don't recall when the thoughts began, in the classroom or not until later; whether there were only feelings, at first, that I gave voice to afterwards. But I do remember that my belief in a basically good world had been shattered, in a way that my own firsthand experiences of loss and hardship had not.

I had always known some ache, one that was in the air, for as long as I could remember – unspoken, but always there. Not about the war. Terrible as that had been in terms of lives lost, the ruin of cities, it had been a war, I thought, like many wars before. The ache was not about death, either. Onkel Jean's, Grandmother's – their deaths were the natural deaths of human fate. My father's death, a soldier's death, even his was different. None of it could be compared to the monstrous deeds I had just heard about.

The teacher's remarks tapped something eerily recognizable: a tone of voice, innuendoes I had sensed in adult conversations that I could not have pinpointed before. I began to dimly recognize that I had been engulfed by a silence. Later, it would occur to me that, by not asking questions, I had perpetuated that silence.

Millions of human lives murderously ended. That had been the nameless horror, known and unknown, secreted away in the hearts of people, guarded like a terrible family secret the elders all knew and no one spoke about.

Strangely, the descriptions of the horrendous details I heard that day did not produce any images. Those would remain beyond imagining. Not until some time later would I see what had been documented in photographs and films: emaciated human beings clinging to barbed wire; heaps of nude corpses; mass graves. Still, those images, brutal as they were, were removed from any immediate horror. That kind of experience would not come until I visited Dachau years later, when, in a sea of people, I felt myself among one of the condemned.

Words, familiar words, became endowed with meanings of horror they hadn't had before – *Viehwagen* – cattle car, *Lager* – camp. New words, too. Words I had never heard spoken – *Gaskammern,* gas chambers, *Kristallnacht, Selektion* – words denoting utter inhumanity. And the names of places – that were once just villages or towns – would forever signify nothing but the evil perpetrated there.

As for my own losses, I couldn't have named them. I didn't yet have the language to articulate them. But they happened that day: the loss of country, the country of which I had felt myself a part, the only country I knew. A loss of trust, even in those I loved. Why had no one told me about what had happened? At times, I would even feel ashamed of the German language that I had so loved and that had been misused in such obscene, brutal, sadistic ways. I also felt the stigma of my inheritance, by association, of guilt.

The bell at the end of class sounded jarring that early afternoon. Absent was the usual stampede of students heading for the door. The teacher remained standing at his desk, maybe to make himself available for questions, maybe to allow us time to absorb what we had heard. No one moved or uttered a word.

I looked out the window. Rain-heavy autumn clouds hung close to the leafless crowns of the oaks on the playground, their branches visible as ghostly configurations through the steamed-up glass. Even the stark fluorescent lighting could not lift the dreary-weather pall that hung in the room.

Finally, the rustling of paper, the snapping sound of satchel locks, the shuffling of shoes on the wood-planked floor. A somber group of sixteen-, seventeen- and eighteen-year-olds filed out of the classroom.

Except for Karin. She took a headlong flight, pushing her way out the door. I thought I heard a scream. Was it her?

I caught up with Karin at the school gate. We started out to the train station, just the two of us, side by side, along residential streets and down Neusser Straße, the same route we always took. We didn't speak. The knowledge of our country's shameful past hovered between us, like a rift. We moved along briskly. Drops of rain splashed on the sidewalk, large like summer rain but cold and whipping.

We made our final turn at the overpass. Trains rolled in both directions. The station entrance lay ahead. We passed a block of ruins that had not yet been touched by the reconstruction efforts of the fifties. Piles of rubble, overgrown with tall weeds, left to neglect. And at the very end, the skeleton of a bombed-out building, an ugly monument to the past.

It rained more heavily now. We still hadn't spoken, when Karin, without notice, started to run ahead of me and darted up the concrete steps of the bombed-out building. I followed her to the bottom of the staircase. She was leaning against the remnants of brick, framing what had once been an entrance. Her head tilted up, she let the rain splash on her face, down through the roofless ruins.

"What he said was the truth, wasn't it?" she said. Her question, it seemed, was directed at the ruins, or the open sky.

"Mein Vater hatte mit alledem nichts zu tun. – My father had nothing to do with any of this," she said, coming down the steps. She pressed her palms together, as if in prayer. "You must believe me," she pleaded.

Karin's birth father had been in the *SS.*

An abbreviation for *Schutzstaffel,* literally Protection Squadron, the *SS* had been a paramilitary unit and Hitler's elite guard. The term itself was as familiar to me as *Wehrmacht* – from which it was separate – and the three branches of the *Wehrmacht: Infantrie, Luftwaffe, Marine.* Yet, the ring of the name itself had an undertone of dread as well as of superiority. There was a kind of awe attached to the SS and, at times, I'd regretted that my father had not been one of them and wondered if he had been less deserving, less of a soldier, less of a man. My contempt for the SS had come later, when I was in my early teens. "The *SS,* they were brutes," Mother had said, talking about Herr Scheer, who had been assigned to a special unit during the war and returned as a drunk. She hadn't elaborated what kind of unit, and I hadn't queried her further. But her tone of voice, the expression of disgust in her face, had been enough for me to realize that the SS had been an infamous force.

I did not know, then, that there had been two separate branches of the *SS:* the *Waffen SS,* which was the fighting *SS,* and the branch of the *SS* in charge of the concentration and extermination camps. Nor did I know of any complicity and the part the *Wehrmacht* played in the persecution of the Jews. That wouldn't come to light until forty or fifty years later.

But I could not exonerate Karin's father. Nor could I exonerate my mother, my two grandmothers, my grandfather, my aunts and uncles. Or any German. Their silence implicated them. And I, who had barely been born, I, too, felt implicated as a citizen of the country that had committed such atrocities.

43

Karin and I remained silent on our train ride and on our walk home. We parted on the sidewalk in front of my house with a somber *"Tschüss.* – Bye."

I pushed open the wrought-iron gate to the driveway. The wet gravel crunched under my step as I hastened toward the house. Through the window, Mother's back-lighted silhouette was visible at her work table, on the far side of the arched opening connecting dining room and kitchen. Seeing her, a rage reared in me, so violent that I slammed the front door shut.

I stormed into the kitchen and dropped my satchel at my feet. Mother looked up from grating raw potatoes. Her hand froze halfway down the metal grater. Her welcoming smile vanished.

"Was ist? – What's wrong?" she said.

"Dass du mir nie was über die Judenvenichtung gesagt hast. – That you never told me anything about the extermination of the Jews."

She wiped her hands on a kitchen towel.

"Is this more nonsense your friend Karin has put in your head?" she said.

Her question irritated me. "Can't you stop picking on Karin?"

It took a while until she said, *"Was hätte ich dir denn sagen sollen?* – What is it that I should have told you?"

"For example, that six million Jews were annihilated in concentration camps."

Again, she paused, uncomfortably.

"Where did you hear that?"

"Does it matter?"

When she didn't respond, I said, "It's a fact. And you knew about it."

"What's come into your head? How dare you!"

I raised my voice. "You had to know about it! You and everybody else!"

"I won't have you speak to me in that tone," she said.

For a moment, I thought she had decided to terminate the discussion. But she went on, *"Ich sag's dir. Ich hab nichts davon gewusst. Damals hab' ich nichts davon gewusst. –* I'm telling you. I didn't know about it. I didn't know about it, not then."

"How can you say that? People were disappearing, and you didn't hear or see anything?"

"I didn't. There were no Jews here. The Jews lived in cities."

"That's your excuse?"

Mother glanced out the kitchen window, as if wondering what to say next or whether to say what came to her mind.

"There were rumors that the Jews were being relocated outside of Germany. In Poland. Hungary. That's what everybody believed."

"It's what you wanted to believe!"

"I knew nothing else. Even if I had, do you really think there was something I could have done?"

"Yes!" I said, emphatically, "You could have spoken up."

"You don't know what you're talking about. This wasn't a free country. We lived in a dictatorship, under a dictator-"

"–who you and my father and all of Germany cheered and applauded." I yelled mockingly, *"Heil Hitler. Heil Hitler."*

"Stop this," she said. "And leave your father out of this. He fought for his fatherland and sacrificed his life for it."

"Yes. . . for an insane and murderous ideology."

Mother said nothing in protest. She adopted an apologetic tone. "We were in the middle of a war. I worried about your lives, yours and Gitta's, whether we were going to survive another night's air raid. I worried about your father at the front. About what to feed you for your next meal. That's what I worried about. Not about whether the propaganda we were fed was correct or not."

"What about before the war?"

"I have nothing against Jews. Never did. . . Tante Irma, after all, was married to a Jew."

"That makes cousin Jochen half Jewish. But you never talk about that. Is it because you're ashamed of it, or want to hide it?"

"He's half Jewish, yes. What's there to talk about? He's Catholic now."

Mother, who was always mild-mannered, who I had never heard raise her voice, was noticeably agitated. A pinkish color had risen to her face.

Not ready to let up, I said, "What about anti-Semitism? There never was any?"

"There were reasons. . . The banks, the big department stores, the newspapers, before the war, they were said to be almost exclusively owned or run by Jews, while the rest of the population suffered. That's why they were resented."

"It was a good reason to round them up and gas them?"

"You're putting words in my mouth," she said.

"That's what it sounds like."

"*Unsinn.* – Nonsense."

"That's all you can say?"

"Listen," she said, "not everything was bad in those days. There were good things, too."

"Millions murdered! And you say, there were good things, too?"

"Yes. In the beginning, at any rate. . ."

"How can you . . . ," I said. I felt mounting rage.

"I'm telling you for the last time. I never condoned the killing of Jews or anyone else. And I did not know about it."

Mother went back to grating the half-grated potato that had turned grayish. I had been dismissed.

I walked to the door. I felt a desire to resume the attack.

I stared hard at Mother: "I hate this country." I choked, forcing back my tears. "And everyone in it."

Contrary to Mother's claim, I would learn much later, when I was already in college, that there had been those in opposition to Hitler's dictatorship: those who had disagreed but not spoken up, a position that would be called *internal exile*; those – some of them well-known writers and artists – who had left the country, to live in *external exile,* many of whom returned to their homeland after the war; and groups of men and women with enough integrity, and even more courage, to put their lives on the line and act. There was the *Weiße Rose,* the *White Rose,* a student resistance movement at the University of Munich, with the siblings Hans and Sophie Scholl at its core. There were Pastor Dietrich Bonhoeffer and other clergy. There were the men who conspired to assassinate Hitler on the 20th of July, 1944, in a failed plot called *Unternehmen Walküre,* Operation Valkyrie, with its key figure of Claus Schenk Graf von Stauffenberg. Not one of the conspirators, more than 150 in all, escaped execution or imprisonment.

My ideals lined up with those of the *Weiße Rose.* I would have joined in their cause, I postulated with self-righteous idealism.

No one, it seemed, dared to speak about the German resistance to the Nazis until well into the 1950s and early 1960s, not until the country had accepted responsibility for World War II and, specifically, for the Holocaust. While acknowledging culpability, most Germans still claimed not to have known about the mass murders of Jews and others, at the time. Reparation payments were made to Israel in accordance with the *Wiedergutmachungsabkommen,* the reparation agreement of 1952, by the Adenauer government. Eventually, the more humane side of Germans in the form of the German resistance could legitimately be given a voice. I might have heard the name of Graf von Stauffenberg at an earlier time, but not until my college years in Munich did I become fully aware of any organized opposition to the Hitler regime. Nothing could compensate for what had happened, yet I felt a certain amount of exoneration learning that not every German was evil.

To her credit, Mother had always been candid about her membership in the girls' league of the Hitler Youth and her position as a group leader. She would talk enthusiastically about their gatherings at the old windmill in Nievenheim that, later, was bombed. In her telling throughout the years, nostalgia for a happier youth would mingle uncomfortably with misgivings about an ideology that, in the end and by her own admission, had engendered nothing but devastation. "It was innocent fun, in those days before the war," she would say, reminiscing about evenings of song and story-telling around campfires, about bicycle outings along the Rhine, about Saturday night dances and the young men who had courted her. "There were more dashing fellows than your father, but in the end, I chose him. He had a bright future."

The discussion Mother and I had that day after school left us strangely at odds. I passed judgment on her and on every German alive, and on those dead, as well – except for my father. In those early days of grappling with the degree of my parents' responsibility, I put my father beyond reproach. Dead before I was five, he remained locked in my early memory of him, beyond guilt or innocence. Mother, on the other hand, would become the scapegoat, on whom I unloaded my muddled sense of the guilt of her generation. As I saw it from my teenage perspective, her participation in the system, however limited, and her silence, had made her guilty by more than association. She had been a blind follower of, perhaps even an apologist for, the evil forces of her time.

I, on the other hand, sought to make myself not culpable through my own puffed-up standards of morality and judgment.

44

The preceding day's downpour had washed the sidewalks clean. Rainwater still glistened in the channels of the streetcar tracks. Clusters of clouds, whipped into fanciful patterns of light and dark, threatened more rain to come. It was colder than it had been the day before.

A short distance past City Hall, Karin and I turned into a narrow shopping arcade. Tucked away in the far corner was *Bücherei Bollen,* a small, but well-stocked, bookstore and frequent stop on our way to the train station. A new display of books in the window caught our eye: two shelves, one above the other, each with a row of identical paperbacks, precariously lined up like dominoes.

Karin read the title out loud, *"Das Tagebuch der Anne Frank."* The German translation of the original Dutch *Het Achterhus,* and the American, *Anne Frank: The Diary of a Young Girl.*

On the cover was a glossy image of a row of tall, narrow buildings alongside a canal, in black, white and gray tones, with a winter tree reaching into a narrow strip of blood red sky.

Das Tagebuch der Anne Frank. There it was.

I announced to Mother that I would be in my room all afternoon and evening, that I had some reading to do, and would not have supper. To placate her, I took a slice of pumpernickel bread and an apple with me. Mother accepted, under protest.

I propped myself against a haphazardly piled up mound of blankets in the corner of my bed. The slanted attic wall met the top rail of the headboard. Though it was still light outside, I turned on the reading lamp, and covered myself with a throw. Its coarse wool prickled against my neck and arms

I turned Anne Frank's diary to its back cover. Above a half-page biography was her photo, in black-and-white; she looked out from that photo, an open book resting in front of her. My gaze fastened on her young face: her pretty smile, her finely chiseled nose. But it was her dark eyes, complementing her black, shoulder-length hair, that I was drawn to over and over. I noticed the crocheted pattern of her sweater, sleeve bunched up above her left elbow, and a round-faced watch on her wrist. The watch struck me as oddly emblematic of the passage of time and of time running out. I examined the photo more closely under the light. Barely discernible was a thin band on her ring finger. Such a small detail! So personal, so intimate a discovery, the sight of it made me cry.

My eyes returned to her eyes. The longer I looked, the more real Anne became, and her death, increasingly unreal.

I opened the book. Leafing past the introduction, I read Anne's preamble, addressing her diary, on June 12, 1942. *"I hope that I can confide everything in you, as I have never been able to confide in anyone, and I hope that you will be of great support and comfort to me."*

It was followed by an entry on Sunday, June 14, 1942, two days after her 13th birthday. *"Among the many gifts,"* she wrote, *"I saw you, my diary, first. It was without question the best present of all."* Her words were animated, when she reported about her birthday party – the many boys and girls who attended, about the Rin-Tin-Tin film they watched, and the fun that was had by everyone. It sounded so much like my own birthday parties and those of my girlfriends; it was easy to make believe that she lived in a normal world.

Less than a week later, on Saturday, June 20, 1942, after introducing her family, she went on to enumerate the *Hitler laws,* as she called them, regulating Jewish life in Amsterdam: *"After 1940, the good times began to dwindle. First came the war, then the capitulation* [of Holland], *then the takeover by the Germans. That's when our misery began. . . Jews were required to wear the yellow star. They had to turn in their bicycles. They were banned from riding on streetcars, and were not allowed to drive cars. All Jews were required to do their shopping between 3 p.m. and 5 p.m., and only in Jewish-owned stores. They were not allowed to be out in the streets after 8 p.m., not even in their gardens or on their balconies. They were forbidden to visit theaters, cinemas or any other places of entertainment. They were no longer allowed to swim, play tennis or hockey, nor participate in any other athletic activities. Jews were forbidden to visit*

Christians in their homes. Jewish children were required to attend Jewish schools. One restriction after another. From then on, this was the kind of pressure we had to live under."

Her entry illustrated the blatant difference between the lives endured by millions of Jews all over Europe and the lives of their non-Jewish fellow citizens. I contemplated Anne's final demise. How, at a different time and under different circumstances, I might have met a fate similar to hers. What if I had been Jewish; or if Christians, like me, had been targeted for persecution and extermination? What struck me even more was the alarming recognition that her life had been interrupted by the murderous deeds sanctioned and committed in the name of my country, of my parents and their fellow contemporaries.

In a second entry on that same Saturday, she addressed her imaginary friend, *Kitty* – the name she had given to her diary – for the first time. Like a girl living in ordinary times, she talked about ordinary things – how she enjoyed playing ping-pong and, afterwards, going for ice cream in one of the cafés open to Jews. She confided in Kitty about the many boys who'd fallen for her, and how she ignored their adoring glances. She concluded the day's account, *"With this, the cornerstone of our friendship has been laid. Until tomorrow! Anne"*

What followed were reports to Kitty about her life, with little or no mention of hardships – a life not unlike my own: she was the daughter of ordinary parents. She lived in an ordinary flat with ordinary furnishings that made me think of Grandmother's old-fashioned parlor suite. She went to school with ordinary boys and girls.

Anne had been born in Frankfurt am Main, in 1929, a distance of about 200 kilometers south of us. A business opportunity had brought the family to Amsterdam. Like me, Anne was German. It was a bond, in my mind, that belonging to a different religious group could not sever. Until she was five years old, we had shared the same language, spoke the same words, sang the same songs. I thought of this as a kinship deeper even than nationality. Did she remember any of it? Or did she follow the understandable impulse to extricate herself from the language of a people who inflicted such suffering upon her, even if that language had been her own mother tongue?

As I read, I ached to bring Anne back from exile – to be a girl like me, a German girl, the girl she had once been and, in my longing, still was. But I had the gnawing sense, already, that my fantasies were driven by a self-serving desire to comfort myself, a desire to roll back time and erase the events that had sent Anne into exile and death.

Mother's steps coming up the staircase interrupted my thoughts. I heard them move along the hallway, expecting them to stop at my bedroom door. I watched the brass door handle, waiting to see it pushed down, as if by an invisible hand. But it did not move – the steps went past my door, then faded.

I picked up the book again and resumed reading. *"So much has happened, it is as if the whole world has been turned upside down."* These were the words that marked the day the Frank family were forced to go into hiding in the annex on 206 Prinsengracht, long prepared in anticipation of such a possibility. It happened on Wednesday, July 8, 1942, after a notice for Anne's older sister, Margot, to report to the SS. *"A call-up. . . everyone knows what that means: I pictured concentration camps. . . lonely cells."* It was followed by anxious details of the family packing up hurriedly and, with the help of concerned friends, escaping from their home late that night. Eventually, the Frank family was joined by the van Pels's, their son Peter – two and a half years older than Anne – and Fritz Pfeffer.

From one day to the next, Anne and her family's life had shrunk to the size of their limited quarters. Their confinement, the reasons for it, and the constant threat of being discovered were beyond my imagination. Though it was tempting, as well, to romanticize hiding in a secret place, safe from an evil world, and left to reading, writing in one's diary, daydreaming.

In entry after entry, Anne reported to the imaginary Kitty about the day-to-day routines in the annex and about some of the challenges of living in close proximity with family and near-strangers. Later in the diary, she wrote, at times excitedly, at other times soberingly, about her budding love for Peter, their times spent alone in the nook under the roof, their first kiss. In enviably mature terms, she elaborated on her plans for the future – the writer she wanted to be – on thoughts about God and the world, and also on her doubts about her relationship with Peter.

On Wednesday, February 23, 1944, she wrote: *"From my favorite spot on the floor I look up at the blue sky and the bare chestnut tree, on whose branches small raindrops glisten, and at the seagulls and other birds gliding elegantly like silver on the wind. . . Through the open window, I looked over a large section of Amsterdam, over all the roofs and on to the horizon. I could barely make out its demarcation blurred in the pale blue. 'As long as this exists,' I thought, 'this sunshine, this cloudless sky – and I may live to see it – I must not be sad.'"*

I lifted my eyes from the page. In my imagination, I craned my neck, looking at the same small piece of sky Anne saw, the same leafless tree and the same roofs of a city that I, too, could not enter. The world was within a stone's throw, but out of reach. An awful dread came over me, of being trapped without hope of escaping. I felt my own room shrinking.

It was raining again. Irregular rivulets of large and small water beads streamed down the window pane. A short row of potted cacti, which would soon be moved inside for winter, stood drenched on the outside sill, dew-like drops suspended from their spines. Raising myself to my knees, I looked out the window: pine trees glistening from the rain, above them the big autumn sky and, below, Mother's lush patches of late-blooming asters between the shrubbery and a path winding to the gate. How different, in reality, was my view from Anne's!

After darkness, I heard the mute clatter of dishes from downstairs and the refrigerator door falling shut, and a few minutes later, Mother calling Gitta for supper. The bread and apple sat on my nightstand, untouched.

What a contrast my daily existence was to Anne's, where even ordinary household noises could have endangered her safety and the safety of everyone else in the annex. Where food supplies had to be brought in by trusted helpers, at odd hours, when the risk of being spotted was minimized. Where a crack of light from a window detected by a neighbor could have given them away.

I picked up reading where I had left off. After only a few pages, on Tuesday, April 11, 1944, Anne wrote: *"My head throbs. I don't know where to begin,"* leading to a tense depiction of a break-in on the ground floor, a part of the building that was operated as a warehouse. *"Everyone's breath was audible, otherwise no one moved. . . steps in the house, the private office, the kitchen. . . Steps on our staircase, then the rattling of the revolving bookcase. These moments are indescribable."* How close the inhabitants of the annex had come to being exposed!

Holding my place with my thumb, I closed the book and revisited Anne's picture on the back cover. I looked into her face, trying to uncover something, but I didn't know what. The photo had been taken during happier times, when the horror of what lay ahead was only dawning. I reflected on the deadly fear that had taken possession of her and of everyone in the annex. Had there been times in my growing-up as frightening as this time in hers? Nothing came to mind. In my own thinking, my life had been sheltered, good, despite the many wartime events that contradicted such an assessment. Then, without bidding, the memory returned of our escape from East Germany across the Soviet-patrolled border. It was followed, almost immediately, by the idea that Anne's and my fate bore no comparison: we had survived; Anne and most of her family had lost their lives.

"Liebe Anne. – Dear Anne," I said inaudibly, my eyes still on her face, *"Bleib verschont!* – Be spared!"

"I want to go on living even after my death!" Anne wrote, giving voice to her desire to become a writer, who would be remembered beyond her lifetime. However, not far under the surface, misgivings about her personal death again and again troubled the vision of her future. As I read her words and imagined her hopes and fears, I became haunted by the idea that I was alive to read her diary while she was not. In an eerie way, it was as if I were reading a book written from beyond the grave. Of the millions of victims, Anne had become the first victim with a name.

I slowed down my reading: I did not want the end to come.

But it did.

It was past midnight when I came to Anne's last letter to Kitty, written on August 1, 1944. *"'A little bundle of contradictions.' Indeed, I have not one but two souls within me. One embodies my exuberant cheerfulness, my habit of making fun of things, my love for life, and, above all, the way I take everything lightly. . . This side usually lies in wait and pushes aside the other, the one that is so much more beautiful, purer and deeper. It's true, no one knows Anne's better side, which is why only a few people care for me."*

Anne's insight thrilled me. Had she read Goethe's poem, *Gingo Biloba*, by chance, as I had in our German literature class? How I identified with its final lines! *Fühlst du nicht an meinen Liedern / daß ich eins und doppelt bin?* – Is it not my songs' suggestion / that I'm one and also two? I had copied the poem into my diary. I marveled at Anne's astute description of her inner division. My own sense of duality had been nothing more than a diffuse unease and a pull in different and opposite directions.

In Anne's last letter to Kitty, the final sentence read: . . . *I look for ways to become how I would like to be and how I could be, if. . . yes, if no other humans lived on this earth. Anne*

It was followed by a short line printed in italics: *"Anne's diary ends here"*.

I went over and over the same four words, in disbelief. I had known the outcome before I began reading Anne's diary, yet it could not be. Yet it had to be.

I did not want to accept what I would learn in the brief postscript that came after a page left empty. I wanted to delay the inescapable end: *"On August 4, 1944, the 'Green Police'* (the Gestapo) *broke into the annex, arresting its eight inhabitants, as well as Kraler and Koophuis* (two of the small group of helpers), *and transported them to German and Dutch concentration camps, respectively. The Gestapo robbed and vandalized the annex. Among old books, magazines and newspapers inadvertently left behind, Miep and Elli* (the two remaining helpers) *later discovered Anne's diary. With the exception of a few passages, of little interest to the reader, the original text has been printed. Of those who had been in hiding, only Anne's father returned. Kraler and Koophuis survived the deprivations they endured in Dutch camps, and have been reunited with their families. Anne died in March 1945, in the concentration camp of Bergen-Belsen, two months before the liberation of Holland."*

I pulled out my own diary from under the mattress where I kept it hidden. I opened Anne's to an entry she had written in the middle of July, 1944. Using my emerald green ink fountain pen, I copied parts of a paragraph: *"It is a miracle that I have not given up all my hopes, even though they seem absurd and impossible to realize. Yet, I cling to them, because I still believe that people are good at heart. . . I see the world slowly being transformed into a wilderness; I hear the ever approaching thunder, which will destroy us, too; I feel the suffering of millions and yet, when I look up into the sky, I believe, that everything will change for the better again. . ."*

I underlined, <u>People are</u> good at heart. I clung to those words. I would always remember them, as they spoke of hope and redemption for all of mankind. I felt personally included in Anne's prayer-like words.

Forty years later, a dream: *I am sitting on the stone floor of a synagogue. Two widely spaced pillars support the low arched ceiling, reminiscent of a crypt. Other people are present, among them my three children, and a rabbi who explains to me that I am here to say the Kaddish, the prayer said by a mourner. He spells out the word. It is a long string of letters, many more than the word itself actually consists of.*

The next night, another dream: *I am back in the same synagogue/ crypt. The ceiling is even lower than it was the night before. Anne Frank and I are alone. Sitting on the floor beside me, she reads out loud from her diary and shows me the pages. I realize that the handwriting is my own. Anne has traced over my words in emerald green ink.*

45

A new spirit descended on our class in the spring of 1957, as we neared graduation. We talked among ourselves and dreamed aloud, agonizing about the directions that would take us into the adult world. It had been drummed into us by our parents and teachers that the choices we made now would determine the rest of our lives. It was a daunting prospect.

Without any sense of a particular calling, I considered the further study of languages, only because Fräulein Köhne, a year earlier, had suggested that I had a talent for them. While language-centered professions – foreign language teacher, translator, interpreter – seemed only distantly appealing, the idea of entering another culture through its language intrigued me. However, I could think of no profession that would actually allow me to do that.

I was in my seventh year of studying English, and my fourth year of French. I had a good grasp of the grammar of both languages. My vocabularies were adequate; but I had no experience in spontaneously expressing myself in either of these languages. Whatever it was I wanted to say or write, I first formulated in German, then translated it word for word. It was a cumbersome process that regularly required the use of a dictionary.

The classroom doors swung open; students piled into the hallway and headed in all directions. I caught sight of Karin as she plowed her way toward me. Craning her head over the heads and shoulders of the last remaining students between us, she called out, breathlessly, "You won't believe this," and, as she pushed closer, "They're offering a work/study program abroad. All we have to do is sign up. They'll make the arrangements."

"Where?" I asked.

"England. Newcastle upon Tyne."

I was almost certain my plan to go to England would not gain Mother's approval, therefore I didn't ask for it. I simply informed her of my decision. Other than an implicit expectation that I would go to college, she had never put demands on me. But a work/study program in a foreign country was not, I was certain, a choice she would readily accept.

Traveling in the 1950s was still exotic. For many Germans, it was also still out of reach financially or, at best, limited to destinations within Germany – most commonly, the North Sea islands and the Bavarian Alps. Mother vacationed in the same spa town of Idar-Oberstein in the Hunsrück mountains every summer. Only the well-to-do frequented the trendy spots in Switzerland, Italy or Spain – as Tante Irma had. Skilled workers, following the prospect of higher wages, took short-term construction jobs abroad with German companies, mainly in the Middle East.

Mother put forth one argument after another. "You're too young." "There are plenty of good colleges in Germany." "It's a waste of time." "You'll get homesick." I countered her objections stubbornly. Nothing could dissuade me, not even her final plea, *"Die Deutschen werden im Ausland nicht gerne gesehen.* – Germans are not welcome in foreign countries."

I discredited Mother's final argument as just another of the far-fetched ploys she grasped for when she found herself in a bind. Once in England, I would be too naïve to recognize, and too arrogant to admit, that there had been truth to what Mother had said. I would manage to conceal, even from myself, the obvious: that neither Karin nor I made friends with English students, despite our efforts.

I had never examined why it was so important for me to study abroad. It seemed the natural, perhaps the adventurous, course to take, and certainly one that would benefit a career in languages.

That it was the first step in a journey that would eventually lead me out of Germany altogether never crossed my mind.

In the spring of 1957, a week after graduation, Mother and Herr Hamacher took me to the Düsseldorf airport, Herr Hamacher at the wheel of his car. Mother's semi-resident *Bekannter* for the past three years, he would remain her companion until his death 25 years later.

Also with us was Tante Maria, my father's surviving sister, who had offered to support Mother in her hour of defeat.

Our little group remained at a polite distance from Karin's family as we waited in the terminal. Mother acknowledged their presence with a barely civil nod of the head. For some never-articulated reason, she held Karin's mother responsible for this ill-conceived journey. Making no attempt to hide her dislike, she commented, "Look at her stepfather, strutting in his uniform. . . and her mother in a fur coat in April."

It would have been out of character – as it would have been for most German mothers, at that time – if Mother had wished me farewell with an embrace. Not that she wasn't a loving woman – she was. But, to her way of thinking, and the thinking of most of her contemporaries, lavishing physical affection on children, once they'd reached school age, spoiled them; while lavishing affection on older children was just improper. It wasn't until her later years that she would indulge in a perfunctory hug now and then. We shook hands at the bottom of the stairs leading to the Lufthansa plane. Mother's eyes were dry, and I was glad of it. She bore the look of one determined to accept the inevitable. There were no tears in my eyes either.

"*Mach's gut.* – Be well," Mother said.

"I'll write to you soon."

I wrote to Mother from the dormitory at the London YWCA on our two-day stopover, en route to Newcastle upon Tyne in the northeast of England. It was the first letter in a lifelong correspondence that from then on would be the central means of communication in a mostly long-distance relationship.

"*All these years of learning English,*" I wrote to Mother on a pad of linen writing paper she had given me as a farewell gift, "*and I don't understand a word people are saying. I ask for directions, which I am able to do without difficulty, yet people's replies sound like gibberish. I ask them to speak slowly, but rather than articulate each syllable, they raise their voice as if I were hard of hearing. I may not know their language well, but half-deaf I'm not. I'm not saying they are unfriendly. In fact, they're very helpful in their reserved way.*"

Describing London, where Mother had never been and never

would be, I wrote, *"We walked up and down Oxford Street, the main shopping street. You wouldn't believe the number of red double-decker buses. And the single-file queues of people at the bus stops. No one cuts in line. The English are so very civilized! The shops aren't nearly as fashionable as those on the Düsseldorf Königsallee, but you can browse without being accosted by a saleswoman. Since you gave me some extra money, I bought a Scottish cashmere scarf. Imagine cashmere!"*

Every week, and sometimes more often, I sent letters home from Miss Bicknell's Preparatory School for Girls, in Newcastle. And each week I would receive a response. And every day, I would listen for the mail slot to open and fall shut again. The sight of Mother's old-fashioned penmanship, her out-of-character use of *Miss,* instead of the German *Fräulein,* in the address, always sent a sweet rush through me. How I wanted to tear her letters open immediately! But I set them aside to savor in a quiet moment, alone in my room.

"I'm glad you have adjusted so well abroad," Mother wrote in her answer to a long letter in which I had described my new life with wildly exaggerated confidence.

In Newcastle upon Tyne, I settled in an upstairs room in Miss Bicknell's Victorian manor, a large house set amidst a garden of extensive lawns and well-kept flowerbeds. A polished brass plaque on the wall next to the front door read, *Miss Bicknell's Preparatory School for Girls.* Three large downstairs rooms had been converted into classrooms, with only the drawing room left for private use. I was the only boarder among twenty day students who came from prominent Newcastle families. Because I wasn't a regularly enrolled student, I was also the only one not required to dress in a school uniform, a dark blue blazer and skirt with a white cotton blouse. Three women teachers, Miss Bicknell one of them, taught all the required classes.

Compared to the small-town environment of my upbringing, the environment I had been transplanted into was status-conscious beyond anything I'd ever known in Germany. Still, my humble background did not deter me from blending in – or pretending to blend in.

According to the terms of our arrangement, I would serve as Miss Bicknell's companion, for the next 15 months, in exchange for room and board; I would take courses in English grammar and English literature with the prep school girls – all several years younger than I was – in order to improve my English to the point at which I would be fluent enough to enroll in university. I also received a small weekly allowance, enough for bus fares into Newcastle and cigarettes – Benson and Hedges, in a tin.

Middle-aged and unmarried, Miss Bicknell looked the part of a robust English country gentlewoman, with a preference for tweeds and lace-up shoes. It soon became apparent that the real reason for my presence was to distract her from grieving over the recent loss of her mother.

"We must get rid of that awful accent of yours," she had said in her high-brow Queen's English on the day I arrived on her doorstep, after we'd exchanged only a few words. Tempering her criticism, she'd then added, "A fine vocabulary you have, I must say."

Before my first class the next morning, Miss Bicknell alerted me, "I've instructed the teachers and the students to correct you diligently." I'd been assigned to classes with the most senior girls, a group of eight snooty thirteen-year-olds, who derived wicked pleasure from mimicking my accent. "Are you *sinking* again, instead of *thinking*?" they would ridicule me when I mispronounced the *th* sound. The almost five-year age difference between us inhibited any meaningful social interaction. There was the teasing, but outside of that, the girls kept to themselves, except for one girl whose name was Imogene. In her typically understated, upperclass demeanor that betrayed no emotion, she asked questions about my impressions of English life, and made it a point to sit next to me in our classes. Once or twice, she invited me to her parents' home. I felt odd around her father, a vice-admiral in the British Navy, whose comment about my father's rank in the war seemed designed to embarrass me. "A sergeant in the Infantry! Not a career man, was he?"

Was it my German accent, specifically, that aroused some meanness in the girls' attitude toward me, someone who came from a country that had been an enemy country not so long ago? If it was, I was too naïve to make that connection, then.

I was a serious student, eager to enrich my vocabulary and to lose my accent. Being immersed in the English language and surrounded, almost exclusively, by native speakers, my pronunciation improved, over time: With the prep school girls and Miss Bicknell correcting me, and after much practice in front of a mirror, I was able to surmount the most glaring hurdles native German speakers typically have to deal with. The *th* sound, absent from the German language, posed the greatest challenge. Gradually, my pronunciation shifted from a regular *s* to a lisped *s,* achieved by putting my tongue between my teeth, finally arriving at the proper sound; the British English *o,* also absent from the German, was easy to achieve, by pursing my lips; the sound of the vowel *a,* with its similarity to the German *ä,* merely needed fine-tuning; *r's* were no problem, as swallowing them made them sound authentic. Adjusting my tongue to the middle of the mouth, where English is spoken – in contrast to German, which is spoken in the front of the mouth – came about as a matter of course. Eventually, my accent lost most of its clipped German inflection.

It didn't take long before I could follow class discussions; it took longer to overcome my shyness to participate. My proudest achievement was playing the two-line speaking role of the *Wall* in a school performance of the play within Shakespeare's *Midsummer Night's Dream.* Left alone on the stage after all the other players had exited, I recited my speech through the hole of the cardboard wall, *"Thus have I, wall, my part discharged so; / And, be done, thus wall away thus go."* My pronunciation sounded flawless to my ear.

Evenings, Miss Bicknell and I sat on either side of the drawing room fireplace, her unsmiling mother gazing down on us from a portrait above the mantle. Her mother's half-finished tatting project propped on her lap, Miss Bicknell twisted and crossed an array of ivory silk bobbins, producing a geometrically patterned strip of white lace. I tried my luck at knitting an ambitious yellow wool cable knit sweater, and failed. The grandfather clock striking ten was our signal to retire to our rooms: Miss Bicknell's, the corner room at the end of the upstairs hallway; mine, one of a number of guestrooms. Small and plainly furnished, it had a bed, a desk and a chest of drawers on one side and a gas fire place, the only source of heat, on the other.

Sundays were special. Often, Miss Bicknell invited me to accompany her on motoring excursions through the towns and hamlets of the Northumberland countryside in her white Morris Minor, top down, weather permitting. On one of the rare sunny days in the North of England, we set out for the Lake District early in the morning, Miss Bicknell in an aviator hat, me with a scarf flapping around my head. An admirer of Wordsworth, she took me to *Dove Cottage,* his home at the outskirts of Grasmere. Afterwards, we sat atop a windy promontory on the lake that gave the village its name, enjoying a picnic of egg and watercress sandwiches, along with milk tea from a thermos.

When it was too inclement for motoring adventures, we called on Miss Bicknell's titled lady friends for high tea in the *stately homes* (an official designation for landmark houses) they occupied. These were historic country houses open to visitors during part of the year, often for an admission charge.

"May I introduce my young German friend," Miss Bicknell would say.

"So very pleased to meet you," was the standard reply, an unmistakable tone of mild condescension in their voices – which I interpreted as a mark of superior breeding. I also thought that, as a teenager, I was not worth their attention. But perhaps there was more to it; perhaps it was a subtle way of expressing an anti-German sentiment that was still well and alive in those days.

My background was ordinary, compared to theirs. I was easily impressed – by the historic homes, the fine antique furnishings and decorations as much as by the inhabitants' understated display of gentility. Which did not stop me from poking fun at their airs and pretensions in later conversations with Karin, who was boarding with a wealthy industrialist family in North Shields, a seaside town 10 miles east of Newcastle. Affecting a nasal twang and ridiculing the banality of their conversations, I would mimic Miss Bicknell's titled lady friends' speech, *"Ohhh, the weathaw has beeen soo extroadenairily oafel."*

Miss Bicknell, who had read literature at Cambridge and came from a family of educators, subscribed to a narrow idea of class that put breeding and ancestry above wealth, and to the idea that proper speech attested to a person's superior status. While this wasn't an attitude that was altogether absent from German norms and was, in fact, somewhat appealing to me, it was the repulsive sense of superiority – akin to the elitism that had been propagated under Hitler's design of the Aryan master race – that made me question her position.

I remember Miss Bicknell bringing up WWII only once, and then only in passing. "Oh, it was a dreadful war, as wars go, but that's history now," she said, brushing off any hostility she may have harbored, adding that the English and the Germans, after all, were cousins. "Queen Victoria's husband, for one. Prince Albert was of Saxon birth, a fellow citizen of yours. He was her first cousin and so much the love of her life, his early death plunged her into deep mourning for the remainder of her days."

Four and a half months into my stay with Miss Bicknell, she called me into her office. I stood by the door, waiting for her instructions.

"It's my opinion. . . and that of the teachers as well. . . that you've achieved a respectable command of English and are ready for university." There was pride behind her withholding smile.

That same day, I went off to enroll at King's College in Newcastle, a satellite campus of the University of Durham, for the upcoming autumn term.

Karin had been assigned to board with a family that, lacking status through birth, compensated for it with a show of newly acquired wealth. This included a limousine with a uniformed chauffeur and a pedigreed great Dane, Sir Patrick McGinty Bagoly. This may not have been his name's proper spelling, but that's what it sounded like to us.

Sir Patrick was Karin's charge. She brushed his fawn-colored coat. She put out his food and water. She cleaned up his messes. Mornings and afternoons, she walked him in the park-sized grounds of the estate. In return, she received an allowance, more generous than mine, as well as room and board. To prepare for admission to university, Karin took classes in English as a second language at a small community college.

On most Wednesday evenings, when Miss Bicknell had social engagements that didn't require my presence, I took the bus to visit

Karin in North Shields. She had an entire suite to herself in her hosts' mansion. An antique four-poster bed dominated one room; in the other, a television set was the source of blissful hours of entertainment on my night off. We would curl up together on the sofa, Sir Patrick sprawled on the floor, and watch the *BBC News,* followed by *TheGeorge Burns and Gracie Allen Show.*

Television was an experience new to both of us. Not until the early seventies, after I'd already been away from Germany for ten years, did Mother resign herself to buying "such an unsightly thing," she wrote in a letter to me. Karin and I, on the other hand, were enthralled by the medium's magic and novelty. We followed political developments on the news with less interest than accounts about the young Queen Elizabeth, and were even more interested when the accounts involved Princess Margaret, who by then had decided not to marry Peter Townsend in favor of staying faithful to the Crown. Karin and I, of course, thought she should have followed her heart. We raised our eyebrows at the silly humor in *The George Burns and Gracie Allen Show,* at the same time as we laughed uproariously.

Most Saturdays, the two of us met to take the bus across the River Tyne into Newcastle proper, where we'd joined the British Council, a social club of foreign students, primarily from the Commonwealth – countries formerly under colonial rule, such as India, Pakistan and Ghana. A smaller number came from the Continent, mainly young women from France, Austria, Sweden and Germany, in contrast to a preponderance of young men from the Commonwealth.

The lounge, appointed with tufted leather seating and portraits of Queen Elizabeth II and other dignitaries, would have been as stuffy as any English club, had it not been for the mixture of young students of all races and cultures from around the world. It was a stark contrast to the more monochromatic environment I'd come from. Although we were of different color, came from different backgrounds and had different accents, we shared that we were foreigners, none of us belonging to the dominant culture. Small groups congregated in various seating areas, engaging in conversations and discussions about whatever moved us: the English class system, the lectures we attended, our professors, politics and sometimes home.

As Karin and I made more friends independent of each other, Karin began drifting away from me, and I, from her. The bus ride from Newcastle to North Shields, involving a transfer and walks at either end, was inconvenient. Our free time was limited. Whereas initially Karin and I may have sought comfort with each other as strangers among strangers, as both of us got more accustomed to our environments, our need for each other lessened. It also may have been the beginning of our interests diverging. Although both of us attended classes at King's College, my interests were more academically directed than hers. After our time in England, that would continue to bear out as I started college in Munich, while she went off to Paris. Soon after, we lost track of each other.

Having grown up in a homogeneous country, a country that the war had further homogenized, with no experience of people visibly different from myself or of non-Christian faith – the Negro chauffeur who had delivered Tante Irma's parcels had been the one exception – people from cultures other than my own fascinated me. From among the many foreign students I met, Sammy, whose home was Ghana, stands out in my memory. His skin color darker than that of the American Negro chauffeur, Sammy was of royal blood. A crowd would gather around him to listen to his far-flung stories and enjoy his funny antics. Both the notion of an African extrovert and African royalty contradicted my ideas of Africa, gleaned from books I'd read about its jungles and native chieftain rulers. Knowing Sammy, showed me how half-baked my concepts of the world were.

I felt accepted and respected at the British Council. I wasn't one to draw crowds around me, but people seemed interested in engaging me in conversations. If a bias against Germans or Germany existed, no one showed it.

Miss Bicknell would have rather I socialized with her prep school girls, whose disinterest in me I reciprocated. She took displeasure in the friends I made at the British Council, as none of these friends were of Anglo-Saxon origin. She tolerated those from the Continent, calling the Continent *Europe,* as if the United Kingdom were a separate entity from the rest of Europe; but anyone from Commonwealth countries she referred to as *from the Colonies*.

"They are of a different race than you," she said. We were having our nightly supper. I had just told her about some of the countries that were represented at the British Council. The ring of their foreignness was exotic and, therefore, intriguing, to me. To Miss Bicknell, they were a source of irritation. Lifting her head to show her superiority, it seemed, she continued in her class-conscious British way, "The races should keep to themselves. It makes for a better world."

I found her prejudice offensive, but made only a half-hearted attempt to advocate for an egalitarian world. "I believe our skin color is a superficial difference. We're really all the same."

Recognizing that I was breaking Miss Bicknell's social norms, from then on, I kept my friendships with students from the *colonies* a secret – especially a budding romance with Sumant Patel, a medical student from India. Sumant, in my eyes, was as stunning a man as I'd ever met – his skin tone golden, his fine features like those a young Buddha. We were aware that we attracted stares when we walked together through the streets of Newcastle – he was dark, and I was fair and blonde – but we didn't care. We were of different races. Sumant was a Muslim, I was a lapsed Catholic. None of it seemed to matter. We attended the bimonthly Saturday night dances at the British Council together, dancing the entire evening. But whatever chemistry there was between us, by the end of the first term, it fizzled out.

And while I disagreed with Miss Bicknell's biases, I admired her forthrightness – even when it was at my expense – her position in life as an educated, professional woman, and the generosity with which she shared her time with me.

As I became more fluent in English and began sounding more British than foreign, I also began absorbing other aspects of Englishness. I dressed in plaid skirts and twin sweater sets. I acquired a taste for English food, despite its bad reputation – roast beef with Yorkshire pudding and peas became my favorite dish. I imitated English bearing – the way I greeted people, "How do you do?" without expecting an honest answer, as any German would. I didn't want to stand out as someone foreign.

In ways I was not conscious of, I began breaking from Germany, and my Germanness. I enjoyed my independence and my freedom from parental constraints, enjoyed being away from the country whose history and people had made me feel ashamed. I idealized England, with its proud people – Miss Bicknell, too – the undulating countryside dotted with manor houses, even Newcastle upon Tyne – not a scenic city by any stretch of the imagination. I didn't mind not having made English friends. If there was resentment toward me as someone German – a saleslady asking about my accent and finding out where I was from, my professors at King's College, the students at the British Council – I didn't allow it to penetrate. I felt comfortable in a foreign country.

It was a day late in the spring of 1958. I'd been in England for a year, was now in my third and final term at King's College, taking Monday-through-Friday classes in English language and English literature. Miss Bicknell and I were out on one of our rain-or-shine late afternoon walks that were recreation for her and a chore for me.

A man and a woman were walking toward us on the same side of the street, still a short distance away. Both were wearing Macintosh coats to protect them from the light drizzle.

"Countrymen of yours." Miss Bicknell said. "Jewish." She whispered, as if telling a secret, or a piece of gossip, or something shameful.

Miss Bicknell had called them "my countrymen." This Jewish man and this Jewish woman were my countrymen. They had been robbed of their German homeland, had been forced to leave the country we shared in order to save their lives. Still, Miss Bicknell's description roused in me a sense of kinship, momentarily bridging the atrocities that separated them from me.

I had never, to my knowledge, met anyone Jewish – not in Germany where, after the Holocaust, most surviving Jews had fled the country; only about 15,000 remained or returned at the end of the war. Neither had I met anyone Jewish in England where, I had learned, many European Jews had found refuge. I did not count cousin Jochen. That he was half-Jewish had not yet occurred to me; it had never been spoken about at home. I had never met Jochen's Jewish father, whom Tante Irma had divorced in the late 1940s. Neither had I ever heard an anti-

Semitic remark made by anyone, not in my family, nor otherwise. I didn't know whether anti-Semitism still existed in Germany, but I knew, of course, that it had been prevalent before and during the war. But I felt that I knew Anne Frank. The memory of her young life as a Jewish girl in an Amsterdam attic had stayed with me, as well as the horrible awareness of Anne as one among millions murdered by the people to whom I belonged.

An entire scenario spun out in my head in the time it took for Miss Bicknell and me to meet up with her neighbors – a fragmented jumble of images, speculations, fears, wishful thinking that, in a matter of moments, coalesced into an upsetting realization: I was about to come face to face with a man and a woman, who had been subject to discrimination and persecution in the homeland we shared, for the simple reason that they were "different" from me. They had fled their country – our country – left behind the good life that, presumably, they had once enjoyed there. It struck me that they, along with countless others like them, must have lost friends or relatives, perhaps even children, in the camps. I had never anticipated an encounter such as this, although I had often asked myself what, in theory, I would feel or say on such an occasion, what people like this couple walking toward me now would feel or say.

I feared it would not be a casual meeting, although that's what I would have wished for: that the history that had exiled this man and this woman would not step between us. I wished that they would not mention the war and the murder of Jews. I wished that allowing the past to remain unspoken would undo that past. I did not recognize, then, that the silence I was wishing for was the same silence for which I had indicted my mother and her generation.

I struggled between a view of myself as both personally innocent and guilty by association. If I had thought that I could refuse the Reich's legacy of horror, I realized – as the couple walked toward me and I toward them – that I could not.

Anne Frank flashed through my mind – not Anne herself, but the belief she stood for in my thinking: that all people are good at heart. With the memory of Anne's words came the hope that this Jewish couple would believe likewise – that they would not condemn me.

Recognizing Miss Bicknell, the couple smiled at her and glanced at me as we drew close. We stopped with only a few feet between us. The man was slender, past his middle years; the woman finely dressed, of fragile build and with strikingly white hair. Heat rose to my neck, raising the foolish fear that I would blush.

Miss Bicknell introduced us.

To them, she said, "Meet my young German friend."

To me, "Neighbors who came here from Germany."

I doubt that Miss Bicknell recognized the weight of her chance introduction. She followed with a comment about the weather, the most common follow-up after any initial exchange. "What an awful day again." For a moment, it was as if the banality of the weather had saved me from an indictment of both myself and all of Germany that I feared might follow.

I waited for the couple to take the lead to address me. I concealed my unease with a timid smile.

The man looked at me. Speaking a cultured German, he asked, *"Woher stammen Sie? –* Where are you from?"

"Aus der Kölner Gegend, – Not far from Cologne," I replied, as casually I as could.

"And what brings you to England?"

"I'm studying English language and literature."

These were the polite, the expected questions, nothing to make me feel uncomfortable.

The woman stood slightly behind him, not saying anything. Only in retrospect did I dare interpret her behavior, and understand that perhaps she was not ready to interact with someone German, not even to play the part.

I didn't ask what had brought them there – I knew. Perhaps, this could have been an opportunity for me to say that I was sorry. But I didn't. Instead, I welcomed the polite posturing in our exchange – mostly from lack of courage but also to protect what was raw, still, in me.

The man smiled at me. Relieved, I smiled back. We made-believe that we were fellow countrymen on foreign soil, glad to have met, and that we would simply continue on our separate ways. A lie that absolved me, temporarily.

I search my memory now for a glimpse of our parting. What I find is the image of a tentative handshake – but only with the man.

We continued our walk on the same side of the street, in opposite directions. It was still drizzling. The air was heavy with the fragrances of spring. I imagined the distance increasing between the Jewish couple and Miss Bicknell and me. I imagined their dark Mackintosh coats, glistening with moisture. Although I felt an impulse to look back, I did not.

Miss Bicknell spoke into the long silence. "What a pleasure it must have been to speak German with someone from your country."

What had remained unspoken, in my encounter with Miss Bicknell's Jewish neighbors, would echo, in years to come, in my initial meetings with anyone Jewish. These meetings would follow a pattern, repeated over and over: my reluctance to mention my German heritage – either until it couldn't be avoided because I'd been asked, or until I felt reassured it would not offend.

My generation had inherited more than just the unredeemed sins of our parents. Those could never be undone, anyway; nor could they be assumed by a generation who had barely been born when those sins were committed.

But we had inherited our parents' silences, too, and had made those silences our own, and so they became silences that only we could break.

46

I left England in the summer of 1958. I had completed three terms, the equivalent of one year, at Durham University, and passed my final English Language exams at Cambridge. After close to a year and a half with Miss Bicknell, I said goodbye. We stood in the front entrance where she had first welcomed me and, in her somewhat rough tone, had commented on my *awful* accent. Now she lifted her chin and blinked several times to hold back her tears, with the same stiff-upper-lip restraint I'd seen her use when she spoke about her mother. I wiped my wet cheeks with the back of my hand, embarrassed to show my sadness. I had grown fond of Miss Bicknell. I'd come to accept her abrupt, sometimes hurtful, manner, discovering beneath the surface the kind woman she really was. I promised to write, and come back to visit her, perhaps even live in England. Though we entered a regular correspondence that lasted for a number of years, we never met again.

I spent the month of July traveling alone through England, zigzagging my way south by train. I stopped in York, Stratford-on-Avon, Oxford, Canterbury, the Isle of Wight, Bath and London. I saw *A Midsummer Night's Dream,* this time performed by professional actors, in an outdoor theater in Stratford-on-Avon; walking around the colleges of Oxford, I daydreamed about reading literature at one of the women's colleges; I sat on a bench across from Canterbury Cathedral, writing postcards home and to friends; on the Isle of Wight, I spent the day on a cold and windy beach; I swam in the Roman Baths in the city of Bath; I took in more sights in London than I can remember. I stayed in hostels and inexpensive small inns, where a typically substantial English breakfast was in included in the rate. I furtively wrapped up what I didn't eat and saved it for lunch. I met a few foreign students along the way, spending a day or two with them, but, mostly, I was alone. At the end of my journey, I took the ferry across the Channel from Dover to Le Havre on a stormy day that kept me lying seasick on a top bunk.

For the final leg home, I took the night train from Le Havre. My stomach still queasy, I fell in and out of sleep sitting up in a window seat. When the compartment emptied in Paris, I stretched out for the rest of the journey to Cologne.

Like a rite of passage, my month of travelling through England was the final step toward adult independence, even though I didn't realize it then.

I took the local train from Cologne to Delrath. I lugged my suitcase down Rheinstraße, turning the corner at Schulstraße. I arrived at Mother's doorstep without a penny in my pocket. I was famished and underweight.

Mother had grown older in the year I hadn't seen her. She looked more provincial, more German, than I remembered. As at our parting, we shook hands, but our handshake suggested so much more than a casual hello.

Once I'd settled in, Mother served a lunch for both of us. Commenting on my undernourished look, she said, *"Du wirst mir noch an Schwindsucht sterben, wenn du so weiter machst. –* You'll die of consumption, if you keep this up." Still, she was as overjoyed to see me as I was to see her.

In the time I'd been away, Mother had completed much of her remodeling of the house. It now bore little resemblance to the house that had been Onkel Jean's. She showed me around, proudly. First, the downstairs with the living room. No longer the average sized room I remembered, an addition with picture windows on three sides now jutted into the garden. It created enough space for another seating area. Across the hall, she swung the door open to a new, built-in kitchen – not the traditional, individual cupboards and sideboards – a novelty back then. "Look. Completely modernized," she said. I followed her to the upstairs. My room had been extended over the downstairs addition. More than double its former size, its slanted walls were gone. So was my childhood furniture, replaced with a contemporary Danish set. A door that hadn't been there before led to a verandah that hadn't been there either. Red-blooming geraniums spilled from planters over a wrought iron railing.

I stepped outside. I looked down into Mother's garden. I remembered Onkel Jean's orchard, gone now. Tears gathered in the corners of my eyes. It saddened me to see the old cherry tree, lone survivor of the many fruit trees that had been there. Its enormous crown shaded the immaculate lawn. It bowed low after years of generous bearing. Even after it became barren, Mother did not cut it down for many years. When she did, she placed a birdhouse on its stump and, in her waning years, watched the birds come to feed, as she sat at her living room window.

"Do you like the changes?" Mother asked, like a little girl waiting to be praised.

"Yes, you have a fine-looking house," I said, complimenting her, as a guest would, visiting for the first time. I didn't want to acknowledge the sense of loss I was feeling, and tried to shove it aside. Beautiful as Mother's house was, it was no longer my home.

I spent the rest of the summer of 1958 alone with Mother. Gitta was in Switzerland for a year as a *Haustochter*, a position similar to that of an *au pair* girl, geared to learning cooking skills and the running of a household. I applied at the *SDI*, the *Sprachen und Dolmetscher Institut München*, an applied foreign language college in Munich. I had heard the college talked about at Durham University as the preeminent private institution in its discipline in Germany. That and its location persuaded me. I was notified by letter within weeks that I had been accepted on a tuition scholarship. Mother offered to set aside 100 Deutsch Marks a month for my upkeep, and Tante Irma, who by the mid-1950s had achieved relative wealth, would contribute 200 Deutsch Marks. If I budgeted prudently, I would have enough to pay for college supplies, rent and food and still have a few Marks left over for extracurricular activities.

In early September, a week before the start of the semester, I took the train to Munich, lugging two heavy suitcases, jam-packed with everything I owned. Still years before high velocity transit, it was a long day's journey. After a night in the *Hotel Drei Löwen*, I went to the *Institut* office on Amirastraße, around the corner from the Odeonsplatz.

Through a notice on the bulletin board, I rented a furnished room on Leopoldstraße, in the heart of Schwabing, the bohemian district of the city. My landlady, Frau Eichhorn, was a past-her-prime opera singer, tall and stout, with a bosom that heaved when she spoke, and a pompadour of auburn hair. She practiced the same repertoire of alto arias from four to five p. m. daily, with the diligence of one preparing for a comeback.

Her lodgers – there were three of us, all students – lived by Frau Eichhorn's strict rules: no radio; ten-o'clock curfew for visitors, who were not welcome in the first place, especially if they were male; permission to take cold showers daily and a warm tub bath once a week. We also had minimal kitchen privileges – anything more than heating water to prepare coffee or boil an egg was out of bounds. Her vigilance was uncanny. Nobody ever broke a rule without getting caught and reprimanded.

As a Durham University transfer student and based on the results of a placement test, I entered the third semester at the Institute.

After a couple of days, I met Susanne T in the cafeteria, both of us sipping black coffee and smoking cigarettes. A third semester English major herself, she helped me make class choices and find my way through the maze of hallways.

I was intimidated by the number of prominent last names among the names of my fellow students, who were mostly women. If their surnames weren't those of recognizable industrialists, like Thyssen or Krupp, or politicians – an Adenauer niece was among my classmates – they were preceded by the nobility particle *von,* meaning descending from, or *zu,* meaning resident at, and often even a hereditary title. I assumed that the students with ordinary names, such as my own name, Schupp, came from distinguished, or at least wealthy, backgrounds. I also assumed that I was the only one with unremarkable ancestry or social standing, despite a family tree going back to 1430.

After the war, Susanne's family had fled Silesia – now part of Poland – where they had been landowners of considerable status and means. Thanks to the post-war *Lastenausgleich* – payments made by the German government to compensate for loss of property in areas ceded after capitulation – they had relocated near Rosenheim, in southern

Bavaria, and now lived on a sizable estate of agricultural and forest land.

Susanne introduced me to Ingeborg von B, also a third semester English major. Ingeborg had spent a year at Smith College in the United States, and was one of the few students with an American accent. Her ancestry was most impressive. It connected her directly to the King of Belgium. Ingeborg had the imposing stature and aloof bearing of a ruling queen, at the same time as she was affable and smart. Susanne, Ingeborg and I took most of the same classes. We sat together and visited during recess and at lunch in the cafeteria.

During lunch hour, the college cafeteria was always packed. Students crowded around the few tables, or they stood in clusters wherever space allowed. Their chattering was magnified by the constant clatter of dishes from the open kitchen.

The three of us – Susanne, Ingeborg and I – were perched on stools at a tall bar table. We were sipping black *Melitta* coffee and smoking cigarettes. Of boyish build, with a pixie haircut, Susanne was trying to look like the vamp she wasn't, waving a holder with a thin cigarillo as she told us about a weekend skiing trip she and a group of friends were planning. Ingeborg, the most intellectual of the three of us, looked as if she were waiting for an opportune moment to change the subject.

When she did speak, her tone was provocative:

"I think this is outrageous," she said, "Our very own Professor Schmidt broadcasting his national socialist background and, at the same time, minimizing and justifying his role."

She placed a book on the table, demonstratively. It was Paul Schmidt's memoir, *Statist auf Diplomatischer Bühne* – An Extra on the Diplomatic Stage. Dr. Paul Schmidt was the founder of the Sprachen und Dolmetscher Institut in 1952, as well as its chancellor and a professor of English. Before and during the war (from 1922 – 1945) he had been ambassador and chief interpreter, first for the Department of Foreign Affairs of the Weimar Republic, then for that department of the Third Reich. Specifically, he had served as Adolf Hitler's personal English interpreter.

Ingeborg raised the question of Schmidt's almost certain involvement with the Nazis and of his possible culpability. Schmidt had been arrested by the US Forces in 1945 and detained until 1948, during which time, he had served as a witness at the Nuremburg Trials. In 1950, he had been exculpated. Many years later I would learn that, in 1967, five years after I graduated the SDI, he would be investigated on the grounds of supporting to obstruct the immigration of 5,000 Jewish children to Palestine. The investigation would end with his death, in 1970.

"I find Schmidt's close association with Hitler appalling, generally, and quite disturbing on a personal level," Ingeborg said. "My family opposed the system. My uncle was connected with the July 20th plot." She was referring to the failed attempt to assassinate Hitler on July 20, 1944.

Susanne, always pragmatic, and echoing a commonly held position, said, "Come on, Ingeborg, they were all involved in some way. What choices did they have? Schmidt happens to have a phenomenal command of languages that opened doors for him. He may have been an opportunist, but that doesn't make him a war criminal."

Ingeborg argued, "As interpreter for Hitler, he must've had a pretty intimate relationship with his boss."

I said, "If the book title reflects the contents, then it would have to be a portrayal of himself as only a minor player. And without having read the book, I assume that's what he set out to prove. What other motive would he have?"

"Let's face it," Susanne said. She leaned back on her stool, and crossed one leg over the other, theatrically. "The SDI has a stellar reputation as language school. That's what persuaded me and, I suppose, most everyone else to come here, not who the founder was." She glanced at us for approval, then went on, "My father was a Party functionary, but what does that mean today?" Neither Ingeborg nor I reacted to her candid revelation. I secretly admired Susanne for having admitted this, but it was not something we would have thought to discuss further. Susanne glanced at the wall clock and got off her stool for the next session. "Just think about it, there would have to be those among our student body who come from fanatic Nazi families. But most, I venture to guess, don't. Take the Adenauers. *Der alte Konrad* had a clean slate, for one. He had to pass rigid Allied background checks to become our first chancellor. The Krupps, the Thyssens and all the other industrialists, for the most part, are another story. And the blue-bloods, look how many of them we have here," at which point she gave Ingeborg a knowing glance. "Well, they had their own agenda and it wasn't to support Hitler. They wanted to run Germany."

"I can't quite accept your so-what attitude," Ingeborg said, but didn't take it any further. Neither did I.

Still, misgivings simmered. While at the time I registered at the SDI, I had been unaware of Schmidt's prominence during the Third Reich, I had heard it gossiped about at some point, but not given it any weight. After Ingeborg's indictment of Schmidt, I thought I might read his memoir, but never did. Let sleeping dogs lie. If it was fear of what I might have found out that kept me from probing further, I dismissed it before it had a chance to register at all.

By not looking into his past, had I not taken a stand?

Even though Dr. Schmidt was popular as a professor and always filled the auditorium and classrooms, I avoided his lectures after attending one or two. Susanne, who was taken by his flamboyant style, commented on my absence.

"Schmidt doesn't interest me," I said.

"Why not? He's absolutely amazing," she raved.

"I find him pompous. And his anecdotal approach to teaching annoys me."

In retrospect, I wished that, by not attending, I had, at the very least, distanced myself from Schmidt and his past. But I hadn't. All I had done was avoid the dilemma entirely.

Prof. Friederich dragged his polio-stricken left leg when he walked. The irregular beat of his quick, thumping step on the parquet floors along the corridors announced him long before he actually entered the classroom and limped his way to the podium.

He was anything but pompous and flamboyant. A bookish-looking man in his early forties, dressed in the same dark suit and blue-and-red striped tie every day, he often carried himself with mortified shyness. When he spoke, he shunned direct eye contact. Eyelids lowered, they alternately fluttered and rested motionlessly. In the still moments, this gave him the appearance of a somewhat neurotic Buddha with monkish features. On the other hand, when he interacted with a student one on one, he took off his glasses and, raising his brows inquisitively, looked into the student's face. This conveyed the sense that he or she was the most engaging person with whom he'd ever spoken. Whenever he and I interacted, he made me feel that I was worth listening to. I was somebody in his presence.

Although Friederich was chair of the German Department and taught advanced German idiom and grammar, he was the preeminent scholar in the English Department. He was renowned for his pioneering work on the gerund, including the -ing verb ending as present participle, e. g. *I am walking*. A uniquely English grammatical form, it is essentially absent from the German and thus creates confusion for the German student of English. Ironically, for a professor of English, his speech lacked both native British and American pronunciation. Nor did he have a German accent. His speech in English sounded academic, almost artificial. Though following British English rules phonetically – the voiceless *r* and the rounded *o,* for example – there was a non-native cadence to his diction.

Sometime midway into my second year, Friederich stopped me in the hallway between lectures.

"I would like to speak to you and Fräulein von B," he said. His eyelids were fluttering, his voice stern. It was my first personal encounter with him. "I will expect you in my office during the next break."

Ingeborg and I were waiting at his door when he came thump-thump-thumping down the corridor. He ushered us in. Opening his briefcase, he removed a folder with test papers. He leafed through them until he found the two he was looking for.

"Meine Damen," he said, "Ladies, this is a matter of grave concern."

Alarmed, neither Ingeborg nor I said anything.

"Also. . . Very well. . . I have every reason to believe that one or both of you resorted to dishonorable means in our last grammar test." He spoke in his always formal manner of speech. "Furthermore, I have positive proof."

I knew I could not have scored well on the test – a litany of questions about the more complex forms of subjunctive conjugation. Without having studied for it at all, I had fallen back on quite a bit of guesswork. But I had not cheated. Ingeborg looked stunned. She was a top student, and didn't need to cheat.

"You both gave the same peculiar wrong answer to a particular test question. Too peculiar to have been a coincidence. And. . . *meine Damen,* you were sitting next to each other." A glint appeared in his eyes.

Still, neither of us spoke.

"I have no option but to fail you both," he said, after a tense silence.

I had nothing to lose. My test, at best, would have scored a C, maybe even a D – in either case, not far from a failing grade. Would confessing make me a hero in Friederich's mind, even if my confession were false? Did I stop to consider that? Did I want Prof. Friederich to think well of me, most of all?

"I copied the answer from Fräulein von B," I said, quickly, before I had time to think about the ramifications. But I regretted the lie as soon as I'd uttered it.

Satisfaction registered on Friederich's face. He took his time to sit down behind his desk, tugging at the creases of his trouser legs.

"I take an extremely dim view of cheating," he finally said. "And, I am truly disappointed in you, Fräulein Schupp."

I pressed my lips between my teeth, the way I did when I was nervous, and fidgeted with the handle of my satchel. Friederich, it appeared, was turning things over in his head. Then, very slowly, very deliberately, he said, "Considering your excellent record, Fräulein Schupp, and in view of your willingness to admit your deception, I shall give you a chance to retake the test. Fräulein von B's score of an A- will remain unchanged."

I should have been delighted with his verdict. It was the best outcome I could have hoped for. My good standing had been preserved in Friederich's eyes. I would be able to study for the test and, almost certainly, improve my grade. But I felt the unease of something amiss. Had I manipulated the situation to my advantage, even though I could not have foreseen Friederich's invitation for me to retake the test?

Ingeborg did not show any response.

I studied that evening and scored a straight A on the test I took in Friederich's office before class the following morning. But it bothered me that I had falsely taken the blame the day before. I told Friederich the truth – that I hadn't actually copied from Ingeborg's test.

"I realize saying this jeopardizes my new grade," I went on, as an afterthought. "But above all, I don't want you to think that Ingeborg von B cheated, because I know she didn't, either. I'd rather you think that I was the one."

Red blotches were burning my neck. A grin spread over Friederich's face. His eyes lit up like a young boy's. He either enjoyed seeing me squirm, or he had something up his sleeve.

"No. You keep your grade," he said. He took off his glasses and looked at me. His speech was halting at first. "As a matter of fact. . . I. . . I. . . I have been thinking about this." After that, his words spilled out rapidly, as if he were in a hurry to finish his thought. "I began to suspect that I might have been mistaken soon after our meeting yesterday, with both you and Fräulein von B being such good students. The rationalist in me rebels, but I concede, coincidences do happen."

I was stunned. I thanked him, ready to leave.

"Wait," he said, "I owe you an apology, and Fräulein von B, as well." Without missing a beat, he rushed on. "On an altogether separate subject, my present research assistant is graduating. I'm looking for a replacement. I thought of you."

Nothing could have surprised me more. No intelligent response came to my mind. "But. . . Fräulein von B is so much more qualified than I am," was all I could think to say.

"I'm not asking Fräulein von B. I'm asking you."

"But. . . I can barely type." What I really wanted to say was that I was undeserving, that I wasn't smart enough.

"Your typing skills are of little concern to me. All that it takes is practice."

It was a huge recognition and honor to be invited to become a professor's assistant, reserved only for the most excellent students. How could this brilliant man believe that I would possibly qualify? I didn't believe I would.

"Fräulein Schupp, what is your response?"

"Well...I...I..."

"I'll take that as a yes. I'll start you out with an easy practice run. Tomorrow."

Initially, Friederich gave me assignments that any secretary with a solid knowledge of English could have done better than I: copying test and instruction material to be mimeographed; transcribing letters and language-related articles from a Dictaphone; typing test results; filing his extensive correspondence in thick, three-ring *Leitz* binders. I did not find the work stimulating, merely tedious and, given my limited typing skills, frustrating. The pay was minimal.

By the end of the semester, Friederich began to involve me in projects that were more compatible with my interest and abilities. My English had become more and more nuanced, my comprehension of it deeper and deeper. The new assignments entailed researching the lexicography of vocabularies and compiling them in dictionary format. Each entry listed the various British English and American English definitions of a given term, along with their German translation or approximation.

Over the next two years, the topics covered *Family, Household, Food; Education; Meteorology; Law; Communication Systems.* While, in themselves, these were not areas of great appeal to me, the work itself was an adventure into uncharted territory. It was exciting to explore the different meanings and usages of a single word, always finding something new and often unexpected.

A day or two after I had turned in my first completed assignment for him – a 300-page manuscript, titled *Family, Household, Food* – Prof. Friederich called me into his office. He shook my hand in his haphazard but cordial manner. He sat down and motioned for me to take a seat across from his cluttered desk. Leaning back in his chair, he shut his eyes. The traffic noise from the street below sounded muffled through the closed window, as did bits of conversation from the hallway.

I looked at him, trying to read his thoughts through his quivering eyelids. After a while, he took a deep, audible breath and held it for what seemed an unnaturally long time, before he exhaled. In a rush of excitement, his words burst forth.

"If it weren't for a host of typographical errors littering the text, I could turn your manuscript over to the publisher with only minor editing. Your research and the development of themes have been excellent."

He smiled mischievously and handed me the title page to the manuscript: below his name, *Wolf Friederich,* he had typed my name, *Marie-Luise Schupp, Co-Author.*

So unexpected was Friederich's generous acknowledgment of my contribution, I responded with a confused, "Honestly?" Then, realizing how foolish and unappreciative this must have sounded him, I said, "Thank you so much. And please know how grateful I am that you entrusted me with this work."

"You deserve it, Fräulein Schupp." He looked at me, proudly, I thought. "And another thing," he added quickly, like an eager father heaping gifts on his child, "I want you to teach two German classes at the Institut's summer course this year, *The Basics of Idiom* and *Orthography.*" Registering my surprise and incredulity, which were greater than my delight and gratitude, let alone my fear of public speaking, he said, "Don't interpret my offer as flattery. You have the competency."

I received my degree two years later, in the fall of 1961, prepared for a career in translation and English language instruction.

Friederich laid out a path for me: that of his freelance collaborator on his research projects, of a regular German Summer School instructor, and substitute instructor during the academic year, with the prospect, after more training, of a full-time teaching position at the SDI.

"A bright future lies ahead for you." He looked at me kindly from behind his glasses.

I saw him in his office the following day, after a restless night of turning his proposition over in my mind.

I was torn for reasons I could barely admit, least of all to myself. My love of languages – German and English – was not in question. My aptitude had been fairly established. Yet, over time, I had come to doubt whether either translating or teaching were my calling. In my course work, I had specialized in legal terminology, but without more than a cursory background in law, and with much of the available work limited to translating contracts, I found it a dull and unfulfilling prospect. Literary translation held greater appeal, though for a translator just out of college, that seemed unattainable. A career as a teacher did not excite me. Under Friederich's tutelage, research had tapped my passion more than any of the other options. However, on its own, it was not viable as a profession, at least not within the framework open to me.

"I don't know what to do," I confessed. "Perhaps I need time." I felt ungrateful for even considering turning my back on everything Friederich had helped me achieve.

Disappointment registered in his expression, but he did not voice it.

I tried not to show my unease during an interminably long moment, when neither of us spoke.

At last, he got up from his chair. We stood across from each other. He said that a request from the local Metro-Goldwyn-Mayer offices had come to his attention. "The film studio is looking for a bilingual coordinator and interpreter on their location work in Bavaria. A four-month assignment. Terrific pay, too. Is that something you would consider as a temporary solution?"

He'd spoken in a tone so caring and supportive, I felt this was the advice of the mentor he had been to me. But what I felt even more was the unconditional love of a father, or what I imagined the unconditional love of a father would be – for the first time in my life.

Friederich only knew the bare bones of my family background – that I had been raised fatherless by a widowed mother, whose husband had been killed in action. But I had shied away from telling him any details of my upbringing. Friederich hadn't spoken much about his background either, beyond his immediate family circumstances, that he had a wife and three children.

A much earlier conversation had thrown some light on his mindset during National Socialist times, at least in the way that I interpreted it. Prof. Schmidt had been mentioned in passing. Without articulating anything specific, I'd let on that I had hesitations about him. When

Prof. Friederich had not come to Schmidt's aid – not defending his political past, nor his off-putting showmanship as a teacher – I'd concluded that there had been no love lost between the two men, either, for whatever reason.

Friederich was an academic, *par excellence,* and a brilliant teacher. Buried in linguistics and languages to the exclusion of almost anything else in the world around him, he even seemed disinterested in the politics of the time. This had led me to assume that he'd had just as little interest, or had detached himself, from the politics and ideology of the Third Reich. His disability would have made him exempt from the military. But even that, he'd never spoken about.

"I'll give you my advice . . ."

At that moment, before he even spoke, I understood, that no matter how much I let him down, he would always stand by me.

"Take the position. Make it a time to consider what to do with your life."

I never returned to accept Friederich's offer. Our last encounter had left me feeling ambiguous. Although I had experienced him as an understanding mentor and a man who had shown me the love of a father, a deep sense of shame lingered on. I couldn't rid myself of the idea of having turned my back on everything he had given me. Neither could I forget that I had never acknowledged this to Friederich.

Still, we remained friends through an active correspondence, my frequent visits in Munich, and, for a brief time, a collaborative project several years later. After the death of his first wife and subsequent remarriage, in the mid-eighties, to his second wife, Hannah, we regularly visited each other in our respective homes – theirs in Munich, mine in California. My friendship with Hannah outlived Wolf Friederich's death of a heart attack in 1999, at the age of 80.

47

The swerve in the course my life would take began on that fateful day in Prof. Friederich's office when I said *No* to his vision of my career. Instead, I took his recommendation to apply at the MGM offices in downtown Munich for the temporary position of bilingual coordinator. I was interviewed by a man named Mr. Wallach, one of the studio executives. Middle-aged and of Austrian birth, he had fled the Nazis, first to England, then to America. He related this to me at a social gathering during the time of our filming. Even though my technical skills – typing and shorthand – were found to be lacking, I met the requirements for interpreting and negotiating, ostensibly with the municipal authorities on location. At the end of a second interview, I was offered the job.

I felt tall as I left the offices with a signed contract in my briefcase. I had been hired by an American film company, at a salary that was higher than anything I'd ever dreamed of. I headed for a small boutique along a side street in the city center, where I had long admired the stylish clothing in the display window. I bought my first suit, a straight skirt and tailored jacket made of sage-colored linen with subtle, beige striping.

Though I wasn't an avid enthusiast of American films, I was in awe of a few of the stars, nevertheless – Ava Gardner, Gregory Peck, Audrey Hepburn, and Sidney Poitier, whom I had admired in *Porgy and Bess*. Now I was a part of the film industry. I felt glamorous by association.

For the first three weeks, I worked in the Munich offices as part of a team preparing for the location work of *The Wonderful World of the Brothers Grimm*, an MGM and Cinerama co-production. Directed by George Pal, it starred Laurence Harvey, Claire Bloom, Karlheinz Böhm, Barbara Eden, Yvette Mimieux and Russ Tamblin. Karlheinz Böhm, an Austrian actor, who had been my idol as a teenager, was the only one in the cast whose name I recognized. The film chronicled the lives of Jakob and Wilhelm Grimm and included three of their fairytales.

In late September, the location work began in Rothenburg ob der Tauber in upper Bavaria. The town, with its medieval architecture and fairytale quaintness, had been spared during the wartime bombings, and provided a backdrop against which the story of the Grimm brothers could be reenacted.

My daily tasks were anything but demanding. I took care of the tedious work of typing up camera reports. Those David Pal, a young cameraman, dropped off before lunch and again late in the afternoon. His short visits and casual chats broke my boredom. I liked the way he dressed in dark crew neck sweaters and blue jeans, different from all of the other men in their tweed sports jackets or blazers. I thought he was good-looking, in an American way, his features rugged like some of the leading men in Hollywood films, with a boyishly awkward smile.

Lindsay Jones, too, made it a custom to stop by my office. He was an overbearing, pink-faced production assistant with the irksome habit of introducing himself as *Lindsay Jones, from Pine Bluff, Arkansas.* He repeated this tiresome phrase every time he opened my door. Once he'd plopped himself on a chair, he'd make suggestive invitations to meet outside of working hours. I rebuffed his advances, not just because of his unflattering looks, but also because of the crudeness of his overtures.

At the end of working hours at 5 p. m. , I sent telegrams by phone to an MGM office in Studio City. I translated and explained the menus for the executives in the finer restaurants at lunchtime. I interpreted the negotiations for filming rights between the local authorities and MGM representatives, occasionally toning down the aggressive language of the Americans, frustrated over not getting their way. When there was nothing to do in my office, I watched the filming or assisted the script supervisor, then known as script girl. Had I been more courageous, I might have approached Karlheinz Böhm. As it was, I just admired him from afar.

After the filming in Rothenburg was completed, cast and crew moved to other locations along the Romantic Road – a medieval trade route lined with towns that had maintained much of their bygone character – and then to locations along the Rhine River, where the

German anthropologists Jakob and Wilhelm Grimm had gathered regional folklore throughout the countryside in the 19th century.

The leaves had barely begun to turn. Early patches of mist lifted from the meadows by mid-morning, giving way to flawless late-summer days. *Altweibersommer* – Indian summer, literally translating as old hags' summer – summer's last fling to celebrate the dying season. There had been many such days that year, more than in average years.

It was early November. Cast and crew had moved on to a lodge in Neuschwanstein, the town that bore the name of the castle built high in the Alps by King Ludwig II, Bavaria's idealistic and, arguably, mad king. *The Dancing Princess,* one of the fairytales, was being filmed on mountain roads when an unexpected snowfall transformed the landscape overnight. What had one day been a magnificent autumn scene was the next day no less magnificent in its wintry guise, but it no longer met the script's specifications. Production would be suspended until the snow had melted.

That morning, a number of the film's crew gathered in the pub area of the lodge at the base of the mountain, occasionally glancing through the windows to check to see if there had been a turn in the weather. Most were sipping coffee or lemonade; the hardier of the men were drinking beer and Schnapps.

David Pal was sitting next to me, by sheer coincidence, I assumed, although I wished it had been by intention. He participated in the general conversation – anecdotes about filming; Kennedy's politics; and the disdain most everyone shared for Germany's national sport, namely soccer – around a large table of mainly crew members. David showed no curiosity in me and made no attempt to engage me in the conversation.

The hours wore on. An attentive waiter frequently returned to take additional orders for drinks. At lunchtime, he served platters of cold cuts and bread. Then, as if he had just noticed me, David addressed me with a question that seemed to come out of the blue but, nevertheless, sounded premeditated. "What do you think about Nietzsche?"

I was baffled. The question seemed bizarre, under the circumstances, given that soccer had just been the topic of conversation. But it also seemed to me a flattering question, one that made an assumption about my intellect that I liked. I didn't know much about Nietzsche, but I did all I could to come across as if I did.

"Thus Spoke Zarathustra?" I asked rhetorically, leading into a few modest remarks any secondary school graduate in Germany could have dredged up. "The *Übermensch*?" If anything, I assumed, that was what he was intimating. After all, it was the often cited infamous term the Nazis had appropriated to describe their idea of the superiority of the Aryan master race. "I find the thought of a superior race repugnant." I wanted to distance myself from Nazi ideology and close the subject. "I'll leave superman to your American comic strips," I added, somewhat sarcastically.

Ignoring my dig, he asked, "So you don't share the Nazi *Übermensch* idea?"

I felt uncomfortably pressed. The legacy of the Third Reich was not what I wanted to talk about. "It's repugnant no matter who espouses it." Changing course, I said, "But I do believe that Nihilism as a philosophy reflects the lack of meaning in modern-day man." I felt very smart.

"Like God is dead?" David asked. His question perplexed me. He had, it appeared, at least as much familiarity with Nietzsche as I did.

Americans didn't have a reputation for philosophical sophistication. I had judged America as a materialistic society that bred mediocrity. My opinions were based, I didn't realize then, on a prejudice I had made my own, taking part in conversations with other Germans; on my limited observations of GIs stationed in Munich – young men with crew-cuts and loud voices – and a few blustering American tourists in bobbysocks, gushing over the sights they took in. Such tourists were then labeled *Ugly Americans,* after the title of a book that had been published a few years prior. On the other hand, I and all of my friends had enthusiastically followed John F. Kennedy's campaign for US president. We had admired him at least as much for his good looks as for his liberal politics. I enjoyed American literature and had frequently attended cultural events and readings by American authors at the *Amerika Haus,* most memorably Truman Capote, who read from his novella, *Breakfast at Tiffany's.*

My negative assessment of Americans wasn't, in the least, supported in my daily interactions with the American film crew and executives.

That morning in Neuschwanstein, in fact, David revealed himself as someone with intellectual prowess I had assumed Americans didn't possess. Neither did I ever feel any explicit resentment against me as someone German. George Pal, the Hungarian-born director, who spoke German fluently, took pleasure, it seemed, in telling me of his association with UFA – the German film company – and his life in Berlin before the war.

David would admit years later that his Nietzsche query had been a ploy. He said he'd been curious about me and had asked Lindsay Jones what he knew. After describing me in unflattering terms as a "cold fish," and suggesting that he count me out, Lindsay Jones had allegedly said to David, "On second thought, try the intellectual approach. It might just work for you."

If I were to pinpoint the defining moment that marked the beginning of our relationship, it would be a moment at the bottom of the lobby staircase on that snowed-in day in Neuschwanstein. Slowly, boredom had descended on the group. One person, then another, had left the table, until almost everyone had disbanded. I got up and, having left the pub area, crossed the lobby. David caught up with me at the bottom of the stairs.

"Can I accompany you tonight?" he asked, in reference to a party one of the production managers had announced for the evening. Everyone was invited. A slightly crooked smile came over David's handsome face. It created a fine, vertical crease in his left cheek. He didn't wait for an answer, but said, "I would like it better if you didn't wear lipstick."

As if following an unspoken ritual taking me into the adult working world, I had started wearing red lipstick. With my first MGM salary, I splurged on a bottle of Chanel No. 5 perfume, which, I thought, epitomized the height of sophistication, and enough expensive creams and lotions to fill a cosmetic case.

David's comment caught me off-guard. "You may have to look for someone else to take to the party."

I turned on my heels and dashed up the broad staircase. From the top landing, I looked back. David was still there. I smiled a barely perceptible smile meant to convey, "I'll see you tonight."

There had been nothing in our exchange to warrant the sweet rush that caught me. Or the impatience I felt waiting to see him again later, and the dazed indecision in front of the bathroom mirror between putting on lipstick and not, between wanting to please and showing independence.

With nothing to distract me from thoughts about David, the afternoon seemed endless. Once the appointed time for the party came, I left my room and sped down the long corridor. When I moved down the staircase, I felt the full skirt of my elegant burgundy and black patterned dress billowing with each step, caressing my hips and legs. Never before had I moved with such self-assurance and poise, confident of my own beauty. David was waiting for me in the lobby. Leaning casually against a wall, he waited for me to approach. I noticed the faint scent of an aftershave – Old Spice, as I would learn much later. I wondered whether he noticed the absence of lipstick on my lips. He didn't say.

The production manager's suite was teeming with people. David and I found a small alcove away from the rest of the party. We sat on the plush, carpeted floor, my skirt flared out around me. We talked throughout the evening, oblivious to everything around us. In the low light of the room, people chatted and danced to soft music. Sometimes a flow of air from a sweeping skirt swirled near us.

Our conversation was around lofty matters. German expressionist art. The early Fellini and Bergman films. Jean Cocteau's *Orphee,* a favorite of David's, which I hadn't seen. We talked about Bach. Again, I was amazed to hear David, the American, speak about classical European music. While my response to Bach's music seemed academic, parroting what I had learned about it in high school – I said that I liked its mathematical component – his response was both original and irreverent. "The repetitions of the same themes remind me of prayer," he said, "like the pattering of endless Hail Marys in the rosary." David had no love for religion, his tone suggested, but he had an intuitive appreciation of music that surpassed my own. How arrogantly I had underestimated every American's level of cultural refinement. How wrong I had been.

The party ended after midnight. When we stepped outside, the earth had warmed and thawed the snow, turning it into soft slush. The cloud cover had broken up. The remaining clusters of clouds were drifting toward the Alps, where they gathered in a concerted effort to rise above the peaks.

We looked into the sky. The moon hung at a precarious tilt, as if it might fall backwards. I was expecting David to say something romantic, about the moon or about the stars trembling in the darkness of the mountains. But he remained silent.

Neither of us slept that night. Instead, we spent the hours talking in David's suite in the lodge. The light from a candlestick lamp on the bureau surrounded us with a soft glow. When we touched, it was without reserve or shame. "I love you," David said before morning, before the sun had come up over the eastern slopes and I, too, said, "I love you."

By noon, the snow was all but gone. A few patches remained in the shady underbrush, but in the sunlight, beads of moisture glistened and intensified the brilliant colors of the autumn foliage.

After lunch, the filming resumed: *Yvette Mimieux is the princess, Russ Tamblin, the prince who rescues her. Her driverless coach tears down the mountain road at reckless speed. Tamblin swings onto the empty coachman's seat from a tree and takes control of the galloping horses.* Take 1, Take 2, Take 3. . . David was behind one of the three cameras. I watched from behind the ropes that cordoned off the filming location.

Later, alone in my office, time passed in a haze. I did my work mechanically, shuffling and reshuffling papers. I daydreamed, reliving the magic of the day and night before. But as the hours crawled past, and David still hadn't come to see me, as he had said he would, the charm began to wear off. What had been ecstasy became tinged with shame and regret. Questioning the intense hours we had spent together, tormented by misgivings that I had been deluded, I tried to shake off the memories.

I wanted to put David out of my mind. I wanted to dismiss him as a Hollywood philanderer, the kind Mother had warned me about when I started the job she didn't think I should take. "Film is nothing but a world of illusion and temptation," she had said.

Dusk had already fallen. Filming for the day had long wrapped. With an air of defiance, I put on lipstick, more heavily than ever before. I was ready to turn off the lights in my office, when I heard an abrupt knock on the door. My flimsy hopes refueled, I said, "Come in."

The door opened. There was David, his arms wrapped around a large cardboard box. He glanced at me, smiling with that already familiar twist of the left side of his mouth. All thoughts about Hollywood philanderers, all my doubts, evaporated.

"You knew I would be here!" he said. I didn't answer. I didn't want him to know I'd been waiting impatiently and had given up hope.

I watched him unpack a portable record player, together with two speakers, and set them up on a side table with practiced motions. He removed a record from its cover and placed it on the turntable. When the initial scratching sound of the needle on the record subsided, the chorus of violins in the *Spring* movement of Vivaldi's *Four Seasons* began rippling from the speakers.

"This music will forever be our measure," he said. I understood it was his way of asking me to spend my life with him.

On my final afternoon at home at my mother's house, I gathered my journals, letters and postcards in Mother's laundry basket. I kept separate the bundle of daily letters David had written from America during the preceding two months. Those I put in my shoulder bag for safekeeping and to treasure forever.

Under the willow tree, in the farthest corner of the garden and out of view of the house, was a stone trough, repurposed as a bird bath. I scooped it empty of its icy water and wiped it dry. I tore the journals apart. Crumpling the pages, I threw them into the trough's sculpted cavity, followed by the letters and postcards – without glancing at a single word. I struck a match. The flames leaped up from the well-aired pyre. When most of it had turned into ashes and only a few singed scraps remained in the embers, I stirred them with a stick to encourage a final burst. The smoke rose lazily. I stood there, following the ascending white and gray ribbons, until nothing remained but the clear, early evening dusk. The private thoughts of years of keeping journals, the letters written to me – all these memories that had been dear to me – in ashes. I felt emptied. And I felt free. Was I aware, then, that I wanted to break with the past?

After I had moved to America, was married and raising children, and people asked me what had brought me to this country, I would say, "Love." Regardless of the always flippant undertone I used, it was so: love alone had propelled me here, with a force that had been irrepressible.

Amerika, Land der unbegrenzten Möglichkeiten, America, land of opportunities. That was the byword, in those days. But opportunity wasn't the promise I had pursued. I hadn't been seeking a better life. My life had been good, a career waiting for me. I hadn't followed the call of the unknown, although had I been any less adventuresome, I would not have dared to cross an ocean and an entire continent. Nor had I been driven by the same pioneering spirit I assumed was the bedrock of the American psyche. No, none of those things had been what persuaded me to leave family, friends, career, country, language, history. I was driven only by my love for a young man, setting me on a course that would change my life and determine my future.

The idea of loss seldom entered my mind. If it did, I quickly nipped it in the bud. Family and friends I took for granted. They would be there, no matter where I was. Country was an abstraction: *Heimat,* that specifically German concept of homeland, a sentimental aberration. And the language, after all, was an inalienable part of my being; I believed it always would be. As for leaving behind a history, I failed to realize that it would follow me.

I didn't realize that there would be a time when I would no longer be able to identify myself as solely German; that I would become a hyphenated German-American. I didn't anticipate that I would come to experience myself as always an outsider, both in the country of my choice and eventually, also, in the country of my birth. Nor did I realize that, the longer I was away from my own language, the more my mastery of it would suffer. At the same time, my command of English would never be complete. No matter how comfortable I would become speaking, thinking, writing in my second language, it would not touch me emotionally as deeply as my native tongue. *Rock-a-bye, baby* would never create the same nostalgic stirrings as did *Schlaf Kindlein, schlaf,* the lullaby my mother had sung at my cradle. I didn't know that my speech would remain accented, a permanent vestige of my foreign birth, and that it would make me conspicuous as non-native. I would never have fathomed that, in the end, the deterioration of my mother tongue would become my greatest regret.

48

I departed from Germany knowing little about my destination: Venice, California. I had a vague notion of palm-tree lined beaches, year-round sunshine and Hollywood, "film capital of the world."

The day I first set foot on California soil, in February 1962, it was foggy; then it rained for weeks on end, and stayed cool and overcast most of the summer. It was an anomaly, everyone said. But for me, it crushed all promises of California weather.

The weather wasn't the only surprise. While I had no clear-cut picture of Los Angeles, I had expected modern architecture, wealth reflected in gleaming façades. I had not anticipated a city on a grid, entire tracts of cheaply constructed, identical homes, shabby ghettos, potholed streets – whole neighborhoods that stood in glaring contrast to the affluent neighborhoods with their often gaudy mansions and wide green lawns.

My new life revolved around David and our small, unglamorous cottage on 21st Place. Built in the 1920s, when wealthy film stars and executives owned vacation homes in Venice, it was right on the sand of the peninsula, south of the boardwalk, close to the Marina Channel that was then under construction.

All during that summer, the beaches stayed empty; so did the boardwalk, except for a handful of beatniks and older people who lived in nearby retirement homes. I would never have admitted, least of all to myself, that I was anything but contented in my new environment. If I felt a shred of homesickness, I didn't acknowledge it. My letters to Mother and to friends perpetuated the image of the Los Angeles I'd had until I arrived. I accentuated the natural beauty of mountains and sea, and minimized anything that would have shown the city in an unfavorable light. I kept quiet about the unsightly oil well pumpjacks that dotted the neighborhood, whose monstrous arms worked relentlessly day and night.

For reasons I neither understood nor questioned, and only later ascribed to "culture shock," I grew less and less communicative outside of our home life. I was painfully shy and quiet in the presence of strangers, not just film people by whom I might have felt intimidated, even at social functions with David's friends. At the same time, I found fault with everyone for not showing greater patience to engage me. After my monosyllabic answers to their inquiries about where I was from and whether I liked it here, they would simply return to conversations among themselves. Sensitive to my discomfort, David accepted fewer and fewer invitations.

Instead, we went on drives after he came home from work and on weekends. David was proud, showing me the magnificent ocean views along Pacific Coast Highway or the enormous size of the Los Angeles basin from high points in the mountainous area of Bel Air, where he had been raised. Some evenings, he took me to see foreign films at the *Coronet Theater* in an old arcade on La Cienega Blvd. Or we hung out at the *Blue Couch*, a West Los Angeles coffeehouse – owned by a young man who wore lipstick and eye makeup – with its offbeat, artistic ambience, including a rococo-style sofa with robin-egg-blue upholstery. Sitting in a cozy corner, we listened to jazz from loudspeakers and sipped hot cocoa. I ate my first hamburger and typically American sandwiches – BLT, Club, Rubin, Montecristo – at the *Patio,* a coffee shop on Wilshire Blvd. in Santa Monica. The coffee shop, I discovered, was a uniquely American institution, with Naugahyde-covered booths, long counters and stools, coffee cups that were endlessly refilled from carafes with a drip-brewed coffee, also typically American. Not only the décor but the menu was almost identical in every coffee shop.

During this time, I had a recurring dream, in which a miniature version of myself kept trying to claw and crawl out of a bowl of popcorn. Popcorn was another American novelty.

My first summer in California was the summer that Marilyn Monroe died. Though I was hardly a Marilyn fan, I found myself obsessing about her suicide, at 36, imagining and re-imagining the despair that might have driven her to it.

Less than a week after Marilyn's death, I heard on the radio that

Hermann Hesse had died. One of my favorite writers, he was of German birth and adopted Swiss citizenship in the 1920s. He lived in Switzerland to the end. Mother, at my request, sent my copy of Hesse's *Steppenwolf,* along with just about every novel he had written. One after the other, I devoured them, propped up on my elbows and wrapped in a towel on the chilly beach, or spread out on our beautiful wrought-iron bed. Immersed in Hesse's writing – in the language and in worlds that were home to me – all concerns of alienation temporarily left me.

Being held hostage by my extreme reserve felt unbearable at times. Yet, I didn't know how to overcome it. The longer it lasted, the more imprisoned by it I became. No matter how determined I was to purge myself of its crippling effects, still, among strangers, I would clam up.

We lived in Venice through the summer, bought a house in Malibu Lakeside, then, at the beginning of 1963, moved to San Francisco, to follow a Gurdjieff teacher, under whose spell we had fallen. On November 22, 1963, the day John F. Kennedy was assassinated, we left the "group" under stormy conditions. We returned to Southern California and settled in Santa Monica in a rooftop apartment above a real estate office. I'd regained enough self-confidence by this time to apply for a position as an editor of marketing reports, for a management consulting firm in downtown Los Angeles. After extensive interviews that included skill level tests and a psychological evaluation, I was hired. The editing work drew on my keen eye for exact language and my love of English, I enjoyed what I was doing, I was recognized for my performance, all of which facilitated my overdue adjustment. Los Angeles began looking less and less foreign and more and more like the home of my choice.

But nothing had prepared me for the view of Germans and Germany in this country. Wrapped up in my own insecurities for a long time, I was protected from noticing anything adverse. Later on, too, my outlook was that of a naïve young woman: Americans presented themselves as friendly, unpretentious and sincere. Had I conveniently forgotten that, less than twenty years ago, Germany had been America's enemy?

I was first struck by overt prejudice when I saw how Germans were portrayed on American television: the exaggerated, stereotypical accent;

the often cartoonish behavior of goose stepping or a rigidity in posture, the choice of military language – *Achtung, verboten, jawohl,* always bullish and loud – even in ordinary settings; the histrionic display of the Hitler salute. I tried to excuse much of it as humorous, low-brow, even ignorant. After watching an episode of *Hogan's Heroes* on television in the mid-1960s, I was hurt, appalled, offended, by the content as much as by the accompanying laugh track. I never watched it again. Still, I couldn't help suspecting that what was depicted on television through the guise of humor, represented prevailing attitudes.

In a seemingly innocent way, I was commonly asked, "How come you don't have that heavy German accent?" It was true, my accent did not sound typically German. My English followed British English rules of pronunciation and inflection and was softer than what might have been expected. Still, it was not unlike the way many Germans living in this country spoke.

Less innocent was the question a Jewish co-worker asked my supervisor, who was also Jewish: "How could you hire a German pig?" I was grateful when, after repeating the offensive comment to me, my supervisor also told me how she'd responded: "Not only did I hire her, she has become a close friend." Barbara Woodward was my first close friend in this country, and our friendship would last for decades, until her death in 2009.

But there would be others I had regarded as friends whose prejudices were wounding. "When are you going to put on your marching boots?" someone once asked. Someone else, once, in a huff, called me a *Nazi.* He apologized afterwards, admitting that he had wanted to hurt me with what he knew would hurt me worse than anything.

Even ostensibly positive characterizations – such as Germans being brilliant technocrats or hard workers – struck me as back-handed compliments. I also didn't know how to reconcile the hostility toward things German, with the abundance of German-built cars on Los Angeles streets – Mercedes Benzes for luxury-minded drivers, Volkswagens for the economy-minded. Music programming in concert halls and on KCFA, the one classical radio station, featured a predominance of German and Austrian composers. This pleased me and, at the time, seemed contradictory and opportunistic.

It wasn't that I perceived myself as being perpetually judged, although concern about being judged was always in the back of my mind, particularly when meeting someone new. Many people did accept me without prejudice, or they did once I had passed their scrutiny. Others, I assumed, did not voice their prejudice. And there were those who expressed admiration for the new Germany.

Things began to shift in my life in the mid-1970s. By then, I had lived in the US for more than a dozen years. I had been a stay-at-home mother with our daughter Alison, born in 1966, and our son Jeremy, born in 1970; I had resumed my work with Prof. Friederich, specifically a compendium of American slang. We did this long distance, by correspondence. As it turned out, the project never came to fruition. David had worked as head of the camera department of a Hollywood studio and as a cameraman on various films and television shows. Pregnant with Daniela, the youngest of our three, born in 1971, I opened *Gallimaufry,* an antique shop in Venice, on a lark. Two years later, I started participating in antique shows throughout California, and would continue to do so until the end of 2013. To my surprise, the business gained a fine reputation and brought me significant success. Initially, I relied on local sources for merchandise; then I began to travel to buy antique furniture and accessories in Vienna several times a year and, later, bought *objects of vertu* in London. For some time, both David and I were involved in running Gallimaufry as a team, and went on buying trips together. Before long, I went on my own.

A collector of Biedermeier furniture and porcelains, who I will call Marvin Wolfson, became a frequent visitor and sometime buyer in my shop. David and I invited him to see our personal collections, and he reciprocated by showing us his. Soon we began socializing with him and his fiancée.

I liked Marvin. He was a tall, lanky man with an often biting sense of humor. Outside of his love for Biedermeier – that specifically German and Austrian style of the early nineteenth century – he had a passion for cooking, film and contemporary art.

Of our many encounters with Marvin, one has eclipsed all the others in my memory: we were at a small dinner gathering at his house in the Hollywood Hills. The fading light of dusk came through the French doors, casting an ashen gray into the dining room. A group of seven sat talking at a long, rustic dining table after the meal. From discussing contemporary art, which included an Ed Kienholz painting that hung on the white-washed wall above the Biedermeier sideboard, the conversation moved to the *New German Cinema* that had come into its own during the early and mid-seventies.

A young film editor, who sat at the end of the table, commented, "It's about time German filmmakers turned from escaping into *schmaltz* to probing contemporary issues and confronting a notorious past."

The editor had not spoken to me personally, but I was the only German in the room. At a loss for something that would sound intelligent and free of bias to contribute, I reached for my empty coffee cup. Marvin noticed – either the empty cup or my unease. He put his hand on my forearm, as if to reassure me. He pressed down ever so slightly, then, without facing me, said, "You have killed my people."

I looked for David across the table to come to my rescue. He wasn't there. By the time he returned from wherever he'd gone and sat down again, the moment had passed, whatever that moment could have been. I had no response to Marvin, neither did anyone else, assuming they had heard his remark. Marvin laughed, self-consciously, suggesting, perhaps, that he regretted what he had said or wished he could take it back. But it couldn't be taken back. It hung in the air. Or did he feel justified in striking out at me, as not only a representative of the country that *had* killed his people, but as a potential killer myself?

A flush of shame came over me. I wanted to dismiss Marvin's charge against me as too outrageous and too insensitive to have been said in earnest. I wanted to attribute it to his sense of humor gone awry, or a drink too many. I wanted to wipe it from my memory before it had a chance to sink in.

I couldn't. His words roared through my head.

Marvin had not said, "Your people killed my people," although, perhaps, that's what he'd meant. He had said, "You killed my people." He had addressed me.

And it reinforced what I myself had come to believe already: that I was implicated in the Holocaust through my German birth alone. In a sense, Marvin had only reminded me of this.

The concept of *collective guilt* in regards to Germany's sole responsibility for World War II and the Holocaust, in particular, had long suffused the *Zeitgeist*. It was espoused by German psychologists, philosophers and theologians, as well as in British and US publicity campaigns in post-war Germany, something I was not aware of at the time. Furthermore, intergenerational guilt was an article of faith repeated in several books of the Old Testament: ". . . visiting the iniquities of the fathers upon the children, and upon the children's children, unto the third and the fourth generations." Although I was no longer a practicing Catholic, biblical texts were too deeply engrained in me to ignore altogether.

Too caught up, initially, in my own shock at Marvin's words, I didn't look for an explanation for his accusation. I failed to recognize the pain and anger he must have felt as a member of a group of people who, through the actions of my country, had been driven to the brink of extinction. Over time, I began to realize that his lashing out at me, in all likelihood, was born out of deep-seated grief. The lives of six million people of Marvin's faith and culture had been obliterated in Nazi concentration camps through forced hard labor, extermination in gas chambers, mass execution, disease. Among them had very likely been members and friends of his family.

Marvin's statement went to the core of something else, as well: it raised the question whether a people who had committed such inhumanities were predisposed to evil. I asked myself whether I, and every German alive today, was a representative and expression of that evil. It was an indictment too huge to fathom.

Oddly, even after this event, I never doubted that Marvin respected and liked me, nor did I stop respecting and liking him. I all but blotted out what he had said that night. Our friendship survived for a number of years, until Marvin, married and with children by then, moved to another state.

In the years that followed, the inner struggle around my German heritage mounted and, in the early eighties, ushered me into Jungian analysis, first with a woman named Sigrid McPherson, a German-born analyst. We had only just begun to explore the burden I felt at being born German when she fell, or jumped, to her death from the second-story window of her home. It was rumored in the Jungian community that she had been caught in a struggle with her own Germanness, that it had escalated into a psychosis and ultimate suicide.

I was in Sacramento, at the time, exhibiting at an antique show. David, grasping the enormous blow this would be for me, flew to Sacramento to deliver the news in person. Strangely, I had dreamed of Sigrid under a white shroud the night before she actually died. I returned to Los Angeles in time to attend her memorial service.

Shattered by Sigrid's death, I battled with the fear that I would remain trapped in the same insoluble dilemma that had killed her. I was in the grip of utter despair and saw no way out of it.

Eventually, I found Dianne Cordic, an American-born analyst, whose pragmatic approach helped reverse the freefall course Sigrid's death had set me on.

It seemed that something even more fateful than love had ridden on the swell that had brought me to America: a deeper reason which, up to then, I had not examined. I came to believe that it had been my fate, unconsciously driven, to leave the safe fold of family, friends and country behind, in order to look back on my personal history and the greater history of Germany. I recognized that I could achieve this in ways that only the *Fremde* allows. The word *Fremde* literally translates as *foreign land*. It has a secondary meaning that resonates underneath the obvious: creating an interior and exterior distance from the comfort and complacency of home.

Under Dianne Cordic's guidance, I plucked from my memory many of the losses, conflicts, silences, and feelings of guilt I had experienced growing up in an undifferentiated muddle of past and present, personal and collective. I came to examine the fractures those experiences had created in me, and the childhood bruises that had not been tended. I learned to weep for myself and for those I recreated, from among the millions murdered, in my imagination while my rage at the actual perpetrators did not subside.

The work with Sigrid McPhearson and Diane Cordic brought me back to recording my thoughts – as I had done earlier, before I'd burned everything personal I'd ever written. I started keeping a dream journal, then a regular journal, in time moving on to poetry and essays. Initially, I wrote both in German and in English but, finding it cumbersome to shift between languages, I eventually abandoned writing in German and kept to English, almost exclusively. English became the written language of my choice.

David and I would separate in 1996, after a 33-year marriage, having raised our three children together. I would continue to say I had come to America for love, because it would have felt like a betrayal of the bond between David and me, and of the storybook courtship with which our life together had begun, had I said anything else. But a time would come when I added, "Love, at any rate, is what brought me here."

49

In the autumn of 1985, there would come a discovery, one that would prompt an unexpected, but welcome, adjustment in my thinking. I was back in Germany visiting Mother, after completing a trip buying antiques in London.

Mother was setting the table for our afternoon coffee and cake. She turned to me, her head slightly tilted, a reflective sadness in her eyes. I had seen this gesture countless times before, always when she brought up my father, his premature death, her lot as a war widow. I anticipated her well-worn remark about the china coffee set: *It was an engagement gift from Josef. In all these years, not a single piece has been broken or chipped.*

To my surprise, she launched into a story I had not heard before.

"It must've been in the spring of 1944. . ." She stopped, as if wondering whether to go on.

"What happened?" I prompted her.

"Oh . . ." she said. She poured the freshly brewed coffee into our cups, and put a cozy over the gold-rimmed pot.

"Tante Irma came to our flat late one evening . . ." She lowered her voice. "She and Frau Schlenger. . . *Eine Jüdin, a* Jewess. . . Irma insisted that Frau Schlenger stay with us. . . In a small place like Delrath. . . you couldn't possibly harbor someone, unnoticed. I tried to reason with her. There were informers in our midst, in this neighborhood, this building. You just didn't know who. I was frightened."

She shook her head. "Why am I telling you this? It's all so long ago."

Ignoring her hesitation, I asked, "Did you let her stay?"

She turned to face me. "What choice did I have? She was Irma's mother-in-law. *Die arme Frau,* the poor woman. How she pleaded with me! *Die Angst in ihren Augen. –* The fear in her eyes."

"How long did she stay?"

"Three weeks, maybe longer."

"And then?"

"Man kann sich das heutzutage gar nicht vorstellen. – It's hard to imagine, nowadays. To go underground, not be able to set foot outside. Frau Schlenger became stir crazy. She parted the bedroom curtains one afternoon, just to see the rain come down. A neighbor spotted her, and later asked me who the woman was. It may have been an innocent question, but I had to let Irma know."

"And?"

"It was too big a risk, for us. . . and Frau Schlenger. Irma came to fetch her after dark, that same day."

Mother put a piece of homemade fruit tart on each of our plates, and generous dollops of whipped cream. She said nothing else, indicating that this was all she was going to say.

If there was more to the story, I wanted to hear it.

"Did she survive?" I asked.

Mother shook her head. "No."

"How did she die?"

"Irma did her best to save her. She moved her from one hiding place to another." Again she paused.

I saw this wasn't easy for Mother, but I couldn't give up, even if talking about this was painful for her.

"What more do you know?"

Mother pressed her lips together.

"I wish I didn't remember," she said, after a while. Her voice became strained. "She was deported. After the war, Irma found out that she had been taken to Bergen-Belsen."

"Like Anne Frank," I said.

"Yes, and like so many more."

Mystified by her late account, I asked, "Why didn't you tell me this way back, when I confronted you?"

"It wouldn't have made a difference," she answered.

"It would have to me."

The fact that her story contradicted her earlier claim of ignorance seemed to be of no concern to Mother. Perhaps, in her mind, one had nothing to do with the other. At any rate, she didn't try to justify herself.

Nonetheless, in my immediate interpretation of the story Mother had just told me, I wanted to reinvent the woman she had been: a woman who would have made an ethical, a political, choice to offer refuge to Jews. I didn't think those had been the considerations that had motivated her to take action. She had not been that kind of woman.

At the same time, I did not assume that my mother had told the story as a plea for absolution. I was at a loss to establish why she had chosen to tell the story at all. Did it amount to a late admission of complicity? But that interpretation, too, I realized, came from my desire to reinvent her. Mother had made no attempt to reconcile her dual positions: the willful unknowing she had clung to during our encounter in the kitchen in Delrath in 1956; and her tacit acknowledgment, all these years later, that she had harbored Frau Schlenger and therefore, must have known about the fate of the European Jewry. I didn't speculate what caused the shift, or how and whether she had found a way to let one co-exist with the other.

What could be said of my mother is that her humanity had prevailed, flawed, but it had prevailed. At the risk of jeopardizing herself and her children, and certainly against her judgment, she had harbored a Jewish woman. Not any Jewish woman, but the mother of her sister's husband, the grandmother of her sister's unborn child. She had acted, not out of heroism, but out of her sense of family. Still, she had acted.

Anyway, by the mid-1980s, admitting personal knowledge of the Holocaust no longer amounted to an act of courage or a defining of character. It was already part of the *Zeitgeist*. On the 40th anniversary of the end of the war, Richard von Weizsäker, the German president from 1984 to 1994, conceded, *"Jeder Deutsche konnte miterleben, was jüdische Mitbürger erleiden mussten. – Every German could have known what their Jewish fellow citizens were made to endure."* He was speaking on behalf of every German alive during National Socialism.

The slices of fruit tart, the whipped cream on our plates had not been touched. Mother and I had each fallen into separate silences. I recalled my blanket indictment of all Germans, back when I first learned about the Holocaust in Karin's Protestant Religion Studies class. It had been informed, over time, by an attempt to understand a part of our history which, ultimately, remains incomprehensible. Without the benefit of knowing that history – the very history out of which I was born, the very history that shaped me – what would my position have been? Would I have been swept up, as most Germans had been, by a tide of propaganda promising to restore a bad economy, national pride, and to create a bright future? Would I have turned a blind eye to what was happening to segments of the population, who were being scapegoated, demonized, enslaved, murdered? Had there been a means of not knowing, of remaining uninformed?

In light of the arbitrary measures taken against those who harbored Jews – from incarceration to execution – would I have found the courage to put myself and my children in harm's way? Had that been my expectation of Mother? Could I make that judgment? It would have been arrogant to even speculate, I realized then, at Mother's dining table.

It was Mother who ended the silence. She said, "Sometimes I am ashamed to belong to a nation capable of committing such acts of inhumanity."

At last, Mother's and my feelings meshed.

I never loved Mother more than at that moment.

PART FOUR

The Search
1994 – 1996

50

1994. It was forty-nine years after the war, five years after the fall of the Berlin Wall, two years after German reunification. I had wept seeing hundreds and hundreds of joyous people on television tear down the wall that had separated them as Germans, both physically and politically. They had helped one another climb over the wall, had pulled down the barbed wire and, with crowbars and sledgehammers, had demolished the 103-mile-long, 12-feet-high solid cement partition inch by inch. Conciliatory acts brought about by the will of the German people, they illustrated the extreme opposites alive in the collective German psyche: a capacity for evil demonstrated by the horrors of genocide during the Hitler regime, and the capacity for reconciliation of a magnitude very few had anticipated and many had hoped for. After nearly half a century without diplomatic ties, the communist East and the democratic West had rejoined as one people under one government. No longer did the *Iron Curtain* divide a country. No longer was it unthinkable to travel between East and West. And for the first time in my imagination, the desire and the idea came to me to return to Rockensußra.

In the autumn of that year, I took the train from Cologne to Erfurt, the capital of Thuringia and the closest big city to Rockensußra. I sat in the window seat of a nearly empty compartment, as fifty years earlier, Mother had sat in a window seat of an overcrowded compartment, her two children on her lap. That had been the wartime summer of 1944. Gitta had been an infant, barely six months old; I'd been a tow-headed four-and-a-half-year-old.

How different my reasons were for this journey from what Mother's reasons had been! She'd been escaping the air raids at home in Delrath, getting her children and herself to safety; I was pursuing a desire, only vaguely articulated, to return to the farmhouse where the curtain had been drawn that divided the time before my father's death from what followed. Perhaps, I hoped to imbue my childhood, retroactively, with a sense of innocence and wholeness. To bring back the ghost of my father.

The monotonous clatter of the train lulled me into reminiscence, daydreaming, half-sleep. I paid little attention to the countryside we traversed, the towns where we briefly stopped. We passed through Bebra and Gerstungen – now just two stations like all the other stations. Before the fall of the wall, they had been checkpoints in the West and East, respectively. Then, crossing the border between the two Germanys would have been difficult, if not impossible, under ordinary circumstances. There would have been exhaustive custom and passport inspections, along with drawn-out delays. At the time of Mother's train journey, like now, there had been no border. Germany had still been one country.

I had been the only passenger in the compartment for most of the four-hour train ride, when a peasant woman of indeterminate age boarded the train. Her drab, poor-quality clothing suggested she was East German, as did her unstyled, mouse-gray hair, worn twisted into an old-fashioned bun. She sat down a couple of rows away from me. As soon as the train pulled out of the station, she spread a green plastic shopping bag on her lap, whereupon she removed a sandwich from its newspaper wrapping. She held it with both hands and took slow bites, savoring them as one would a delicacy. The smell of pumpernickel bread and liverwurst permeated the compartment.

The woman, it appeared, was unaware of my presence and undisturbed by my curious glances. I speculated about the dissimilarities in our lives – hers poor and, until recently, oppressed by a communist system; mine, free and affluent, by comparison. Most likely, she had never left the immediate area of her village or gone beyond a couple of train stops away, while there was no limit to the world that was open to me.

Early that evening, the train pulled into Erfurt. Following the announcement that this was the train's final destination, the passengers filed out of the compartments. They walked along the station platform, leisurely, but for one or two who rushed toward the exit. This was not the rush-hour scene one would expect at a train station in a major city, but one that still betrayed remnants of communist sensibilities free from capitalist pressures and values. Here, it seemed, time was not yet equated with money.

Almost immediately, I felt disoriented, my own sense of time shifting, alternating between time present and time past, the two merging in distorted perceptions. The station itself – brick walls pitted with holes from artillery fire, missing glass in the roof panels – took me back to the endless hours of waiting for connections on our trek home from Rockensußra after the war.

It was a short taxi ride to my hotel. Along the way, we passed empty lots filled with heaps of rubble, weed-overgrown – scars of wartime destruction, long erased in the West. We passed façades of crumbling stucco with black, curtainless windows, interspersed with communist-era buildings, already shabby from neglect.

The taxi pulled up in front of the hotel, an ultra-modern structure, unmistakably built after the reunification. It jogged me back into now. Wide glass doors opened to an elegant western-style lobby. My room on the fifth floor was tastefully appointed with birch-veneered furniture.

In the middle of the night, I woke from a vivid dream: *I wander through the inner city of Erfurt. The shops are closed, some are barricaded with graffiti-defaced plywood. A matronly woman greets me from a recess, where an open door leads into a second-hand shop. She waves for me to enter. As my eyes adjust to the dim light, I discover one exquisite treasure after another among a clutter of worthless objects. The woman takes my hand and escorts me through a meandering passage into a church. We kneel at the baptismal fountain to the left of the altar. I dip my fingertips into the holy water and cross myself. Looking up, I'm awestruck by the photographic image of the exterior of a basilica projected onto the sweeping ceiling of the apse. As if emerging from it, three white doves, their wings spread, slowly glide from sight.*

Walter Gornick was waiting in the lobby when I stepped out of the elevator at nine the next morning. My driver and guide for the day, he had described himself on the phone the previous evening as a man of medium build in his early forties; he had said that he would wear a brown leather jacket. At first glance, his clothing did not fit the stereotypical idea I had of cheap East German fashion, until I noticed his rather shabby shoes. He welcomed me warmly, not as one would a stranger, but as the fellow German I was. We exchanged a few words about the weather as he escorted me to his *Brabant,* the GDR state-manufactured car with minimal comfort and high emission rates.

"It will take us about an hour to get to Rockensußra," he said.

Once we were outside the city, a mist hung in the valleys. We drove along two-lane roads through farmland and rolling hills. Now and then, we passed dilapidated, half-timbered houses that looked abandoned but probably weren't. The asphalt glistened with moisture seeping up from the waterlogged ground. The car navigated around the many potholes filled with yesterday's rain. There was very little traffic in either direction. A few farm vehicles in front of us pulled over to let us pass. Although the countryside was bucolic like the countryside on the other side of the border, the contrast in the condition of the roads and buildings we passed was striking, as was the minimal traffic we encountered.

We conversed little beyond what we each thought was polite, or necessary. Both of us spoke in our native German, but his was tinged with the accent of the region, mine with the occasional awkwardness that comes with lack of practice. I briefly related that my mother, my younger sister and I, had lived as evacuees in Rockensußra during the final year of the war and a few months after. That my father had fallen in action during that time. That I wanted to revisit the place where we had received the news of his death.

"*Das muss arg gewesen sein.* – That must've been hard," Walter Gornick said. He turned briefly to look at me, adding, "My maternal grandfather, too, was killed during the war. In Leningrad." Then, encapsulating his life since the reunification, he recounted that, as a result of streamlining employment in the new market-driven economy, he had lost his job as an engineer. The factory was now defunct. "It's been two years since the merging of the two Germanys," he said. "For many, the honeymoon is over. We were accustomed to a system where the little we owned was provided by the state. It's been a challenge to make the shift to self-initiative." He paused, before he went on in an accusatory tone, "The kind of ruthless capitalism imposed by West German investors has caused bitterness. The economic imbalance between East and West is hard to swallow." His voice became hesitant, as if sharing something shameful, "I ended up in a depression."

"I'm so sorry," I said. "Are you getting help?"

Again, he turned to me, "Help? Where? My wife left me. Couldn't stand living with someone who's a loser."

More than an hour passed, some of it in silence, some of it answering each other's questions about our divergent lives.

"Rockensußra." Walter Gornick pointed to the yellow sign on the side of the road. It read: *Rockensußra, Stadt Ebeleben, Kyffhäuserkreis.* Then he added, "A dot on the map, where nothing has changed. Everything will be as you remember it."

Two women in dark work clothes with kerchiefs over their heads looked up from spreading asphalt on the cracked surface of the road. They stepped aside and, leaning on their rakes for a welcome break, watched us drive by.

There was a farm on the right. I saw it, the half-timbered façade and gabled stucco walls, and a spark flashed in my memory: the Köppel farmhouse.

"Da ist es. – That's it," I gasped. "Just where I remembered it was."

Walter Gornick stopped the car. I took a moment to look at the house. But the closer I looked, the more the similarities vanished and the differences stood out. This farmhouse was diminutive compared to the one I'd known. Where I expected to see low-growing hazelnut bushes, pine trees towered above the gable, obstructing the view of the upstairs window. The meadow, the barn, the brick wall, none of it matched my recollection. Only an elusive sense of *déjà-vu* remained. Something vague and nostalgic, like a memory that lingered just barely outside of my grasp. I groped to retrieve it, but it receded. The harder I tried, the more the resemblance to the house of the past faded. Then the remembered image disappeared altogether.

"I don't think this is it," I said. I felt shaken.

Walter Gornick noticed. "We'll find it," he said.

We turned left into the village proper, down an unpaved street. None of the small, attached houses along the way looked familiar. Their doors and window shutters were closed. I recognized the barn where I'd gotten separated from Mother among huge heaps of army surplus and, panicked, had run home. We passed the brick church and the village green, beyond which an access road led into the fields. Not a soul was in sight.

"There has to be someone we can ask," I said.

"The women working on the road?"

They were gone when we returned to the spot where they had been only minutes earlier.

I felt as if I were trapped in another time zone. "How eerie!" I said.

When Walter Gornick didn't respond, I wasn't sure whether he was joining me in this strange place of altered time, or whether he was dismissing me as someone imagining things.

He pulled a quick, determined U-turn – to demonstrate, perhaps, that he was taking charge. We drove back the short distance to the same intersection where we had just been. On the corner that had been as deserted as the rest of the village only moments ago, a group of three women now stood chatting. There was nothing to suggest where they had come from so suddenly. Yet, they looked settled, as if they had been there for a long time. They were young women, with traces of the kind of bitterness in their faces that comes from hardship. Their lips were thin, like those of old women. They looked at us suspiciously, as Walter Gornick slowed the car, and I rolled down the window.

The tallest of the three, a woman with a leg cast, adjusted her crutches and stepped next to the passenger side of the car. She squinted her eyes, less with curiosity than distrust.

"*Guten Morgen,*" I said, "We're looking for the Köppel farm. Can you help us?"

After a brief hesitancy, the young woman lifted one of her crutches and pointed to the gabled, half-timbered house across the highway. It was the same house that, earlier, had quickened my memory.

"*Da drüben* – Over there," she said, her voice tentative, as if she were questioning whether she should give me the information. She turned to her friends for reassurance, but their faces remained blank.

"I've come for a surprise visit," I said, in an effort to show that my intentions were harmless.

This seemed to set her mind at ease. *"Der alte Köppel ist schon Jahre tot.* – Old man Köppel has been dead for years," she said, "His son Kurt took over the farm." There was pride in her voice when she added, "I'm his daughter-in-law."

The other two women, who'd been watching with caution, now came alive. They began talking among themselves in low voices, their hands covering their mouths. They lowered and tilted their heads to get a good look at us.

"Let me take you there," the young woman offered.

Walter Gornick and I both got out of the car. Before I had a chance to say anything, he said, "I'll wait for you. There is a pub across the street."

The young woman flung herself on her crutches and, skillfully avoiding potholes, negotiated her way across the highway. I followed.

She stopped at the bottom of a gentle hill. Supporting herself on the crutches, she straightened her body. She looked up the hill, away from the house, and waved to a man in overalls coming down the meadow.

"That's Kurt," she said.

His black rubber boots parting the mist-covered autumn grass, the man in overalls lumbered toward the spot where I stood waiting. He was of husky build. Gradually, his broad face came into focus, the ruddy complexion, the graying hair. His look was reserved, not jovial as his type might suggest, but of a man unaccustomed to welcoming strangers. He paused, leaving a safe distance between us, and a silence. A few crows circled over the meadow. Cawing, they flew dauntingly close before they alighted on the rim of a water-filled trough.

I took a few steps in the direction of the man, who, it appeared, was assessing me, or expecting me to say something. I extended my hand, feeling awkward as I introduced myself with a phrase I had rehearsed, "I don't expect you to know who I am." Here, I paused to swallow an unexpected emotional surge. "When you were nine and I was four, we were playmates, on your farm, right here."

What happened next was more surprising than anything I could have imagined. A boy, forty-eight years ago, had said to me on parting,

"I know you'll never come back." Now, this grown man, who hadn't known I was coming, called out my name: "Marie-Luise!" He reached for my hand, taking it in both of his.

"Kurtie." I said, quietly.

I did not immediately recognize the boy in the man. I searched his face until, taken back in time, I became the little girl I had been, and I saw the nine-year-old: feisty, with a runny nose and gentle eyes. He'd liked playing rough, though not in a mean way. I'd been his shy little girl who'd needed protecting. He'd chased away the boys when they pulled my straggly braids. He'd comforted me at the barn when I thought I'd lost my mother for good. He'd picked me up when I'd bruised my face sledding into a rock. Wiping my tears with his coarse woolen glove and tickling my belly, he'd made me laugh despite my smarting pain and fright. "You're a sissy," he'd said, teasingly. He'd shown me how to make impressions of angels, their wings spread, in the freshly fallen snow.

A soft drizzle started coming down. I turned to look for the woman on crutches, to thank her, but she was nowhere to be seen. Her friends, too, were gone. All was deserted again, save for the car by the roadside and Walter Gornick leaning on the open door.

Kurt and I stood alone in the meadow. "What brings you back here?" Kurt's question seemed redundant. Didn't he know?

I glanced at the farmhouse behind me. "My father's death . . . We were notified of it . . ."

"I remember," Kurt interrupted – so quickly, it was as if that day had been on his mind, too, as if no time had passed between that day and now. "I answered the door for Johann Hartlieb. . . ahead of you and your mother."

"Johann Hartlieb? That was his name?" I said.

"*Ja, der Totenmann.* – Yes, the Death Man. That's what we called him behind his back."

Kurt threw a look at the path where the uniformed man had waded through the snow on the day after Epiphany 1945.

He said, "I hid under the staircase. I heard everything. I was the first to tell my mother and sisters."

Kurt stomped his feet, shaking the wetness off his boots. He crossed the drive of hard-packed dirt between the meadow and the house. He didn't need to extend an invitation for me to follow. He had entered my memory; we were returning together into our shared past.

The same heavy, wooden door led inside the house. As dank as I remembered it, the hallway was sharply reduced in size from the one imprinted in my memory. The past became tenuous, mercurial. What had been then, and what was now, shifted back and forth. I took a few steps on the black-and-white tiled floor. I paused on the spot where, nearly half a century ago, a little girl had searched for her mother's hand.

We kept silent, Kurt and I. I tried to remember the little girl who had stood right here. Kurt took the few steps to the nook under the staircase where young Kurtie had hidden. We were each re-enacting the event. Kurt, his part of the remembering; I, my part of the remembering.

Kurtie had not been part of my memory. Mother and I had been alone in the hallway, alone with the man whose name I had just learned. Memory had cheated me. Kurtie had heard the same words: *"Ich habe die traurige Pflicht, Ihnen mitteilen zu müssen, dass Ihr Gatte gefallen ist. –* It is my sad duty to inform you that your husband has been killed in action."

After that, our memories truly parted: I would stay, holding fast to my sobbing mother's skirt; Kurtie would steal away from under the staircase. He would open the door to the front room, softly, and bring the women the news he had overheard.

My memory at first refused to incorporate Kurtie in a reality that, unbeknownst to me, we had shared. Protecting memory's selfishly immutable nature, I tried to discount Kurtie's version. I felt robbed of an experience that had been only mine, and Mother's. But something greater was true as well: the memories, Kurtie's and mine, different from each other, had connected our lives through time. They belonged to both of us.

Assuming the role of leader, just as Kurtie had when we were little, the adult Kurt ushered me up the stairs. I paused on the landing where, sitting with my legs pulled to my chest, I'd eavesdropped when Onkel Jean, who's arrived from Dresden on his way home to Delrath late one night, had spoken to Mother about the end of the war nearing.

Kurt followed as I made my way down a dark, narrow passage, the ceiling barely clearing my head, and opened a door. Ducking, I stepped into the room that, I believed, had been the bedroom Mother, Gitta and I had shared. It was a smoke room, not much larger than a walk-in closet. How could I have been so mistaken? It unsettled me. I navigated around rows of oval sausages strung on wooden rods and slabs of bacon hanging from hooks in the ceiling. The window on the far wall was open. Pine trees shaded the side of the house. They allowed no more than a glimpse of the highway, and nothing of the fields in the distance.

Had I not heard the faraway rumble of Russian tanks from this very window? Had I not seen them approach along the highway? Had my imagination invented the terror I remembered feeling, hiding under the bed with Mother and Gitta?

I turned to Kurtie. "Was this – ?"

I stopped midsentence. I did not want to finish the question I was about to ask, lest the answer might invalidate my memory. I needed my memory of this room to remain intact. I needed it even if it were based on what had not been real.

"When you were here, this was your bedroom," Kurt said, answering the question I had left unasked. "We turned it into a smoke room some years ago." Joining me at the window, he went on, "You wouldn't remember these pine trees either. They were saplings when my father planted them after the war."

My memory of the room was safe again.

Kurt leaned his elbows on the window sill. "My sisters," he said, with obvious pleasure. "News spreads fast around here." He waved to three older women coming up the path to the house.

Following the sound of Kurt's voice, they looked up. They cupped their hands around their mouths and called out, *"Gertruds Tochter? –* Gertrud's daughter?"

I waved. Yes, I was Gertrud's daughter. And they waved back.

There was nothing familiar to me in their faces. These were the aging faces of plain farmwomen, their graying hair combed back. They wore cheerless cotton smocks, looking not at all the way I would see them, months later, in a dream: *The sisters are young again. It is summertime in a meadow of tall grass. Wavy brown hair frames their smooth, laughing faces. Holding hands, they dance in a circle. Their white gowns flow in the wind. Too late, they alert me to an avalanche of mud pouring down the hill. It buries me waist-high, threatening to carry me away. The sisters extend their hands and pull me to dry ground.*

The three sisters greeted me exuberantly, as if they, too, had been expecting me. I followed them into the front room, where Kurt's wife, whose name I learned was Helga, was busy tidying up for the visit that had come to her attention, also. A Formica and Naugahyde dining set had taken the place of the hand-hewn table with the assembly of odd chairs I remembered. Sitting at that table, Kurtie had whittled toy blocks for the cabin he wanted to build, while I had drawn pictures. A modern sofa and coffee table dominated the small space. I recognized the crudely made dresser in the corner closest to the door. The framed photos of the Köppels' dead sons were gone. They had made room for an oversized television set.

"The last photo taken of our father," Kurt said, pointing to a wood-framed photograph on the wall, of an old man leading a horse. There was admiration and love in Kurt's voice. A larger-than-life presence even in his old age, the image of the family patriarch stirred a buried fear inside me.

I glanced at the window. It matched the image that was engraved in my memory. On a snowy morning in January 1945, I'd peered through the same mullioned glass panes and seen the man plod through the snow; months later, on a warm spring day the war had ended – May 8, 1945 – I'd sat on the same sill, legs dangling. And Mother, looking into the distance, had promised that she would take us home. "All we have to do is follow the sun west."

We all sat down around the coffee table, on the sofa and on chairs Kurt pulled up.

Christa, the youngest of the sisters by many years and not much older than I, was the first to speak.

"You and I were playmates," she said, though, in my memory, she had been all but absent.

"There is a picture of the two of us somewhere in here." She rummaged through a large tin stuffed with photos. Near the bottom, she uncovered a small black-and-white snapshot of two fair-headed little girls, squatting by a manure heap, their skirts lifted. And another, of Mother, dressed in a pleated skirt and blouse, hair twisted into a chignon, posing under a tree.

"Your mother was a beautiful woman. So elegant," Waltraud, the middle sister, said. She was the one closest in age to Mother.

"Fate dealt her a hard blow when your father didn't come back from the war." The changing look in her eyes suggested empathy: perhaps, she remembered losses of her own: perhaps, she was trying to span the years since their youth and imagine Mother as she might look now, nearing eighty. "She must've remarried," she said.

"No," I replied, "She remained a widow." I decided to say no more, out of respect for Mother, who would not have wanted me to say more.

Anna was the oldest of the three sisters. More talkative than the others, she recounted the family's collective memory of our time in Rockensußra.

"We were shorthanded here on the farm. The fields and the stables had been men's work. Then, our two older brothers were drafted and, soon after, killed in Stalingrad." She paused. "Our poor mother. . . never got over it. . . Our father couldn't manage the work on his own. So the women chipped in, except for your mother. She wasn't made for hard labor in the fields." Here, she chuckled. "She earned her keep, and yours, by doing chores around the house and taking care of the children."

I hadn't seen Kurt leave, but I did notice him coming back into the room. No longer in his work overalls, he'd changed into clothes that probably were his Sunday best: a maroon and white knit sweater, a pair of pants too loose in the seat and too short in the legs, and scuffed, brown leather shoes.

He was carrying a large platter with a hefty sausage tied into an oval. He placed it on the coffee table the sisters had set for an impromptu, late-morning repast.

"Fresh as can be. We slaughtered a hog only last week." A broad smile spread across his face.

The sight and smell of the sausage tapped into the same unease I had felt looking at the old man's photo on the wall. Old man Köppel's stature had been imposing and his speech, thunderous. No one in the household had dared ignore his orders. Everyone had lived in fear of him.

I remembered the particular noon meal, when Herr Köppel had called me a *spoiled brat,* and I'd forced down the home-butchered pork sausage I detested so much. I remembered, too, all the other times I'd pushed the sausage pieces to the side of my plate, and Mother had stashed them in her apron pocket. The memory released my enduring distaste for the sausage.

"Prepared in the family tradition. Same recipe handed down through the generations," Kurt said. "Eat as much as you like. What's left we'll pack up for the road." And so I ate, just to please my host, and I complimented him on his butchering skills.

"Our father had a falling out with your mother," Anna said, "He accused her of stealing his sausage. We didn't dare tell him that it was only your scraps she was saving."

For the first time, I connected the dots: Mother had saved the sausage bits. They had been the bribe the Russian-speaking women had offered the Soviet soldier when we had gotten caught fleeing across the border. In return, the soldiers had let us pass, unharmed. I told the story.

Smug pleasure lit up Kurt's face. He looked around to make sure everyone was listening. "Just imagine. Our sausage saved their lives."

For the remainder of the meal, Kurt and his sisters took turns telling their individual life stories. Five decades of living condensed into bare-bones:

Old age took their father twenty-two years ago. He was survived by his wife, younger than he by ten years. Frau Köppel had died in 1979.

Kurt and his wife had three sons. One of them lived in the house behind the barn that the men built with their own hands.

Anna had six children. One daughter was killed in a tractor accident at twenty-three, two weeks after the youngest sibling, a late arrival, was born. An adult son died of cancer the previous year.

Christa had one daughter. A son had died of congenital heart disease at seventeen.

Waltraud had two daughters.

"Our eldest is Marie-Luise," Waltraud said. "We named her

after you."

Waltraud smiled at me, and I smiled back at her. Something tender stirred in my heart: no matter how much time had passed since the war, my presence in this family had continued in the person of a namesake, a godchild of sorts.

Tears came to my eyes, as I searched for something appropriate to say. *"Was für eine Ehre.* – What an honor." I wished I'd thought of something less formal.

"I can't wait to tell her that you came to see us. She is a trained optician, works in Erfurt, but lives here in Rockensußra. She's intelligent. Like you."

"Tell us about you," Anna said.

And then I, too, told about my life. "I've lived in California for many years."

Everyone gasped with amazement. "Are you an actress?"

"No," I laughed, "I married an American. He works in films. We have three children, all of them grown now." I felt hesitant telling them about my privileged life and so limited my story to the bare outlines.

"What about Gitta? She was a handful in those days," Waltraud asked.

"She and her husband have a teenage daughter. They built a house on a lot next to our mother's. Mother likes it that one of her daughters lives nearby."

Changing the subject abruptly, as if something important had slipped his mind, Kurt said, "Johann Hartlieb. He's still alive. Must be close to a hundred."

He got up from his chair. "I'll go fetch him."

The sisters threw him disapproving looks, insinuating that the man who'd brought the awful news was not one of us.

He glanced at me.

"Maybe not," I said, as an old dread won over my desire to meet this man, who, however unjustly, held a sinister place in my memory. I'd not seen him again after he'd walked back into the snow, but some nights, he'd returned in a bad dream. Always, he'd come to take Mother away. Waking up frightened, I had reached for her warm body next to me in the bed we shared, relieved that it had only been a dream. During waking hours, I'd sometimes imagined him prowling under the hazelnut bushes below our bedroom window.

Later, when I regretted my decision, I wrote Johann Hartlieb a letter, saying that I wished I'd looked him up when I was in Rockensußra.

"My dear child," he would say by return mail, *"I have grown to be old and none the wiser. My life has been one of fulfilling my duty, even when it brought sorrow to others. Not all men die as heroes."*

After close to three hours of reminiscing, the conversation began to shift. Away from the memories that bound us, it drifted into the more recent political upheaval in Eastern Europe. Kurt and his sisters spoke animatedly of the discontent with the inequities, after reunification, between the eastern and western states of Germany, the disappointment that the promise of prosperity had not been fulfilled, not yet.

Once the memories had been exhausted, the stories told, the reunion was over. The world we held in common belonged to the past, and to the war that had shaped all of us. I felt indebted to Kurt and his sisters, who had cheerfully contributed their memories. They had invited me into their home so that I might revisit my past. They had served a generous meal to celebrate the occasion. It was time to say goodbye.

It was early afternoon. Walter Gornick was waiting near his *Brabant*. He had declined to join the reunion with the Köppels, when I'd invited him earlier. "That's your occasion," he'd said. Now, he helped me get situated in the passenger seat, and shook Kurt's hand.

"Have a safe journey. Come back soon," Kurt called over the sound of the car engine. The women stood outside the front door, waving goodbye. I, too, waved, knowing I would never return to Rockensußra, never see Kurt and his sisters again.

I leaned back in the seat. A light mist on the windshield cast a gray film over the harvested fields and blurred the outlines of the villages we passed. The smell of Kurt's leftover sausage, wrapped in layers of newspaper, filled the interior of the car. The hum of the engine sounded muffled, as though it were coming from some other place.

"Did you find what you were looking for?" Walter Gornick asked.

"I don't know. . . how to answer . . ." I spoke haltingly. I was near crying. His question, it seemed, heightened the poignancy of my visit to Rockensußra.

"I'm sorry," he said, after a polite silence.

Had I found what I was looking for? I wasn't ready to answer that question, not even to myself.

Rather, the word *Vater* – Father – ricocheted through my mind. It had an unfamiliar and faraway ring, as from an archaic or dreamlike vocabulary. A word that had been lost to me long ago, it lacked meaningful resonance. As the word itself was strange to me, my father himself was a stranger, also. When he had died as my father, had I died as my father's child?

It would have been simple to leave it at that. But already, something was beginning to take shape at that moment of utter abandonment. Something distant still, like a mute call or a foreshadowing that this was not the end of the search for my father. A thought struck me, like an epiphany: that inasmuch as my father had abandoned me, the child he had left behind had abandoned him. Neither were to blame. Not his death, nor the innocence of her age. While his life had been stopped short, I had gone on living to become the person I was, no longer the child he had known.

The car rolled to a stop in front of the hotel in Erfurt. Walter Gornick shut off the engine. I turned to thank him for his services and handed him the envelope with his fee and a thank-you note.

As the revolving door to the hotel lobby swallowed me, I turned to catch a last glimpse of the *Brabant* pulling away and Walter Gornick waving.

I opened the window in my room. I looked out over the city whose streets I had never walked. The autumn air chilled my face. Early dusk spread over the city. A thick layer of pinkish gray lay over the red roofs and on the weather-beaten façades of the buildings within my view. Against the horizon rose a cluster of smokeless chimneys and the turned-green copper roof of a basilica, reminiscent of the one in the dream I'd had the night before.

51

December 26, 1994, marked the 50th anniversary of my father's death. Alone in my Venice, California study, I read most of the three hundred and fifty letters he had written to my mother and she, in turn, had given to me on a visit home. The first one was dated May 1939, the final one, December 19, 1944, six days before he was killed.

I wanted to remember the man who had been my father, honor him in this way. I also wanted to establish his guilt or innocence beyond his membership in the *Wehrmacht* and his participation in the war.

Throughout my growing-up years, Mother would talk about details of my father's history as a soldier. My parents had been married for less than a year, when my father joined the *Wehrmacht* in May of 1939. It was ten months before I was born. He was assigned to the *58. Infanterie Regiment der 11. Division,* an army regiment, and was stationed in the Ruhr valley city of Remscheidt, less than 50 kilometers northeast of us.

My father enlisted voluntarily – perhaps even enthusiastically – despite military exemption status as a promising young executive in his company, *Rheinland,* a prominent insurance company, and contrary to Mother's wishes. This caused an enduring rift between my parents. What Mother construed as my father's needless sacrifice of family and career – and ultimately of his life – had sparked a bitterness that she harbored into her old age. *"Er war ein begeisterter Mitläufer.* – He was an enthusiastic follower, full of romantic and idealistic notions. He alone bears the blame for his fate," she often lamented when talking about what she felt was his misguided decision and her widowhood. "When it was too late, he regretted his foolishness."

While in the early days I never heard my mother talk about the war in political terms, and about Nazi ideology directly, she always spoke freely about my father, how she perceived his involvement, and how his decision to enlist ruined her life. But I do recall one story she recounted about a small wartime social gathering in the home of our downstairs neighbor, when one of the guests called Hitler a *Schweinhund,* a swine. "Even among friends, it wasn't safe to say that," Mother said. "That person was hauled off the following day."

By the time my father joined the military, Germany's alliance with Italy and smaller countries had been established; Austria had been annexed; Czechoslovakia had been taken over, as a quasi-giveaway resulting from the Munich Agreement between Germany, Italy, France and England; *Kristallnacht* – when Jewish businesses and synagogues were vandalized, and Jews were murdered and incarcerated in concentration camps – had passed; the non-aggression pact with Stalin would be signed later that year, in August 1939; little more than a week afterwards, on September 1, World War II would break out with the invasion of Poland.

My father's regiment was deployed in that invasion and, later, in the campaigns in France and, finally, Russia.

His earliest letters, those written before the outbreak of the war, dwelled on details of Mother's day-to-day concerns: questions about her and her parents' wellbeing; instructions to give away a jar of his tobacco that might otherwise get stale; the vivid description of a film he had seen – a love story that had aroused his yearning for his wife. Most letters were tender evocations of his love for Mother, and assurances that she need not fear for his life. Each one ended with an expression of hope to be reunited with her soon.

In letters my father wrote from Poland in September and early October 1939, I came upon two unexpected references. The first one, written in September 1939, said: *"We are 17 kilometers outside of Warsaw. My beloved, Krieg ist grausam – war is cruel. I will spare you the gruesome details. . . In a few days, we should reach Warsaw. I hope that will bring this war to an end. It is terrible to see so much human misery. I pity the Polish people."*

In a second letter two weeks later, when Warsaw had been taken by the *Wehrmacht,* and the city had been heavily destroyed by *Luftwaffe* bombings and artillery attacks that, together, claimed the lives of 18,000 Polish civilians, he wrote: *"Mein liebes Trautchen* (an endearing form of

Gertrud, and my father's favored name for Mother) – *My dear Trautchen, you need not fear any longer. All is quiet now, as in peace times. Only the buildings, ravaged by bombings and gunfire, bear witness to this horrible war. And in the countenance of the population, the grief of the last days and weeks remains as visible testimony. It is sad."*

I wondered whether, in light of censorship, he had taken risks writing these passages. I wondered, too, whether they were the words of a conflicted man. I dared not construe them as a turn in my father's thinking. But even if they weren't a disavowal of the war and of Nazi ideology, as I wished, I construed them as spoken from humanness and compassion. None of the letters, up to that point, had provided insight into the ideological convictions he might have held.

However, when writing from Division Headquarters in East Prussia three-and-a-half years later, on June 17, 1943, he echoed the official line with apparent fervor. Deploring the low morale in some circles, he wrote, *"We must trust in our leadership. While things look bad in the West, and the sacrifices demanded of everyone are very great, we must not forget that our leadership is well aware of this, and will take the appropriate measures to bring the killing to an end. Up till now, the Führer has mastered even the most hopeless situations. He shall lead us to a victorious outcome."*

Here was the first letter that expressed belief in Hitler as the trusted leader. While it was disturbing to read these lines, I still hoped that they might not voice his own conviction but were written from a place of duty.

During the second half of 1944, after he had been deployed to the front, confidence in his own survival had eroded. The *Kurland Armee,* as his division was known, had been defeated by the Soviets after the one-thousand-day siege of Leningrad, as St. Petersburg was then called. For several months, the Armee had been retreating toward the Baltic states, with the intent of reaching East Prussia and, from there, defending the Reich.

A letter he wrote on August 1, 1944, ended with these words: *"My dear little darling, at present, I still hold the position of clerk in the company, and as such am behind the firing lines and less exposed to danger. My poor Trautchen, we are not certain whether my situation will change and whether I will be spared. . . We have been successful in defending the isthmus of Narwa. But I don't know how long we can hold on. My dearest, should fate take me, it would be sad for you and for our children. But let us not dwell on it, my dear one, because up till now fortune has smiled upon us."*

This would have been the letter Mother often referenced when she said that my father foresaw his death in the war. I read it over and over, knowing what the outcome would be, an outcome he didn't know at the time, nor would he ever know. And I thought of Mother, how his words of despair would have affected her. How she would have wept on his behalf, as well as her own and that of her children.

Ten days later, his spirits visibly boosted, he wrote, *"I am firmly convinced that there will be a decisive turn before the year is over. Not that it will bring the end of the war, but that we will move toward it with giant leaps. . . I also believe that the Russians will not be successful in crossing the borders into the Reich. With the decision of the leadership to engage in total war, our front will be reinforced with personnel and greater supplies of weapons and ammunition. . . which will put us into a position of more offensive warfare and a decisive victory over the enemy."*

Reporting on the advances and battles, in which he had participated later in 1944, my father limited himself to unadorned observations of the hardships in a soldier's existence: long marches in hostile environments; lack of sleep; and an occasional mention of skirmishes.

In the third of six battles fought in the Baltic region, my father was killed. It was December 26, 1944.

Long past midnight, I closed the folder with my father's letters. He was dead, one of the eleven million German men alone who had fallen in the battles of WWII. An unimaginable number! I thought about Josef Schupp, as the father I had hardly known and lost and as the husband and family man I had gotten to know a little more that day. He was the man, I thought, who Mother had described as "an enthusiastic follower," but a man, too, who was conflicted in his beliefs. I also thought about him as a soldier who, along with all the others, had died for a wrongful cause. After the war, they had not been celebrated as heroes or remembered in memorials. It hadn't been something I had missed or expected as a child. It had been the norm, after all. Only later, in the 1950s, when the names of all of Delrath's fallen soldiers were engraved on a wall behind the church's Marian altar, and later yet, sometime in the 1960s, when a memorial was built near the Delrath post office, did it occur to me that any kind of recognition of these men had been absent. Nor had these dead soldiers been exonerated, even though they themselves had been casualties of the same destructive forces that had claimed the lives of millions more. They hovered, like unredeemed ghosts, in the great silence after the war.

As an adult struggling with the extreme events of WWII, I came to regard the war as separate from the Holocaust – a differentiation through which I conveniently absolved my father from what was the greater evil. My reading of his letters had fleshed out the man Mother had portrayed and whom I recalled through only a few sweet memories. He had been a devoted father, a loving husband, a willing soldier, a man swept away by the ethos of his times. If another man could have become visible through his letters, I did not see him.

Mother, on the other hand, came to be the scapegoat, on whom I unloaded my muddled sense of the guilt of most of her generation. As I saw it from my teenage perspective, her participation in the system, however limited, and her silence had made her guilty by more than association. She had been a blind follower of the evil forces of her time.

52

I trace the beginning of my journey to Kurzeme to the end of September 1997, the moment I set foot aboard the *St. Petersburg* with my old high school friend, Dieter Wegener. A cargo ferry, originating in the harbor of the east German island of Rügen, the St. Petersburg would take us on an eighteen-hour, overnight voyage to the Lithuanian port of Klaipeda.

We were headed to the western-most plains of Latvia, *Kurland* – the German name for the Latvian *Kurzeme* and the English *Courland,* where my father had been killed in the third of six battles that sealed the Soviet victory over Germany in the Baltic region.

Other moments could also have marked the journey's beginning: Hamburg, where we started the 300-kilometer drive to Rügen. Estimated to take less than three hours by car, it had turned into more than half a day of alternately crawling through congested towns and racing at break-neck speed over tree-lined highways. We caught the ocean ferry only because it was delayed by two hours past its scheduled departure time.

Or the Lithuanian town of Klaipeda, for example, our point of entry into the Baltic region.

Or, Liepaja, in the Kurzeme region, where the actual quest began.

There were less concrete beginnings, as well, further back in the past. When, for example, as an eight-year old, I'd pleaded with Mother to bring my father's remains back home and give him a proper burial in our local cemetery, with a gravestone bearing his name. She had dismissed my arguments as childish.

Or, further back still, in Rockensußra on that snowy morning in 1945 – the place and the day that prefigured this journey – when we learned that my father had fallen in the trenches of Kurland.

During the nearly three years since my visit to Rockensußra, the yearning to search for my dead father had deepened gradually into resolve. I had decided to make a journey to the battlefields of *Kurland* – a vague location identified on the official death notice as 30 km southeast of Frauenburg, the German name for the Latvian town of Saldus. I wrote a letter to Dieter in Germany, asking him whether he would take on the task of researching the movements of my father's regiment and the region where he had been killed. Dieter, who had become an historian, agreed.

As the wartime events and the geography of Kurzeme took shape in Dieter's investigation, he mailed the results to me via post. When his reports arrived, I gave them no more than a cursory look. I found myself withdrawing from these practical concerns. Instead, I allowed myself to return to the landscape of *Kurland* as it had first unfolded in my imagination on the day in Rockensußra when the uniformed man had come to deliver the news that my father was dead: a landscape of misty plains, hills with vague contours, and brooding skies at dusk.

Reflecting on it during this planning stage, I saw myself traveling alone through the countryside of my imagination. Compelled by an inner necessity, and by romantic and idealistic sentiments, I wanted to retrace my father's history as a soldier. I would walk the ground he had walked, breathe the air he had breathed, look up into the same sky, listen for the bullet that struck him.

Dieter must have realized that, caught up in my own world as I was, it would be unwise for me to travel on my own, and, unbeknownst to me, made arrangements to travel with me.

Dieter and I had corresponded during my college years in Newcastle and Munich, and had met often during my visits home to Delrath. Then, we had gone for walks on the dikes of the Rhine River, continuing, as it were, where we'd left off as good friends after our graduation. He had invited me to tony restaurants in Düsseldorf or Cologne to demonstrate his worldliness. I had shown him my early, tortured writings. When I read him a poem about a young woman entrapped by a green moon, he looked at me as if he were hearing the voice of a crazed mind.

We'd continued our correspondence after I'd gone to America and gotten married. Later, when David and I lived in Amsterdam for a time, Dieter had come to call on us at our second-story canal flat. It was May 1966. My belly already big with my first child and stretching the seams of the blue and white paisley Empire-style dress, I'd opened the door. There he'd been with a bouquet of thirteen red roses – signifying, he said in a private moment, the number of years he had known me.

We'd never made promises but, always, I knew, and, I believe, Dieter did, too, that we would keep in touch throughout our lives. Impervious to absences dictated by physical distance and to the divergent directions our lives had taken, a friendship endured that had begun in our early teens and survived the awkwardness of jilted love, even our marriages – Dieter's that had ended a number of years before; mine, that had ended the previous year. Both of us were in new relationships. None of it mattered. Older now by forty years, Dieter looked the part of the dreamer he had always been. His silvery white hair, short beard and rimless glasses brought to mind the professorial type. No longer resembling the provincial ingénue of the early days, I, too wore glasses – round, tortoiseshell-rimmed – my hair streaked blonde and cut in a bob, and too vain, still, to wear sensible shoes.

Dieter's appreciation of classical music was matched only by his passion for European history. The tumultuous events of 20th century Europe – World War I, the Weimar Republic, the rise of National Socialism and World War II – had continued to hold for him an abiding interest. It went back to our high school years, accompanied by a grappling with ideological issues and the loss of national pride. Back in those early days, my own struggle had still been in its infancy.

"Your thinking is simple-minded," he'd once said on the way to the train station after school. I had just pronounced all prewar Germans to be reprehensible Nazis harboring grandiose desires to conquer the world. "Even if you're right," he'd said, "there are historical determinants that are worth considering. True, your father gave his life to an insane cause, and that narrows your responses to emotional clichés. . ."

Angry, I'd interrupted him. "Say what you will, you won't be able to convince me otherwise. Besides, any kind of defense makes *you* sound like a Nazi." We'd reached the crossing barriers close to the ticket office, waiting for a freight train to pass. Dieter had looked at me, reproachfully. I'd seen the hurt in his eyes, but had felt too stubborn and righteous to apologize.

Now, forty years later, on the ferry crossing from the German mainland town of Stralsund to the island of Rügen, I remembered the unfortunate exchange and the injustice I had done to Dieter. His eyes were on me as I stood leaning against the main deck's railing. A strong wind touched my face, coloring my cheeks, blowing my bobbed hair. He said, *"Du siehst gerade aus wie das junge Mädchen von früher. –* Just now, you look like the young girl you once were." No, he had not read my mind, not remembered what I had remembered. But he too had gone back into the past. I said, *"Ich bin so froh, dass du mitgekommen bist. –* I'm so glad you've come with me."

The murky brown water of the Rügen harbor sloshed high against the walls of the *St. Petersburg* as I climbed up a steep and wobbly ladder into the belly of the massive gray ship. I felt swallowed by the dimensions of the journey. Time seemed to be shifting, the way it had in Rockensußra: time past alternating, or mingling, with time present; the sea swelling as our vessel dipped into horizonless waters and then rose again toward endless skies.

There were only a few other passengers, mostly men, on board. They huddled in small groups around tables in the dining area and adjoining bar. Some spoke in Russian, some in German, some in Eastern European languages I couldn't quite place. "A storm's moving east over the Baltic Sea from Scandinavia," a man said in broken German. Another laughed grimly, "The luck of the draw!"

Three or four men sat alone at the bar, drinking beer, smoking cigarettes, and watching the rising and dipping sea through the portholes. They only half-listened to the bartender telling about the Polish ferry disaster that had happened on the same coastal route five years earlier.

"No, the *St. Petersburg* -" he said, and was interrupted mid-sentence by a roar so loud it sounded like the hull of the ship slowly breaking apart. My mind went blank. An all-overpowering presence of doom took over. Panicked, I looked at Dieter, who sat across from me at the small bar table. He reached for my hand.

All eyes turned on the bartender. Everyone was waiting for an explanation that would save us from imminent disaster. A minute or more passed before the deafening noise faded away. Then, only the monotonous hum of the vessel's engines turning could be heard. A grin crept over the bartender's face: with both index fingers pointing skyward, to indicate, maybe, that he was crediting the storm or God for this fortuitous turn of events, he said in his Berlin-accented German, *"Mäusjen still.* – As quiet as a mouse." After a suggestive pause, he went on, *"Nur keene Aufrejung!* – Not to worry. It happens during storms." Without explaining what had happened to cause the roar, he went on, "But the *Jan Heweliusz,* that was a real tragedy. Fifty-four drowned. The seas were rough, rougher than tonight. Believe me, the *St. Petersburg,* she wouldn't sink."

The ferry rocked from side to side with gentle motions. Dieter and I moved to a bolted-down dining table next to a porthole. I sat on one side, he on the other side. We ate our one-selection, cafeteria-style dinner. We each held on to our plates of pork roast, mashed potatoes and a peas-and-carrots medley with one hand, and held a folk with the other.

Afterwards, Dieter spread a road map on the table. He took off his glasses, and, eyes close to the map, reviewed routes and locations he had previously highlighted. Now and again, he pointed and commented on the journey ahead, but I paid no mind. I trusted Dieter. I had given myself over to his itinerary and to his plan. Lost not so much in thought as in an absence of thought, I looked out through the porthole into the night-darkening sea.

We said goodnight early. I staggered to my cabin, steadying myself against the ship's rolling motion, holding onto the polished chrome rails along the stairs and walls. Homeopathic pellets eased the queasiness in my stomach and the pressure around my eyes.

Nestled under a comforter on the narrow cabin bunk, knees pulled to my chest, I abandoned myself to the billowing sea that soothed me into sleep.

I dreamt: *The nameless place where Dieter and I are headed comes into bird's-eye view. A cluster of concrete high-rise buildings emerges through the mist like an island, amidst row upon row of paint-worn, wooden crucifixes.*

A violent shuddering and a wild roar from the sea below jolted me out of my dream and almost out of my bunk. I waited. Then, as with the episode before dinner, it turned quiet again.

I rose from my bunk. I reeled from side to side, making my way to the porthole. It was almost dawn. The sky loomed darker than the sea. Sleet whipped against the glass and gathered on the deck in night-glistening pools.

By morning, the storm had calmed. I leaned against the railing at the ship's bow. A fine mist sprayed my face. The ferry plowed on in its northward course, the coast of Lithuania on one side and a spit of land paralleling it on the other.

Land and sea were cast in gray and black: an ashen tree line, jagged and sparse, crouched against a huge sky the color of steel. Columns of smoke, barely lighter than the color of the cloud cover, rose from distant chimneys. I scanned the sky for sea birds. There were none.

Gray, too, was the view as the ship neared Klaipeda. Much of the harbor was a depository of antiquated Soviet warships, remnants from World War II: rust-gray tankers left moored to rot, and their seaworthy counterparts in shades of smudged gray.

53

Dieter at the wheel of our rental car, we entered the Lithuanian city of Klaipeda. We passed rows of nondescript structures and endless walls of unpainted concrete. Drizzling rain intensified the sense of post-war and post-Soviet desolation. Here and there the blood red of a brick building, a reminder of a more prosperous time, momentarily suspended the colorlessness of the cityscape. A few pedestrians, some with umbrellas, some without, bustled along the sidewalk.

We followed the highway north toward Latvia. A center divider, the width of half a football field, separated the two south lanes from the two north lanes. For the greater part of the drive, our red, compact German Ford was the only vehicle traveling in either direction. A weather front brewed darkly to the west, as clusters of clouds drifted to the east in a pale blue sky. Fields of waterlogged soil and patches of leafy vegetables stretched beyond the horizon. Isolated farmhouses, aged and weather-beaten, stood solitary in the landscape. The woods beyond the fields looked aglow with the colors of autumn, except to the west where their silhouettes merged with dark banks of cloud.

We drove in silence, each of us surrendering to the northern beauty of this countryside, both gentle and austere to the unaccustomed eye. The sun, less generous than in more southern latitudes, shone upon the meager fields; the sky rose higher as if to touch eternity; shadows grew longer.

Around midday, we entered the deforested no-man's-land between Lithuania and Latvia. After a kilometer or two, a colony of barracks came into view.

"When we go through border formalities, don't be intimidated. Remember, we are leaving one democratic country to enter another." Dieter's voice, in the confines of the car and after the long silence, rang like an intrusion.

"Of course," I said.

We stopped at the first of four barriers, guarded by heavily armed border patrol. The difference between crossing a national border in peacetime and traversing a war zone narrowed. The officers' uniforms looked as intimidating as those of military personnel, heightening the sense of danger.

On the side of the road, just a short distance away, I saw a dugout, camouflaged under a mound of sod, like the bomb shelters I had seen as a child, although I didn't remember where. And suddenly, a flash of Nazi history's most infamous symbol, the black double zigzag lines of the *SS* insignia on a yellow sign, jolted me.

I pointed at the offending symbol. "Dieter! What am I looking at?"

He frowned. "The high voltage sign?"

"I'm sorry," I said, "my mind's playing tricks on me."

Passport inspection and customs formalities consisted of a series of tightly followed procedures. "Soviet-style bureaucracy. The residue of forty-five years under communist rule," Dieter said, quietly, as we parked the car.

We didn't need to be familiar with the languages the border agents spoke. We only needed to follow one officer's wordless hand motions, or another officer's movement of the eyes directing us to the next official, or the next barrier.

A young, baby-faced agent, the black peak of his military cap pulled deep over his forehead, pointed to a two-story structure midway between the Lithuanian and Latvian authorities.

"*Paldies!*" Dieter said. The Latvian word for thank you was the only one he knew.

Amidst the loud sputtering of an engine, we walked up a short staircase to enter the building. *Shut door behind you,* a sign read in five languages. Inside, our footsteps on the wood-planked floor reverberated through the open space. The room teemed with staff, both men and women, in brownish green uniforms. Bent over paperwork, they sat in pairs at war-surplus metal desks. They moved up and down a staircase leading to a spacious loft. Some stood stiffly along the upper banister, scanning the activities below. Some were in cubbyholes, only their disembodied hands visible through small windows.

"*Touristen,*" Dieter said in German, responding to a question that neither of us understood, though he apparently interpreted correctly. His tone was composed and ordinary, not at all in line with my on-edge frame of mind. He remained unaffected by the formalities that warped my sense of time. Dieter was here, in the present; I was not.

The dismissive motion of an official's hand in the general direction of the door conveyed that we had permission to leave the building.

Back in the car, we passed scrutiny one last time on the Latvian side – a glance first at Dieter, then me, to compare our identities with the photos in our passports – and the final barrier rose.

In Latvia now, we continued our drive north. The forested plains, the high skies, the weather gathering to the west – no different from south of the border. But there was something odd in this landscape, where past and present time seemed to alternate: one moment, it held the particulars of the present reality – borne out by an occasional car coming from the other direction – the next, it receded into wartime – a landscape imbued with the mystery of my father's fate.

"Think of it! The blood of thousands and thousands has stained this very earth," Dieter said. An engaging storyteller and seasoned historian, well prepared for this journey, he chose this particular moment – a moment that, for me, was floating in unmeasured time – to go back into the history of the region. In his engaging, anecdotal style, he told of the many wars, invasions and occupations this small country and its neighbors, Lithuania and Estonia, had endured.

He took pleasure in recounting the charmed life of Marta Skavronska. "Whether she was a Polish peasant's daughter, as some sources say, or a gravedigger's daughter, her great beauty was undisputed. A Protestant minister and his wife raised the young Marta. At seventeen, she was married off to a Swedish dragoon officer during the Great Northern War of the early 18th century. But after only eight days, she fell into Russian hands and was made to work as a laundress and servant." Dieter filled in many of the details that eventually brought the young woman to the Moscow court. "There," he concluded the story, "this girl from such humble beginnings drew the attention of Tsar Peter the Great. In time, she became his mistress and later was crowned empress, Catherine I."

I was swept up by Dieter's colorful stories and historical data, then brought back into 20th century history when he mapped out German and Soviet involvement in the Baltic states: Germany's occupation of the western half of Latvia in First World War, followed by twenty years of Latvian independence between the two wars; the 1939 Molotov-Ribbentrop Pact of nonaggression between Germany and the Soviet Union, after which the Soviets annexed Lithuania, Latvia and Estonia; finally, two years later, after Germany had violated the nonaggression pact with its attack on the Soviet Union, the Baltic region was invaded by the *Wehrmacht*.

"Initially, the occupation by the Germans was welcomed by the native population," Dieter said.

This surprised me. "But why?"

"They saw it as liberation from Soviet tyranny." Then he added, "Local right-wing militias even helped the German *Einsatztruppen* – SS paramilitary death squads – round up the local population of Jews. 34,000 Jews were killed in Latvia alone."

Dieter and I fell into silence. My thoughts remained with what I had just learned. Prior to this time, I had only been vaguely aware of the killings of Jews by Germans in the Baltic states. Everything I had known about the dimensions of the Holocaust had been momentous. The number of individual men, women and children murdered was too enormous to even fathom. Now, Dieter, in his short history lesson, had summoned into mind another 34,000 Jews killed in just one small country. I wondered whether there would ever be a time, when every last victim had been counted.

We had entered an area of forest on both sides of the road, when Dieter returned to the wartime events of this region. "On his very road, the 11th Division of the *Heeresgruppe Nord* moved from headquarters in East Prussia through the Baltic states. They crossed the River Narwa into Russia and eventually lay siege to Leningrad for a thousand days."

Dieter described a monstrous beast comprised of troops, trucks, tanks in steady motion, advancing through densely forested terrain. One moment, I became caught in the efforts of these men, marching for their country, willing to lay their lives on the line; the next moment, I condemned and accused every one of them. And I saw what I did not want to see: that I still held my father innocent while holding a faceless mass of German men guilty.

My father had not participated in the initial march north through the Baltic states that led to the conquest and one-thousand-day siege of Leningrad. He had remained stationed, out of harm's way, at Division headquarters in Allenstein, a small town in *Ostpreußen,* East Prussia. I turned away from Dieter and gazed out the window at the passing trees.

Ostpreußen, a bittersweet name: it rang of magic and longing and fate gone awry. Distant images arose of woods like the ones we were traversing – pine trees, beeches, birches. . . *Birken.* The sound of their name called back East Prussia, where Mother and I had gone to visit my father. I remember: *those slender black-and-white barked trees, the peek-a-boo trees, behind which I playfully hide from my father. He lets me believe that I have disappeared from his view, and I giggle, pleased to have fooled him. "I see you," he then says and takes both my hands into his, the tree between us, and we dance around it. Our feet tapping in the April snow, we twirl and twirl until I feel dizzy, and he lifts me into his strong arms. Still giggling, I kiss his cheek and say, "When I grow up, I will marry you."*

The ghost of East Prussia lingered on, casting my memory forward in time: *I am ten or eleven years old. Mother and I are next to each other on the sofa in our living room. A photo album, titled "Ostpreußen 1943" – written on the flyleaf in my father's script – is on my lap. We take our time looking at page after page of snapshots: My father at his desk in his barracks office, looking up from a typewriter, bulky earphones strapped to his head. Mother and I on a snow-packed forest road, posing next to a snowman; Mother sitting on a fallen trunk, looking into the camera, arm resting on my shoulder. We look happy. My favorite photo is the one of me with my father: I'm wearing a knitted hat and a coat that's gray in the photo, but that Mother says was red, with a white fur collar; my father is in his dress uniform. We both face the camera. My hand reaches up to hold his hand.*

Mother pauses as this or that picture calls up a memory. Her voice is mournful, and I like it that way, because that's the voice in which she always speaks about my father. "If we hadn't gone to East Prussia, Gitta would not have been born." "Why not?" I ask. I know why: I have counted the months from our visit in April 1943 to Gitta's birth the following January 24. But I want Mother to say it. "Things just would've been different. That's all," she says, annoyed with my question. She snaps the album shut.

After three more hours of driving, the forest gradually gave way to gently rolling countryside. Dusk brooded over the small settlements we passed. Traffic increased, with more cars and trucks in both directions. A low skyline rose into view. We were nearing Liepaja, capital of Kurzeme, where we would spend the night.

54

I woke up early the next morning to a persistent sound, like the sound of metal scraping against metal. Suspended at intervals by hushed pauses, it rose from the street below my fourth-floor hotel room. I lay in bed, listening, trying to identify it, waiting for it to stop.

When it didn't, I got up and parted the curtains to look outside. What had been a dismal view of concrete against concrete the previous evening had been transformed overnight into a picturesque cityscape in winter. The crumbling stucco of the façades appeared less bleak. The state flag of red/white/red stripes billowed atop the snow-laden roof of the imposing, colonnaded theater at the far end of the square. Snow weighted down the foliage on the trees.

Yesterday's busy city thoroughfare had been rendered impassable under a blanket of snow. It was pristine, except for the sidewalk directly below, where an old man's shoveling became the scraping sound I'd heard. He was digging a channel through which the odd pedestrian could pass. Every so often, he would stop and, leaning on his shovel, take a break.

After a hasty good morning in the hotel restaurant – a room that resembled a banquet hall of old-fashioned splendor – Dieter asked me, "Do you realize the significance of this snowfall?" While the concern in his voice took me by surprise, the question itself did not.

The unseasonal late September snow replicated the wartime weather conditions in December 1944.

Snow covers the trees of the forest where our unit has been dug in, the winter sun makes the white of the rolling hills glisten, but I am blind to all this beauty and devoid of the spirit of Christmas, my father had written in his second-to-last letter to Mother on December 14, 1944.

"Isn't it like a nod from the past, the same weather as back then?" I said, in answer to Dieter's question.

Dieter was looking past me. He stood up from the table and stepped to an alcove window with a view onto the square. He gazed into the serene winterscape. From a distance, the sound of the old man shoveling snow, then silence while he rested for a moment, could be heard.

With his back turned to me, as if he couldn't bear the news he was about to deliver, Dieter said, "It most likely means the end of this journey."

He pointed out the all-too-obvious ramifications I had ignored: "The traffic in the city is paralyzed. We have no winter tires, no snow chains." He needed to say no more.

The snow would hold us captive in this hotel. At best, we would be able to venture to the end of the channel the old man was digging along the sidewalk.

Oddly, Dieter's prediction didn't stun me, nor did I question its accuracy. Rather, it thrust me into reviewing the expectations I'd had of this journey. I had harbored no secret hopes of finding evidence of my father, where he might have fought or where he had been buried. Instead, I had longed to be in these woods and plains where he had spent the last days of his life, whatever that experience might be. But utter defeat? That I had not considered.

I recalled the images of the dream on the *St. Petersburg* two nights earlier – crucifixes and a group of high-rise buildings. Now this city, made impassible by the snow, separated me from the thousands of nameless dead left by the war, buried under snow that covered the past. Perhaps, the dream was all that I would take home from this journey.

Dieter and I sat across from each other at the breakfast table. The morning hours inched on. We were served all sorts of delicacies, from fancy cold cuts and caviar to fine pastries. "What an ironic contrast to a soldier's ration of potato and cabbage soup in an army just months from defeat!" I said.

"Yes," Dieter agreed, "most likely barely enough to keep these men going."

Whether Dieter was waiting for a break in the road conditions or not, I had resigned myself to the dismal prospects of the circumstances. There was nothing to say. We ate our breakfast, each of us lost in our own thoughts.

A few other hotel guests, all of them men in dark suits and ties, came and went. A waitress remained attentive to our needs, cheerfully filling our cups with fresh coffee and tea.

A wintry light suffused the square outside. Shadows hung in the recessed doorways. Passers-by trudged along the sidewalk, heads lowered against the wind and cold. They endured this out-of-the-ordinary weather as a matter of course, I reflected, in the same way, perhaps, that they had lived through year upon year under communist subjugation, and, before that, the war.

By noon, nothing had changed, when, like a phantom out of nowhere, a city bus appeared. It crawled to the curbside stop on the far side of the street. Its wheels, caked with snow, left knee-deep ruts in their wake. A single passenger got off. He plodded along the sidewalk and slipped into a storefront a few yards away.

The driver checked the rearview mirror – out of habit, it seemed, for there were no vehicles approaching, not from anywhere. The bus started up again. It drove for a foot or two, before the wheels began to spin and dig themselves into the fresh snow. The engine revving loudly, the bus backed up, then moved forward, sputtering. Again, it stopped dead.

Dieter stepped to a window and I joined him, watching the same dogged maneuver over and over. In the end, the driver's persistence paid off. The bus pushed ahead and, taking off, left behind defiant puffs of exhaust.

This, apparently, was the signal for the city to come alive and resume its daily routine. One car and then another and another – their roofs, hoods and trunk lids still weighted down with snow – followed in the tracks the bus had carved out.

"If they can, we can," Dieter said. He cocked his head playfully and reached for my hand as if asking me to dance. He gathered up the folders and road maps he'd examined.

"Let's get our coats," he said.

A parking lot attendant shoveled the snow from around our car and cleared a pathway to the street, while Dieter scraped the roof and windshield. The engine started with a single turn of the ignition key. We drove off the lot. The wheels ran smoothly in the channels of snow left by the earlier traffic. Turning corners, our car went into gentle swerves, then straightened itself again.

A short drive, and we came to the end of the inner city. A humpback bridge took us south onto a wide boulevard, lined with run-down mansions and majestic trees on both sides. The autumn-leaved branches drooped precariously under their wintry weight. The cloud cover had begun breaking up into billowing clusters, exposing patches of sky so blue it startled the eye.

In April 1944, three months after Soviet forces ended the German siege of Leningrad, my father had been deployed from headquarters in East Prussia to the front lines in Estonia. Withdrawing from the advancing Soviet army, German forces had retreated as far as the River Narwa at the border between Russia and Estonia. A *Feldwebel,* the US equivalent of sergeant, my father was in charge of a squad of men. It was his first time as a combat soldier since the beginning of the war.

A letter he wrote at the end of April described the adversities he and his men endured: *Our regiment has changed position. We have been marching for weeks, covering 40 km from dawn to dusk each day, over roads covered with ice, then mud, as the weather changes. My joints are sore. We have no shelter.*

"Your father's unit traveled southward on this very road in the late autumn of 1944," Dieter said. "Buses had been confiscated in Riga for the purpose of moving troops."

After the German defeat in Leningrad, my father's division had been engaged in a last-ditch effort to retreat from the encircling Soviet army to East Prussia and, from there, to defend the Reich.

The shoddy surface of the road became visible as the traffic turned the snow into sleet, while the fields on either side glistened under a cover of white. We came to a village of weathered clapboard houses. Small groups of men and women stood leaning against their brooms and shovels as they waited for a line of vehicles behind a slow-moving tractor to pass. Dressed in colorless peasant garb – the women wearing aprons over their winter coats and kerchiefs around their necks, the men in brimmed hats and overalls – they looked untouched by the present. When our eyes met, I thought I saw indifference in some, curiosity, even distrust, in others. Did our late-model car, among mostly shabby, older vehicles, give us away as foreigners? Were we regarded as trespassers? Perhaps naively, I conjectured that these villagers were suspicious of the reason we had come to this remote area of their country. In a moment of past overlapping present, I feared that they recognized me as the daughter of the enemy.

Their parents, who had been children then, and their grandparents, might have watched the convoy of buses filled with German soldiers passing on this road. Then, too, snow had fallen early in the season.

I see my father in the window seat of a bus. He wipes the steamed-up glass clear with his palm, then gazes out onto the same wintry countryside. Like me, he exchanges looks with the villagers along the roadside, sees the fear and hostility in their eyes, knows that he is the enemy.

At moments like these, did my father think about the futility of the war, of comrades he'd seen fall in action, of civilians, like those on the roadside, or their family members and friends, who had lost their lives in the crossfire of skirmishes?

In a letter around this time, he had confessed to Mother: *Against all faith I have left in my heart, I do not believe that I will see the end of this war alive. I refused to listen to the voice of reason when you warned me of my foolish and selfish decision to enlist. I offer you my deepest apology.*

He had written this passage – often quoted by Mother – weeks before his 33rd birthday on December 7, twelve weeks before he was killed. Six battles would be fought in Kurland. He would survive the first two battles as a fighting man. He would be killed on the sixth day of the third.

At a junction, barely discernible in the snow, Dieter turned the car off the main highway onto a country road. No vehicles had traveled through the fresh snow. "Do we dare?" he asked, but did not seem interested in an answer.

Without tracks to guide us and with only the faint indication of a road, he steered the car in the direction of a forested belt halfway to the horizon. The land looked uninhabited but for an occasional power pole or a bus stop, although not a single dwelling could be seen. If Dieter was nearly as unnerved as I was about getting lost or stuck, he handled it with calm.

After a crawling drive of an hour, we came to the hem of the forest. Alongside a river and near a bridge spanning it, a group of four or five farmhouses lay nestled among the trees. And a thin streak of smoke was escaping from a chimney. A sign of life, finally.

"The bridge at Kesteri," Dieter said. He pulled up to the side of the road. "This was the Division's lifeline for supplies. Here, at this bridge over the river, your father's regiment defended against the Red Army."

This was not my vision of a battlefield but the quaint scene from a storybook. I crossed the road and leaned over the paint-chipped iron railing of the bridge that spanned the river, the same railing that would have been there half a century ago. Turbulent water crashed against rocks and swirled in protected pools. The roaring sound of the river engulfed everything.

While I stood there, I tried to imagine the peasants who'd lived in these modest farmhouses at the time of the war, probably scratching out a modest living from fields that had become a battleground. Men too powerless to protect their families and homes from the onslaught of war, women clutching their children in fear of their own and their children's lives.

They flee over the fields unsheltered after harvest, shots ringing around them. Soldiers scurry to take cover behind rocks and bushes and in the nearby woods. My father gives orders to his unit. More shots ring out. Men on the German and Soviet sides are wounded and killed in the crossfire. But not my father. Not yet

We resumed the drive. "After a ten-day fight to take the bridge of Kesteri, your father's regiment retreated in a southeasterly direction, forced by the Soviet's enclosing circle," Dieter explained. Lowering his head, he peered through the windshield, trying, it appeared, to discern some indication of a road in the snow. We were following, he said, the Regiment's general route.

Dieter stopped at another barely discernible intersection. He inspected his maps. "This is the edge of the Tirs mud lands," he declared with a sweep of his arm.

Leaving the car parked at the side of an untraveled service road, we trudged through inhospitable terrain. Undergrowth perforated the foot-high snow covering across the uneven contours of the ground. We entered a stand of dwarfed trees, where snow-bent branches touched to create a low canopy.

"Your father's regiment held its position here against Soviet troops that had broken through the front line at the river further north," Dieter began. "Heavy rains had drenched the terrain for weeks. There were no fortifications to speak of. The battle lasted nearly two weeks and ended in a temporary stand-off."

Hunching over, I peered into the half-darkness of the canopy, while Dieter walked to higher ground. I contemplated entering the low tunnel that, like a fairytale, was inviting and forbidding at once. I was held back by something unvoiced, not fear, exactly, but a cryptic warning not to go any further.

I pictured my father: the gentle face I remembered from photographs. Not the face of a weary man recounting his plight in a letter to Mother: *I'm at the front line. Without even water to rinse our hands. We live in cramped holes. Lifting our heads above ground could mean the end. There is nothing to brighten our existence.*

We left the battleground at dusk. The snow was as gray as the sky. By the time we reached the main highway back to Klaipeda, it was nearly dark, and the endlessness of the countryside shrank to only a few meters of snow glinting in the car's high beams. Once in a while, the red taillights of a vehicle ahead became visible. After a while, they were swallowed again in the deepening night.

I thought about this landscape, how what had happened here had shaped my life, and so many other lives. I wondered whether not only the soldiers on both sides who had died here, but also those who had survived, had left a part of themselves behind. I wondered, too, about the Latvian people, how their lives and the lives of their offspring had been changed by this senseless war.

Kurland was no longer a mere point on the map.

55

The night passed dreamlessly. By morning, a solid mass of clouds hung over the roofs on the ocean side of Klaipeda. The pathway the old man had cleared the previous day had been iced over by night frost.

Dieter and I held on to each other as we shuffled gingerly down the street to an outdoor farmers' market. What would have been a short walk on a good day was a long and painstaking venture on a path as slippery as a frozen lake.

Some of the stalls were closed. Others displayed regional autumn vegetables and fruits on long tables: heaps of cabbages, potatoes, apples, pears.

At a stall tucked away in a corner, a flower seller sat hunched under a canopy. Her face was aged and weather-lined. Her eyes were the startling blue of the sky. A dark jacket and a brightly patterned scarf around her head protected her from the biting wind and cold.

I pointed to each of her three buckets of evergreens, purple asters and roses, indicating that I wanted to buy all she had left to sell. She looked at me, skeptically.

"*Ludzu,* please," I said and, signaled the number "3" with my thumb and two fingers.

Her gnarled hands wrapped first one, then the other two bunches in newspaper, fastening them with rubber bands. She placed them gently into my arms. I poured a handful of coins into her palm.

The old woman scanned the coins. She looked at me, questioningly, implying, "This is too much."

I shook my head. "*Paldies.* Thank you. For you."

She smiled at me with a toothless smile. "*Paldies,*" she said, then stuffed the coins into a small cloth shoulder bag.

"Three bouquets?" Dieter said, giving voice to his bewilderment.

"I wanted to make the old woman's day," I said. I had no other explanation. I didn't know yet what other reasons would present themselves by the end of the day.

It took the better part of two hours to reach Saldus, a town less than 100 kilometers east of Klaipeda. Dieter pulled over in front of an old brick building. Two flag poles at the entrance flew both the Latvian and German national flags.

The sight of an office building, and especially of the black-red-and-gold striped German flag, begged the question, "What are we doing here?"

Dieter put his hand on mine. "I've made advance arrangements to meet with the man in charge of the Saldus outpost of the *Volksbund Deutsche Kriegsgräberfürsorge*. They're working in this area."

I was familiar with the *Volksbund,* the German War Graves Commission, a volunteer organization whose mission it was to establish and maintain German military cemeteries. They had done so extensively in Western Europe, both between the two World Wars and after the Second World War.

Dieter clasped my hand firmly, "Please, for your own sake, let go of any expectations this may raise for you."

"I have no expectations," I said. "I never did."

A noisy elevator took us to the second floor. We walked along a shabby corridor. The only light came from a gabled window facing the street. At door number 7, a barely legible inscription identified the *Volksbund.*

Inside the bare-bone quarters of an office, we were greeted by a tall man in his late forties. He introduced himself as Franz Berger. The benevolent expression in his eyes, his grayish blonde hair, combed back in the style of the forties, called forth my father's memory, the likeness I remembered from the framed photo Mother had kept on our nightstand in Rockensußra. I quickly reminded myself not to read childlike longings into this encounter.

With obvious enthusiasm for the unique contribution of his organization, Herr Berger said, "Of course, you're familiar with the work of the *Volksbund* in Western Europe. With the fall of Communism, we have been able to extend our mission to countries formerly behind the Iron Curtain."

He gestured to the framed posters that covered every wall in the office. They depicted cemeteries with countless graves in geometrical configuration, most of them set in lush countryside.

"Our particular outpost is responsible for the installation of one of a number of cemeteries in the Baltic region," he went on. "Our student volunteers worked through several summers, sifting the ground to exhume the remains of German soldiers, both from known burial grounds and previously unknown sites. The latter were brought to our attention by villagers old enough to remember the war."

In a tone more somber than before, he went on, "The reburials were completed just a few weeks ago. Eight thousand men, what was left of them. Four to a plot."

Then, shifting back to a matter-of-fact delivery, he said, "As part of the final phase, Latvian stone masons have been commissioned to fabricate the headstones, plain crosses from indigenous black quartz, and inscribe them with the names of the dead soldiers."

As I listened to Herr Berger's account, the world shrank to the size of this office with its posters of cemeteries covering the walls. The organization's mission and my journey's purpose merged – both reaching back into the past and bringing it forward into the present. The *Volksbund's* work went beyond individual concerns: preserving history for posterity, for no gain other than to remember the dead – regardless of how complicit they had been in that history – and to heal the wounds of the living. *Work for Peace.* That was the slogan on the *Volksbund* logo. It was printed in multiple languages on each poster.

For the first time since he had spoken, Herr Berger turned to me directly. "Frau Pal, I was expecting you, of course," he said. "In preparation, I sent an inquiry to our headquarters in Kassel. As luck would have it, I received a faxed reply just this morning."

He extended a sheet of paper in my direction. Then, heeding a different impulse, he placed it in front of himself on the desk. He followed the typed lines with his index finger and read out loud, *"Josef Schupp, geboren am 7. Dezember 1911 in Blexersande/Oldenburg, Erkennungsmarke 160-5. /I. R. 2."*

He raised his head to catch my eye. "Josef Schupp. That's your father. Correct?"

I tried to answer. No sound came from my throat. I nodded.

His finger moved to a small paragraph of short typewritten lines. He read, "Exhumed at Smiltnieki cemetery, September 18, 1996." He looked up momentarily, "That would have been just about a year ago," and returned to the page, "Interred at *Deutscher Soldatenfriedhof Saldus.*"

Had I learned that my father had risen from the dead, my response could not have been any more disbelieving.

Dieter glanced at me. "It means that your father's remains were located and reburied in the new cemetery."

I am eight. Mother and I are walking among the gravesites of the military cemetery adjacent to the Knechtsteden monastery. The gravel crunches under our feet. She reads the names on the markers out loud. She remembers a schoolmate; a boy who was the brother of her childhood girlfriend; a young man who had been sweet on her. Here and there, she pulls a weed from a manicured plot and tosses it aside. It troubles me that, among all these graves, there isn't one for my father. "I'll go to Kurland one day," I say to Mother. "I'll find his grave and bring him back." I barely know where Kurland is. It's only a word in my vocabulary and a vague point on the map, way east. "You're an idle dreamer. There is no grave," Mother says. Her response angers me. "If there is no grave, then he's alive," I say, defiantly relying on what I know is false logic. Mother replies, "You must learn to become realistic. When those men fell they were buried haphazardly under a handful of dirt. What else could they have done in that god-forsaken war?"

"Where . . . ?"

Before Dieter could finish his question, Herr Berger cut him off. "A senile local woman remembered that German soldiers had been buried in a field adjacent to the Smiltnieki cemetery," he said. "Not a reliable source, by any means. But it was a lead our group pursued nonetheless." He paused, shrugging his shoulders. "We go after straws in the wind. This time it paid off. We uncovered the remains of four hundred soldiers, nearly all of them with identification tags. They were packed together in rows of shallow graves. . . according to this fax, your father was among them."

His eyes moved past Dieter to a trunk the size of a child's coffin, its lid propped open. It was filled with layer upon layer of military identifications tags and medals in see-through envelopes. They appeared to be in various states of corrosion. Some of the medals' ribbons were still intact, their colors as bright as they'd ever been.

I bent down and picked one at random. I ran my fingers over the numbers and letters that had belonged to one of the four hundred unknown soldiers – now known. For the blink of an eye, the years vanished, and a young soldier fell to his death. I had a faint sense that he was within close reach.

I put the envelope back. I thought of my father. Buried in this trunk of hundreds of identification tags, would there be one that had been his, *160-5/I. R. 2?*

Turning to Herr Berger, I started to ask the question I had felt too hesitant to ask. "The state of decay, what . . . ?" Tears stopped me from finishing it.

The question's morbidity left Herr Berger unfazed. Describing what was commonplace to him, he said, "Generally, what remains of a human skeleton after fifty years in a climate such as this are the skull and the primary bones. The secondary bones, the ribs, for example, will have caved in and fully decomposed. Often we find clues to determine the cause of death. In your father's case -"

Herr Berger cut himself off mid-sentence.

Out of respect for a vulnerability he detected in me?

What he left unsaid, I knew: the cause of death had been stated in the notification we had received in Rockensußra. "A bullet hole in the skull." *Kopfschuss.*

I don't recall whether it was then or not until after we had left the *Volksbund* office that the myth my mother had created and I had perpetuated crumbled, replaced by a new reality: my father had been buried – under more than a handful of dirt. Not in a marked grave, but a grave nonetheless, one he had shared with his fallen comrades. Whatever earthly remains there were of him, they had been recovered. After half a century of obliteration and non-existence, his identity and material presence in this world had been restored. It gave his death a finality it had never had before.

56

Outside of Saldus, a two-lane road took us through agricultural plains, their autumn crops obscured by snow. After a short drive, the dark shape of a cross became visible in the distance. It loomed taller as we drew nearer. Soon it dominated the landscape.

At a barely discernible fork in the snow-packed road, a poster-size sign read, both in German and Latvian, *Work in Progress. German Military Cemetery. 1939/45. Saldus.* It pointed us to a parking lot on the right.

We left the car in the empty parking lot. Ahead of us was a chapel, built in the flat-roof bungalow style in keeping with local architecture. Instead of a conventional steeple, an unassuming, peaked gable over the entrance marked it as a place of worship. An attached portico, the length of the building, led to the cemetery proper that spread out behind the chapel.

Snow drifted tentatively. As if obeying a time-honored ritual, Dieter and I walked side by side up the cobblestone path that divided the immense cemetery into two burial fields of equal size. Our steps were measured, solemn, taking us to the cross at the far end of the burial grounds. The dark soil, dotted with patches of autumn grass, created a jarring contrast to the white cover of snow in the surrounding landscape. Not many months had passed since this earth, still lumpy and soft, had been dug up to receive the remains of the eight thousand soldiers. Yesterday's snow had melted away.

In one of these as-yet unmarked graves my father was buried – what remained of him: a skull with a smooth bullet hole and an assemblage of bones. I didn't know which of the small plots was his. It didn't matter.

Eight thousand men. Their involvement in a wrongful war, and in a monstrous system that had propagated untold horror and suffering, had robbed them of personal honor. Their valor, loyalty, obedience, even conscience – nothing counted. These soldiers had been individual human lives, all of them caught up in a war they couldn't, individually, control; and, while some of them may have committed terrible acts, more terrible even than soldiers are routinely made to do, others had simply been swept into an historical maelstrom that had all but erased their individual lives, denied them so much as a place in memory. In the eyes of history, they all were but villains. The death of each one of them had been stripped of meaning.

Nothing could ever change this. However, the *Volksbund Deutsche Kriegsgräbersfürsorge*, without condoning their actions or the past, had paid these men a basic tribute. In this cemetery, their lives had been restored to memory and given a kind of dignity. The people of Latvia, who had endured the torment of war at the hands of these very soldiers, in a profound gesture of reconciliation, had welcomed them to stay here for eternity. This piece of earth, more than a thousand kilometers away from their German homeland, had become their final resting place.

Where the burial fields ended, the terrain sloped upwards. At the highest point rose the cross we had seen from a distance. Forged from black iron, fitted together with massive bolts, it towered more than three stories high. It cast no shadow. A drift of untouched snow hugged its base.

The air was so still, the only sound I could hear was the sound of my breath. Snowflakes touched my cheeks and, melting, left tiny tears on my skin.

In my coat pocket was a copy of my father's last letter to my mother. I had brought it with me, entertaining the romantic idea of shredding it and casting its pieces somewhere in the landscape of Latvia, in my father's memory, in a place where his presence might be evoked.

I passed it to Dieter. He unfolded it and, recognizing what it was, let out a barely audible sigh.

"*At the front, 19 December, 1944,*" Dieter read out loud. He kept his voice low. It sounded monotonous and faltering, at times: "*Mein geliebtes Trautchen. There hasn't been a sign of life from you. You must know how concerned I am. I pray that you and our children are in good health* and high spirits, and that I will have news from you soon. . . Reports have reached us that our troops launched an offensive at the Western Front. Let us hope that the enemy will be repelled beyond our borders and annihilated, so the end of this war may draw near. . . My beloved. Nur noch fünf Tage bis Weihnachten. Es wird wohl das schlimmste für mich werden seit der Krieg begann. – Only five days till Christmas. It will be the most dismal for me since the war began. My only joy now is to remember Christmases past. . . Circumstances may not allow me to write. It might be many days before you hear from me again. But do not worry. Make the best you can of the holidays, especially for our little ones. Hold them tight on my behalf. Yours forever, Josef." A postscript followed. It was underlined, the handwriting larger, as if urgent: "Auf Wiedersehen! – Remain well!"

These had been my father's last words to my mother: this, the very letter she had received on a January day in 1945, three weeks after he had been shot dead on the day after Christmas. Fifty-two years later, I'd heard my father's words delivered in Dieter's voice. My father's actual voice had not left an imprint in my memory, nor had I ever given thought to how his voice may have sounded. Mother had sometimes mockingly compared my singing voice to his: "You can't carry a tune, just like your father."

But I heard, as Dieter spoke my father's words, the low, gentle lilt of the Rhineland my father speech would have likely had. And so, in that moment, Dieter became my father speaking, conveying a soldier's hope for a victory that would lead to the end of the war, and the despair of a man who loved his family. For the first time, my father became more than just my dead father, more than a widow's husband, or Hitler's willing soldier. He became a man in his own right, a man who had lived his own life, made his own choices, and died his own death.

"Mein Gott," Dieter said, as he handed the letter back to me. I folded it along its creases, and wedged it into the bouquet I was carrying – one of the three I'd purchased from the old flower seller. Made up of evergreens and moss, it resembled a funereal arrangement. I placed it at the foot of the cross. I sprinkled a few handfuls of snow over it.

"Papa," I said. Papa was the name by which I had called my father when he was alive, but never again in the more than fifty years that had gone by since his death. The name Papa, and all it meant, had vanished with him.

In that moment, the pain of his absence receded. I felt closer to my father than I ever had before. I released him to the earth of Kurland.

57

We left the cemetery. It was still early in the afternoon. On the old military map that Dieter consulted, the hamlet of Stedini was a barely visible dot next to the winding line of a secondary road. As the crow flies, it was about 15 kilometers west of the Saldus military cemetery. There was no indication of it on the present-day road map.

"So Stedini no longer exists," he said.

We took off anyway, in the direction of where Stedini would have been. I leaned back in my seat and stared into an amorphous sky, only marginally taking notice of the scenery we passed: overhead power lines; the skeletal ruins of a medieval monastery up on a hill; a man pushing his bicycle through the snow; an oak leaf on the windshield flapping wildly. Whatever thoughts floated through my mind, they were too incoherent to articulate. Whatever feelings arose, I was numb to them. Perhaps it was a time of prayer, perhaps not even that.

We drove along roads of iced-over snow and countless curves. A cautious driver, Dieter mostly kept the car from swerving, and on the rare occasion that it did, corrected it masterfully. At intersections, he stopped to check and compare the military and current road maps.

After an hour's drive, we pulled over alongside low barbed wire fencing. The fence was rusty and sagging. Dieter looked at the maps again and, ducking his head slightly to increase the field of vision proscribed by the windshield, surveyed the terrain in all directions. The scraggly outline of a massive oak tree dominated the view to the right of us. Wooded areas bordered the foreshortened horizon and the far side of the road. Nothing else. No sign of civilization as far as the eye could see.

Dieter turned off the engine, signaling that this was as far as we were going.

"Stedini would have been somewhere right here," he said.

We stepped down into a small ditch next to the fencing. Dieter scanned the immediate surroundings. There was decisiveness in his gesture when he lifted the barbed wire for me to crawl under. He followed with a jump over it that almost cost him his balance. We walked up and down rolling hills covered with snow, coarse tufts of dead grass protruding here and there. Beneath the deceptively benign surface, the mud was almost ankle deep.

The landscape was startlingly similar to the landscape I had seen in a dream some months earlier: *I'm wandering aimlessly through a winterscape of gentle slopes. The snow is not deep enough to cover the ground entirely. It is neither dark nor light. I'm looking for my father's comrade, who has witnessed his death. But I see no one, not anywhere.*

In actuality, my father's friend had called on Mother after being released from a Soviet prisoner-of-war camp. That had been several years after the war. He'd assured her that her husband had not suffered.

Trying to show to Dieter that we had, indeed, found Stedini, I described to him the landscape of my dream that so closely matched the landscape in which were standing. He didn't seem swayed. Dreams were not his purview. He preferred solid facts. Still, I trusted my dream.

"If you're right, this is the battlefield of Stedini," he conceded after consulting his maps one last time, and in the absence of more persuasive evidence, "Your father's regiment would have held the front line right here, with Soviet troops attacking from the woods on the far side of the road. Stedini itself would have been nearby."

Dieter took a book from his inside coat pocket. He read the title out loud, *"Weg und Schicksal der 11. Infanterie-Division* – Movements and Fate of the 11th Infantry Division." He went on to elaborate that, during his research at the *Bundesarchiv,* the Federal Archive, in Koblenz, he had come across this work of Werner Buxa. As regiment commander, Buxa had chronicled the movements and battles of my father's division.

"I contacted him earlier this year," Dieter said. "He invited me to his home in Ölbronn-Dürrn. He was in late his seventies and already in frail health. At the end of our hour-long conversation, Buxa presented me with an autographed copy of his book." Buxa died in May of the following year.

The road and the barbed wire fence behind us, Dieter and I stood on a low incline on the battlefield. A line of trees hemmed the horizon.

Dieter opened the book to a marked page and began reading a highlighted passage: *"Russian artillery and shell fire broke out at daybreak on 21 December, launching the Third Battle of Curzeme. Fierce fighting ensued that lasted for four days, until abruptly, around 5 o'clock on Christmas Eve, enemy fire ceased. An uncanny silence set in, which heralded the spirit of Christmas against all prior hope. The Division Commander made his rounds of the regiments in their fortifications. Emergency lights flickered among pine branches. On the lids of ammunition crates, soldiers had drawn Christmas trees with green marking pens from their map kits. And the men in regiment after regiment joined in singing the words and melody of 'Silent Night, Holy Night,' until their voices rang throughout the snow-covered forest under a starlit sky. It was the 6th Christmas of the war, the final and most devastating."*

It was eerily quiet in this vastness of land and sky – not a breeze, not the sound of a distant airplane, no evidence of human civilization. Then I heard, beneath that silence, the low hum of *Silent Night*. The voices of hundreds and hundreds of soldiers had vibrated through these very fields and woods. In a moment of reprieve, the war had been suspended by mutual consent, differences had been washed away. Enemy armies had been moved by grace so profound it arced across the decades, touching us in this moment.

I thought of the presence of disparate forces within us, and the promise, demonstrated by these men, of reconciling what was irreconcilable. It required more than a recognition of good and evil cohabiting in our souls at a safe distance from each other; it required the recognition of these opposing elements commingling in dangerously close proximity within each of us. As grace had touched these men, grace quickened a sense of recognition in me that God was never absent, not even in war.

I wandered through the fallow fields, a bunch of red home-grown roses in my hand, the second of three bouquets the old woman had sold me. Dieter went off exploring the terrain, map in hand, measuring distances by sight.

I couldn't have said how much time had passed when I saw Dieter waving to me from a level field where the rolling mounds came to an end. I trudged to where he stood waiting for me. With each step, my short boots became heavier as snow and mud stuck to them. Dieter said nothing, at first, but let me see for myself the mossy remnants of a brick foundation. Several more were in close proximity. These had once been homes.

"Stedini!" There was triumph in Dieter's voice, but also sadness. He cocked his head and looked at me. "I knew it had to be nearby. But this kind of devastation! I didn't expect it." The hamlet of Stedini, by all appearances, had been obliterated during the fighting that took place here.

Dieter and I walked deeper into the fields, until we came to a depression the size of a small pond in the ground. Snow and water had collected at its bottom.

"A crater. Fifty years later and, still, the remains of war," Dieter said.

Behind the crater were sections of corral fencing that leaned in the direction of the prevailing northern winds. It no longer served its original purpose of separating the farms that had once been here – had been here for centuries, perhaps. Somewhat to the left of the crater ran a shallow ditch – evidence, real or imagined, of a wartime trench.

Words from the notification of my father's death came to me. I knew them verbatim, as did Mother, who'd read them so many times: *"On that particular day, Soviet troops attacked the position of the company several times. Your husband who, in the course of combat fought with valor, was spotted by an enemy sharpshooter from a range of about 50 meters."*

I turned in the general direction of what would have been the Soviet position and estimated that a 50-meter distance put the sharpshooter at the edge of the wooded area on the far side of the road we had traveled on.

I imagined *the sharpshooter lying low to the ground in the shallow ditch, his helmet smeared* with snow. *I imagined him pressing the stock of the gun against his cheek, setting his sight.*

The fatal shot has not yet been fired. My father is still alive.

In the blink of an eye, his fate might have still been reversed and the future altered.

I waited for a sweet moment, then allowed what followed in the notification: *". . . and sustained a shot to the head. Your husband died instantly and did not suffer."*

In my imagination, the shot that killed my father had always remained in a kind of darkness – not utter darkness, but dusk just before darkness – obscuring what had happened and keeping me from envisioning the actual event.

In all probability, the fatal shot had not been obscured in the crepuscular light of early evening, but had struck my father in broad daylight, on a glorious winter day. The not knowing – not knowing deep in my heart, or not wanting to know – had cast its long shadow into the future. That future had just now come to an end. The fatal shot had been sustained on this field. This had been my father's last battleground.

I was standing in the spot, or in a spot very close, very much like it, where the shot had rung out.

I looked up into the sky – my father's last, split-second view, perhaps, as he fell backwards into the trench. The cloud cover, dense only a short while ago, had broken up. Huge, pearl-white masses traveled from horizon to horizon.

I bent down and lay each of the red roses of the second bouquet in the snowy white ditch.

58

Dieter looked westward into the afternoon sky. He shielded his eyes from the lowering sun in order to gauge how much time was left before dark.

"Eighteen kilometers," he said, "We should be able to make it in daylight."

After another hour's drive, the graveyard bell tower of the village of Smiltnieki, at last, came into view. "You can't miss it," Herr Berger had said, giving us directions to the place where my father had been buried for fifty years. "It's the only structure as far as the eye can see."

A solitary landmark, built of dark red brick, it rose on top of a steep hill. Had there been a funeral procession, the gradient would have slowed down the horse-drawn hearse and the attending mourners.

Under trees, where the sun never touched, mounds in the snow gave evidence of the dead. Centuries old graves, where generations of local peasants lay. Not arranged in any particular pattern, the graves followed the natural order that the roots of the trees and the contours of the earth prescribed.

Separated from the graveyard by a low wooden fence, a large barren area stretched toward the roadside. The ground beneath the snow, only recently disturbed, felt soft and uneven underfoot. Clumps of dead grass and last season's patches of growth had turned winter-gray.

The final section in the notification of my father's death read: *"Your husband was one of my best non-commissioned officers. Although he joined the company only a few days prior, he was well liked and respected by his superiors and subordinates alike. He has been laid to rest in the Division's cemetery. . ."*

Mother had dismissed the claim that my father had been buried – in a military cemetery, no less. *"Wem machen die das vor? Das sind doch nichts als Lügen und Propaganda.* – Who are they trying to fool? That's nothing but lies and propaganda." Eventually, she had erased the mere suggestion of such a likelihood.

I had believed Mother. But she had been wrong. According to Herr Berger's documentation, my father had been buried here, adjacent to the Smiltnieki graveyard, after the battle at Stedini that ended on January 1, 1945. One among four hundred soldiers, he had been exhumed by *Volksbund* volunteers a year ago, and reinterred at the newly installed Saldus cemetery.

I welcomed the scene that unfolded in my imagination, dispelling the one inherited from Mother of fallen soldiers being shoddily covered with dirt: The battle in Stedini had ended in German defeat. Heaps of casualties, piled on *Wehrmacht* vehicles, had been transported to this location. At some point, the vehicles would have met up with the snow-packed road on which Dieter and I traveled half a century later.

The winter-frozen earth, resistant to the cut of the spade, has been trenched to less than a meter deep. One by one, the fallen soldiers are lowered into rows of communal graves, shoulder touching shoulder touching shoulder. Their uniforms and helmets are their coffins; the identification tags near their hearts all that is left of their identities.

In my mind's eye, the Division pastor moved along the soft edges of the ditches, muttering a prayer for the dead. He sprinkled holy water, scooped up spades full of earth, casting it into the makeshift graves, where the soil came to rest on the bodies with timid thuds.

By the end of the battle on New Year's Day 1945, the casualty toll in Kurzeme had climbed to 44,141 dead or wounded on the German side alone. This according to the Werner Buxa account.

Standing amongst a group of tall birches, I was reminded again of the birch woods of Ostpreußen, where my father had been stationed until his deployment to the front that changed his fate. I was reminded, too, of my last encounter with him, when, full of life, he had held my hands, the trunk of a tree between us, and danced with me. I yearned for the soles of my shoes to touch a clump of earth, a worm, a rock that had touched my father, knowing both how slim and how great the odds were.

The setting sun tinted the western horizon orange and red. Rays of late light illuminated the cloud-scattered heavens. The field of snow and lumpy earth glowed with reflections of gold and pink. A leaf floated to the ground noiselessly. The cool air touched my face. This was the moment when my father's fate and my own fate converged. I became the daughter who had lost her father in Rockensußra, on the day after Epiphany 1945; in ways beyond imagining, she had found him in the western reaches of Latvia. Under this earth, a soldier with a bullet hole in his skull had been buried for fifty years; from now to eternity, he would rest under the massive cross overlooking his final burial site, and the final burial sites of 8,000 soldiers like him, at the military cemetery of Saldus. I couldn't help but think that he had been waiting for me.

And I felt indebted to my dear friend Dieter for guiding me on this journey; our bond was now inseverable.

I walked to the middle of the field. There, with my bare hands, I piled up a mound of snow-drenched earth and in it planted my last bouquet, an arrangement of evergreens and asters – their bright mauve color reminiscent of the north German heather country where my father had been born.

Along the outer perimeters of the burial field grew masses of star-shaped clusters of sedum-like succulents. Their petals were the color and shape of common pebbles, like those in my dream from long ago that intimated this journey: *In the nearby meadow, my mother, young and lovely as I remember her from my early childhood, rakes pebbles into piles. I pick up the smoothest and shapeliest, gather them in my apron pocket. I arrange them on my father's bare plot to spell his initials: JS*

Until the ground had been disturbed and the dead exhumed, the succulents, it appeared, had covered the entire plot. They had begun spreading again, from the bordering hems toward the center. In seasons to come, they would once more carpet the entire field with a blanket of sedum-stars – a mirror image of the star-filled heaven.

I bent down. The ground yielded willingly to my hands scooping up clumps of succulents and their earth-embedded roots.

A *memento mori,* I will carry them with me on my journey home. I will plant them in my California garden.

I ask that they may thrive in foreign soil – under the same sun.

Marie Pal-Brown was born and raised
in a small town near Cologne, Germany.
After completing her education in
England and Munich, she emigrated to
California. With a background in applied
language studies, she has coauthored three
works of lexicography. Her poetry has
been included in various anthologies.
She resides in Long Beach, California, with
her husband, the actor Garrett M. Brown.